"MAJORGRAPHS"

From the Tennessee Evolution Trial — By Henry Major

(1) JOHN T. SCOPES, Defendant; (2) JOHN T. RAULSTON, Presiding Justice; (3) A. T. STEWART, Attorney-General; (4) WILLIAM J. BRYAN; (5) JUDGE B. G. McKENZIE; (6) JUDGE GORDON McKENZIE; (7) W. J. BRYAN, JR.; (8) SUE K. HICKS, Attorney for the Prosecution; (9) BUTLER, the Author of the Tennessee Anti-Evolution Law; (10) DR. JOHN RANDOLPH NEAL, of Knoxville, Tenn., Chief Defense Attorney; (11) CLARENCE DARROW; (12) ARTHUR GARFIELD HAYS, of the American Civil Liberties Union; (13) DUDLEY FIELD MALONE; (14) DR. GEORGE W. RAPPLEYEA; (15) REV. CHARLES FRANCIS POTTER, Pastor of West Side Unitarian Church, New York; (16) DR. WM. GOLDSMITH, of Southwestern University.

Compliments of ALMA ART AGENCY

500 FIFTH AVENUE, NEW YORK CITY

(Copyright, by Major, July, 1925)

KEEPING THE FAITH

KEEPING
the FAITH

God, Democracy, and the
Trial That Riveted a Nation

BRENDA
WINEAPPLE

RANDOM HOUSE
NEW YORK

Published in the United States by Random House, an imprint and division of Penguin Random House LLC, New York.

RANDOM HOUSE and the HOUSE colophon are registered trademarks of Penguin Random House LLC.

Scripture quotation, 2 Timothy 4, has been taken from the Christian Standard Bible®, copyright © 2017 by Holman Bible Publishers. Used by permission. Christian Standard Bible® and CSB® are federally registered trademarks of Holman Bible Publishers.

LIBRARY OF CONGRESS CATALOGING-IN-PUBLICATION DATA
Names: Wineapple, Brenda, author. | Tennessee, defendant in error. | Tennessee. County Court (Rhea County)
Title: Keeping the faith : God, democracy, and the trial that riveted a nation / Brenda Wineapple.
Description: New York : Random House, 2024. |
Includes bibliographical references and index.
Identifiers: LCCN 2023050454 (print) | LCCN 2023050455 (ebook) | ISBN 9780593229927 (hardcover) | ISBN 9780593229934 (ebook)
Subjects: LCSH: Scopes, John Thomas—Trials, litigation, etc. | Evolution (Biology)—Study and teaching—Law and legislation—Tennessee—History. | Bible and evolution. | Fundamentalism. | Democracy. | Constitutional law—United States. | Bryan, William Jennings, 1860–1925. | Darrow, Clarence, 1857—1938.
Classification: LCC KF224.S3 W56 2024 (print) | LCC KF224.S3 (ebook) | DDC 344.768/077—dc23/eng/20231031
LC record available at https://lccn.loc.gov/2023050454
LC ebook record available at https://lccn.loc.gov/2023050455

Printed in the United States of America on acid-free paper

ENDPAPER CREDITS: " 'Majorgraphs' from the Tennessee Evolution Trial," courtesy of W. C. Robinson Collection of Scopes Trial Photographs MS.1091, University of Tennessee, Knoxville—Libraries (foreground left); "Subpoena Issued to John T. Scopes," courtesy of Sue K. Hicks Papers, Scopes 2235, University of Tennessee, Knoxville—Libraries (foreground right); *Teenage Girls with Monkey Dolls,* courtesy of W. C. Robinson Collection of Scopes Trial Photographs, University of Tennessee, Knoxville (top left image on left endpaper)

randomhousebooks.com

2 4 6 8 9 7 5 3 1
First Edition

To Michael, again and always

Ignorance and fanaticism is ever busy and needs feeding. Always it is feeding and gloating for more. Today, it is the public school teachers, tomorrow the private. The next day the preachers and the lecturers, the magazines, the books, the newspapers. After a while, Your Honor, it is the setting of man against man and creed against creed until with flying banners and beating drums we are marching backward to the glorious ages of the sixteenth century when bigots lighted fagots to burn the men who dared to bring any intelligence and enlightenment and culture to the human mind.

—CLARENCE DARROW

The only way to be orthodox in anything is not to think.

—WILLIAM PICKENS

We colored men so often see ourselves described and painted as monkeys, that we think it a great piece of good fortune to find an exception to this general rule.

—FREDERICK DOUGLASS

I fear the plutocracy of wealth. I respect the aristocracy of learning; but I thank God for the democracy of the heart.

—WILLIAM JENNINGS BRYAN

I have fought the good fight, I have finished the race, I have kept the faith.

—2 TIMOTHY 4

Contents

PART 5: THE TRIAL: FLYING BANNERS
AND BEATING DRUMS, 1925

PART 6: THE TRIAL: A DUEL TO THE DEATH, 1925

PART 7: A LITTLE LEARNING, 1925–1926

EPILOGUE: THE FOUR WINDS OF THE SKY

The Trial of the Century

DAYTON, TENNESSEE, WAS A SLEEPY little town at the foot of the Cumberland Mountains, with Chattanooga to the south and Knoxville to the north. Giant maple trees shaded the two principal streets, Main and Market, and along Market, farmers could still tie up their teams at the hitching rail. There were flower boxes in the windows of the homes and pretty gardens in their backyards. If the place was known for anything, it was for the strawberries that left by railroad car each spring to be distributed nationwide. That's all, until the blisteringly hot summer of 1925 when as many as two hundred journalists descended on a town they'd never heard of. They'd come to Dayton to cover what otherwise might have been a forgettable local matter—something about evolution and a young high school teacher named John Thomas Scopes.

That it turned out to be the trial of the century was, at least in retrospect, entirely predictable. America was a secular country founded on the freedom to worship, or, for that matter, the freedom not to worship. The very first amendment to the Constitution asserts that Congress shall make no law establishing religion or prohibiting its free exercise; it drew a hard line, in other words, between church and state. As Thomas Jefferson put it in his *Notes on the State of Virginia,* "it does me no injury for my neighbor to say there are twenty gods, or no god. It neither picks my pocket nor breaks my leg."

But for many Americans, religion—specifically Protestantism—was the only safeguard against moral bankruptcy. Religion should not be separated from government; on the contrary, it should sit at its very center. For to them, America was a Christian nation with a sacred mission, conceived for and by devout men who believed they were endowed by their Creator with certain unalienable rights. Any legislation separating church and state might well be construed as antireligious, iniquitous—and even unpatriotic.

One nation, under God. One God, one nation: In 1954 President Dwight D. Eisenhower maintained that including the words "one nation, under God" in the pledge of allegiance would strengthen, he said, "those spiritual weapons which forever will be our country's most powerful resource." Without our swearing allegiance to religion, the Reverend George M. Docherty had suggested to Eisenhower, "little Muscovites," all of them godless communists, could easily be reciting the very same loyalty oath.

That religion and government, religious Fundamentalists and religious liberals, or even an older and a younger generation did and would vie with one another was not news. But in 1925, their antagonism possessed a force and a focus that surprised even the journalists who rented rooms in the small Tennessee town hoping for a scoop. After all, two gladiators, the ubiquitous politician William Jennings Bryan and the criminal lawyer Clarence Darrow, each of them national celebrities for decades, were going into battle over God and science and the classroom and, not incidentally, over what it meant to be an American.

For just a few months before the trial began, the Tennessee legislature had passed a law, known as the Butler Act, that forbade the teaching of "any theory that denies the story of the Divine Creation of man as taught in the Bible, and to teach instead that man has descended from a lower order of animals." The fledgling American Civil Liberties Union, an organization that promised to protect the constitutional rights of citizens, claimed that the Butler Act violated the First Amendment's guarantee of religious liberty. It flouted the First Amendment's prohibition against establishing a state religion. And the Butler Act denied the right of professionals—educators—to decide for themselves, as professionals, what they should be teaching.

When the ACLU offered to defend anyone willing to test that Tennessee law by breaking it, John Scopes stepped up. Ordinarily shy, this unpretentious twenty-four-year-old admitted that not only had he taught evolution, you can't teach biology without it. And in any case, the textbook that he'd used in his biology class, a textbook that the state of Tennessee had authorized, mentioned evolution only in a few pages. It said nothing about divine creation or the Bible. It had merely said that evolution was change. That was it.

Young Scopes was immediately indicted for violating the Butler Act; the trial date was set for the summer of 1925. Then the commotion began. Soon it seemed every automobile in the country, every itinerant preacher, and every snake-oil salesman was headed for Dayton, Tennessee.

"This trial was bound to take place somewhere," a Dayton resident philosophically observed. "It's an issue that is coming up everywhere in the United States." As he suspected, the issue had nothing to do with whether John Scopes had broken the law. No one disputed that, not even Scopes himself. And the issue wasn't about the theory of evolution per se. Very few people reading or writing about the Scopes trial, or even those directly involved in it, understood how evolution occurred or even how to define it. So something greater was at stake than whether a young schoolteacher had taught from an authorized textbook that mentioned evolution.

To the celebrated criminal lawyer and self-described agnostic

Clarence Darrow, who volunteered to defend Scopes, the Tennessee law raised issues that went to the heart of democracy. It asked who controlled how Americans could be educated, and where and with what means, and what limitations on freedom could be or should be placed on the freedom to learn, to teach, to think, or to worship. None, he said. Agreeing with him were the other members of the defense team: the Irish Catholic Dudley Field Malone and Arthur Garfield Hays, a secular Jew, who were both from New York; they were joined by the local Tennessee lawyer John Randolph Neal, the son of a colonel in the Confederate army.

But to William Jennings Bryan, a figure as recognizable as Darrow, and as irrepressible, the issue was faith. The issue was God. A three-time presidential nominee and crusading leader of the Democratic Party, Bryan arrived in Dayton intending to save men and women—and children, most especially—from the warped ideas that would turn them into atheists. Though he knew little about science and even less about evolution, Bryan intuited with stunning accuracy the frustration and anger and anxiety of the people he represented and claimed to speak for, particularly the religious Fundamentalists. Confident of his mission and sure of himself, he trusted that he could pluck out from the public schools, and even the public colleges, the science that so offended him and threatened them. This science had a name: "evolution."

For by 1925 evolution had become a lightning rod, and the Scopes trial channeled the turbulence of the preceding decades, years of hunger and panic, of bombings and lynchings and riots and then a world war, the so-called Great War. There had been labor stoppages, assassinations, deportations, and great economic disparity. Some men were making so much money at the expense of so many others that a new term was invented for them—"robber barons"—and a new phrase, the "Gilded Age," would characterize the era. But the Gilded Age was gilded only for a very few.

The farmers of the Midwest and South, in debt, could barely make ends meet. They had even formed a political party to demand such reforms as the public ownership of railroads, which had been gouging small shippers and growers. Immigrants had been pouring into the cities, crowding into tenements and working in sweatshops until Congress in 1924 passed legislation slamming the door shut on many of them. In the South, Black men were being routinely turned away at the polls, and when Black men and women moved northward, creating vibrant communities in formerly white neighborhoods, they were often chased out of their homes, their businesses and newspapers burned to the ground. The Ku Klux Klan had revived itself, in fully hooded regalia, to terrorize Blacks and Jews and Catholics, while Klan members sat in state legislatures, in governors' mansions, and in Congress. Women were still not allowed to vote. In 1917, when they peaceably picketed the White House, they were quickly arrested. That same year, America was sending its men to Europe to fight and die in a world war known for brutal, senseless slaughter on a scale never before imagined.

What's more, discoveries in archeology, philology, and anthropology were suggesting that the Bible had been written not by the hand of God but by a number of authors in a number of languages over a span of maybe a thousand years. Physicists seemed to be saying everything was relative and in flux. The old order was collapsing. The compass no longer pointed toward heaven.

Darwin and the theory of evolution were not, in themselves, news either. More than six decades had passed since his *On the Origin of Species* first appeared in 1859, and five decades since his *The Descent of Man*, which was published in 1871. Darwin had proposed that all living things were linked and that, over long periods of time, they had evolved from far earlier organisms in a slowly changing drama. Random biological mutations in a species would cause new characteristics to develop, and some of these characteristics could offer an advantage for that species' survival. Take the giraffe: its ancestors resembled deer, but when food became scarce, as in times of drought, those with longer necks, even just an inch or two longer, could eat the foliage that others with shorter necks couldn't reach. Darwin called this process "natural selection." Through natural selection, Darwin said, characteristics that increase the chances of survival will reproduce themselves and, over time, a new species may "evolve" while the previous one dies out.

As the biology textbook that John Scopes taught from had pointed out, evolution meant change.

Yet for many the idea of evolution and of natural selection was hard to swallow. If humans evolved from earlier forms— were descended from monkeys, as Darwin was interpreted to say, which he did not—what about Adam and Eve? Didn't God create them in His own image? And if a random mutation allowed some species to survive and others to become extinct, then accident, not design, ruled the biological universe. Where was God, then? Or, if God existed and allowed only some select species to survive, was God immoral? Natural selection seemed to imply nothing more than struggle, conflict, and a rage for dominance.

The great Darwin popularizer, the English polymath Herbert Spencer, made some of this go down easier. In 1864, he coined the term "survival of the fittest" and applied Darwin to the society at large. "This survival of the fittest," Spencer wrote, "is that which Mr. Darwin has called 'natural selection,' or the preservation of favored races in the struggle for life." To Spencer, natural selection was not a random process at all but rather a way of ensuring that only the "best," or the "fittest," people and races would (and should) survive. Only the winners in the competitive struggle for existence deserve to be winners. Nothing was random after all.

This process of allowing some species to survive and others to die out actually demonstrated God's purposeful guidance.

"God intended the great to be great and the little to be little," the liberal American preacher Henry Ward Beecher agreed with Spencer. Sidestepping the implications of a universe ruled by chance, Americans might then transform Darwin into a prophet of progress and upward mobility.

In fact, to some, that meant government shouldn't meddle with this "natural" process by introducing, say, social programs that protected or educated the worker, the poor, or the illiterate. A perfect rationalization for laissez-faire capitalism, "social Darwinism," as it came to be known, was embraced in the latter part of the nineteenth century by the captains of industry. They assumed it was logical—even scientific—that they, the fittest, should enjoy wealth and privilege. "When men are ignorant and poor and weak, they can't help being oppressed," Beecher announced. "That is so by a great natural law."

Of course not everyone accepted social Darwinism, which was not Darwinism or, for that matter, particularly scientific. Many, like William Jennings Bryan, confused social Darwinism with the theory of evolution. Bryan argued that evolution offered nothing more than a soulless world where only the most brutal survive. Over and over he adamantly claimed that "evolution robs the individual of a sense of responsibility to God and paralyzes the doctrine of brotherly love." And, if left unchallenged, the theory of evolution would deprive men and women of peace and comfort—and moral accountability—in the here and now, and it would take away the promise of happiness in the hereafter.

Evolution thus was said to endanger children, education, ethics, and of course religion itself. It removed God from the order of things. "Evolution is atheism," cried evangelicals like Billy Sunday, who drew huge paying crowds.

"The evolutionists bring their doctrine before the public in a jeweled case and praise it as if it were a sacred thing," William Jennings Bryan declared just before the Scopes trial began. "They do not exhibit, as Darwin did, its bloody purpose; they do not boast that barbarism is its only true expression."

THE OLD ORDER was indeed changing, and to many Americans change was defined as capricious, unpredictable and, if not stopped, wholly sinister. For the Great War, too, as F. Scott Fitzgerald lamented, had left "all Gods dead, all wars fought, all faiths in man shaken." Only drift, anarchy, and despair remained.

Campaigning for the presidency in 1920, Warren G. Harding had promised "a return to normalcy," implicitly admitting that no one felt anything had been normal in a long time. Even that disillusioned generation of the 1920s—the people whom Gertrude Stein called "lost"—were not lost at all. They were experiencing a crisis of faith that had been ongoing for decades, and that was erupting, full force, in Dayton, Tennessee. "When science strikes at that upon which man's eternal hope is founded," one of the lawyers prosecuting Scopes poignantly declared, "then I say the foundation of man's civilization is about to crumble."

ARGUED ON BOTH sides by those who genuinely sought to make life more tolerable, more meaningful and just, the Scopes trial was cathartic, as trials generally are. It aired the uneasiness about what science seemed to portend, the pitilessness and hopelessness of it all. It aired the uneasiness about the coming role, if any, of religion in public life. It aired the uneasiness over the role of the state, if any, in dictating a civic religion that could supplant science or scholarship. In principle, then, the Tennessee law could also prevent public schools from learning about the Sumerians or the early history of Egypt, civilizations that existed before the creation of the world, as dated by the Bible. Geology would be out; botany and zoology and astronomy would be out.

There was something else too, something less tangible. Those who flocked to Dayton and read about Dayton and made fun of Dayton were coming face-to-face with essential questions about life and death, questions that no one could completely answer— not the evangelist and not the agnostic, not the scientist and certainly not those skeptics who were called modernists. "At bottom, down in their hearts, they are equally at a loss," a reporter covering the trial suspected.

So the Scopes trial was the trial of the century in a century of infamous trials: The prosecution of Sacco and Vanzetti, two Italian American anarchists accused of robbery and murder in Massachusetts; the prosecution of the Scottsboro boys, nine Black teenagers who allegedly raped two white girls in Alabama; the case against Bruno Hauptmann, said to have kidnapped and murdered the baby of famed aviator Charles Lindbergh and his wife Anne Morrow Lindbergh; the trial of Ethel and Julius Rosenberg, accused of handing over atomic secrets to the Soviets; and the televised trial of Black football hero O. J. Simpson, accused of killing his wife, Nicole, and her friend Ron Goldman in cold blood: trials of the century.

But here, in the small town of Dayton, Tennessee, in the summer of 1925, there was no murder, no robbery, no rape, kidnapping or spies. This was a different kind of trial.

BANNERS WERE HUNG all over town. One instructed, "Read Your Bible," while another asked, "Where Will You Spend Eternity?," and yet another reminded folks that "You Need God in Your Business." The local jewelry stores featured monkey watch fobs, and several of the shops sold toy monkeys. The meat market handled all kinds of meat, except monkey, a sign in the window declared. The local drugstore offered a drink called "monkey fizz," and the proprietor of a dry goods store, whose name happened to be Darwin, suspended a scarlet banner on his storefront to advertise that "Darwin is right inside."

It did seem like a circus. There were lemonade and hot dog stands set up around the courthouse, and evangelical preachers sermonized day and night on the courthouse lawn. Men in black felt hats sang spirituals on street corners, and Thomas Theodore Martin of Mississippi, field secretary of the newly founded Anti-Evolution League of America, rented a storefront to flog his own book, *Hell and the High Schools*. The Anti-Evolution League had nailed up several posters depicting a party of apes: "Shall We Be Taxed to Damn Our Children?" it wanted to know. Two chimpanzees had been brought to town; their trainers offered them as exhibits for the defense, and when Scopes's lawyers politely turned them down, the trainers displayed the chimps in an empty store. At the railroad junction, the brakemen on passing trains would holler, "All out for Monkeyville."

Henry Mencken, the acerbic journalist from the Baltimore *Sun*, came up with the term "monkey trial," and it stuck.

No wonder men and women regarded the Scopes trial, then and later, as a misbegotten and bizarre farce played out in a country that lacked the saving graces of culture and sophistication. The Scopes trial had to be nothing more than a promotional stunt engineered by small-town opportunists and, in the end, not much different from flagpole sitting. The entire affair was monstrous nonsense, George Bernard Shaw lashed out; Tennessee was an outpost for "morons and moral cowards." The German press called the whole thing an American circus, but their local dailies reported on it. Newspapers in Switzerland, Italy, Russia, and Japan covered the trial, and in China, sixteen provincial papers carried the latest bulletins from Dayton. "Faith cannot be protected by law nor propagated by force," the London *Sunday Times* editorialized with disdain.

"This is twentieth-century America?" wondered a dazed correspondent, and the London *Daily News* marveled that a one-horse town like Dayton could produce such weirdness. "I would have given anything if I had only invented the Dayton affair off my own bat," the English writer Rudyard Kipling remarked. "It was inconceivable." Ernest Hemingway slid a send-up of the Scopes trial into *The Sun Also Rises,* and after the trial, Sinclair Lewis began work on his satirical novel *Elmer Gantry* about a phony evangelical preacher.

It was easy to shrug off the trial as a bunch of benighted white Southerners, ignorant about science and narrow-minded about religion, fighting to fend off one and to safeguard the other. It was easy to see Dayton as an intellectual wilderness, Tennessee as an offense against civilization, and America the land of Puritan bigotry. Eastern newspapers reported that the people of Dayton resented being called peasants, hillbillies, and yokels. That didn't stop anyone, and especially not Henry Mencken, whose witty, caustic, and frequently unfair point of view about the trial dominated much of the coverage. Drubbing Southerners as rustic theologians and dunderheads who lived in the "Bible Belt," a term he also invented, Mencken also shrewdly pointed out that Dayton hadn't cornered the intolerance market. "It was not in rural Tennessee but in the great cultural centers which now laugh at Tennessee that punishments came most swiftly, and were most barbarous," Mencken wrote. New York City, not Dayton, had fired teachers for protesting the recent Great War.

The far more traditionalist or conservative writers who hoped to keep Darwin out of the schools were no less objective, often characterizing evolutionists and, in particular, the lawyers defending Scopes as invading vultures come to feast on the people, customs, and religion of the South. In this, the American Civil Liberties Union was for them the chief offender, with its "horde of pacifists, pro-Germans, German agents, defeatist radicals, Reds, Communists, I.W.W.'s, Socialists and Bolshevists." The Scopes lawyers, the ACLU, and any fellow travelers—even scientists—intended, it was said, to destroy such civic institutions as the American Legion and the Ku Klux Klan.

xxiv PREFACE: THE TRIAL OF THE CENTURY

The lines were drawn.

But when an out-of-town reporter asked a local man, Daniel Costello, what the people of Dayton really expected from the trial ("Rental for rooms? Advertising for coal mines or crops?") Costello replied, "They are going to have some of the greatest scientists and the greatest speakers of the world there for the trial," he said. "They are going to get a college education for nothing." The citizens of Dayton, the reporter concluded, were willing to face the world's ridicule in order to learn.

Their teachers were to be the two illustrious men headlining the case. Large personalities, comfortable on a public stage and consummate performers, Clarence Darrow and William Jennings Bryan were famous, they were infamous, and they had been sparring for years.

William Jennings Bryan was the de facto voice of religious Fundamentalism and a leader of the Democratic Party for almost three decades. Nicknamed the Great Commoner, Bryan had for a lifetime represented the forgotten, the poor, the plain, and anyone left out of an increasingly corporate America. He believed in salvation by faith and reform by democratic action—that is, through legislation that would thwart the temptations of drink and war and godless science.

Often dismissed as a demagogue or a buffoon whose claim to fame was really failure—failure to win the White House—Bryan was mocked as the man who intended to make "Tennessee safe for Genesis." But he was revered in many quarters of the country; people still hung on his every word; thousands went to Florida, where he was living, to hear him preach outdoors under the palms on any given Sunday. Aligning himself with conservative clergy although he still considered himself the progressive Democrat he'd always been—on the side of the people against the plutocrats—he had taken his crusade against teaching evolution in public schools on the road, much as he had when he railed against the sale and consumption of alcohol and campaigned for Prohibition. He was a force to be reckoned with.

And no fool, he had long detected the rampant anxiety and gnawing doubt beneath the easy money and dubious morals of America in the 1920s. For this, he now blamed not just the unequal distribution of wealth but the theory of evolution and Charles Darwin. "His works are full of words indicating uncertainty," Bryan complained, as if doubt and anxiety might be placed at Darwin's feet. As a corrective, Bryan opted for the consolation of a theocracy—a nation of Christians that legally enforced moral behavior and could thereby revive the values that he associated with a white, rural, decent and upstanding America. This would in turn restore, within the context of a centralized government, the pastoral life he imagined had once existed. The alternative was unthinkable.

"Mr. Bryan may protest as much as he likes that he is not a member of the Ku Klux Klan," warned the New York *World*. "He is fighting with all the powers he possesses for the fundamental object of the Ku Klux Klan"—that is, for an established national church, which was un-American, lawless, and predicated on the assumption that white people were a superior race.

Bryan's main antagonist, the star criminal lawyer Clarence Darrow, was himself both beloved and despised. With remarkable success, he'd defended socialists and anarchists, labor organizers and bomb-throwers. Just the year before the Scopes trial, he'd prevented the execution of two teenagers, Nathan Leopold and Richard Loeb, who had killed for the thrill of it. That had been another spectacular trial, and *Time* magazine would name Darrow "one of the most dangerous lions of the U.S. bar." Though no great lawyer in any academic sense, Darrow would fight desperately in the service of a lost cause, as historian Bruce Catton observed. He was charming. He mesmerized juries with his impression of humility, some of which was genuine, and with his unmatched logic and down-home wisdom. If Mark Twain had been a lawyer, people said, he would have been Clarence Darrow.

"The powerful orator hulking his way slowly, thoughtfully, extemporizing, through his long broken story," Lincoln Steffens remembered Darrow, "hands in pocket, head down and eyes up, wondering what it is all about, to the inevitable conclusion, which he throws off with a toss of his shrugging shoulders: 'I don't know—We don't know—Not enough to kill or even to judge one another.'" To Darrow, life was tragic but precious. What he said about a friend might be said of him: to Darrow, "the earth was a great hospital of sick, wounded, and suffering."

Still, there were those who dismissed Darrow as a crafty, publicity-hungry celebrity lawyer or atheist revolutionary without piety or scruple. To them, Darrow was a man who liked to think he was champion of the underdog and bamboozled others into believing it. Attorney for the damned, he'd stop at nothing. He must've gone to Dayton to stick pins in Bryan—and God—for the hell of it, or just to jack up his fee.

Darrow presented himself as tousled from head to toe, and no matter how expensive his suits, they crumpled with ease around his large frame. He refused to play the city slicker. Though as tall, Bryan stood erect and over the years wore what seemed to be the same black alpaca coat he had worn back in the 1890s, with the same string tie and comfortable shoes. He stooped to stylishness only when he draped a natty cape over his shoulders, though in Tennessee, walking the streets of Dayton in the oppressive July heat, he liked to appear in a white pith helmet, which protected his head from the Southern sun. Unlike Darrow, who lived much of his life in a spacious Chicago apartment lined with books, Bryan was a successful real estate entrepreneur who built himself more than one mansion set back from any crowded street.

Both of them had been born around the time Charles Darwin's *Origin of Species* was first published in the middle of the nineteenth century. They had grown up during and after the Civil War and in its shadow. Darrow's family had been free-thinking abolitionists; Bryan's father was a religious-minded, Southern-sympathizing Democrat who dropped to his knees three times a day to pray and advocated what was called popular sovereignty, or the notion that citizens should decide for themselves whether, say, they wanted their state to allow or prohibit slavery—not whether it was immoral.

These two were men of the nineteenth century, coming to terms with the twentieth in the best ways they knew how. "There is a contest pending today that is not one of religious liberty, but one of economic liberty," Darrow had declared in 1900. But Darrow was wrong if he thought the fight for religious liberty was over. It was far from over.

To Darrow, religious liberty was connected to all sorts of liberty: the right to speak, to assemble, to write, to work. For like Bryan, he considered himself a descendant of Thomas Jefferson, who believed in the rights and dignity of the mass of ordinary citizens over and above corporations and banks and even government.

But Darrow and Bryan differed in certain respects about what government should control and how it should exercise that control, if at all. They had both pushed for government ownership of such utilities as electricity, but Darrow opposed any intrusion into the conduct of private life. He loathed Prohibition. To Bryan, Prohibition was a public good. And Bryan would have the teaching of evolution outlawed in the same way as the sale and consumption of alcohol had been—likely by constitutional amendment.

Yet both Bryan and Darrow placed their faith in democracy. To Bryan, democracy meant majority rule and states' rights. The people in each state should decide for themselves, for instance, what should be taught in state-supported schools. That was the irony of Bryan's progressive spirit. He was the man who stood by the little people, the neglected, the poor and the weak, the man who insisted that women should be allowed to vote. Yet he was the man who wanted to make people believe what he believed, by decree if necessary.

To Darrow, there could be no democracy without reason, which is to say, without education and an educated people. For he imagined, or at least he hoped, that people might lead better, fairer, more just lives if they knew more. "It was he who was the Great Commoner," not Bryan, mourned the Black newspaper *The Chicago Defender* after Darrow's death. For this was a man who in 1903 had declared that he could envision "a universal republic, where every man is a man equal before his Maker, governor of himself, ruler of himself and the peer of all who live; where none will be excluded; where all will be included." Though he may not have said so, Darrow did not relinquish this dream, which was not unlike Bryan's own: the dream of a universal republic, a place where miracles had once taken place and still could. To Darrow, life was a miracle to be preserved; he acted as though it was his duty to preserve it.

PASSIONATELY DISAGREEING ABOUT whether the theory of evolution contradicted the biblical story of divine creation, and whether human beings are related to monkeys and whether science teachers should be allowed to teach science, Bryan and Darrow did not invent the positions they took. Rather, they came to symbolize two different and warring sides about culture, ethics, religion and the state. And they articulated these positions brilliantly and with unfailing energy on the stump and in the courtroom.

For the controversy over evolution had long been stoked both by the Fundamentalist Protestants and the press, with many pundits looking disdainfully at the South and Midwest, and just as many looking with contempt at the self-appointed urban intelligentsia, loosely termed "modernists." The Scopes trial was thus bound to be a media event that, for all its nuttiness, would encapsulate the exuberance and agitation, the snootiness and the fissures, of America in the twenties. "Most of the newspapers treated the whole case as a farce instead of a tragedy," Clarence Darrow later reflected.

Lining up behind Scopes were the liberal-minded men and women, whether in the church or not, who believed in the scientific method and progress. Often they unfortunately included those self-appointed arbiters of culture, hip and disillusioned, who in their magazines and editorials sneered at what they regarded as Bible-thumpers. And the Fundamentalists, as a group, were those who held fast to the Bible, to its unimpeachable wisdom, to the veracity of every word and every miracle.

The two poles did not meet. Neither the so-called modernists nor the Fundamentalists could see Darrow or Bryan whole. Prejudice encountered prejudice; intolerance, intolerance. And though this compelled Darrow and Bryan, and those like them, to adopt extravagant positions, they were speaking of that longstanding debate between reason and faith, or what passed for reason and faith, which was a debate not easily resolved by extremes.

There was something tragic about the trial—Darrow was right—but something noble too. The Scopes trial reached back to the era just after the Civil War, when industrialization, immigration, and urbanization threatened institutions, like the church, that had once seemed—whether or not they were—coherent, comforting, and foundational. And the Scopes case stretched forward to the next century, the twenty-first century, our century, when once again schools would try to outlaw certain modes of teaching or remove books from library shelves or even rewrite them in part or whole. The Scopes case asks, then and now, where the country was headed, where it should be headed, and

how to make it better and kinder in light of privation and prejudice and disillusionment and war—particularly that Great War
that didn't end all wars, as the slogan promised, but rather killed
more than twenty million and severely wounded twenty million
more.

"Democracy has shaken my nerves to pieces," said the heroine of a Henry Adams novel. "I believe in democracy," a wise
friend had told her. "I have faith; not perhaps in the old dogmas,
but in the new ones; faith in human nature; faith in science."

"Free thought is the most important issue that has been
raised," the British biologist Julian Huxley remarked during the
trial. "That is the real danger to a young democracy that has not
got to the full pitch of its development—that it is likely to be
swayed by crowd psychology and violence in expressing its opinions and forcing them on other people."

Democracy was on trial in Dayton. As it would be again in
our time: teachers being told what or how to teach; science regarded as an out-of-control, godless shibboleth; books tossed
out of schools and libraries; loyalty oaths; and white suprema-
cists promising that a revitalized white Protestant America would
lead its citizens out of the slough of moral and spiritual decay to
rise again, regardless of what or whose rights and freedoms
might be trampled. "The truth is, and we know it: Dayton, Tennessee, is America!" the renowned Black historian and editor
W.E.B. Du Bois astutely summarized. "A great, ignorant, simple-
minded land, curiously compounded of brutality, bigotry, religious faith and demagoguery, and capable not simply of mistakes
but of persecution, lynching, murder and idiotic blundering."

Dayton was America, and America in 1925 was a place of
skyscrapers and tenements and radios, of motorcars and mus-
tard gas, of billboards and cherished Bibles, of dispiritedness and
the vexed search for something, something good, to believe in.

Part 1

1858–1914

Doubt was the beginning of wisdom, and
the fear of God was the end of wisdom.

—CLARENCE DARROW

Chapter One

The Beginning of Wisdom

1858–1914

CLARENCE DARROW, THE FAMOUS LABOR lawyer from Chicago, had stood tall in the public's eye for almost two decades, and even those who didn't much like him respected his vigorous defense of what seemed to be hopeless cases. That was until he himself was put on trial, twice, in 1912 and 1913, for attempting to bribe a juror. Though he was acquitted the first time, the second trial ended in a hung jury. His reputation seemed beyond repair. Then came the 1920s and his second act, and Clarence Darrow was over sixty years old.

EARLIER, IN 1887, when Darrow first arrived in Chicago, it was a city of immigrants, of Poles and Hungarians, Irish and Italians, Germans and Jews, a smoldering place of grime, noise, wind, and graft with more than a million people and still growing, a city where the smell of blood wafted from the stockyards and animals screeched in the slaughterhouses.

Chicago was perfect for Clarence Darrow, a young and ambitious lawyer from the provinces eager to put village life behind. Before Darrow arrived, Bryan had been in Chicago studying law for two unhappy years and yearned, he said, to return to the rural life he idealized. But Darrow adored the city, with its noise and energy and people living there from all over the world. America's rail lines converged in Chicago. "Corn, hogs, wheat, iron, coal, industrialism—a new age moving across a continent by railroads," the novelist Sherwood Anderson would recall. In his novel *Sister Carrie,* Theodore Dreiser sent his hungry heroine Carrie Meeber to Chicago, where she gazed longingly at bright merchandise she couldn't afford in that city of Armour, Swift, McCormick, Pullman, and Marshall Field, the Chicago barons. John D. Rockefeller had endowed the new University of Chicago. "Education ran riot at Chicago," Henry Adams said drily.

The civic leader and social reformer Jane Addams had opened the doors of her Hull House settlement in Chicago's sweatshop district and offered hot lunches, university extension courses, and lectures, along with gymnastics and language classes, to the immigrants who had flooded into the city. Hull House residents prodded the city council into building a public bathhouse and agitated for the inspection of factories. This too was Chicago. The homeless slept on the floors of City Hall. British author H. G. Wells said Chicago was like a prospectors' camp, and German sociologist Max Weber compared the city to a human with its skin removed.

Darrow embraced all of it. For him, there was no going back.

CLARENCE DARROW HAD been raised in Kinsman, Ohio, a village about two miles east of Farmdale, in the northeastern part of the state, where he'd been born in 1857. His parents, abolitionists, helped fugitives escape slavery to find safe harbor in Canada, and every Sunday Darrow's father would read to his brood of children from the sermons of the abolitionist preacher Theodore Parker. And it was a brood. Seven children had survived infancy, including Clarence, and together they lived in a wood-frame octagon house, a style which the phrenologist and reformer Orson Squire Fowler had been promoting as an efficient and healthful and ventilated use of space, with more light and fewer dark hallways. (P. T. Barnum had one built in Connecticut.)

By most mid-nineteenth-century measures, the Darrows were fairly eccentric. One of Darrow's brothers was christened Channing Ellery after William Ellery Channing, the antislavery preacher; another was named Edward Everett Darrow to honor the orator, diplomat, and former Massachusetts governor, Senator Edward Everett. "Seward" was Clarence's middle name, out of his parents' admiration for New York senator William Seward (later Abraham Lincoln's Secretary of State), who had proclaimed "there is a higher law than the Constitution"—that of inalienable human freedom.

Clarence Darrow believed that too, up to a point. Human law was made by human hands.

Darrow's father, Amirus, had studied for the ministry at the Meadville Theological Seminary in Pennsylvania but somewhere along the way lost his faith. Locals in his village dubbed him "Deny" Darrow because he denied that the Bible was the literal word of God. A frustrated, dreamy, and well-read man with too many children to feed, Amirus Darrow reminded Clarence that John Stuart Mill was just three years old when Mill began to learn Greek. Young Clarence preferred baseball. But Amirus taught him a lesson he never forgot: "Doubt was the beginning of wisdom, and the fear of God was the end of wisdom."

Darrow was a sensitive child. He wouldn't venture inside his father's workshop at night because Amirus, a cabinetmaker, was also the local undertaker and kept a supply of caskets right there in the corner. When Clarence was told his pet chicken had to be killed and eaten before it grew old and tough, he ran outdoors and would not come back inside while the chicken was cooking. Nor would he eat anything for the rest of that day. Nor would he eat chicken ever again.

Darrow told his first biographer that his mother, Emily Eddy

Darrow, regarded displays of affection as a sign of weakness. Claiming he barely remembered her—untrue—he said, "I know that I must have loved her, for I can never forget the bitterness of my despair and grief when they told me she must die." The fifteen-year-old Clarence stared for a very long time at her open coffin in the darkened front parlor and, in later years, found no comfort in homilies about immortality or the soul. No one had the right, especially not the state, to deprive anyone of anything as precious, fragile, and fleeting as life.

After just a year at Allegheny College, Darrow returned to Kinsman, the depression of 1873 having wreaked havoc on the family fortunes, such as they were. To earn money, he taught in a nearby school, and on the way home he often stopped by the tinsmith's shop, since the tinsmith happened to be the justice of the peace. Darrow later reminisced that he enjoyed hearing the local lawyers rail at each other. Perhaps that was why he enrolled for one year in the new law department at the University of Michigan. The next year, 1878, he was admitted to the bar. Two years after that, he and a young local woman, Jessie Ohl, were married and in 1883 had a son, Paul, whom they adored.

Darrow opened a small practice in Andover, Ohio, another small town, where he presided mainly over horse trades or adjudicated personal grudges. But the country boy was making good. Wanting more exposure and likely more money, he moved his family to the far larger town of Ashtabula, a railroad hub located on the shore of Lake Erie. There he realized, after he successfully ran for city solicitor, that he had a taste for politics. And deeply moved by Judge John Peter Altgeld's tract on the criminal justice system, *Our Penal Machinery and Its Victims,* Darrow began to develop his lifelong interest in the causes of crime. The poor and the helpless were arrested the most, he noticed. The deck was stacked.

He wanted to buy a house. Though he had five hundred dollars and promised to pay the remaining three thousand, the

Portrait of Clarence Darrow's father (Amirus Darrow),
Clarence Darrow's son (Paul Darrow), and Clarence
Darrow, circa 1888

COURTESY AIP EMILIO SEGRÈ VISUAL ARCHIVES, DARROW
COLLECTION, NIELS BOHR LIBRARY & ARCHIVES

sellers of the house rejected his bid; they assumed he'd never be
able to earn enough to come up with the rest of the money. Darrow decided right then (he claimed) that he would leave Ashtabula
and forget about a reasonably comfortable but inglorious life.
Two of his siblings were in Chicago. John Peter Altgeld was in
Chicago. Darrow would go to Chicago. He would meet Judge
Altgeld.

Altgeld had arrived in America in 1847, when he was just
three months old, after his parents had immigrated from Germany. As a young man, he worked on his father's farm in Ohio
and, during the Civil War, enlisted in the Union army. He read
law in Missouri and though elected county prosecutor there, he
moved to Chicago around 1877 and started investing in real es-

tate. He did well, but his real love was politics; he called it his recreation, which also meant he never rested. And he was as sharp a politician as anyone in sharp-elbowed Chicago. He catered to no one, feared no one, he was a man who "plays the game, for the benefit of the people," Darrow recalled.

In 1886, Altgeld was elected to the Superior Court of Cook County and was soon named chief justice. In the spring of that same year, just before the Darrows arrived in Chicago, the large farm implement manufacturer the McCormick Harvesting Machine Company fired a number of employees. When fellow workers walked out in protest, the company hired nonunion men and employed a special police force to guard the new workers, who were called "scabs." Inevitably fights broke out between picketers and scabs, but on May 3, the police opened fire and killed four of the striking men.

The next night, after the mayor had issued permits, a legal protest rally convened in Haymarket Square. The organizers of the rally had hoped for a better turnout, and when it began to rain, those who had come began to head home. Everything had been peaceful.

That the final speaker of the evening was more incendiary than the preceding ones may explain why the police began to advance on the thinning crowd. Suddenly an unidentified person threw a bomb. No one ever discovered who it was or what really happened next. Everything seemed to take place at once and in a matter of seconds. The police shot their own men as well as several people in the crowd. At least four of the spectators were killed. Seven policemen died, and hundreds of people—onlookers and police—were wounded in what became known as the Haymarket affair, a tragedy, really, that inflamed the nation.

Almost immediately, those men suspected of being union members or thought to be anarchists were rounded up. Eight of them went on trial—not as accessories before the fact and not for throwing the bomb; no one knew who did that. Still, the judge instructed the jury that if the defendants had conspired to overthrow the government, whether on that night or any other night, they were to be found guilty, not just for conspiracy, but for murder.

All eight defendants were convicted and sentenced to death. One committed suicide. Four were hanged. The remaining three waited on death row.

By the time Altgeld was elected governor of Illinois in 1892, he and Darrow had become friends, having met shortly after Darrow moved to Chicago. The two men formed a bond that lasted for the rest of Altgeld's short life (he died suddenly in 1902 at the age of fifty-four); Altgeld influenced Darrow just as profoundly as his father had, though in this case about the city's apparent neglect of the poor and its seeming indifference to the economic disparities so plainly and heartbreakingly visible in Chicago.

For Governor Altgeld despised the whole idea of social Darwinism, with its justification of inequality—the rich deserve their wealth, since they're the fittest—and he was a strong supporter of organized labor, which, to Altgeld, stood opposed to corporate power, with its exploitation of workers. He backed a minimum wage; he backed factory inspection laws. He rode the streetcars in Chicago like everybody else even though he'd made a fortune (later lost) when he built and then managed the construction of the Unity Building, the first seventeen-story structure in the world. He advised young Darrow to do what he had done: earn enough money so he could defend whomever he chose no matter how poor they might be.

Altgeld had urged his friend Chicago mayor DeWitt Cregier to appoint Darrow assistant counsel in the mayor's office in 1889 and, in two years' time, Darrow was running the city's legal department. Just two years after that, he was working for the Chicago and North-Western Railway. He was taking Altgeld's advice.

In the meantime it had become obvious to many, particularly Darrow, that the Haymarket convictions were unfair. Darrow insisted that Altgeld review the Haymarket case. "If I do it," Altgeld replied, "I will be a dead man politically." He did, and he was. He concluded that the jury had been packed, the judge biased, the evidence thin. Whatever else these men might have been guilty of, Altgeld declared, they were innocent of the bombing. He pardoned them.

The reaction was swift and predictable. "A lying, hypocritical, demagogical, sniveling Governor of Illinois," *The Chicago Tribune* exclaimed, "is a sympathizer with riot, with violence, with lawlessness, and with anarchy." Theodore Roosevelt said Altgeld had condoned murder. The journalist Henry Mencken remembered that as a boy, he'd been told Altgeld was "a shameless advocate of rapine and assassination, an enemy alike to the Constitution and the Ten Commandments—in short, a bloody and insatiable anarchist."

IN 1894, the thirty-seven-year-old Darrow resigned his lucrative position as corporate lawyer to defend Eugene Victor Debs, the gangly president and founder of the American Railway Union.

George Pullman of the Pullman Palace Car Company had cut wages but not the high rent on the small houses in his supposed utopian town, located in eponymous Pullman, Illinois, near Chicago, where workers were forced to live. The union demanded raises for the employees and a shorter-than-sixteen-hour workday. If Pullman refused, the union threatened a general boycott of any train that hauled Pullman's palatial sleeping cars. Pullman refused. "What in God's name does Pullman think he's doing?" asked millionaire Mark Hanna, no friend of labor. "A man who won't meet his men half-way is a God-damn fool."

The switchmen duly uncoupled Pullman's cars. When the men were fired, about forty thousand workers nationwide went on strike, paralyzing the rail system, creating massive gridlock and effectively shutting down transportation from coast to coast. Fruit and vegetables and meat rotted in the cars. Future president William Howard Taft said Debs and his union were letting the country go hungry.

But since the trains moved the US mail and since Pullman cars were attached to the mail trains, President Grover Cleveland felt justified in sending federal troops to Chicago to break the strike. No Illinois official had asked for federal intervention, and certainly Governor Altgeld hadn't. "Forty years ago the slave power predominated; today it is capitalism," Altgeld fumed. "It sits in the White House and legislates in the capitol." A federal judge then issued an injunction preventing Debs and the union from telegraphing or otherwise contacting anyone about the strike. Altgeld knew, too, that this was an interference in the matters of the state—and a misuse of the interstate commerce law initially written to protect farmers and small business from the railroads' price fixing.

No matter. Federal troops arrived, and soon railroad cars in the yards were burning, men dragged from towers, stones and spikes thrown, men killed. Debs and other strike leaders were arrested. The strike soon collapsed.

A generous, devout, and himself a very calm man, Eugene Debs had urged the workers to remain calm. But he was charged with conspiring to interfere with the US mail and obstruct commerce. He was also charged in civil court for ignoring the government injunction. When Darrow defended Debs on the civil charge, he noted that the government injunction was so broadly worded that it would make all strikes illegal. Regardless, Debs was found guilty and sentenced to six months in jail; the case was appealed to the Supreme Court, which upheld the injunction. The court said the injunction had not been misused because the mails had in fact been disrupted.

As for the more serious criminal charge of conspiracy, Darrow argued that there was no evidence that Debs had conspired to stop the mails. He went on to claim the very idea of a conspiracy charge was ridiculous. A conspiracy charge depends on witnesses, whose testimony is filled with hearsay, which, by the time it is stricken from the record, had already persuaded a jury to believe that more than one person, even if not present at a crime, might have been involved in it.

Darrow also subpoenaed George Pullman and all his management. None of them showed up. Pullman himself could now be charged with contempt, and so it seemed Darrow might win the case—until one of the jurors fell ill and the judge, declining to seat the alternate, declared a mistrial. The government dropped the charges against Debs.

Darrow's reputation as a friend of labor skyrocketed. He subsequently served as a negotiator between a streetcar company and striking employees, and he pushed for municipal ownership of the city's rail lines. He delivered speech after speech on behalf of eight-hour workdays and against child labor and capital punishment, which he abhorred. He said women should have the vote: "Freedom is a farce" without it. (He would later change his mind about suffrage, believing women were meddlesome do-gooders intent on legislating morality.)

In 1898, in another soon-to-be-famous trial, Darrow defended Thomas Kidd, general secretary of the Amalgamated Woodworkers International Union, and two other men, all of them charged with criminal and civil conspiracy against the Paine Lumber Company. It was alleged that they plotted together to ruin the company. (The implication of the charge was that no strike should ever be allowed; it could destroy business.) Darrow countered. Since no one could remember hearing these men conspire, the three defendants weren't able to confront their accusers.

Darrow also pointed out that in a free country anyone could voluntarily lay down their tools and walk off the job, and that's exactly what the employees of the Paine mills had done.

With a penchant for courtroom drama, he went on to paint a harrowing picture of boys overworked, women overworked, and "men who rise in the morning before daylight comes, and who go home at night when the light has faded from the sky and give their life, their strength, their toil to make others great and rich."

Darrow won. The jury acquitted the defendants.

Darrow was now well-known as a radical-leaning labor lawyer, though that seemed to many redundant; all labor lawyers were radicals. For there was the coal miners' strike too, and Darrow was involved.

The United Mine Workers had begun to organize the Pennsylvania anthracite miners, who supplied the coal most families used for heating their homes. In the spring of 1902, about 150,000 of the miners walked off the job, demanding higher pay and better working conditions. The Western Mine Owners' Association, together with the coal-carrying railroads, refused to negotiate. Coal prices spiked. With winter approaching and businesses panicking, the new American president, Theodore Roosevelt, who had taken office after William McKinley's assassination in 1901, had to do something. He telegraphed union officials and operators and invited them to the White House.

When the talks failed, Roosevelt created a commission to mediate between union leaders and mine owners. Appearing before this commission were Henry Demarest Lloyd, the trust-busting journalist who had taken on Standard Oil and now represented the union, and Clarence Darrow, who spoke for the miners.

His voice cracking, Darrow stood before the commission to explain what unions meant, and what they meant to him.

I love trade unions, because I believe they are one of the greatest agencies that the world has ever known to bring about this time; one of those agencies for the building up of character and the building up of men, and toward forming that ideal republic

which has been the hope and the aspiration and the dream of
every great soul that ever lived and wrought and died for his
fellow-man.

The applause was so loud and lasted so long that the commission had to recess.

The commission then recommended a framework for arbitration in further labor disputes, for implicit recognition of the
union itself, and for wage increases. It was a victory for the
unions—and for Clarence Darrow.

Another prominent case followed. In 1907, Darrow defended
"Big Bill" Haywood (so named for his size) after Haywood was
arrested with two other men, leaders of the Western Federation
of Miners, for allegedly conspiring to assassinate Frank Steunenberg, the former governor of Idaho. They were likely suspects
since Steunenberg, an avowed enemy of the union, had called for
federal troops back in 1899 to crush a strike in northern Idaho's
mining district. Six years later, on December 30, 1905, a bomb
strapped to the front gate of Steunenberg's house blew up when
the former governor pulled the gate open. Steunenberg was
pitched backward, flesh torn from his bones. He died in a matter
of hours.

"Big Bill" Haywood and two others were arrested as conspirators even though they had been in Denver at the time of the
blast. Extradited and sent by special train to Boise—some say
they were kidnapped—the three men had been held in jail for a
year by the time Darrow arrived.

Haywood later remembered Darrow standing in a rumpled
gray suit, his eyeglasses in his hand, while talking without notes
for eleven hours and fifteen minutes. He spoke of the way the
railroad tycoons would celebrate if the jury convicted Haywood.
"If you decree his death," he warned the jury, "amongst the spiders and vultures of Wall Street, will go up paeans of praise."

"Vultures of Wall Street": reporters had their story.

Then Darrow continued more tenderly. "If you free him, there are still those who will reverently bow their heads and thank these twelve men for the character they have saved." Darrow went on:

> Out on our broad prairies, where men toil with their hands; out on the broad ocean, where men are sailing the ships; through our mills and factories; down deep under the earth, thousands of men, of women, of children, men who labor, men who suffer, women and children weary with care and toil, these men and these women and these children will kneel tonight and ask their God to guide your judgment. These men and these women and these little children, the poor and the weak and the suffering of the world, will stretch out their hands to this jury and implore you to save Haywood's life.

Haywood's life was spared. His alleged co-conspirator George Pettibone was acquitted and the charges against the other man, Charles Moyer, were dropped. It's hard to know if the verdicts were the result of Darrow's speech or if there just wasn't enough evidence to convict. It's also hard to know whether Clarence Darrow had pressured the state's key witness to recant. The scrupulous historian J. Anthony Lukas, who studied the trial at length, considers it a possibility.

It is a possibility—especially from the retrospective vantage point of what was to happen five years later, in 1912, when Darrow was accused of jury tampering in Los Angeles, when he defended the two brothers who had blown up the *Los Angeles Times* building.

DESPITE HIS POLITICS or perhaps because of them, despite his seeking a public forum or because he did, Darrow was frequently considered a possible candidate for some office or another. He was said to be square, honest, and able. Square and able, to be sure. The matter of honesty was somewhat debatable. He was, after all, Altgeld's secret fixer, granting favors, offering deals. As he said of Altgeld—and might have said of himself—"He was absolutely honest in his ends and equally unscrupulous in the means he used to attain them."

Supporting municipal control of utilities during his single term as state representative in 1902, Darrow helped pass a bill in the Illinois legislature that gave the city of Chicago the right to manage its streetcar companies. In fact, he had run not as a Democrat, as Bryan had, but on the Public Ownership ticket. Then Darrow seemed to do an about-face when he represented the lawyers of a private streetcar company in a personal injury case—likely for a hefty fee. "When bought, Darrow stayed bought," John A. Farrell, his most recent biographer, declared.

Darrow knew what he was doing and saw his situation somewhat differently. "I came to Chicago," Darrow explained to a friend, "determined to take my chances with the rest, to get what I could out of the system and use it to destroy the system." If he wanted to take the cases that mattered to him and to protect the people he wanted to protect, he would have to take cases that paid well. "I cannot defend them without bread," he said. "I cannot get this except from those who have it." By his estimate, he charged no fee to at least one-third of his defendants. The number is certainly higher.

Doubtless he walked a thin ethical line, and he knew that too. "Judged by the ordinary commercial and legal standards of ethics I did right," he wrote this friend, referring to the streetcar case. "Judged by the higher law, in which we both believe, I could not be justified, and that I am practically a thief. I am taking money that I did not earn, which comes to me from men who did not earn it but who get it because they have the chance to get it."

More to the point, as he told another friend, "I never have been able to get over the dread of being poor."

Jane Addams, who saw Darrow often at Hull House, recalled, "I remember during those earlier years having to go among my friends and acquaintances, with my hand out, helping to raise funds to pay some of the big fees that Mr. Darrow demanded in labor cases." The Darrow of later years, she said, was different: "Mellowed by life and more than ever interested in advocating causes—in defending victims—." There seemed to be two Darrows. There was that true-blue hero of labor, and there was the opportunist and cheat.

"Who Is This Man Darrow?" journalists liked to ask. The maverick publisher Elbert Hubbard said he loved Darrow because he was such a blessed crook. "He affects to be a brave man, but admits that he's an arrant coward; he poses as an altruist, but is really a pin-headed pilferer; pretends to work, but is an artistic loafer and acknowledges he is a parasite," Hubbard went on. "People think he is bounteously unselfish and kind, whereas he dispenses and supplicates solely for Darrow & Co. He eloquently addresses the bar, bench and jury in public in the name of justice, and then privately admits the whole thing is a fraud and means nothing, including his plea."

Hutchins Hapgood, a friend of Gertrude Stein who had worked under Lincoln Steffens at the New York *Commercial Advertiser*, talked at length with Darrow in 1906 while researching a book about the rising labor movement. "Darrow, indeed, is a man wonderfully typical of one aspect of the life of the Middle West today—dreamer, practical man, lawyer, politician, friend of labor, friend of women, friend of literature and experiment!" Hapgood wrote. "A rich personality, often distrusted, generally inconsistent in all but humanity, too complex to be philosophic, but a gathering point for all the 'radical' notions of the time."

"He was human as pie a la mode," a reporter who knew him well once noted. "To me, of course that makes him all the better copy than if he had been a plaster saint."

Clarence Darrow, circa 1900
COURTESY CHICAGO HISTORY MUSEUM, ICHI-031827

Unfussy, Darrow was said to care little about his appearance, but that was not entirely true. In the early days, he was nattily dressed, spiffy from bowler hat to walking stick although there were times, said an onlooker, that he evidently wasn't on speaking terms with a brush or an iron. He smoked heavily, his blue-gray eyes were sunken but keen, and his sallow and leather-like complexion made his lips seem almost purple. He could also look like a mischievous boy. He talked brilliantly for hours about unions and justice and the economic reasons for crime. He could just as easily speak about Leo Tolstoy and A. E. Housman. He read Walt Whitman not entirely for his poetry but for his belief that there is some truth in error and some good in evil. We're all freckled, he liked to say.

He worked six days a week, and on the seventh, instead of resting, he shoved a sheaf of papers in his pocket and lectured at various clubs, at Hull House, or the Star Theater, when he joined Jane Addams to denounce the pogroms against the Jews of Russia. "The streets of the city, the politics, newspapers, courts, conspiracies, greeds, triumphs of bad things over good, victories of greed over dreams—all these he has seen if any man has," *The Chicago Tribune* declared.

After they had been separated for about three years, he and his wife divorced in 1897. "Clarence's first experience was more tragic than can be known by everyone and should not be needlessly idealized, say, any more than needlessly mistreated," his second wife, Ruby Hamerstrom Darrow, later said. During the separation from Jessie, Darrow furnished poignant travel pieces to *The Chicago Chronicle* while visiting Europe, writing of the fairy lights that dance over the Grand Canal in Venice, and the sewage, and the silent mountains, which he described as immovable and thus so very different from a fickle humankind.

When he returned to Chicago, he lived near Hull House where he met several of the women there, women committed to their own sexual and economic independence as well as to far better working conditions for immigrants and the poor. There were always rumors about his liaisons with many of these women, particularly during those years. Ruby Darrow was quick to defend him: "He was everywhere, with everyone, men as well as women, almost boyish in his acceptance of things as on the surface." To her, Clarence Darrow was no rake; he simply found himself "much more strongly entwined with them than ever intended by himself."

A dark-haired former journalist who wrote a column for the

Chicago *Evening Post* under the pen name Ruby Stanleigh, she and Darrow married in 1903, and for the rest of her life she protected and perhaps coddled Darrow, although their life together could not have been easy. When Darrow later published his autobiography, *The Story of My Life,* his friend Rachelle Yarros, a pioneering obstetrician who had also been a resident at Hull House, said Darrow shouldn't call his book an autobiography since he revealed nothing of his love life, which deserved one whole chapter at least. "What a goddamn fool!—and I'd be another if I did such a silly, unthinkable thing," Darrow told Ruby. "A whole chapter, eh,—I could do a whole library." He quickly apologized for the library remark.

Mary Field (Parton) and Ruby Darrow
COURTESY CHICAGO HISTORY MUSEUM, ICHI-182049

But apparently no one, then or later, blamed Darrow for his flirtations and his supposed affairs, whether with social workers like Gertrude Barnum or the writer Mary Field. These women accepted him, even those hurt by him, and they became friends, often for a lifetime. "Perhaps he felt the need of physical nearness—the emptiness of life—The isolation of the soul and tried in closer physical proximity to forget his isolation," Field speculated. She stayed involved with him and him with her. He introduced her to his friends when she moved to New York and sent her money when she needed it, encouraged her to write, and continued to feel close to her after she married the journalist Lemuel Parton in 1913. For Darrow was seeking an intellectual as well as sexual companionship—though the sex was of course important. "Sex [is] the only feeling in the world that can make you forget for a little while," he confided to her.

Kansas journalist William Allen White remembered that Darrow "was not an indiscriminate petticoat chaser, nothing like it. But he loved, like the wind, where he listed."

Darrow had devoted friends and a devoted wife, all of whom adored him. And he was a very lonely man.

NO ONE EVER quite knew what Clarence Darrow might do or say. When Jewish peddlers were stoned and beaten, their push-carts stolen or smashed while the police casually looked on, Darrow told them to organize. "Stand up and demand your rights as citizens," he said. Law was a luxury bought and sold, he declared, and those who pay the most receive the most.

There was nothing wrong with Blacks and whites marrying. "Is there any reason . . . why people should not meet together upon perfect equality in every relation of life and never think of the difference," he asked. "The excuses given are pure hypocrisy; they are not good excuses; they are not honest excuses."

"I am pessimistic about the white race," Darrow lectured in 1901, "and when I see the injustice everywhere present and how the colored race is particularly subjected to that injustice and op-pression, I admit that I am pessimistic as to the future of the colored race, and fear the dreams we have indulged in of perfect equality and of unlimited opportunity are a long way from any realization."

Invited to the second annual conference of the National

Negro Committee meeting at the Cooper Union auditorium in New York City in 1910, Darrow simultaneously delighted and horrified his audience. On the platform, along with Darrow, were journalists Ray Stannard Baker (white) and Ida Wells-Barnett (Black). A longtime activist, Wells-Barnett powerfully denounced the murder and lynching of Black people while Baker claimed the races needed to exercise patience and better understand each other.

Then the Reverend Percy Stickney Grant introduced Darrow, who strolled over to the lectern and leaned forward with something of a slouch. His hair fell over his forehead in that seemingly lazy way of his. He began slowly, repeating what he'd told the Jewish street peddlers of Chicago: Organize. Demand your rights as citizens. Everyone should demand their rights. As Americans.

"The laws don't go far enough in protecting everybody," Darrow declared.

"It's false philosophy that teaches the negro that he can get along all right without the ballot so long as he is allowed to put a dollar in a bank," Darrow continued. Referring to two white abolitionists, Senator Charles Sumner and the outspoken orator Wendell Phillips, Darrow continued. "The good cause [abolition] which Sumner and Phillips fought so bravely for fifty years ago is dead."

The white speakers on the dais blinked with embarrassment. Darrow was too bold.

The younger people in the crowd were ecstatic. "He was so brave and so fearless that he did not realize he was either," said Joseph N. Welch, the lawyer who, years later, during the hearings of the House Un-American Activities Committee, asked Senator Joseph McCarthy if he had "no sense of decency, sir." Darrow went on to denounce lynching and segregation, and he denounced Booker T. Washington and his Tuskegee Normal and Industrial Institute, which he labeled one of those schools that taught the Black man "to lay brick for the white man," Darrow joked without humor. "What the negro needs is not more work but more wages."

Darrow resumed his speech. He said that in Cairo, Illinois, a mob of about one thousand people had lynched and mutilated and burned a Black man named William James, who had allegedly raped and killed a white woman in Springfield, Illinois. As Darrow reminded his audience, who needed no reminding, "A black man has been lynched almost in the shadow of the statue of Abraham Lincoln in the town that Lincoln lived in."

"Back of the acts of the Cairo and Springfield mobs is prejudice—the prejudice built up by the clergymen in the pulpits and the lawyers in the courts, pleading the cause of the rich." The courts were no better than mobs.

The Reverend Percy Grant fidgeted.

"Negroes are being crucified because the Lord made them black," Darrow bellowed. No other reason, and no good reason.

Darrow's speech had entered dangerous territory. Reverend Grant wanted to get Darrow away from the lectern.

"No Horace Greeley wrote or spoke against it. Our most talented men, nowadays, use their brains and voices merely to help the corporations rob the poor. Step by step the South has reconquered the North."

W.E.B. Du Bois would later recall, "I was drawn to Clarence Darrow because he was absolutely lacking in racial consciousness. He was one of the few white folk with whom I felt quite free to discuss matters of race and class which usually I would not bring up."

Others scoffed. "No well-balanced negro or white man, of course, takes Darrow seriously."

ON OCTOBER 1, 1910, an explosion ripped through the *Los Angeles Times* building in downtown Los Angeles. At least twenty-one people, several of them jumping from windows, were killed and more than a hundred others injured. John and James McNamara, prominent members of the Bridge and Structural Ironworkers' Union, were charged with planting the bomb, but labor officials assumed the McNamaras were being framed by union-busters who'd dynamited the building themselves. The rabidly anti-union General Harrison Gray Otis, owner of the *Times,* was known to cruise around with a small-caliber cannon perched on the hood of his limousine.

Clarence Darrow had not wanted to take the McNamara case. He was fifty-four and dreaming, or so he said, about a life surrounded by books, books to read and books to write. But then Samuel Gompers, the head of the American Federation of Labor, and Darrow's friend Ed Nockels, secretary of the Chicago Federation of Labor, knocked on the door of Darrow's Chicago apartment and said that if Darrow didn't defend the McNamaras, he'd be considered a traitor to the great cause of labor that he'd so bravely championed for so long. The McNamaras were victims of capitalist greed, and the cause needed him.

At first Darrow seemed to think the McNamaras were innocent. He wasn't alone. Samuel Gompers and Big Bill Haywood and Eugene Debs had evidently believed that too. So when James McNamara confessed to Darrow during the trial that he and his brother were guilty, Darrow was stunned. And distressed. "I felt as does a doctor, who realizes that his patient must die," he claimed.

At Darrow's suggestion, the McNamaras changed their not-guilty plea to guilty to avoid the death penalty. Darrow was arranging a deal that would send James McNamara to prison for life for the *Times* bombing, and by pleading guilty to a different bombing, John McNamara would receive a prison sentence of fifteen years.

Something happened just at that time. Before the deal was

finalized, Bert H. Franklin, Darrow's lead investigator, was arrested in a sting operation that had been stage-managed by the Los Angeles district attorney. Franklin had been caught apparently attempting to bribe a prospective juror, and Clarence Darrow seemed to be involved. Just as a five-hundred-dollar bill was changing hands at a Los Angeles intersection, Darrow, who had been walking nearby, rushed across the street, waving his hat as if to interrupt the transaction.

Darrow's whereabouts could have been a coincidence, but his waving his hat looked pretty suspicious. Even worse, Franklin himself soon pleaded guilty to the charge of attempting to bribe a potential juror, and he fingered Darrow as the mastermind of the scheme. Darrow was indicted.

Some said Darrow had convinced the McNamaras to change their plea to save himself: that is, with the McNamaras pleading guilty, Darrow could argue he'd have nothing to gain from bribing a juror. Why bribe a juror if there was to be no trial? Darrow explained that he arranged to change the plea *before* his arrest, not *after*. Having learned the brothers were in fact guilty, all he'd wanted to do was keep them alive. They'd surely get the death penalty otherwise. By pleading guilty, they'd avoid that.

Lincoln Steffens corroborated Darrow's story and added that the Los Angeles district attorney had been jubilant over the plea deal. "It was all the compensation he desired," Steffens explained, "to have the chance to 'get' Darrow."

Darrow's bribery trial lasted thirteen weeks. Defending Darrow was Earl Rogers, later the model for Erle Stanley Gardner's fictional defense lawyer Perry Mason. A vain and increasingly alcoholic son of a Methodist minister whom Eugene Debs called a "notorious corporation corruptionist," Rogers was deft, brilliant, and notoriously good at converting murder charges into claims of self-defense. And he had help, inadvertently, from Bert Franklin. Franklin had initially testified that Darrow was unaware of any bribery and had nothing to do with it. But because Franklin changed his story, and now incriminated Darrow, Rogers was able to crush Franklin on cross-examination.

There was no hard proof of bribery, just Franklin's waffling testimony, and anyway the whole scheme, as Franklin had described it, didn't make sense. "Will you tell me how any sane, sensible man who knows anything about the law business—and this defendant has been in it for thirty-five years—could make himself go to a detective and say to him: just buy all the jurors you want," Rogers scoffed. "I put my whole life, my reputation, I put everything I have into your hands. I trust you absolutely. I never knew you until two or three months ago and I don't know much about you now. But there you are. Go to it."

Slumping listlessly, Darrow lit cigarette after cigarette. He was uncharacteristically curt with journalists. He insisted on delivering the closing argument even though in court he looked like he'd already been beaten. Yet when he rose, he was no longer ashen-faced or doleful. He was the self-possessed attorney whom thousands of people had come to hear.

Speaking simply, as always, while looking straight at the jury, as always, Darrow explained that he had never wanted to take the McNamara case. He had done so only because he had always been a friend of labor. And since there would be no reason to bribe a juror when the guilty plea had already been arranged, he explained why he was being persecuted.

"I am on trial because I have been a lover of the poor, a friend of the oppressed, because I have stood by labor for all these years and have brought down upon my head the wrath of the criminal interests in this country," he said with feeling. "That is the reason that I have been pursued by as cruel a gang as ever followed a man."

With a whiff of his characteristic humor, he added, "I am as fitted for jury bribing as a Methodist preacher for tending bar."

It was vintage Darrow, a roller coaster of different emotions: anger, sorrow, persecution, more sorrow, stoic resignation.

"Life is a game of whist, and the cards are shuffled by a devil," Darrow said, quoting a poem by Eugene Ware. "I do not like the way the cards are shuffled, but I like the game, and will sit up all night and take a hand and then play the best I can. I have tried to play honestly, and I will play that way to the end, whatever that end may be."

People in the courtroom sobbed. Darrow wiped his streaming eyes with a handkerchief and then, when it was too soggy, with the sleeve of his coat. As he finished, the bells of a nearby cathedral tolled. In just thirty-four minutes, before anyone had time to take a breath, or Darrow to exhale, the jury acquitted him.

The Los Angeles district attorney immediately filed a second indictment, claiming Darrow had tried to bribe yet another juror on behalf of the McNamaras.

Again great crowds thronged the courthouse, but during the second trial, Darrow mounted the disastrous defense Earl Rogers had dissuaded him from attempting earlier. Darrow now argued that the McNamaras weren't murderers at all but rather representatives of a great cause, the cause of those who cared for the weak and the poor and the children who were worked to the bone. Responsibility lay with the capitalists who scooped up all the resources of the world—the Rockefellers, the Morgans, the Goulds—"that paralyzing hand of wealth which has reached out and destroyed all the opportunities of the poor."

The sweeping denunciation of the rich, eloquent but histrionic, cost Darrow his acquittal. The jury was hopelessly deadlocked.

The district attorney set a date for a new trial and then, mysteriously, the date disappeared from the calendar. Perhaps there was no point. Perhaps Darrow had promised never to return to

Los Angeles, which might have been a reason for the trial: to get rid of him. Or the intention, deliberate or not, was to discredit him with the unions and, by shaming him, discredit the unions. Whatever the reason, "he seemed a beaten man," recalled journalist Hugh Baillie. "It seemed the end of a great career."

MANY WERE NOT sure if Darrow would stoop to bribe a juror to save a client's life. Even his recent and astute biographer assumes Darrow wasn't exactly innocent. But the present editor of Darrow's letters considers the matter underexplored, the evidence unreliable, and the prosecution witnesses impeachable.

Whether innocent or not, Darrow had been riding high. He'd come off several huge victories for labor and for himself, which perhaps made him heedless when he should have been prudent and careless when he should have been cautious. And his taking on the McNamara case only confirmed the rumors that had dogged him for years: that the big-city lawyer lapped up publicity and that he was greedy—Darrow received a $50,000 fee—and that he was vain, arrogant, and something of a showboat who would do anything to win. Maybe so.

Yet Clarence Darrow had also passionately believed in the cause that the McNamaras were fighting for: the right to unionize and agitate for decent working conditions and better wages.

DARROW WAS IN debt. He lost big and important clients, like the Hearst newspaper chain. He lost smaller clients. He lost the spring in his step. He felt betrayed by the labor movement. "Won't you & can't you do something to bring the old time people to my support," he asked Eugene Debs during the bribery trial. "It is awfully hard to be deserted in this crisis by those who should stand by me." Debs was touched and saddened. "There is undoubtedly a strong feeling against you among Socialists,"

Debs sorrowfully admitted. "You may be sure that all my heart is with you and that I am going to see what can be done to set the tide moving in your direction." Not much happened. Gompers wrote Darrow off, hypocritically it seemed. "Almost firmly convinced of the innocence of the McNamaras, we strained every nerve to raise as near as possible the amount of money you suggested would be necessary for their defense," Gompers told Darrow with some disdain. "I am free to say to you that in my judgment any general appeal for funds to defend you or the men under indictment would fall upon indifferent ears."

Darrow was depressed. "Poor broken Darrow," his friend Mary Field noted in her journal, "with the great marks of suffering on his face, looking like an oak that has been cleft by a lightning bolt."

Darrow's law firm in Chicago had been bled dry. Darrow had been in Los Angeles for two years, leaving his partner, the poet Edgar Lee Masters, and his other partner to manage the office. The lucrative days of ten years earlier, when he and Masters launched the firm, were long gone.

Certainly Darrow and Edgar Lee Masters had started out amicably enough. Both had been influenced by Altgeld. Both opposed injunction laws. Both supported the labor movement, and they had backed Bryan for president in 1896 and 1900. Both men read widely. Both dreamed of a literary career. Writing under a pseudonym, in 1907 Masters praised Darrow as likable, conscientious, and "an old-fashioned soul, easy and lounging and full of generosities."

In private, though, the situation grew increasingly tense. Masters resented Darrow's being away from the office, spending too much time on pro bono work, or delivering too many lectures. And Masters was generally dissatisfied. He was not yet the famous poet that he aspired to be; his international bestselling collection of poems, *Spoon River Anthology*, wouldn't be published until 1914. He was splurging on women who weren't his wife. When Darrow recommended that Masters invest in a bank stock that then failed, Masters blamed Darrow. And he suspected that Darrow was bilking their firm. Darrow had received $50,000 for the Haywood trial but returned only $14,000 to their practice.

Masters intended no compliment when he said that Darrow reminded him of Abraham Lincoln. "According to some of the descriptions of Lincoln, those who speak of Lincoln's cunning and his acting ability," Masters wrote, "I think he was more like Lincoln than anyone."

"NO ONE CAN find life tolerable without dope," Darrow told Mary Field. To him, dope could be anything: drugs, alcohol, sex, public approbation—or, as often in his own case, the courtroom and his legal work.

But the bribery trials had shaken him.

"I will never close my eyes again," he told Mary Field, now Mary Field Parton. "What an everlasting enigma is life, and how we do get lost in its dark maze. No sooner do we plant our feet on something that seems like solid ground than we find the sand shifting under us & we look for something else. I wonder how much of truth, these things that I have been frantically working for through all the years. Well, it furnished me an interest in life & made me forget myself and I guess this is its chief value."

Disillusion and shifting sands: Darrow was ready for the 1920s.

Chapter Two

A Cross of Gold and the Man with the Hoe

1860–1908

Bowed by the weight of centuries he leans
Upon his hoe and gazes on the ground,
The emptiness of ages in his face,
And on his back the burden of the world.
Who made him dead to rapture and despair,
A thing that grieves not and that never hopes,
Stolid and stunned, a brother to the ox?
Who loosened and let down this brutal jaw?
Whose was the hand that slanted back this brow?
Whose breath blew out the light within this brain?

—EDWIN MARKHAM, "THE MAN WITH THE HOE"

WILLIAM JENNINGS BRYAN BOUNDED ONTO the stage, buoyed by shouts of "Bryan, Bryan, Bryan." It was the summer of 1896, and he was about to deliver what would become one of the most famous speeches in American political history.

It was the third steamy day of the Democratic National Convention, which had the feel of a revival meeting. Handsome and self-assured, William Jennings Bryan, at the age of thirty-six, in his dark alpaca coat and bowknot tie, looked like a church deacon. His hair was very dark, his nose aquiline, his mouth straight, and his lips thin. He was tall, slender, and he held his head high before the crowd of some twenty thousand as he looked out onto the banners and flags flapping in the mammoth Chicago Coliseum, where not long before Buffalo Bill's Wild West show dazzled audiences with cowboys on horseback, their shiny guns drawn as they raced at breakneck speed around the arena.

A reporter happened to have seen the young Bryan lounging in a corner not long before he mounted the stage. Bryan was sucking a lemon to keep his throat clear when an usher carrying a basket of flowers accidentally bumped into him, messing up his tie. One of Bryan's friends reached out to readjust it. "Be sure," Bryan instructed, "that the ends do not come out even." He smiled and then added, "Be careful to make it look careless."

Behind him on the stage were huge pictures of the Democratic icons of yesteryear, Thomas Jefferson and Andrew Jackson. Bryan waited for the applause to subside and just before it did, he raised his hand, as if to bless the crowd. He then spoke in a language they understood. His was the voice of the have-nots, the farmers, the common people, and the forgotten. He was their defender.

The issues seemed clear: financial reform. And silver.

Coming on the heels of a gold shortage and a devastating economic depression that had swept major parts of the country three years earlier, since 1893 a silver-backed dollar seemed to offer relief, particularly in the South and the West. The heavily mortgaged farmers, deep in debt, had seen prices for their wheat and cotton dropping lower and lower. In the meantime, wages for industrial workers failed to meet the rising cost of fuel and housing. What was needed was an expanded currency that put more money in circulation and didn't cater to rich and greedy bankers of the East with their diamond stickpins; what was needed was a currency that would help the rural poor and the

miner and the factory worker, the small merchant and the struggling women and men of the Plains who just couldn't make ends
meet.

Get rid of the gold standard. And get rid of those complacent
Democrats who were in favor of it, those so-called gold bugs.

What was needed was a currency based on silver. William
Jennings Bryan, former Democratic congressman from Nebraska, was a sterling silver Democrat.

He was also bold and brash. Bryan had surprised many when
he bragged that he might well be the presidential nominee that
year. He was shrewd. He knew that no one could upstage the
final speaker. So he made sure that on July 9, the third day of the
Chicago convention, when it came time to address the crowd
about the party's platform, he'd go last.

When it was his turn, he leapt onto the stage, clearing two
stairs at a time.

His trousers were a little baggy, but his silky baritone rang
pure and true. "The humblest citizen in all the land, when clad
in the armor of righteous causes, is stronger than all the hosts of
error," Bryan began. "I come to speak to you in defense of a
cause as holy as the cause of liberty—the cause of humanity."
This cause, the cause of silver, was a sacred battle, a moral crusade, and Bryan had anointed himself as its leader, serious, committed, and sincere.

Though the day was hot, and the Coliseum hotter, no one
moved so as not to miss a word uttered by the Boy Orator of the
Platte, as Bryan was known. (The Platte was the major river in
Nebraska, the state Bryan had represented.) Of course, though
many believed otherwise, Bryan and his speech hadn't sprung
out of nowhere. Whether at a country fair or a political rally,
he'd been practicing parts of this speech in the West each time he
appeared before a crowd; if anyone had already heard it, they
didn't care. Audiences were spellbound when he seamlessly used

the lyrical, cadenced phrases of Scripture to suggest he knew what they faced and how hard they'd been working and that he'd help them as soon as he went to Washington.

Today he was lashing out against Democrats and Republicans who clung to the gold standard. "We do not come as aggressors," he explained with increasing vehemence. "Our war is not a war of conquest; we are fighting in the defense of our homes, our families, and posterity. We have petitioned, and our petitions have been scorned; we have entreated, and our entreaties have been disregarded; we have begged, and they have mocked when our calamity came. We beg no longer; we entreat no more; we petition no more. We defy them!"

He spoke on behalf of the country's heartland, the men and women of small cities and farms who felt ignored, overlooked, irrelevant. Admonishing those Democrats in the crowd who would disagree, he challenged them.

"You come to us and tell us that the great cities are in favor of the gold standard," he exclaimed. "Burn down your cities and leave our farms, and your cities will spring up again as if by magic. But destroy our farms and the grass will grow in the streets of every city in this country."

He epitomized the new, the real, the true. He was the decrier of the rich and the rapacious.

Soon came the unforgettable climax: "Having behind us the producing masses of this nation and the world," Bryan declared, "the laboring interests, and the toilers everywhere, we will answer their demand for a gold standard by saying to them: You shall not press down upon the brow of labor this crown of thorns—you shall not crucify mankind upon a cross of gold!"

As he spoke, his hands first surrounded his head, as if he was pressing a painful crown of thorns on his huge brow, and then he opened his arms wide, spreading them out at right angles, his whole body in the shape of a cross.

There was a silence. Bryan felt a little nervous, but then the entire arena broke into a roar, with cheer after cheer rising and falling and rising again, the delegates to the convention standing on chairs and waving their hats, straw hats and wide-brimmed hats, and men and women crying, hugging each other. Somehow Bryan was soon hoisted on the shoulders of men in the crowd as the roar grew louder, and men and women tossed into the air anything that wasn't nailed down, handkerchiefs and canes and newspapers. The roar continued, no one knew how long. Bryan, calm and smiling, took his seat. The speech had mowed the audience down like straw, said an onlooker. "A suffering people had found the key to its deliverance," the Chicago writer Francis Fisher Browne gushed.

In a single speech, with his defense of the worker and the farmer and the common people struggling every day to make ends meet, Bryan had vaulted into a fame that would last until his death. That fame came early, and it would persist, perhaps longer than it should have. This natural performer with a romantic heart and religious soul knew how to shape a metaphor, and he'd just begun what would seem a perpetual presidential run to deliver the nation from the moneychangers, as he would frequently say. No matter that skeptics detected more than a hint of antisemitism in the speech. Bryan would deny it. "We are not attacking a race," he said. "We are attacking greed and avarice, which know neither race nor religion."

Regardless, right now, in Chicago, in 1896, this was his moment. He had done it. He won the Democratic nomination for president. This boy orator from Nebraska who delivered hope to those who believed gold was the cause of their misery intended to push the current president, Grover Cleveland—also a Democrat— out of his own party. For Bryan was standing up to the bankers in the East and the entrenched business class. Bryan was the candidate of rural America, of the West, of the unheard men and women of the Plains. If elected, William Jennings Bryan, at a mere thirty-six, would be the youngest American president ever.

Clarence Darrow was at that convention as a delegate for Illinois. He was sitting with Governor Altgeld, who was said to be the brains behind the Democratic Party's platform. Grover Cleveland's Democrats didn't like Altgeld any more than they liked Bryan, although Altgeld was a kingmaker. But Altgeld had not come to the convention to coronate Bryan.

As for Darrow, he didn't think a silver-based currency the most important campaign issue. There were fair-labor laws and the municipal ownership of utilities to fight for, and there was the matter of big corporate trusts to break up and an income tax to pass—all part of the platform but not mentioned in Bryan's speech. To Bryan, silver came first.

Darrow and Altgeld listened carefully to Bryan's speech. "I have enjoyed a great many addresses, some of which I have delivered myself," Darrow later said, "but I never listened to one that affected and moved an audience as did that." Altgeld too said the speech was the best he'd ever heard. But he wasn't ready to turn over his decisive forty-eight Illinois delegates to Bryan, not just yet. He held on to them until the fifth ballot, when it was obvious the Bryan wave was unstoppable. Then he and Darrow would campaign hard for Bryan, though as Darrow remembers, the day after the convention, the sallow-looking Altgeld was paler than usual.

"I have been thinking over Bryan's speech," Altgeld confided. "What did he say anyhow?"

FROM A VERY young age, Bryan liked to campaign. For two years, he had represented Nebraska's First District in the House of Representatives, and then he eyed the Senate. He knew his chances for a seat were slim, so he took a nominal position as editor of the *Omaha World-Herald,* buying some stock in the paper and promising a couple of signed editorials each week to bring together "their kindred forces against the common enemy—the Republican party." The editorial job lasted only two years. He preferred campaigning directly though, as he said, the newspaper was "one of the foremost agencies in the formation of public opinion," which he intended to sway. In 1896, the paper vigorously supported Bryan for president.

Bryan for President, campaign poster, 1896
COURTESY LIBRARY OF CONGRESS

Bryan campaigned tirelessly that year, addressing some five million people while traveling about eighteen thousand miles from state to state and back again. But the price of silver was rising and gold production increasing, which was bad news for Bryan's silver campaign. And millionaire industrialist Mark Hanna was behind the scenes nimbly pulling strings for his friend William McKinley, who sat sturdily on his front porch in Canton, Ohio. So when the ballots were counted, Bryan lost the presidential election to McKinley even though almost fourteen million people had come out to vote. But he carried no big city. It was a Republican sweep, too, in Illinois. Altgeld lost the governorship and Clarence Darrow, who was running to represent Chicago's Third Congressional District, was also defeated.

Bryan and his wife weren't worried. Mary Bryan was as devoted to her husband's career as he was. The couple had married in 1884, soon after Bryan completed law school, and in 1887, they moved to Lincoln, Nebraska, where prospects not just for a legal but a political career seemed promising. Mary too studied law and was admitted to the bar although, as she liked to say, only to assist her husband. She was Bryan's main consultant, and his only one. "Bryan was a law unto himself," said Arkansas senator James K. Jones, who managed or tried to manage Bryan's campaigns.

After Bryan's defeat in 1896, he and Mary compiled several of Bryan's recent speeches and added them to Mary Bryan's biographical sketch of her husband. Called *The First Battle,* it sold roughly two hundred thousand copies: an impressive number, netting the Bryans a notable reserve of cash, which would naturally help finance the second battle. For president, of course.

THE SHELVES IN Bryan's home in Lincoln, Nebraska, contained little poetry beyond collections of didactic verse. There was little fiction apart from the popular novel *Trilby* and Victor Hugo's *Les Misérables.* "It was Hugo's vague hyperbolic generalizations on sociological questions that he marked and quoted," the novelist Willa Cather remembered. As a student, she'd visited his library, which he opened to the undergraduates at the university. Mostly, there were partisan tracts of a forgettable kind, often published by propagandistic presses, committees, or leagues— books by quacks, Cather recalled. There were no magazines, no volumes of Huxley, no Darwin. "The shelves might have been filled by a Virginia country judge before the war," said another visitor. Even Bryan's clothes seemed antebellum.

That was no surprise. His father had never given up the fight, which in his case was for states' rights. During the Civil War, Silas Bryan was denounced as a Copperhead, meaning he was a Northern Democrat with decided Southern sympathies, which he was happy to publicize. Elected to the Illinois state senate in 1852 on a campaign to prevent the immigration of "free negroes into this state," Silas was reelected in 1856 but in 1860, the year his son William Jennings was born, he lost his seat. That also was the year that Republicans sent Abraham Lincoln to the White House.

Silas was livid. To him, Republicans were illegitimate because they were a special-interest party formed solely to protest the extension of slavery into the territories. States are sovereign entities, Silas argued, and must retain their jurisdiction over persons and property. As for slavery, well, if the people of any state "held property in man," then that state should be "free from any accountability for the existence of the institution of slavery, either to their country or their God." So the federal government had no right to pervert our great Constitution about a subject over which it has no jurisdiction—simply "to advance their peculiar views on the negro question."

Even worse than the Republicans were the abolitionist fanatics, he fumed, devils all of them.

Almost six feet tall, with a thin mouth and amply receding hairline—his son William would eerily resemble him—Silas Bryan was an intimidating man. Born in Culpeper, Virginia, Silas moved to Illinois after the death of his parents when he was fourteen. He lived with a sister and attended McKendree College, a Methodist institution in Lebanon, Illinois, before teaching school in the southern part of the state. Soon named school commissioner, he was also studying law, which would provide him with an entree into a public career with prestige.

After he passed the bar and opened a law practice in Salem, Illinois, Silas married his former student, Mariah Jennings, twelve years his junior, who offered unswerving support as he began his political ascendancy. He spent eight years in the state legislature, and though he lost his seat in 1860 he was also elected circuit judge, a position he held for twelve years and which allowed him to run around the state praising Jefferson Davis and repudiating what he thought was the government overreach of the Republicans.

During the war, he said the Emancipation Proclamation would lead to abolition, miscegenation, annihilation, and ruin. Slavery had not caused the war; abolition had—foul, creeping abolition. As Silas Bryan put it, a Black person was better off, better cared for, and far happier with a white master. Reportedly he also denounced the draft laws, worked with conspirators in Canada to burn federal buildings, and signed on to the Sons of Liberty (the Order of American Knights), which was a kind of Ku Klux Klan forerunner.

In 1864, when his son William was four, Silas again ran for Congress, predicting that the abolitionists would be stricken for their sins, their eyes propped open so that they might look upon the Peace Democrats and be saved. He lost that election too. In 1872, he tried again even though he was lampooned as an unreconstructed rebel "who belongs to the dead and never to be recovered past." Losing yet again, he claimed to have been swindled by a "Corruption Fund."

William Jennings Bryan was twelve years old at the time and listening to his father.

Silas did not run in 1874, saying his chances would be better later, but they weren't. Again, he lost in 1878. "Is there no relief from this man's ambition this side of Congress or the lunatic asylum?" his opponents wondered.

Silas was called an old fogey and rebel fossil "who for forty years has three times a day dropped on his knees, with his face turned to the Eastern Star, and prayed for the restoration of the Democracy and his election to Congress." There was some truth to that. A deeply religious man, Silas Bryan, like his son, believed religion and politics were close to the same thing. "Every step in our progress has pointed to a result—the advancement of the Christian religion and the establishment of the Republican Governments," he insisted. Silas opened his court sessions with a prayer and three times a day thanked the Lord for having saved him from pneumonia when he was a child, when he wasn't praying, it was nastily said, for the restoration of slavery and his election to Congress.

There was a family altar in the Bryan home, and the family prayed together at mealtimes, Silas often reading aloud and then discussing the Book of Proverbs. Committed to following his father in all things, William for a while considered becoming a Baptist preacher. When he learned that he'd have to be baptized—immersed in water—his father allowed him to join the Presbyterian Church. In later years Bryan was quick to say his views on religion and politics were his father's: all civic offices should be filled by direct popular vote (about this, Silas had changed his mind). The younger Bryan opposed federal interference in the states, except in the matter of religion. He fought against what he deemed the gold interests of the East as hard as his father had, and he was a temperance man who didn't drink, curse, smoke, or chew tobacco. And like his father, he proudly did not change with the times. As Silas was described, so might one describe William Jennings: "His devotion to the doctrines of the Democratic fathers [is] next to his adoration of his God."

Both father and son also appreciated what they considered the gifts of Providence but what others might call their shrewd investments. In addition to an annual salary of $1,000, as a circuit judge Silas presumably received a docket fee for each suit filed in his court, and he successfully dabbled in real estate, as William would do, both of them conspicuous in the display of their good fortune. In 1866, Silas purchased a farm—essentially an estate, similar to the plantations he recalled from his Virginia youth. The estate came with 520 acres that included timberland of cedars and maples, a pasture, a prairie, and a fourteen-acre deer park because Silas liked deer. Considered the showcase of Marion County, at its center was a grand two-story brick home with two open porches, a large central parlor with a piano, spare rooms for guests, and a dining table set with silver. Silas employed servants (Black) and occasional farmhands though he liked his eldest son, William, to work around the place.

Silas wanted to instill in his son the value of hard work. Everything else was frivolous. When young Bryan wanted piano lessons, Silas said that piano lessons were all right for his sisters; instead, Bryan should "learn to make music on the hack saw." William remembered how proud he was when he told his father he weighed as much as he did. "When you have four pounds more of brains," Silas tartly replied, "we will weigh the same."

William was twenty in 1880 and at Illinois College in Jacksonville when Silas came to consult a friend, a physician, about his diabetes. He also intended to meet his son's girlfriend, Mary Baird, a tall, slender woman one year younger than William who was studying at the Jacksonville Academy. But Silas never met his future daughter-in-law. He died in Jacksonville quite suddenly from a stroke.

Businesses closed in Salem and children were dismissed from school so everyone could march in a procession to the courthouse where Silas's body lay in state. Bryan never spoke publicly of his father's death, though afterward he read Silas's speeches over and over. "I felt so unworthy," he told Mary, "to take my father's place." Referring to himself in the third person, Bryan also reflected that "noble aims make noble men, and his father, who still lives to aid him, often said that one could by diligence, make himself just what he wished to be, and that our duty was to make ourselves worthy of any office within the gift of the people."

William Jennings Bryan wanted very much to take his father's place. And surpass him, which he would.

IN 1898, A forty-seven-year-old schoolteacher, squarely built and bearded, boarded the Oakland ferry bound for San Francisco one Saturday. He was going to see Jean-François Millet's painting "Man with a Hoe" at the Nob Hill mansion of Charles Crocker, the railroad baron. Crocker and his wife had conspicuously purchased the painting for a rumored 700,000 francs (or $150,000), and they invited the public for a viewing. Having fallen in love with a reproduction he'd found in a magazine, Edwin Markham was thrilled.

For almost an hour, the Oakland schoolteacher stood in front of the Millet painting, "the endless pity of it," he soon said, "burning all the time into my soul." It was more terrible than anything Dante had described in the *Inferno,* he would say, and if just as hopeless, more human. "I saw in it the ruin of man, the ruin wrought by the powerful over the patient, of the strong masters over the silent workers."

Rushing back to Oakland, Markham dashed off the first draft of a forty-nine-line blank verse poem in his black notebook. "It has enough dynamite in it to blow up most of the social traditions of our civilization," he remembered thinking. He assumed no one would ever publish it.

He was wrong. William Randolph Hearst featured the poem in his paper, the San Francisco *Examiner,* placing it smack in the middle of the editorial page. The poem was immediately reprinted across the country and then the world and eventually translated into almost forty languages. Not everyone loved it, of course. Markham's friend, the writer Ambrose Bierce, wrote in *The Examiner* that the poem had less vitality than a sick fish, and *The Chicago Tribune* featured one of the many hilarious parodies circulating, this one called "The Man with the Lawn Mower." And the poem stung Collis P. Huntington, another of California's railroad barons. "Is America going to turn to Socialism over one poem?" he groused. "The good workman can generally find work and can safely trust to that law of the 'survival of the fittest,' under which men who lead industrious and moral lives, who have honesty of purpose, and practice an intelligent economy, always thrive."

Huntington offered $400 for a poetic response to the poem, and he provided the title: "The Man without the Hoe."

David Starr Jordan, founding president of Stanford University, said the man with the hoe was just a poor degenerate wretch who'd inherited a slanted brow and brutish jaw from a slant-browed mother and brutish father.

But William Jennings Bryan adored the poem. It was the cri de coeur of the people, the working people, written by the working man for the working man.

And who was responsible for this poor man's suffering, for the injustices he endures, for the burdens he carries? Bryan asked. "Is it the fault of God or of Nature that our tax laws are so made and our tax systems so administered that the poor man pays more?" No.

"Is God or Nature responsible for a financial system which raises the purchasing power of the dollar in the hands of the money changer, while it increases the burden of debt to the man who owes?" Bryan asked. No.

"Is God or Nature responsible for private monopolies which corner the markets?" No.

"Is God or Nature to blame for the substitution of force for reason and might for right in government?" No.

"Is God or Nature responsible for the nation's entrance upon a career of conquest?" No.

Of course not. "Humanity's protest against inhuman greed," Bryan explained, " 'The Man with the Hoe' . . . is a sermon addressed to the heart."

In 1900, William Jennings Bryan was running for president again.

MASSACHUSETTS SENATOR Henry Cabot Lodge was a remote and prickly Boston Brahmin who believed himself motivated solely by the good of the nation. The good of the nation included its financial interests but not just its financial interests. Lodge said the United States should go to war with Spain and support the insurgents in Cuba for purely humanitarian reasons. The consummate sensation-mongering publisher William Randolph Hearst launched his own campaign against Spain, claiming that the sinking of the armored USS *Maine*, at anchor on the Cuban coast, had been the work of the Spanish—even though the deadly explosion had likely been caused by an internal accident on the ship. Evidence didn't stop Hearst, who continued to whip up his readers and inflame Congress, which passed a resolution threatening war if Spain did not get out of Cuba. The resolution also stated that the United States did not intend to annex the island.

But war there was. Without irony, Secretary of State John Hay called it splendid and little. Splendid it wasn't, but it was short. It was over in fifty-five days. Disease killed more men than combat had. That didn't stop Theodore Roosevelt from bragging about his own valor. Having resigned his position as Assistant Secretary of the Navy in 1898, Roosevelt raised a cavalry regiment, about four hundred men whom he dubbed the Rough Riders, the only regiment to see combat. Their famous charge up Kettle Hill took under an hour, and Roosevelt emerged a hero.

Just as eager for a slice of heroism was William Jennings Bryan, who enlisted in the Nebraska National Guard and raised a regiment, the Third Nebraska Volunteers. Though he had denounced imperialism, he believed this to be a war of liberation. We look forward to a time, Bryan told cheering audiences in 1898, when swords will be beaten into plowshares. For now, though, there can be no peace without guns. Bryan's regiment, which never saw any action, was devastated by typhoid.

When Bryan realized the war against Spain was one of naked colonialism, he resigned his commission and hurried to Washington where Congress was debating a peace treaty with Spain that, if ratified, would net the United States the islands of Puerto Rico, Guam and, for a small price ($20 million), the Philippine

Islands. Anti-imperialists slammed the treaty, which would allow an indefinite American occupation of the Philippines. Filipino nationalists wanted independence; in fact, Emilio Aguinaldo had already formed a provisional constitutional government. Then something odd happened. Paradoxically or, to some, hypocritically, the anti-imperialist Bryan was buttonholing senators and urging them to ratify the treaty.

An outspoken anti-imperialist, Massachusetts Senator George Hoar accused Bryan of knowing that the Filipino nationalists were forcibly resisting any American occupation when he lobbied for the treaty's ratification. It was a treaty, Hoar continued, that was neither legal nor moral. Filipinos and Americans were dying by the hundreds. The sovereignty of the Philippine Republic was being summarily ignored. And what was Bryan's argument? Once ratified, the United States would be rid of Spain forever, Bryan argued, and it could eventually grant the Philippines their independence. In the meantime, an American occupation would ensure that the government there was stable. What was that? Hoar wanted to know: that the right thing is to do evil in order to do good? Create a monster—imperialism—in order to vanquish it?

To other anti-imperialists, Bryan's position seemed callously opportunistic. Bryan cornered South Dakota Senator Richard Pettigrew and said the American occupation of the Philippines would deal a fatal blow to the McKinley administration. "I was so incensed by his effort to induce me, on the score of expediency, to change front on a matter of principle and stultify myself," Pettigrew recalled, "that I finally told him emphatically that he had no business in Washington on such an errand; that his stand reflected on his character and reputation as a man, and indicated a lack of knowledge of human affairs which must make his friends feel that he was not a suitable person to be President of the United States."

That's what Bryan wanted: to be president. "He was seeking political capital and he was willing to take it where he found it,"

Pettigrew remembered. Bryan was just another political bucca-neer who pushed aside anything or anyone in his way.

Already an agile politician with an electric smile, Bryan was also given to self-persuasion: his cause was just because he was a just man, a Christian man, a man of peace.

And successful, thus far. The treaty was ratified by one vote. As for a stable government in the Philippines, not a chance. A horrific guerrilla war would last three bloody years, atrocities committed on both sides. Bryan hated the bloodshed—and his country's abandoning, as he said, its principles of democratic government.

There was more. Bryan wanted, eventually, an independent Philippines because he believed in national self-determination. But he also believed, as he put it, there was no other choice. The idea of a Filipino as an American citizen appalled him. "To advocate the incorporation of the Filipinos as embryo citizens to participate in the election of members of congress and senators and presidents, is not to be thought of, for it would involve this country in a race question even more difficult to handle than the tremendous race problem with which the nation is now grappling," he wrote.

That "tremendous race problem" was what Bryan called "The Negro Question." "When conditions force the two races to live under the same government in the same country the more advanced race never has consented, and probably never will consent, to be dominated by the less advanced," he stated. The influential Black journalist John E. Bruce observed that Bryan didn't wish to alienate white Democrats in the South, regardless of what tactics they might use to disenfranchise Black men. Theodore Roosevelt also took note. "It does seem to me that Mr. Bryan cannot be acquitted of hypocrisy when he prattles about the 'consent of the governed' in the Philippines and profits by the denial of this same so-called right in North Carolina and Alabama."

Bryan's racial bias was not terribly unlike that of his friend Benjamin Tillman, though it was quieter and less conspicuous. Tillman, a senator from South Carolina, earned the nickname Pitchfork when he once promised to go to Washington and stick a pitchfork in old Grover Cleveland's "fat ribs"—to prod him into helping (white) farmers. For Tillman was also a white supremacist who proudly announced that in the South "we are not ashamed" of stuffing ballot boxes, and he'd show off, with pleasure, the rifle he used to massacre Black people at the polls. An Anglo-Saxon is an Anglo-Saxon, said Pitchfork, who "walks on the necks of every colored race he comes into contact with."

Bryan praised and admired Tillman and sought his advice. Like Tillman, Bryan also thought the "more advanced race" (Anglo-Saxon) "always exercised the right to impose conditions upon those less advanced."

When Theodore Roosevelt, as president, invited the educator Booker T. Washington to dine at the White House, Bryan stated emphatically that social equality should never be tolerated. He'd never advocate "social equality between the white man and the black man."

"No advantage," Bryan rationalized, "is to be gained by ignoring race prejudice."

"What are you or what am I, that we should undertake to advocate any social law that shall place us above men like Frederick Douglass or Booker Washington?" the old-time abolitionist Thomas Wentworth Higginson immediately wrote Bryan. In 1900, the Colored Citizens' League condemned both Bryan and Tillman.

THE BRYANS WERE ready to convince anyone who doubted that he could in fact win the presidency in 1900. He even welcomed a visit from William Allen White, the young Republican journalist who had panned him four years earlier.

White enjoyed the visit, up to a point, but left convinced that despite the serious limits of Bryan's curiosity and intelligence, the real problem was a shabby approach to learning: "He is not seeking the truth; he has it, and is seeking to make converts." He was also good at begging a question. All debaters and perhaps all politicians deflect, White said, but they at least know it. Not Bryan. "No fluttering wings of doubt that would have brushed by another man's eyes and made him stammer and hesitate in his climaxes, disturbed Bryan," White observed. And there was something stubborn about him. "Facts never budged him," White later recalled. "Wild horses could never drag him from a stand."

In 1900, though, Theodore Roosevelt, another tireless barnstormer, was McKinley's not-so-secret weapon, for on the ticket as vice president, Roosevelt flashed his toothy grin as he traveled from whistle-stop to whistle-stop, hot on the trail of Bryan, whom he considered "the very lightest weight this country has ever seriously considered for such an office." Fortified by Roosevelt's chronic vitality, a strong economy, and Bryan continuing to flog the silver issue, President McKinley won by a larger margin than he had four years earlier—and with a decisive victory in the Electoral College (292 to 155). Bryan even lost his home state of Nebraska as well as South Dakota, Utah, Washington, Wyoming, and Kansas.

Yet after the election Bryan continued to campaign, this time in his own newspaper, published weekly from his hometown of Lincoln and that he called, after his own nickname, *The Commoner*. With a circulation of more than a hundred thousand, it ran for twenty-two years, beginning in 1901, and provided Bryan with a bully pulpit. So too the paid lectures he delivered on the Chautauqua circuit, which for decades had delighted and edified audiences with speakers who ranged from American presidents to comedians to gospel singers and evangelists like Billy Sunday.

Bryan standing before *The Commoner* office
COURTESY NEBRASKA STATE HISTORICAL SOCIETY
PHOTOGRAPH COLLECTIONS

Bryan was a marquee attraction. "I remember well a Sunday when he spoke at Shelbyville, Illinois," reflected the muckraking journalist Charles Russell. "I estimated at 30,000 the crowd that filled the vast Chautauqua auditorium there and stretched far and far beyond it." Special trains often ferried listeners from nearby towns, businesses would close, and a tent would be raised to handle the droves of people, especially in the summertime, who came to hear Bryan when the weather was often so hot that Bryan, unruffled and unconcerned, kept a block of ice handy.

He received a standard fee of $250, plus half the gate over $500, but he refused to take money if the lecture fell on a Sunday. Overall he did make a good deal from his appearances, and often he gave the same uplifting lecture, over and over. No matter. For the audience who may have already heard it, repetition was comforting.

As a former presidential candidate, Bryan was a celebrated name abroad too. In Rome, he had an audience with Pope Pius X; in London he met British prime minister Arthur Balfour as well as Sidney and Beatrice Webb, leaders of the British Labour Party, and with Mary he visited Yasnaya Polyana, home of Count Leo Tolstoy. He admitted to never having read Tolstoy's novels or his works of philosophical atheism, but he adored the man's generous religious nature. The kingdom of God is within, Tolstoy sermonized, and at the time of Bryan's visit, he was working on a study of the abolitionist William Lloyd Garrison and the principle of nonresistance, which Bryan would make his own, though he'd reshape the principle to his own ends.

Back home, Bryan had decided to sit out a 1904 presidential run. "Conditions were not propitious for a third trial," as one of the pundits at the Democratic National Convention noted— putting the case in positive terms. "He must hold on to the reins without taking the risk of a ride." In fact, the more conservative wing of the Democratic Party had grown far more powerful. The twenty-four-year-old journalist Henry Louis Mencken, in Saint Louis to cover the convention, noted that Bryan in 1904 "had lost his grip" on the party although the galleries—thirty thousand men and women—shouted long and loudly for the Commoner.

Except for silver, not all Populist issues were dead, and the millionaire friend of labor, William Randolph Hearst, his ambition as huge as his purse, was angling for the presidential nomination. He had every reason to assume Bryan would support him, since he had put his wealth and his newspapers at Bryan's disposal. In 1896 Hearst had donated offices at the *New York Journal* as an informal Bryan headquarters, and in 1900, when Bryan asked for more help, Hearst opened a new daily paper in

Chicago, the *Chicago American,* to bolster the Commoner's profile in the Midwest. After Bryan lost, it was Hearst who sent Bryan, all expenses paid, to Europe as a correspondent.

Hearst's expectations were high when a haggard-looking Bryan rose to speak at the Democratic National Convention in 1904. Bryan's voice was barely audible since he'd been in bed with a fever, and as Henry Mencken recalled, "In his frayed alpaca coat and baggy pants he was a pathetic figure." But Mencken added, "That is precisely how he wanted to appear." Like Darrow, Bryan too was a performer. For in a matter of minutes, the mellifluous voice came surging back.

Though everyone assumed Bryan was about to second the nomination of Hearst, the Commoner mentioned him only in a brief, convoluted, halfhearted way. "If it is the choice of this Convention," Bryan declared, "though he has money, pleads the cause of the poor; the man who is best beloved, I can safely say, among laboring men, of all the candidates, proposed; the man who more than any other represents opposition to the trusts—if you want to place the standard in his hand and make Mr. Hearst the candidate of this Convention, I and Nebraska will be with you in the fight."

Bryan had betrayed Hearst, or so Hearst believed, and rightly it seems. Bryan much more vigorously endorsed the colorless Missouri Senator Francis Cockrell, an ex-Confederate brigadier general who couldn't possibly win—especially since he was running against an incumbent who happened now to be Theodore Roosevelt, who became president when McKinley had been assassinated in 1901. And Roosevelt was hugely popular.

Bryan may have been hoping for a deadlocked convention, one where he could liberate the Democratic Party from the conservatives within it. But Bryan was considering what would best serve Bryan. "Some of you have called me dictator," he cried out. "It was false. You know it was false. I had opinions and expressed them."

"You may say that I have not fought a good fight," Bryan said, rolling out his final remarks in the cadence of a Saint Paul. "You may say that I have not run a good race. [A longer pause, with dead silence in the galleries.] But no man [crescendo] shall say [a catch in the baritone voice] that I have not kept the faith!!!"

The Democrats nominated Alton Parker, a conservative judge from upstate New York, who was bound to lose not just because of Roosevelt's popularity but because William Jennings Bryan had helped guarantee his loss. Bryan didn't want any Democrat except himself to be president. Disheveled and hoarse as he had initially appeared, Bryan knew what he was doing, as Mencken said. "His soul was marching on."

BRYAN HAD BROKEN ground for a stone-and-brick mansion he was building just east of Lincoln, Nebraska, which he called "the Monticello of the West." The place cost $20,000 (roughly $600,000 today), Bryan admitted, but he had installed electric lighting, steam heat, and up-to-date plumbing—as well as prize poultry, cattle, and in the paddock sleek horses. Its dining room seated twenty-four, enough for a small convention. Christened with the name Fairview, his Monticello manse sat atop a hill from which Bryan and his guests could survey his fifty acres and vast stretches of farmland.

A suburban trolley passed by the front gate, and as it approached, the conductor would yell, "Bryan Station."

By 1908, Bryan was worth about $100,000 (circa $3 million in 2023), money amassed from real estate investments; from *The Commoner,* the newspaper that Bryan's brother Charles was efficiently managing; and from Bryan's hard work on the lecture circuit, which he adored. He readily spoke of salvation by faith, and of peace and love. Politics seemed remote but only because Bryan styled himself the ambassador of Christian populism; whatever else he may have been, William Jennings Bryan was a

Fairview, the Bryan home, Lincoln, Nebraska
COURTESY NEBRASKA STATE HISTORICAL SOCIETY
PHOTOGRAPH COLLECTIONS

crusader. "I fear the plutocracy of wealth," he liked to say. "I respect the aristocracy of learning; but I thank God for the democracy of the heart."

The speech Bryan delivered most frequently was the popular "The Prince of Peace," which he performed from 1903 onward in state after state, from Vermont to North Carolina and in Kentucky, Indiana, Missouri, Texas, and Utah. Said an early and unsympathetic biographer, Bryan "runs the death of Little Nell a close second for the booby prize of literature." But it wasn't literary esteem that Bryan sought. It was a torchlight parade, and when he arrived by rail or buggy, he expected to be greeted by the local dignitaries and swarms of people. He delivered "The Prince of Peace" in countless cities and abroad too—in Tokyo, Manila, Cairo, and Jerusalem, all the while claiming, wherever he spoke, that he had no intention of running again for president, which of course wasn't true. In 1908, when the Democrats nominated him for a third time, he used the speech as a campaign pamphlet, distributing at least two million copies. He was the Prince of Peace—not President Roosevelt's anointed successor, William Howard Taft, who was a Unitarian, which meant, to some listeners, including Bryan, an infidel. Roosevelt was so annoyed with this kind of bigotry that he publicly denounced it.

Bryan, presidential nominee again in 1908,
in a typical gesture
COURTESY GETTY IMAGES

Bryan lost again, powerfully, and while he trusted he was more fully becoming the Christian statesman that he aspired to be, he looked askance at such religious groups as Catholics and Mormons, who seemed to have voted for Taft. Protestants, he said, are opposed to sectarian politics but, he asked, "How long they will think this policy wise if opposite organizations make themselves a political power, can not be said." It wasn't a question; it was a warning.

Nor had the Prince of Peace changed his mind about race. Black men and women were denied admission to Bryan's kingdom of peace and love. In Charleston, West Virginia, Bryan said Black people should not be seated in the opera house, where he was speaking—not even in the gallery. Usually, he wasn't so peremptory, but he did believe, and repeatedly said, that each region in the country should be left to handle its own racial issues. Debating Senator Albert Beveridge of Indiana, Bryan reiterated without apology the importance of states' rights. If California wanted to segregate their schools, leaving Japanese children to fend for themselves, so be it. When the ardently progressive but by no means unprejudiced Beveridge accused Bryan of pandering to the same home rule arguments that had perpetuated slavery, the Commoner was sanguine. Northerners could not possibly understand white Southerners. "The people in the Northern states do not come in contact with the black race as the people of the South do," he insisted.

Bryan made clear what had been obvious all along. Like his father, Silas, he felt he'd been born in the greatest of all ages and in the greatest of all countries—and thankfully "not in the darkest of the continents and among the most backward of earth's peoples." In sum, he was a proud member of the "greatest of all the races, the Caucasian Race."

SOON BRYAN WAS adding a few tidbits about Charles Darwin and evolution to his mix of adages, anecdotes, and biblical homilies. Not pharisaical, not yet, he added that no, he would not quarrel with Darwin. Darwin just wasn't his cup of tea. "I cannot believe that man came from monkeys," he joked in 1907. "I don't say a man must not accept that belief, but he can't graft any such family tree on me." Laughter.

"I have no objection," he merrily continued, "for if a man has not the right to choose his ancestors, what right has he?" More laughter.

"I have as much right to assume as a scientist," he pointed out, "and I prefer to assume a designer back of the design. I prefer to assume a creator back of creation." Implicitly inviting his audience to agree, he'd cite how a big watermelon grew out of a watermelon seed, or he'd sometimes point to a radish, which he kept in his pockets so he could munch on them now and then. "Did you ever see a radish grow?" he might ask. "Where did it get its coloring matter, its flavoring extract? You can't explain it. But I like radishes and I eat them. You do not refuse radishes and other things because you cannot explain them. Mystery never bothers us in the dining room, only in the church."

"We cannot understand all the mysteries of the Bible, but if we live up to what we do understand, we will be too busy to work out those which we don't."

And there was comfort to be had in divine creation: "If the Father deigns to touch with divine power the cold and pulseless heart of the buried acorn and to make it burst forth from its prison walls, will he leave neglected in the earth the soul of man, made in the image of his Creator? If the Father makes the acorn burst into new life," Bryan reasoned, "will He leave the soul of man to die?"

He may have lost the White House three times, but he was still on the stump, aware of the grassroots nature of reform, looking backward toward the agrarian past—that man with the hoe—and looking forward to a renewed religious present of brotherly love and economic equity. He continued to speak out against corporate privilege and predatory wealth, against those greedy captains of rapacious industry, talking and writing in a vernacular that was part biblical and part corn-fed and that his listeners and his readers could understand. He supported them—and they, him.

As he happily remarked, some folk considered him the reincarnation of Christ, which was to say that the Commoner believed sincerely and amiably, nobly and egotistically, that he was keeping the faith.

Part 2

Prejudices
1876–1923

The world always blames the thunder-bolt, it forgets the storm
that had been gathering through the years.

—CLARENCE DARROW

Chapter Three

Huxley, Nietzsche, Mencken

1876–1917

Give me the liberty to know, to utter, and to argue freely
according to conscience, above all liberties.
—JOHN MILTON

IN JUNE 1860, JUST SIX months after Darwin's *Origin of Species* was published, a huge crowd gathered at Oxford University to hear Archbishop Samuel Wilberforce, a superb debater, match wits with the pugnacious and eminent scientist Thomas Henry Huxley. Which of them, the bishop or the scientist, was equipped to understand and explain the origin of the human species?

Huxley, a burly man with big fluffy side-whiskers, would eventually be remembered in America—as well as England—as Darwin's Bulldog. That is, when he first read *Origin of Species*, Huxley exclaimed that it struck him "like a flash of light, which, to a man who has lost himself in a dark night, suddenly reveals a road." From then on, he would defend the book and Darwin, his bashful friend.

But Wilberforce was smug. He intended to ridicule Darwin and demolish once and for all the theory of evolution, which was utterly incompatible with his belief in God. God had created humans, pure and simple, in His image. There was no slow evolution, over time, through natural selection. That was unthinkable. And that was that.

The archbishop paused. He turned to Huxley. Was Huxley descended from the monkey on his grandfather's or his grandmother's side?

Huxley whispered to the person seated beside him, "The Lord hath delivered him into mine hand." He rose from his chair.

Huxley turned to the archbishop. "If I would rather have a miserable ape for a grandfather, or a man highly endowed by nature and possessed of great means and influence, and yet who employs those faculties for the mere purpose of introducing ridicule into a grave scientific discussion"—Huxley took a breath—"I unhesitatingly affirm my preference for the ape."

Seated in the audience, a Lady Brewster is said to have fainted.

HENRY LOUIS MENCKEN would claim that there could have been no Scopes case had Thomas Henry Huxley not lived. To Mencken, the polymath British scientist was an intellectual colossus, with his boldness, his vast erudition, and his crushing logic. "No man can think in English today," Mencken said, "without paying some sort of tribute to him."

"His mind was an almost perfect instrument, as formidable as a 16-inch gun and balanced like a watch," Mencken continued. "When he unlimbered it against enemies the carnage was terrific. And every fraud in the world was his enemy."

As usual, Mencken overstated the case, but Mencken was adamant—and correct—about Huxley's wide-ranging intelligence and pellucid prose style. With proportion, clarity, and cool analysis, Huxley fought for what he believed: not just for Darwin and evolution but against superstition and willful ignorance. "Sit down before a fact as a little child," Huxley advised, "be prepared to give up every preconceived notion, follow humbly wherever and to whatever abysses nature leads, or you shall learn nothing."

Huxley contested anything transcendental, mystical, or religious with a rationality that was hard, reassuring, and unshakable. And it was Huxley who apparently coined the term "agnostic" in 1869, meaning one who "believes only those propositions which can be demonstrated with logically satisfactory evidence." Toward all else, Huxley remained open-mindedly skeptical—and unconcerned about blowback. "If I had at my side all those who, since the Christian era, have been called infidels by other folks," he said, "I could not desire better company."

He was also a fine writer. "No man has ever written more nearly perfect English prose," Mencken said. "My style of writing is chiefly grounded upon an early enthusiasm for Huxley, the greatest of all masters of orderly exposition. He taught me the importance of giving to every argument a simple structure."

Mencken also described Huxley as being "like all men who discover in themselves a talent for controversy, he eventually found a delight in it for its own sake."

Mencken was describing Mencken.

WITH HAIR CAREFULLY parted down the middle and in his mouth a corncob pipe or, more likely, a chewed-up cigar, Henry Mencken was said to look like a teenage troublemaker. Slightly overweight and round-shouldered, he measured five feet eight and a half. His eyes were the color of a clear blue pond; his cheeks, cherry-blossom pink. His black shoes were highly polished. He liked music, particularly Bach's B minor Mass and Schubert's "Cello" Quintet and anything by Haydn or Beethoven. Wagner's *Die Meistersinger* was to him the greatest single work of art ever produced. Mencken saw the world in primary colors.

He was also a consummate stylist, a disturbing polemicist, and a remarkably influential invective-slinger. "He calls you a

swine," the journalist Walter Lippmann remarked, "and he increases your will to live." By the 1920s, Mencken was associated
with modernism, which had become a cultish catchphrase
broadly signifying a rejection of consumerism, mediocrity, and
institutional authority—and whose elements were worshipped
almost as assiduously and intolerantly as anything the Fundamentalists worshipped. Mencken was its evangelist, adored by
the postwar generation. "So many young men," Ernest Hemingway wrote, "get their likes and dislikes from Mencken."

Not everyone was so enamored. "The gleam of fanaticism is
in Mr. Mencken's eye while he inveighs against the bigotry of the
priests and the stupidity of their followers," theologian Reinhold
Niebuhr trenchantly observed in 1930 when reviewing Mencken's *Treatise on the Gods,* a book on religion. "It really tells us
little more than how one fanatic feels about other fanatics of a
different stripe."

For Mencken was conservative in many ways. Something of
a homebody, he never really left his native Baltimore, or at least
not for long. His family had emigrated from Germany a generation earlier, and his father, August, had opened a cigar factory in
Baltimore with a brother. Business was good. The Menckens
owned a nearby summer place, and the four Mencken children
were well cared for. But August didn't know what to do with
Henry, the oldest child. He'd graduated at sixteen at the top of
his class at the highly rated Baltimore Polytechnic Institute high
school but didn't want to go to college.

Obsessed with the printing press his father had given him as
a Christmas present, by the time he turned fifteen, Mencken was
hooked on journalism. August offered to send him to Johns
Hopkins University. Henry wanted to be a reporter. To August,
journalism, insofar as it was a profession, Mencken later recalled, "was above that of a street-walker but below that of a
police captain."

Henry was shipped off to the family cigar factory. Then in the winter of 1898, when Henry had not yet turned nineteen, his father suddenly took ill and died fewer than two weeks later. "Looking back," Mencken would reminisce, "I am convinced that his death was the luckiest thing that ever happened to me, though we were on good terms, and I missed him sorely after he was gone." One biographer speculates that August's sudden death deprived his son Henry of a proper rebellion, which he displaced onto other so-called father figures. Certainly he lampooned teachers, ministers, politicians, lawyers, judges, legislators, authors, and reformers—authorities or vaunted authorities—with fiendish delight. All authorities were fair game, except of course when he was the authority.

Shortly after his father's funeral, Henry shaved, put on his best suit, and showed up at the offices of the *Baltimore Morning Herald* asking for a job. There wasn't one, and he was politely turned away, but he resolutely came back every day, ready to go, just in case. Soon he was handed an assignment as a cub reporter without pay, and he proved so efficient, reliable, and articulate that he was hired to cover crime, the police courts, the waterfront, city hall, and the saloons. In 1900, when he was nineteen, he went to the Democratic National Convention in Kansas City though he wasn't even old enough to vote.

By 1903 he was promoted to city editor, then managing editor, and in 1905 to editor in chief. He worked six days a week, fourteen hours a day. At the same time he turned out articles for rival papers and wrote some short stories as well as some fiction and a small, forgettable volume of poetry. Ellery Sedgwick, the encouraging editor of *Frank Leslie's Popular Monthly* magazine, which had published a story of Mencken's, offered him the position of associate editor. But he'd have to move to New York. Mencken refused. "I was disinclined," Mencken would recall, "to desert my mother in Baltimore, and the comfortable home she had provided for me, and take up a lonely life in a town I disliked."

Mencken stayed in Baltimore for the rest of his life. After his mother died in 1925, he continued to live in the same house at 1524 Hollins Street where she lived and where he was raised. He did carry on a long-distance relationship with a woman named Marion Bloom for over ten years but would not commit himself—or give up living at home. "If I had to leave it," he wrote of Hollins Street, "I'd be as certainly crippled as if I lost a leg." In 1930, he married the tubercular Sara Haardt, and though they moved into their own place, when Sara died five years later, Mencken went back to the family seat.

Henry L. Mencken, Bad Boy of Baltimore
COURTESY LIBRARY OF CONGRESS

All the while he produced at an astonishing rate. He published a book on the plays of George Bernard Shaw in 1905. The next year, after the *Morning Herald* failed, he began writing columns for the Baltimore *Sun* about a myriad of subjects, from local politics to vaudeville to music to free speech to brothels, American cooking, and Henrik Ibsen. His prose was plain, direct, colloquial, and devoid of circumlocution. "A language is not the master, but the servant of people using it," he said. Mencken was not yet the scold who skewered reformers or radicals. Women should be allowed to vote, he said. "Isn't the present sovereignty of the male sex an obvious survival of ignorant and barbarous ages?" He admired William Jennings Bryan, who had valiantly battled the plutocrat, although by 1904, Bryan seemed washed up. "The king was dead," Mencken very prematurely predicted.

He declared capital punishment unspeakably savage. With controlled contempt he congratulated the people of Mississippi for perfecting their "native art of lynching." They had hanged Elmo Curl from a tree for supposedly insulting a young white woman, and think of it, Mencken wrote: no one was drunk or disorderly or had even bothered to fire a gun. "Their lynchings are now conducted in a refined and businesslike manner—not by the rabble but by gentlemen selected for their public eminence and private worth," Mencken acidly explained. "The candidate is conducted to his predestined oak with ceremony and dignity."

"Lynchings, of course, are still painful events, particularly to those who are lynched," he concluded, "but if we must have them let us welcome any effort to make them measurably less barbarous."

The persecution of Leo Frank in 1913 sickened him. Frank, who was Jewish, had been accused of murdering a young woman who worked in his factory, and though found guilty and serving a life sentence, he had been kidnapped and lynched. The clergy who denounced Frank from the pulpit were just as guilty as the mob, Mencken bitterly wrote. "These noble men of God, having tasted blood in the vice crusade, were ripe for an even larger demonstration of their powers."

As for Frank, "he was handy and he was a Jew," Mencken added in disgust. "The rest is known to us all."

THOSE WHO TOOK their cue from Mencken failed to notice his deeply rooted and often obnoxious biases either because they enjoyed his iconoclasm too much or because they basically shared it. Henry Mencken could pierce a conventional assumption with a single thrust, and with deadpan hyperbole, he rendered accepted pieties absurd. Now, he said, give women the vote if only to kill off the suffragettes. In fact, all reform movements annoyed him and none more than the Anti-Saloon League and the vice crusaders, whom he dubbed smut-hounds—sad voyeurs who amused themselves by pruriently sniffing out dirt. He then dismissed socialists, inspirational speakers, pedagogues, preachers, the professoriat and, as he said, "the sort of patriotism that makes noise."

Often Mencken shocked on purpose. Just as often he was reactionary, unfair, and bigoted, flouting with a cheery cantankerousness what he liked to call "prejudices," which would be the title, later, of his six essay collections. "My prejudices are innumerable and often idiotic," he declared. He was right. He flaunted his misogyny, racism, and antisemitism almost as if goading his readers into battle. Unpredictable and brazen, often ironic and just as often odious, Mencken could write that "the Jews could be put down as the most unpleasant race ever heard of," yet he was one of the first to denounce the persecution of the Jews in Germany and the American refusal to help them. President Franklin Roosevelt might express sympathy, Mencken observed, but would not do anything that "would cause him inconvenience." He quoted from a column by his friend George Schuyler, a Black journalist. "Imagine Roosevelt saying 'he could scarcely believe' that such atrocities could take place in this day and time when white people had just got through burning a schoolhouse and running Negroes out of Smyrna, Ga., and had just finished jabbing red-hot pokers into a Negro youth in Ruston, La.!' "

Mencken swayed back and forth, cruelly hateful, shrewdly prophetic. He could be on the mark or vile. That he was gifted, there is no doubt. That he was limited, there is no doubt. James M. Cain, the detective novelist who early on worked at the Baltimore *Sun,* remembered Mencken as "an enchanting Mephistopheles, whose ideas were utterly reprehensible, and utterly irresistible."

"What amazed me was not what he said," the novelist Richard Wright observed, "but how on earth anybody had the courage to say it."

WHEN MENCKEN DISCOVERED Friedrich Nietzsche, he discovered in the German philosopher a rationale for his own iconoclasm. "Error was his enemy," Mencken exclaimed, "and he was ever merciless in combatting it, even when the combat meant a war upon himself." Nietzsche was a truth-teller, Mencken was a truth-teller, and both men struck out at sanctimonious moral codes.

Mencken studied German—what he learned at school was inadequate, and it was never spoken at home—so he could introduce Nietzsche to American readers in two books: a little one, *The Philosophy of Friedrich Nietzsche* in 1908, and then *The Gist of Nietzsche,* an anthology of Nietzschean aphorisms. "It is the fashion among the adherents of the old order to berate him for his ferocity," Mencken explained, "but some day, perhaps, the world will learn to give men of his kind the honor that is their due."

The honor due had to do with Nietzsche's definitions of morals, which, as Mencken put it, are merely human laws "given divine sanction in order to lend them authority. In the course of time, perhaps, the race outgrows them, but none the less, they continue in force—at least so long as the old gods are worshipped. Thus human laws become divine—and inhuman. Thus morality itself becomes immoral."

Instead of the old gods, there was Nietzsche's "superman" or "Übermensch." To Mencken, this meant the genius, the superindividualist, the mighty iconoclast and Nietzschean superstar who proudly rises far above the sappy morality of the bourgeois, as Mencken described it, "that burned the books of the ancient sages, and morality that halted the free inquiry of the Golden Age and substituted for it the credulous imbecility of the Age of Faith. It was a fixed moral code and a fixed theology which robbed the human race of a thousand years by wasting them upon alchemy, heretic-burning, witchcraft and sacerdotalism." By contrast, and as Mencken understood and peddled Nietzsche, the "superman" could never conform or be chained by conventional moral strictures. He (and it was a "he") was free.

Mencken's Nietzsche, "the high priest of the actual," was tough-minded, modern, anticlerical, anti-authoritarian, and antibourgeois. That would be Mencken himself, offering "a counterblast to that childish sentimentality, that pathos, that emotional denial of reality which marks democracy at its worst." Mencken would distinguish himself from the masses, specifically the working class, or, as he told a friend, those men he remembered from his father's cigar factory.

Mencken's Nietzsche was also a Darwinian—at least in the way that Mencken understood Darwin and Thomas Huxley. For Mencken, it would be absurd to label any struggle for survival as evil, even in humans. "Among human beings," Mencken wrote, "as well as among the bacilli in the hanging drop and the lions in the jungle, there is ever in progress this ancient struggle for existence. It is waged decently, perhaps, but it is none the less savage and unmerciful, and the devil always takes the hindmost."

"Without this constant strife—this constant testing—this constant elimination of the unfit—there can be no progress," Mencken claimed. "The strong always exploit the weak." Sounding like a robber baron who thought himself the "fittest," Mencken said that "charity merely converts the unfit . . . into parasites—who live on indefinitely, a nuisance and a burden to their betters."

Ugly stuff, especially since Mencken surely understood but chose to ignore what Huxley called "the unfortunate ambiguity of the phrase 'survival of the fittest.'" But Huxley was clear. That unfortunate phrase, "survival of the fittest," has nothing to do with being better or worse, he said; it has only to do with being the "best adapted to the changed conditions," whatever they may be.

"THE JOY OF life comes in overcoming difficulties," Mencken once remarked. Revealing more than he perhaps intended, he also explained to a friend that his Nietzschean individualism coincided with his own work ethic: there was much joy to be had in "a riddle solved, an enemy vanquished, a fact proved, an error destroyed—in such things he finds the meaning of life and surcease from its sorrows." Mencken thus saluted what he believed to be the Nietzschean strongman, "the intelligent, ingenious and far-seeing man who would acknowledge no authority but his own and no morality but his own advantage."

Whether Mencken entirely believed all this is another story. He despised what he saw as vulgar materialism. "My own private view (the child, I must admit, of a very ardent wish) is that the idea of truth seeking will one day take the place of the idea of money-making," he declared. He lived cheaply. His favorite place to eat was the lunch counter in the basement of Baltimore's Rennert Hotel. As for the country and the way it was changing or the fact that workers were organizing, he told a friend that "whether we adopt Socialism or accept things as they are, we must come eternally upon periods of stress and storm, and during these periods the strong will prevail over the weak, and every manmade law that seeks to stay them will be swept away."

He was the big, acerbic bad boy of Hollins Street.

BY 1908 MENCKEN had begun writing a monthly book column for *The Smart Set,* "a magazine of cleverness," as it called itself. A forerunner of *The New Yorker,* the magazine aimed to entertain the affluent, sophisticated cognoscenti or those who wished they were. It was a perfect fit for Mencken. His own style had become epigrammatic, finely balanced, often abrasive, often pithy. And often very funny. He said he hoped "to make a dent in the cosmos with a slapstick."

Mencken might claim Mark Twain's *Huckleberry Finn* the best novel written by an American. Huck, the urchin with a heart of gold, dislikes violence, hates meanness ("human beings can be awful cruel to one another"), and, best of all, steers clear of religion. Yet Mencken could be critical even of Twain. "There are chapters in *Huckleberry Finn* in which he stands beside Cervantes and Molière," Mencken observed. "There are chapters in *The Innocents Abroad* in which he is indistinguishable from Mutt and Jeff."

He adored Joseph Conrad, especially *Lord Jim.* He admired Thackeray and George Meredith. He praised the writer Israel Zangwill, and Frank Norris's *McTeague,* and wrote of Oscar Wilde with elegant compassion. He detected promise in the novels of Marjorie Patterson and delighted in the reminiscences of journalist George W. Smalley although, as Mencken pointed out, no one tells the truth in a memoir. "Who has the courage to pull his own tooth?"

He praised fluency in the work of Helen Mackay and said of Henry James's early essays that James had actually written some of them in English. He praised George Moore and John Muir. Dreiser's *Jennie Gerhardt* was better than the great *Sister Carrie*. John Millington Synge was one of the most talented playwrights of the generation. And Upton Sinclair, like all socialists, was too serious, but Sylvia Pankhurst's *The Suffragette* convinced Mencken that women should be able to vote.

Usually he stayed away from poetry though he described Edwin Markham as an artist turned propagandist. As for Whitman, "old Walt for all his absurdities was yet a poet at heart," Mencken wrote. "Whenever he ceased, even for a brief moment, to emit his ethical and sociological rubbish, a strange beauty crept into his lines and his own deep emotion glorified them." He couldn't read the romances of Sir Walter Scott without snoring or the sentimental passages in Dickens without swearing, and the Christian Scientists, he remarked, "have an answer to my answer to their answer, and I have an answer to their answer to my answer to their answer."

In the spring of 1914, Mencken was promoted to coeditor of *The Smart Set,* sharing the job with the urbane, hotel-dwelling, and impeccably dressed drama critic George Jean Nathan. Together, they published such writers as James Joyce, Willa Cather, Sherwood Anderson, Eugene O'Neill, and then Hugh Walpole, Padraic Colum, Elinor Wylie, and Arthur Symons.

"I AM AN extreme libertarian," Mencken always maintained, "and believe in absolute free speech, especially for anarchists, Socialists and other such fools." In 1915, he spearheaded the protest against Anthony Comstock's New York Society for the Suppression of Vice when it tried to ban Dreiser's novel *The Genius.* Mencken didn't much like the book—its structure was too loose—but he despised censorship. "Of what value is the right of free speech if it is not the right to say things that the majority dislikes to hear?"

And Mencken did just that. He spoke out, especially after the assassination of Austrian archduke Franz Ferdinand plunged Europe into war in 1914: Allies, like Britain and France, were fighting the Central Powers, which included Austria-Hungary, the Ottoman Empire, Russia, and Germany. At first, he wrote of the war with a bellicose enthusiasm that bordered on the obscene. War would shake people up with "the cleansing shock of adversity," he said. Somehow war would make Americans strong, though America was not involved. "The American people, too secure in their isolation and grown too fat in their security, show all the signs of deterring national health," Mencken taunted. "They are afraid of everything, including even themselves. They are afraid of women, they are afraid of alcohol, they are afraid of money." Readers were appalled.

Then again, so was he. For soon, in America, which was presumably neutral, all things German had become suspect. German-born Harvard psychology professor Hugo Münsterberg, who wanted to keep America out of the war, was said to be a spy for the kaiser. Mencken seethed. Baltimore's German Street was renamed Redwood Street, and sauerkraut renamed "liberty cabbage." The German language was considered barbarous, and German books would be burned in Oklahoma on the Fourth of July. "The country is in a state of moral mania," Mencken told Theodore Dreiser, also of German descent. Mencken himself would be watched.

Fiercely Mencken denounced the British propaganda circulating in America: tales of German soldiers slicing off the hands of Belgian children or crucifying Canadian soldiers with their bayonets. Americans were told to refuse the services of a German waiter, and if the waiter insists that he is Swiss, demand to see a passport. "Eagle-eyed scientists," he wrote, "discovered ground glass in pumpernickel, arsenic in dill pickles, bichloride tablets in Bismarck herrings, pathogenic organisms in aniline dyes."

Mencken refused to be neutral. "Neutral? Not on your life!" he burst out in one of his columns. "I am no more neutral in this war than the Hon. Winston Churchill or Gen. Joseph Joffre." Letters of outrage and protest poured into the Baltimore *Sun*. "Herr Heinrich L. Menchener" was a hyphenated American— that is, not a real American but a German—and a screech.

Then on Friday, May 7, 1915, the *Lusitania,* the largest ship of the British Cunard Line, was destroyed by a German submarine. En route from New York to Liverpool, it was hit in the afternoon, just as passengers were finishing lunch and could see the hills of Ireland from the deck. Of the 1,959 passengers and crew, a staggering 1,195 people died. Dead babies were fished out of the sea, and 885 bodies were never found. Only 11 of the 139 Americans aboard survived.

Mencken was not sympathetic. He pointed out that the people aboard the *Lusitania* were being used as human shields because the British ship was carrying munitions, and the ship's captain had steered it into waters in which two other British ships had recently been sunk.

Some thought Mencken was secretly gloating.

"It is a first principle of this tinpot 'Americanism' that any man who dissents from the prevailing platitudes is a hireling of the devil," he replied. "It is a second principle that he should be silenced and destroyed forthwith. Down with free speech."

Mencken was writing for the Baltimore *Sun* less frequently, and though he said he was ready to leave newspaper work—not quite true—his last column appeared that October. In early 1917, the paper sent him briefly to Germany as a war correspondent, advertising him as pro-German. He returned home after a few months, and as soon as his stories ran, he and the *Sun* parted company for a short time.

Mencken was hired by the New York *Evening Mail* until its publisher, Edward Rumely, was charged with operating a newspaper controlled by the kaiser, which it wasn't. The financing came from a German American. Convicted of trading with the enemy, Rumely was pardoned—although not until 1925.

"I HAVE BEEN engaged in propagandist writing of one sort or another for seventeen years past," Mencken admitted in 1916. "My writings have always failed of success when they were chiefly made up of praise, however well deserved; they have always been successful when they dealt principally in abuse, however ill deserved." More than ever, he loathed provincialism and puritanism and a public that preferred pipe dreams and propaganda to common sense or evidence. "Boobus Americanus" he called them.

He sat in his office on the top floor of his Hollins Street home to write about the aspect of America he loved: its language. In it he placed his flickering faith. Perennially fascinated by how we say what we say, Mencken wrote of the myriad contributions of Yiddish and German and Hebrew and Italian and Hungarian and Russian to the English written and spoken by Americans, and he wrote about how those contributions affected anyone who spoke it. Under his foul bluster, some real, some feigned, Henry Mencken affirmed, beautifully and with bright eloquence, that "in all human beings, if only understanding be brought to the business, dignity will be found, and that dignity cannot fail to reveal itself, soon or late, in the words and phrases with which they make known the high hopes and aspirations and cry out against the intolerable meaninglessness of life."

As it is with most cynics, Mencken's mockeries were rooted in an idealism never really relinquished.

Chapter Four

Making the World Safe

1912–1918

Once lead this people into war, and they'll forget there ever
was such a thing as tolerance.

—ATTRIBUTED TO WOODROW WILSON

I N 1912, DEMOCRATS THOUGHT THEY just might recapture the
White House. Former President Theodore Roosevelt and the
incumbent president William Howard Taft had fallen out, and if
Roosevelt ran, he and Taft would split the Republican vote, leaving an opportunity for a Democrat to win. William Jennings
Bryan was not averse to throwing his hat in the ring, even if it
would be for the fourth time.

But when the Democratic convention met at the end of that
June, the Nebraska delegates weren't pledged to Bryan but to his
friend Missouri Representative James "Champ" Clark, the
Speaker of the House and the Democratic front-runner—until,
that is, Bryan climbed on stage.

At fifty-two, he looked older, plumper, and less handsome.
His dark eyes were bright as he began to speak, and in an act of
unforgivable disloyalty, at least as far as Champ Clark was concerned, Bryan suggested that Clark was the tool of Wall Street

capitalists and the corrupt Tammany Hall crowd. Bryan would refuse to support anyone that New York backed.

"I never have known a case of political treachery equal to or even approaching that of William J. Bryan," a political observer reported. Champ Clark never forgave him.

No one ever really knew if it had been conscience or ambition that had motivated Bryan. Likely it was both. If Bryan could finagle a deadlocked convention, as he was said to have done before, in 1904, he could emerge the Democratic standard-bearer.

Whatever Bryan ultimately wanted, and though he'd not been elected to public office for twenty years—since 1890, to the House of Representatives—he was still a man to be reckoned with in the party, like it or not: the party's prophet and nemesis, said a supporter of New Jersey Governor Woodrow Wilson; at the helm of the Democratic Party, Bryan had led it to defeat three times.

The gray-eyed Wilson, formerly the president of Princeton University, was a Democrat but not a Bryan man. He'd gone so far as to remark rashly—and famously—that he wished his party "could do something at once dignified and effective to knock Mr. Bryan once and for all into a cocked hat," meaning he'd like the Democrats to count Bryan out. But not even Wilson could ignore Bryan. At a Democratic Party dinner in Washington, Wilson partly surrendered. "If anyone has said anything annoying about any of the other candidates, for which he is sorry, now is the time to apologize," Wilson coyly declared, bowing in the direction of Bryan. The applause was enthusiastic. "Bryan's face was that of a man who had met his Waterloo," said a Wilson man. "Here was the rising of a new political star, which he well knew meant the setting of his own." Amid the great applause, Bryan rose from his seat, accepted the halfhearted apology and admitted, in some confusion, that it was time for the Democrats to nominate someone new.

Woodrow Wilson ran for president in 1912, and Bryan loyally campaigned for him. In fact, Mary Bryan reported that "people through the country regard him as a hero," referring to her husband. Bryan might be impractical, wrong-headed, or muddled, but he did have a devoted following and a commitment to progressive reforms. Wilson understood that Bryan was a real political asset and, besides, Bryan in a Wilson cabinet wouldn't be able to run for president in 1916. "When you are on a football team," Representative James M. Cox remarked, "you never kick the shins of one of your own players."

Mary B. Bryan, circa 1912
COURTESY LIBRARY OF CONGRESS

Elected with a large 42 percent of the vote, Wilson as President appointed Bryan his Secretary of State. To Washington and diplomatic sophisticates, the appointment was absurd. "Wilson didn't knock Bryan into a cocked hat, after all," newspapers reported. "He knocked him into a silk hat." Secretary Bryan appeared ignorant of foreign policy or history. The British journalist Sidney Brooks predicted Mr. Bryan would administer matters of state with the same "valor of ignorance with which he espoused Free Silver." Much as he liked Bryan, John Bassett Moore, a State Department expert in international law, complained that Bryan was often absent from Washington, busy delivering paid lectures while affairs of state languished, and consular vacancies remained unfilled. Bryan kept losing important papers by stuffing them into his coat pockets and then sending his coat off to the cleaners. "Chaos prevails," Moore groaned and resigned from the State Department in 1914.

Bryan was the butt of endless jokes. A determined teetotaler who decided everyone else should be one too, at his first formal reception, Bryan piously served grape juice, not claret, and had some colorless liquid poured into everyone's tumbler. The Russian ambassador took a sip and announced he hadn't tasted water for years.

The ribbing about his "grape-juice diplomacy" didn't bother Bryan, though he did take offense when foreign diplomats lied or, from their point of view, shaded the truth, which they felt it was their job to do. And Bryan cared less about having qualified, experienced consuls, clerks, or advisers appointed than about picking the men he dubbed "deserving Democrats"—Democrats, that is, to whom Bryan felt grateful or whom he wanted in his debt. Bryan was also vigilant about protecting the administration from those men he considered infidels. When Wilson offered the Chinese ambassadorship to Harvard president emeritus Charles William Eliot, Bryan wanted to know how a Unitarian who didn't believe in the divinity of Christ could guide the Chinese toward Christianity. Eliot turned down the post.

But as Secretary of State, Bryan fought hard for passage of Wilson's domestic legislation. Duly proud of his accomplishment, Bryan could and did brag about the progressive policies and reforms he'd backed for years: legislation about federal control of the country's monetary system, resulting in the Federal Reserve Board, and antitrust legislation. Bryan also managed to negotiate bilateral peace treaties between the United States and thirty countries to ensure what was called a "cooling-off period" should tensions escalate between them and the United States. (Germany and Austria-Hungary did not sign.)

Still, Bryan supported a treaty that compromised the independence of Nicaragua (the Bryan-Chamorro Treaty), sent the navy as a show of force to Santo Domingo harbor, and allowed the occupation of the port of Vera Cruz, Mexico. More than one hundred Mexicans were killed. And though the United States occupation of Haiti did not occur during Bryan's tenure as Secretary of State, "Pacifist Bryan" had implored Wilson to post warships there.

As Wilson remarked, Bryan had to be restrained when dealing with small republics like the Dominican Republic or Haiti, yet he used the "soft pedal" in negotiations with Germany. For after the sinking of the *Lusitania* in 1915, Wilson wanted to send a stiff reprimand to Germany demanding the Imperial government abandon its submarine campaign and guarantee the safety of noncombatants—American citizens—wherever they had a legal right to travel or trade. Berlin should also apologize and offer reparations. Bryan worried that the note was too confrontational. Shouldn't there be a cooling-off period? Wilson listened, yet sent the reprimand to Berlin anyway.

Berlin replied that the *Lusitania* had been carrying munitions as well as Canadian soldiers, which would account for the size of the explosion. It was the ship's owners, the British Cunard Line, not Germany, that was responsible for the deaths. Agitated, Bryan asked why, if America was indeed neutral, the cabinet could criticize Germany and not censure England. British interference with noncombatant trade and ports violated international law and, more important, prevented food from reaching the German people.

The matter at hand was the sinking of the *Lusitania,* the tragedy, the loss, the enormity of it all, Wilson icily replied.

"If I run again for the Presidency, it will be only to keep Bryan out," Wilson soon confided to a friend. "For he would make a very bad President: he would be ruinous to the country, ruinous to his own reputation. He always wants to think the best of everybody but he's the worst judge of character I ever knew, a spoilsman to the core and a determined enemy to civil service reform."

Wilson had sent a first note to Berlin. He began to prepare a second one. When the cabinet reconvened on June 4, 1915, Wilson read aloud his response to Berlin. Bryan was silent. He was still troubled. He closed his eyes. He had hoped the note would have been softened. He'd hoped there could be some negotiation, both with Germany, for its destruction of the *Lusitania,* and with England, for its interference with international shipping. But Wilson's stiff reply did not offer any such cooling-off period or plan for mediation.

Convinced that Wilson's reply to Berlin—saber-rattling—would lead to war with Germany, Bryan resigned.

Wilson tried to convince him to stay. Bryan was tearful, his voice shaky. "I have never had your full confidence," he said.

Several members of the Cabinet would take Bryan to lunch. "I go out in the dark," he said, his eyes wet. Bizarrely, he then added, "I have many friends who would die for me."

A CHRISTIAN STATESMAN out of work is a real menace, Edgar Lee Masters grimly observed. But Bryan still had a job. He was the Prince of Peace. He was at liberty to denounce war. "A pistol-toting nation is about as certain to get into trouble as a pistol toting person," he declared in the fall of 1915.

Bryan delivered antiwar speeches from coast to coast. He spoke to the eight thousand people seated in the municipal auditorium in Houston; and in Ann Arbor, Michigan, students by the thousands came to hear him. He was famous, he was the Commoner, he was the teetotaler who dared serve grape juice to foreign diplomats, and he could call for peace in as many as ten rallies a day. "Bryan is as usual an ass, but he is an ass with a good deal of opportunity for mischief," former President William Howard Taft remarked.

Bryan's peace platform exasperated even people fond of him and certainly those who were banging the war drum, like Kansas journalist William Allen White, who thought Bryan's pacifism abject and cowardly. And it appeared that Bryan's quixotic resignation undermined President Wilson's position. The resignation made the American government look weak, and the country divided, in its attitude toward Germany.

Woodrow Wilson privately called Bryan a traitor.

Yet Bryan stayed loyal to the administration, and the next year, in 1916, fully backed Wilson when Wilson ran again for president. Wilson was the only man who'd keep the country out of the war, Bryan claimed, toeing the party line.

That proved not to be true. Wilson was elected, and Germany resumed unrestricted submarine warfare although it had pledged not to do so. After several merchant ships were attacked, in the spring of 1917, Woodrow Wilson addressed a joint session of Congress to ask for a declaration of war against the Imperial German government. "The world must be made safe for democracy," Wilson stated, brandishing one of the eloquent slogans that he became famous for. "Its peace must be planted upon the tested foundations of political liberty." The first American troops began landing in France in June.

Bryan immediately offered his services to the government, as he had in the Spanish-American War, should it need him. It didn't.

Bryan always chose, Edgar Lee Masters would note, "the lower path of expediency and party regularity when issues of great moment were pressing and much was at stake."

And so—perhaps as part of a larger strategy—Bryan found a new cause. Instead of peace, silver, the direct election of senators, or a federal income tax, he talked up temperance. He would wage his next great battle against alcohol and the "liquor interests," which were bent on creating havoc, devastating families, destroying lives.

"I had some glimpses of what a national campaign on this subject would be," Bryan's wife, Mary, presciently observed. "A veritable religious crusade."

This was just the right job, a crusade, for a Christian diplomat out of office.

In one month alone, Bryan gave at least sixty speeches opposing the manufacture and sale of intoxicating beverages. If alcohol wasn't harmful, why did colleges ban it? If alcohol wasn't harmful, why was the government trying to pass a law forbidding its sale to soldiers? For think of what alcohol does, Bryan would say. It takes the son from the mother, the husband from the wife, the father from the children. Homes were wrecked, lives ruined.

Banning the sale of liquor did not infringe on an individual's rights. No one can assert a right that interferes with the rights of others, Bryan explained, rationalizing his new platform. And lest anyone think that his campaign to outlaw alcoholic beverages was anti-German because many brewers were German Americans, not a chance. It was the liquor business itself that had turned the question of prohibition into what he called "a race question." He wasn't targeting German distilleries; he was targeting all makers and distributors of alcohol.

The cold and overcast December morning in 1917 that the House of Representatives was to vote on a prohibition amendment, Bryan paid for a large advertisement, one-quarter of a page, four columns in all, in Washington newspapers, urging the representatives to pass the amendment. When the House voted in favor of it, Bryan rushed from the gallery to the floor so that he could shake the hands of party leaders. It was the greatest moral and economic reform in years, he declared. Outlawing the sale, manufacture, and distribution of alcohol, the amendment would pass the Senate the next day and then go to the states for ratification.

"This reform is needed," Bryan wrote, "to ensure *national* prohibition in this country." Nothing short of a ratified constitutional amendment on prohibition, and its strict enforcement, would satisfy him.

Next stop, suffrage. That too was a moral question, he said, especially since Bryan considered women his great ally in his fight against the saloon, the breweries, the distilleries, and the drunks.

GOVERNOR WILSON HAD promised American women the vote, but once elected president he did not urge Congress to pass the Susan B. Anthony Amendment, as the suffrage amendment was called. In 1917, tired of waiting, the National Women's Party declared that if the European war was now to be waged by Americans for democracy, democracy should begin at home.

On the Fourth of July, 1917, women from the National Woman's Party marched in front of the White House, waving flags of purple and gold and white. The police rushed them and seized their flags. Taking their cue from the police, bystanders charged at the women. Ten days later, on Bastille Day, more women showed up. They did not smash windows, they did not throw rocks, and they were not violent. They merely picketed in front of the White House gates. But sixteen women were arrested.

A valued member of the Wilson administration, the beguiling lawyer Dudley Field Malone, who would later join Clarence Darrow as co-counsel at the Scopes trial, defended the women, much to Wilson's surprise. Malone said the women had not been disorderly, adding that any other police department could have simply broken up the crowd to prevent it from blocking traffic. If there weren't enough police, it wasn't the women's fault.

The judge would have none of it. He declared the women guilty of obstructing the sidewalks and sentenced them either to pay a $25 fine or to spend sixty days in the Occoquan Workhouse. The women chose jail.

Doris Stevens, suffragist
COURTESY LIBRARY OF CONGRESS

Dudley Malone had met one of the women, the outspoken suffragist Doris Stevens, when he was campaigning for Wilson.

Originally from Nebraska, Stevens was raised a staunch Republican—back in 1896 her family proudly wore McKinley buttons—but by 1917, at twenty-nine, she was an energetic leader of the National Woman's Party, traveling coast to coast, appearing in smartly tailored suits or white shirtwaists, her picture often in the papers. At the Democratic National Convention in 1916, she had seized Navy Secretary Josephus Daniels by his coat lapel as he was about to slip out of the room.

"What will you do for the Susan B. Anthony Amendment, Mr. Secretary?" she asked.

"I've hardly given the matter a thought," Daniels hastily replied.

"You told me several months ago in New York," Stevens answered, "that you'd give the matter a thought at once." Nervously, Daniels looked around for the exit. "I'll do anything I can for you," he said before scooting out the door.

Daniels didn't do anything, and no one else had done much either. So she was at the Bastille Day demonstration in 1917, and she too was sent to the Occoquan Workhouse. Stevens called the whole episode "administration terrorism."

Her lawyer, Dudley Malone, was an impressive, intelligent, and handsome young man who'd become involved in politics almost as soon as he left Fordham University Law School in 1905. His parents were Irish immigrants, and he strongly identified with Ireland and supported Irish independence. A mesmerizing orator with what was called a "high-powered temperament," in 1908 he married Mary O'Gorman, the daughter of New York justice James O'Gorman, and with his father-in-law's help, Malone was appointed assistant corporation counsel to the city of New York. O'Gorman was also instrumental in launching his son-in-law into politics, for soon after he was elected to the United States Senate, he arranged for Malone to meet Governor Woodrow Wilson.

That Malone was a Democrat independent of Tammany ma-

chinery appealed to Wilson, and Malone made himself indispensable. It was Malone who helped make peace with Bryan
over Wilson's dismissal of Bryan in that "cocked hat" remark.

Dudley Field Malone, 1913
COURTESY LIBRARY OF CONGRESS

Wilson trusted Malone, and once he was elected president,
Wilson appointed Malone, by then just thirty years old, to serve as
Third Assistant Secretary of State under Bryan. But Malone was
gone from Washington in less than a year. Perhaps Wilson thought
Malone would be more useful to him as collector of the port of
New York, where he could protect Wilson's interests in the party.
Which Malone did. That meant he was able to declare, in 1915,
that the *Lusitania* was not carrying arms. Five years later, Malone
recanted and admitted the *Lusitania* had been carrying 4,200
cases of cartridges for the British. The administration had covered
it up. By then Malone had irrevocably broken with Wilson.

For when the women who'd been arrested on Bastille Day were found guilty, Malone went straight to the White House. He reminded President Wilson that women had been trying to secure the vote since before the Civil War, when they were assured that if they could wait until after the war was over, the nation's men would work together with them on it. What had happened? Nothing. What was happening? Nothing. If such a promise to men had been ignored, wouldn't you, Mr. President, be the first to come to their assistance?

If the president really believed in the suffrage amendment, Malone continued, he could get it through Congress. Wilson hedged. Malone left the White House, his pink cheeks coral-colored. A rumor spread through Washington that Malone would resign.

"I think it is high time that men in this generation, at some cost to themselves, stood up to battle for the national enfranchisement of American women," Malone said, and then repeated his speech to waiting reporters.

Though Malone did manage to secure presidential pardons for Stevens and the other jailed picketers, they were reluctant to take crumbs, as they put it, from Wilson's table until Malone convinced them to think of the pardon as the president's admission of guilt. They walked out of Occoquan proudly and vowed to keep up the fight, the pickets, the agitation. In the next two years, more than five hundred women would be arrested, with about half of them serving time.

But Malone did resign from his position as collector of the port of New York during the first week of September. Ridiculed as a sentimentalist utterly obsessed, Malone was said to be in love with Stevens. How else to explain why a young, talented man would give up such a privileged, never mind lucrative, position for what seemed to many men a minor matter, suffrage, especially during the war, and besides, it was simply the brainchild of "deluded creatures with short skirts and short hair."

"I know of nothing that has gone more to the quick with me or that seemed more tragical than Dudley's conduct," President Wilson wrote a confidant. "I was stricken by it as I have been by few things in my life." Malone never saw Wilson again.

MALONE HAD PUBLICLY rebuked Wilson for his treatment of the women picketing the White House, but it wasn't only the right to petition that was under siege.

With war declared, men between the ages of 18 and 45 were compelled to register for the army, and Congress passed an Espionage Act, stipulating that anyone "who shall willfully make or convey false reports or false statements with intent to interfere with the operation of the military" could be charged. Congress also passed a Sedition Act to prohibit "disloyal, profane, scurrilous, or abusive language" or any language at all that might "incite insubordination, disloyalty, mutiny or refusal of duty."

Under these laws and on his own initiative, Postmaster General Albert Sidney Burleson decided which words were patriotic enough. Nicknamed the Cardinal, Burleson carried a black umbrella wherever he went, clicking it on the pavement. People could hear him coming.

Postmaster General Burleson refused to deliver any printed matter that he regarded as subversive—as many as one hundred publications. Burleson banned socialist newspapers like *The New York Call,* the Jewish daily *Forward,* and the *American Socialist.* The Black newspaper *The Chicago Defender* was warned that the government was watching. Burleson banned the *Catholic Register* because it wrote that Ireland ought to be free. As Henry Mencken angrily noted, this gave Burleson "absolute power . . . He may deny the mails to anyone that he doesn't like, for any reason or no reason. No crime is defined; no hearing is allowed; no notice is necessary; there is no appeal."

Burleson banned *The Masses,* which boasted it had "a Sense of Humor and No Respect for the Respectable." In one of the courtrooms on the third floor of an old post office building, Dudley Malone defended the editor of and the contributors to *The Masses* accused of conspiring to violate the Espionage Act. They were merely exercising free speech in a free press and their right to dissent.

William Jennings Bryan wholly supported the new espionage laws and their execution. "If a few are permitted to resist a law—any law—because they do not like it, government becomes a farce," he wrote. "Resistance is anarchy." He'd waste no sympathy on anyone arrested for "unpatriotic utterances," which, as far as he was concerned, was an abuse of free speech.

But many were hounded, accused, or arrested: pacifists, non-conformists, dissidents, radicals, men and women, and among them such unlikely compatriots as the industrialist Henry Ford and the socialist Eugene Debs; both believed the United States should stay out of European affairs and their wars. In New York City, speakers against the war were pulled off their soapboxes. In Wisconsin and Pennsylvania and Kansas and California, men were tarred and feathered in what were called "tar and feather bees" if they did not buy Liberty Bonds and in Missouri if they uttered what sounded like pro-German statements. Congress refused to seat the socialist Victor Berger after he was elected to the House of Representatives. The Russian immigrant Emma Goldman, who helped start something called the No-Conscription League, was arrested, and when a jury found her guilty of sedition, put her on a train to the federal penitentiary in Atlanta. Socialist Kate Richards O'Hare, who liked to dress in red (to match her hair), was sent to a Missouri prison for giving an antiwar speech. The socialist Rose Pastor Stokes was convicted of the same crime.

In the spring of 1918, an ailing and frail Eugene Debs stood on a platform in Canton, Ohio, to denounce the war. "They have always taught you that it is your patriotic duty to go to war and slaughter yourselves at their command. You have never had a voice in the war."

Two weeks later, at his trial, he famously declared, "While there is a lower class, I am in it; while there is a criminal element, I am of it; while there is a soul in prison, I am not free."

Before pronouncing sentence, Judge David Westenhaver asked Debs if he would like to repent. "Repent? Repent for standing like a man?" Debs replied.

Debs's appeal reached the Supreme Court. The court upheld the conviction.

Although Clarence Darrow fervently supported America's involvement in the war, he traveled twice to Washington to try to convince Postmaster Burleson that Burleson didn't have to gag free speech or muzzle the press to win it. After Debs's arrest, when he offered to defend Debs, Debs turned him down precisely because of Darrow's spirited, heated defense of the war, which astonished many of Darrow's friends, who opposed it.

"Clarence Darrow was a super-patriot," Debs later noted with sorrow. "I do not understand this in Darrow; it has puzzled me and perplexed me, I confess not a little, but I would never have dreamed of damning him for it."

"I love him and with good reason," Debs added. "No one rejoices more than I to hear his merit, his splendid qualities of character, his crowning virtues appraised at their true value."

Regardless, he didn't want Darrow's help.

"While I was strongly for America entering the war," Darrow later said, "still I felt that the courts had gone mad and were heartless in their horrible sentences."

After the war, Darrow went straight to President Wilson asking him to pardon Debs. "To keep in prison one who felt it his duty to disagree, after the need has passed, would not be self-defense but a punishment undeserved."

Clarence Darrow, circa 1915
COURTESY CHICAGO HISTORY MUSEUM, ICHI-031827

"The work of the world today is to heal the deep wounds of war," Darrow pleaded. Wilson refused.

"It is he, not I, who needs a pardon," Debs said of Wilson. "If I had it within my power, I would offer him the pardon that would set him free."

Though Darrow could have predicted his appeal to Wilson would fail, he wasn't afraid of failing. "I have long ceased to have any illusions about the human race," he said. "They are more uncertain and less important than bees, or perhaps any other animals."

Eugene V. Debs leaving the Atlanta penitentiary
COURTESY LIBRARY OF CONGRESS

Debs ran for President from his prison cell in Atlanta in 1920 and received more than nine hundred thousand votes. The next year, the new President, Warren G. Harding, commuted Debs's sentence to time served. He didn't, however, pardon the old socialist; he just made sure Debs would be home for Christmas.

Chapter Five

Rebirth of a Nation: The Ku Klux Klan

1919–1922

Europe was devastated by the war, we by the aftermath.
—JUSTICE LOUIS BRANDEIS

It will not do to make a war fought for democracy result in autocracy.
—CLARENCE DARROW

THE WAR HAD MADE NOTHING and no one safe.

The Great War that the United States had entered in the spring of 1917 was brutal, its rhetoric inflated and hypocritical—and it was over nineteen months later, on November 11, 1918. In total there were more than twenty million deaths, and twenty-one million more had been wounded. The scale of loss was indescribable. Soldiers arrived home shell-shocked and suffering.

"I had not thought death had undone so many," the expatriate poet T. S. Eliot grieved.

Himself ailing and frail, Woodrow Wilson had lost what prestige he had after such a gruesome war abroad and at home, with the suppression of civil liberties, the feverish propaganda and the intolerance. After the war, America was refusing to join the League of Nations, Wilson's visionary plan for a permanent council to resolve differences among nations, which had begun with another slogan, that of a "war to end all wars" and which the League presumably would do. Clarence Darrow opposed the League, as did others. To Darrow, it represented a group of dominant nations dictating terms to those countries with far less power. To the intellectual Randolph Bourne, it made obvious the country's latent colonialism. To Dudley Malone, who also opposed the League, speaking to a crowd of more than three thousand in the ballroom of the Pennsylvania Hotel in New York City, Wilson was a traitor to his own principles.

"Whereas we went to war to make the world safe for democracy," Malone declared, "it has been made safe only for the 'Big Four'"—that is, the United States, Britain, France, and Italy. The League was not a "league" at all, and it did not represent democracy. It would break the hearts of millions who lived in countries like Latvia, Ukraine, and India, which were controlled by foreign governments.

If Americans went into the war "to make the world safe for democracy," Malone repeated in conclusion, "then the men who sleep in Flanders fields and in the soil of France have died in vain."

"NO SINGLE NATION got out of the war all it hoped for and expected," the writer Harold Stearns observed, "and we, who said we expected nothing, got precisely that—except high prices, taxes, debt, an inflated currency, the dislike of the world, and industrial unrest thrown in as a side bargain."

Prices were high. Then went higher. With returning veterans looking for work, unemployment jumped. There were no jobs, and it seemed the entire world, or at least Europe and the United States, were again rocked by strikes. In 1919, there were 2,665 strikes by more than four million people. In Seattle, a strike of shipyard workers turned into a citywide general strike that lasted five days. There were strikes by railroad workers and carpenters in Chicago, and streetcar operators and cigar makers in New York City. A nationwide steel strike involved some 365,000 workers. In September, in Boston, when the poorly paid police were prevented from forming a local union, as many as 90 percent of the patrolmen walked off the job. The city stood terrified, storeowners locked up their stores, and President Lowell of Harvard University urged his students to serve as strikebreakers. Though the police were ready to negotiate, the Commonwealth's Governor Calvin Coolidge called out the national guard. "There is no right to strike against the public safety, by anybody, anywhere, any time," Governor Coolidge tersely declared. The remark made him famous.

Bryan was sympathetic to the workers but not to the unions. He had hoped the police would have been given back their jobs—they were not—but blamed them for trying to unionize in the first place. And to him, the coal miners' attempt to coerce the public by threatening to strike, which would mean a cold winter, merely cost them the public's sympathy. It was too bad industrial disputes couldn't be resolved. Too bad there wasn't a cooling-off period. It was a time for brotherly love, not class warfare.

It was a bit late for that. Wilson had called the Boston police strike a crime against civilization; so too the eventual strike by the coal miners in November: they were seen as Bolshevik plots, all of them. For after the October socialist revolution, led by Vladimir Lenin in Russia, deposed the Romanovs, and Czar Nicholas II abdicated in the fall of 1917, many Americans, like John Reed and Lincoln Steffens, were attracted to the revolutionary and what seemed utopian Bolshevik regime. (More skeptical, Clarence Darrow speculated that the Russian Revolution would eventually produce the inevitable tyrannies of any government established on a set of economic theories.) Years of labor unrest and then a world war suggested to many that the old order had deservedly collapsed, and with that came the hope of something more equitable than the depredations of capital that they believed had brought America to war in the first place. The war had made nothing and no one safe, and as Clarence Darrow put it, the war had jarred something ugly loose in American society.

"All the complex machinery for harassing those who opposed the war is now converted into an engine for punishing the foes of capital," Henry Mencken angrily wrote. "Today it is almost worth a free citizen's liberty to be caught reading Marx, or to express the opinion that Debs has been in jail long enough, or to argue that even a Russian Jew deserves to be given his day in court, confronted by his accusers, before he is deported to God knows where, or clubbed by the police, or murdered in cold blood by mine guards."

It was rumored that Soviet Russia was smuggling spies into the country and planned to overthrow the US government. Jane Addams; Charlie Chaplin; former US Representative Jeannette Rankin, who had voted against the war; Reverend Henry Sloane Coffin; James Weldon Johnson; and Clarence Darrow: all were labeled "Reds" or too sympathetic to "Reds," an umbrella term for socialists, radicals, Bolsheviks, anarchists, even immigrants. The Daughters of the American Revolution circulated a blacklist, "The Common Enemy." "Communism, Bolshevism, Socialism, Liberalism and Ultra-Pacifism," it declared, "tend to the same ends." In Seattle, Mayor Ole Hanson said all radicals— "bearded Americans," he called them—should be deported. "My motto for the Reds," said General Leonard Wood, "is 'S.O.S.'—ship or shoot. I believe we should place them all on a ship of stone, with sails of lead and that their first stopping place should be Hell."

On April 28, 1919, a bomb was opened by a clerk in the office of Seattle mayor Hanson. The bomb failed to detonate. The next day another bomb was delivered to the home of former US Senator Thomas Hardwick. This one did explode, severely injuring a maid. On May Day, sixteen bombs were discovered in at least thirty-four packages sitting in a New York City post office, not having been delivered because of insufficient postage. Bombs were then found in various post offices across the country. Justice Oliver Wendell Holmes Jr. was an intended target, as were J. P. Morgan and John D. Rockefeller.

On June 2, 1919, just before midnight, there was a huge explosion at the Washington home of Attorney General A. Mitchell Palmer on R Street near DuPont Circle. The body of the bomber, who had tripped and blown himself up, was scattered in pieces all over the street. Nearby, a pamphlet was found; it said, "We are ready to do anything and everything to suppress the capitalist class."

Attorney General Palmer now took even more concentrated aim at the new enemy purported to lie within the country. "To be a red in the summer of 1919 was worse than being a Hun or a pacifist in the summer of 1917," the novelist John Dos Passos would tartly note. By the end of that year, more than two hundred men and three women, including the anarchist and *Mother Earth* editor Emma Goldman, had been loaded onto the "Soviet Ark," the nickname for the USAT *Buford,* and deported to Russia. Ignoring due process, Attorney General Palmer's agents had rounded up thousands of people and appointed the twenty-four-year-old John Edgar Hoover to head what became the General Intelligence Division of the Justice Department. Hoover, who'd been a cataloger at the Library of Congress—though a zealous one—within a month just as zealously amassed information on as many as sixty thousand suspected radicals and so-called alien anarchists.

Government now "prohibits the free exchange of ideas. It suspends lawful assemblage," Henry Mencken railed in 1920. "It employs intimidation, perjury, lynch law, terrorism, bribery, spying, all sorts of shoddy and despicable villainy." The New York State legislature created a committee, chaired by state Senator Clayton Lusk, to report on seditious activities. "Names! Names of all parlor bolsheviki," he demanded. He sent his spies to meetings in Harlem to ferret out members of the International Workers of the World (the "Wobblies," or IWW) and other suspected subversives. Lusk and his henchmen targeted the *Messenger* magazine as "A Radical Negro Publication." Any Black leader "to the left of Booker T. Washington" was untrustworthy. Attorney General Palmer was pleased.

Not Clarence Darrow. "If the world cannot stand up against Bolshevism and meet it by free speech and a free press, then Bolshevism has a right to rule," Darrow insisted. "It will not do to make a war fought for democracy result in autocracy." When defending twenty men arrested for supporting the Seattle strike, including William Bross Lloyd, a founding member of the Communist Party of America, Darrow explained to the jury that Attorney General Palmer and his men had "started on a mad career to make this world safe for Hypocrisy."

To Mencken, Palmer probably did more than anyone, "save only Mr. Wilson himself, to break down democratic self-government in America and substitute a Cossack despotism, unintelligent and dishonest." By victimizing "palpably innocent people," Mencken continued, Palmer's "gaudy raids" made cynics of those progressives who'd been disillusioned by war, unfulfilled promises, hopes dashed and dreams perpetually deferred.

MENCKEN WAS PARTICULARLY appalled by the American Legion, which had been organized, it claimed, "to uphold and defend the Constitution of the United States of America; to maintain law and order; [and] to foster and perpetuate a one hundred per cent Americanism."

The war had made nothing and no one safe. The Ku Klux Klan of the 1860s had reemerged in 1915, the same year the D. W. Griffith's three-hour film *The Birth of a Nation* was released. Based on the novel *The Clansman* by Thomas Dixon, one of Woodrow Wilson's classmates at Johns Hopkins, the film was privately shown at the White House. The epic spectacle was a propagandist melodrama: a hysterical tale of Reconstruction where real-life abolitionists like Thaddeus Stevens appear as diabolically licentious congressmen determined to destroy an innocently Aryan South; where Blacks are made to seem ignorant or grotesquely evil—and licentious; and where the Ku Klux Klan, as a glorified cavalry arrayed in flowing white costumes, rides to the rescue of a beset white woman. Woodrow Wilson described the whole grim, bigoted film as "history written with lightning." The National Association for the Advancement of Colored People, calling it vicious, tried to have it banned.

But *The Birth of a Nation* helped reawaken the Ku Klux Klan. Organized along pseudomilitary lines, with their so-called Invisible Empire of Wizards, King Kleagles, Klaverns, Grand Dragons, Grand Goblins, Cyclopses, and with their fiery crosses and nighttime rides, the new Klan recruited men and women in the South but also in the Midwest and in the North. Its secret password was "White Supremacy," which it changed to "America Forever," boasting that it represented "100 per cent of Americanism, punishment and ousting of the bootlegger, the gambler and moral pervert; sanctity of the American home, protection of women and children, perpetual rule, political and social, of native-born white Americans."

The Klan rounded up men and women, mostly but not exclusively Black, to tar and feather or beat or burn. In Georgia, Mary Turner, eight months pregnant, was shot, lynched, and burned. In 1919 there were at least ten other reported lynchings in Georgia. The rest of the South was no different. It takes courage for a Black person to live in Mississippi, declared the Black writer and activist William Pickens, who was also the dean of Morgan College in Baltimore, Maryland.

While Black men and women had been moving North in

what became known as the Great Migration, "the North is no paradise," warned W.E.B. Du Bois in *The Crisis,* which he edited for the National Association for the Advancement of Colored People. During the war at least 130,000 Black soldiers had been in combat at the Western Front, but they were unsafe when they returned. During the bloody "Red Summer" of 1919, more than a hundred Black citizens—some of them returning soldiers in uniform—were hunted down by white mobs. There were massacres in Wilmington, Delaware, and Syracuse, New York. In Omaha, Nebraska, a white mob lynched Will Brown and burned his body and then attempted to lynch the mayor when he tried to intervene. In Chicago, a young boy swam into the "white" zone at the Twenty-ninth Street Beach and was stoned until he sank. All over the city, for the next ten days, Black people were dragged out of streetcars, shot at from automobiles, stoned, and pummeled. At least 23 Blacks and 15 whites were murdered. The Chicago courts returned indictments against 57 Blacks but only 4 whites.

Black men and women had defended themselves in Chicago, and they defended themselves in Washington after unarmed Black men and women had been chased, beaten, and killed. In September 1919, the writer James Weldon Johnson, field secretary for the National Association for the Advancement of Colored People, took a train from New York to Washington and interviewed the chief of police, Major Pullman, who insisted that Blacks returning from the front had been responsible. *The New York Times* further ventured that these Black men were Bolsheviks anyway, and that they'd been reading too much Red literature.

The Ku Klux Klan plays upon fears "of Rome, of Bolshevism, of the Jews, of the devil," Henry Mencken noted, adding that "the Ku Klux Klan is essentially a Methodist organization, and has intimate relations with other notorious Methodist organizations, including, in some states, the Anti-Saloon League." To

James Weldon Johnson, Field Secretary of the NAACP
and soon its first Black Executive Secretary
COURTESY LIBRARY OF CONGRESS

him, the Klan was a privatized Prohibition police whose alarm-
ing popularity, Mencken also noted, grew out of the war's repression of pacifists, enemy "aliens," and "Reds," all in the name
of political purity. Now this repression took the form of religious or "racial" purity.

The Klan disapproved of Catholics because they revered the
pope and of Jews because they weren't Christian. "One of the

chief causes of suffering and evil in the world today is race hatred," former president William Howard Taft morosely declared,
his remarks aimed at Henry Ford's antisemitic diatribes in his
paper, *The Dearborn Independent,* that fanned fears about
worldwide Jewish conspiracies. Soon there would be quotas at
Ivy League schools limiting the number of Jews permitted to
enter.

The war had made nothing and no one safe.

LOTHROP STODDARD, the wealthy son of a prominent Massachusetts family, warned a wide readership that the barbarians
were at the gate: yellow men, brown men, black men and red
men, radicals and Bolsheviks and Wobblies and socialists and
Jews and Catholics. People from Serbia, Poland, Lithuania, Slo-
vakia, Italy, and Russia weren't "white" either. His bestselling
The Rising Tide of Color Against the White World-Conspiracy
was published in 1920, the same year that the newly reorganized
Ku Klux Klan murdered forty Black people in Florida when they
tried to get to the polls, and the same year the Republican presidential nominee, Senator Warren G. Harding, was accused of
having "Negro blood."

The revived Klan had amassed something like five million
members, many of them serving as governors, congressmen, and
state and local officials. The Klan had its own slate of candidates
for offices and helped to elect governors in California and Oregon as well as Georgia and Alabama. Klansmen, wearing long
white sheets and pointy headdresses, carrying torches and banners and fiery crosses, paraded down the streets of Georgia, Alabama, North Carolina, South Carolina, Louisiana, Oklahoma,
Texas, and Florida.

Their main offices were located in Atlanta, Georgia, where
Colonel William J. Simmons, Imperial Wizard, held court. Formerly a circuit rider of the Methodist Episcopal Church, the

Wizard was clean-shaven, and he would smile slightly as he leaned back in his big, polished chair. Behind him stood a gigantic American flag. Soon, though, he was replaced by a shady dentist from Dallas, Hiram Wesley Evans, who had risen in the organization after kidnapping Alex Johnson, a Black bellhop at the Adolphus Hotel, and engraving "KKK" on his forehead with acid. Evans shifted Klan headquarters from Atlanta to the nation's capital. By then there were claims that at least four hundred thousand members of the Klan lived north of the Mason-Dixon line.

On May 31 and June 1, 1921, Black men, women, and children were killed in Tulsa, Oklahoma, when a thirty-six-block area of the thriving Greenwood section of the city was laid waste, stores looted, men gunned down. "It was real war: murder, fire, rape, theft. The same sort of thing that gained the *Croix de Guerre* in the World War," W.E.B. Du Bois's magazine noted. Machine guns had rolled into Greenwood, and eight airplanes were flying overhead with at least one dropping an explosive. By four A.M., at least two dozen Black businesses had been burned to the ground along with the new Mount Zion Baptist Church, a library, a school, a hospital, and more than one thousand houses. White men, some of them having put on their war uniforms, carried cans of oil to set the fires. By the time the fires died out, more than ten thousand people were homeless. The Tulsa police force and National Guard units did not arrest the white mobs, just the Black men, who had fought back but were outnumbered and outgunned.

The ostensible cause of the mayhem was the threatened lynching of a nineteen-year-old Black elevator operator, Dick Rowland, who had supposedly tried to assault a young white woman. The real cause was the fact that so many of the city's Black population had become prosperous. And these prosperous Black men and women were said to be radicals, mainly because they denounced Jim Crow laws.

"What is America going to do after such a horrible carnage—one that for sheer brutality and murderous anarchy cannot be surpassed by any of the crimes now being charged to the Bolsheviki in Russia?" asked Black civil rights leader Walter F. White, the executive secretary of the NAACP and a friend of Clarence Darrow. White had contacted another friend, the executive editor of the New York *World,* which then ran an exposé of the Klan. The story had the opposite effect. About five thousand new Klan members a day signed up. In Georgia, Tom Watson, former Populist and now outspoken anti-Semite, anti-Catholic, and anti-Black reactionary, won a seat in the United States Senate.

After riots broke out in East Saint Louis when unions objected to the hiring of Black workers, Missouri congressman Leonidas C. Dyer, fed up, introduced an anti-lynching bill in the House of Representatives. Nothing came of it.

In 1921, after Arkansas newspapers announced that a Black farmer, Henry Lowry, who had confessed to murder, was to be publicly lynched and burned, Dyer tried again, explaining how the Ku Klux Klan "drips with venomous attacks, particularly against Jews and Catholics" while it aims to "terrorize certain classes of people in this country; and one, especially, is the negro population of America." Dyer's bill also permitted the federal government to prosecute if the state failed to act.

To those congressmen who argued an anti-lynching bill was unconstitutional, or that it expanded the federal government, or that it violated states' rights, Dyer said the federal government had no trouble banning the sale of booze; it had sent its "hooch-hounds" nationwide to track trade even of bathtub gin. So how could defending Black Americans—citizens—be unconstitutional.

The president of the National Association of Colored Women, Mary Burnett Talbert, raised almost seventy thousand dollars to help promote the Dyer bill and circulated pamphlets with titles like "A Million Women United to Suppress Lynching" and "The Shame of America": "Do you know that the *United States* is the *Only Land on Earth* where human beings are *Burned at the Stake*?"

In early 1922, the House of Representatives finally passed the Dyer bill. It would allow lynch mobs to be charged with capital murder, and for the cases to go to trial in federal court.

The bill died in the Senate.

William Jennings Bryan was relieved.

Although his hairline had demonstrably receded, when William Jennings Bryan spoke, he seemed the orator of old, a progressive, a Commoner, and a man of the people still very much in favor of reform. But he called the Dyer bill inexcusable, iniquitous, partisan, and wrongheaded because, after all, it demonstrated "more sympathy for the colored man who has attacked a white than to the woman who is the victim."

The Dyer bill, Bryan blandly continued, would "turn the attention of the colored people away from the crime to focus it upon the method of punishment." Lynching in the South isn't as bad as it used to be, he claimed, and besides, it was a partisan issue. Far more important to him was the question of liquor. "In the south the whites have given the black the benefit of the white man's civilization," Bryan declared, "while in the north those engaged in the liquor traffic have tried to drag civilization down to a beer level."

Prohibition, Scripture, and the Crown of Righteousness

1920–1923

> I have fought the good fight, I have finished the race,
> I have kept the faith. There is reserved for me the crown
> of righteousness.
>
> —2 TIMOTHY 4

THERE WERE MOTORCARS AND MOVING pictures. There were telephones. There were Victrolas and dance records. There were airplanes that seemed to bring the world closer, and there was radio that did bring the world close, right into the parlor. And there was Prohibition.

The Eighteenth Amendment to the Constitution, which outlawed the manufacture and sale of intoxicating beverages, had been ratified on January 16, 1919, and would go into effect the following year, enforced by the Volstead Act, which defined as illegal any beverage that contained more than half of one percent alcohol.

There was William Jennings Bryan, who argued Prohibition would diminish poverty, uplift the immigrant, break up the liquor lobby, reduce industrial accidents, and render America's moral leadership secure.

Pleased but unsatisfied—since there was always more to be

done—in the summer of 1920, when the Democrats met in San Francisco for their annual convention, Bryan emerged from his rooms at the grand St. Francis Hotel with one purpose in mind. He wanted the party platform to contain a bone-dry Prohibition plank—and no modification of the Volstead Act. The current wave of permissive talk about maybe allowing cider, beer, and wine to be consumed in the home troubled him. The Volstead Act should not be relaxed. Bryan couldn't have cared less that he was called a crank or laughed at as the Beerless Orator.

The truth was that even among Democrats Bryan now seemed a backward-looking man of the nineteenth century, a Populist of yesteryear wrapped in an old alpaca coat and wearing his predictable string tie. Yet no one denied he was still fighting the good fight for such reforms as government ownership of utilities or the abolition of a peacetime draft.

But he was, by his own admission, not a revolutionary. "I am stemming the tide of radicalism," he explained, "because after me may come—the extremists." He was a progressive Democrat, not a Bolshevik.

He'd briefly broken with Woodrow Wilson—although it was Bryan's peace plan, Bryan claimed, that Wilson had brought to Paris, so it was Bryan's peace plan that would make Wilson immortal, with its emphasis on free trade among nations, freedom of the seas, a reduction of armaments and, above all, a general association of nations that would guarantee their political independence and territorial integrity. That association would become what was known, in different form, as the League of Nations.

Bryan also said Democrats should heed those senators who might be reluctant to ratify the League unless the role and the obligations of the United States were clarified. In this, Bryan presented himself as much more flexible than Wilson, and that may have been easy because Bryan really wanted to talk only about a subject much nearer his heart than the League.

"Remember that it is better to have the gratitude of one soul saved from drink than the applause of a drunken world," he cried out from the stage.

Texas Representative James Luther Slayden, listening to the Commoner, was unpersuaded. He gathered that the Oval Office was what lay near Bryan's heart.

That may have been true, and likely Bryan wouldn't admit this even to himself. His rich voice rose and fell, his torso swayed, his arms lifted, and his bald dome shimmered with perspiration. At sixty, Bryan might be a little heavier, but his face glowed, as if he had come home to the place—the speaker's platform— where he most belonged. He wouldn't use the brand-new loud-speaker system. His voice and message would echo unamplified through the packed auditorium, and he could win over the delegates and spectators.

"I stand for the home against the saloon," he cried again. "We shall not fail." He grinned broadly, pleased with the rolling waves of applause. He bowed. Tears streamed down his cheeks.

What started as cheers, though, ended in shrugs. "As he raged and leaped around the platform in his frayed alpaca coat, weeping for the orphans poisoned by whiskey, the widows debauched and brought down to infamy by absinthe and champagne, the felons fed to the gallows by malt liquors, light wines and gin, it was almost beyond human power to resist him," Henry Mencken wrote from the convention floor. "But to sob with him was one thing and to vote with him was quite another thing."

"Mr. Bryan, while applauded for his consummate oratory," William Allen White remarked, "was politely given his hat and shown to the door."

The "drys" were against him, and the "wets" didn't want to make alcohol a partisan issue. "I never thought they would beat me so badly," Bryan was heard to mutter in astonishment, as he was ushered out of the convention. "My heart is in the grave."

. . .

"WHAT STRENGTH HE will develop, no one can tell," former Interior Secretary Franklin K. Lane surmised. "He evidently has determined that he will not be pushed aside or disregarded."

Defeated for the moment, Bryan returned to the new palatial home in Miami that he had built, and there, at Villa Serena, among the bougainvillea and wisteria, and with Mary at his side, he recovered himself. The time had come for something else, just as important, just as galvanizing, just as successful as Prohibition. The country was in the throes of moral shell shock, racked as it was by strikes and unrest and suspicion and Bolshevism, and someone had to lead the nation back to the path of righteousness and peace and godliness. It had to be him in unflinching battle against the forces arrayed against him, something that could be funneled into an unassailable moral crusade to fight against the wicked piracy in business and industry and the pernicious materialism that had caused the war, all the fruit of Friedrich Nietzsche, Bryan concluded, and not the doctrine of the Nazarene.

As he began to frame that menace, to give it shape and color, he started to envision the form his new campaign would take. "Four years from now it will be my kind of convention," he promised.

Defeated for now but secure in his moral mission, William Jennings Bryan would not sulk in his Florida tent.

WALTER LIPPMANN, the young journalist-editor of the magazine *The New Republic,* confided to a friend that "hysteria has turned to apathy and disillusionment in the general public, and cynicism in most of my friends." John Dos Passos wondered "was civilization nothing but a vast edifice of sham, and the war, instead of its crumbling, was its fullest and most ultimate expression."

"No wonder so many Young Intellectuals," Mencken observed, "depart precipitately for Paris, Munich and the Italian hill towns!" Young people boarded boats headed for Europe to a place where the exchange rate was good and there was no Prohibition or puritanism, a place with cafés and gardens and riverbanks—a place of freedom. James Weldon Johnson said in Paris you could be free "from special scorn, special tolerance, special condescension, special commiseration," and Gertrude Stein said, "it was not what France gave you but what it did not take away." In his *Civilization in the United States,* Harold Stearns, now an expatriate too, collected essays by thirty men and women who despaired of their country, its spiritual poverty and its prejudices: the United States, a nation besotted by the Ku Klux Klan and its grotesque regalia.

In the aftermath of war, in a world that seemed strange and strangely out of joint, the time had come for a return to the apparent fundamentals of the Christian faith—or at least to the fundamentals of faith as defined by an orthodox group of ministers, laypeople, and teachers. *The Watchman Examiner,* a national Baptist weekly, said these "Fundamentalists" were those "who cling to the great fundamentals and who mean to do battle royal." Biblical scholars associated with what was called the "Higher Criticism" had determined that the Bible was the handiwork of various individuals writing over a span of years and presenting varying accounts of different events. They might even understand the Bible as poetic and allegorical. Such notions were just "weasel words," Bryan liked to jeer.

To the Fundamentalists—and Bryan was one of them—the Bible was the literal and infallible word of God. Immaculate conception was a fact. Jesus was the Son of God who offered himself up to death, and then he rose from the dead.

Bryan wholly embraced this orthodoxy: belief in the divinity of Jesus Christ, belief in the Virgin birth, belief in the resurrection, and belief in the Bible, word for word. To him, the Bible could not be a "man-made book." Never. "When one asserts that the Bible is not infallible, he must measure it by some standard which he considers better authority than the Bible itself," Bryan explained.

Bryan insisted that he represented the common folk, those devout people who heard Christ and took him into their hearts. The Bible speaks to them. It speaks for them. It speaks in a universal language, not the language, he sarcastically added, of " 'thinkers.' " To him, then, the Virgin birth was "no more mysterious than the birth of each of us—it is simply different," he declared.

Scripture had always been part of Bryan's speech, as in his reference to the "crown of thorns" in 1896. But now Bryan was also placing the Bible at the center of an emotional crusade that he felt indispensable during this postwar period, with its widening gap between the pious believers and the denizens of Babylon, where loose women drank in speakeasies, Reds ran amok, and bootleggers machine-gunned each other down on city streets. Such immorality had to come from somewhere, Bryan argued. He knew where. Darwin.

"I believe the brute in man is brought out largely by the theory that makes man believe he is blood relative to the brute," Bryan declared. If you say that men and women are the children of apes, why not slaughter them. And if you don't take the Bible literally, you have no hope.

Darwinism, evolution, and any notion of the survival of the fittest—to Bryan, all the same thing—had caused the recent and ghastly war. "God is dead," Nietzsche had declared, and when Nietzsche named Darwin one of the greatest men of the age, Bryan deduced that Nietzsche epitomized the logical outcome of the theory of evolution: "the flower that blooms on the stalk of evolution," he would write with contempt. Connecting Darwin and Nietzsche and both of them with the idea of the survival of the fittest (social Darwinism)—to Bryan, the strong muscling out the weak—Bryan decided that any theory that claimed humans were not created ex nihilo by God in God's image was an affront to all morality, all justice, all idealism, all love.

To Bryan, Nietzsche wanted to substitute the worship of God with the worship of a "superman," which Bryan defined as a "lawless human being, living without restraint and free to do as he pleased, regardless of consequences to others." And since, to Bryan, Nietzsche praised war, denounced sympathy, and labeled democracy a refuge for weaklings, "Nietzsche's philosophy would convert the world into a ferocious conflict between beasts," Bryan warned, "each beast trampling ruthlessly on anything and everything that stands in its way." That way, the way of Darwin and Nietzsche, lies despair—or madness; and as if to make his point, Bryan liked to add that Nietzsche had died insane.

Though originally he worked hard to maintain America's neutrality, once Congress declared war, Bryan fiercely denounced Germany and its kaiser. "Down beneath all the German propaganda, all the German cruelty and treachery in the war, are the teachings of Nietzsche and his following," Bryan continued. "In the philosophy of Nietzsche there is a defense for every Hun atrocity, every violation of pledge, every cruelty practiced on the battlefield and every trickery in the field of diplomacy." To ensure a lasting peace—a world without national rivalry, animosity, armaments and German imperialism—Bryan then argued that the world needed Christianity. "That man bears the image of God and not the likeness of the animals below him," Bryan said in 1920, "is the foundation stone upon which he must build."

And now, during a return to a "normalcy" that was not normal, Bryan saw debauchery, venality, materialism and, above all, atheism. For it wasn't just the Germans who were responsible for the threat to civilization. Bryan blamed the "cultured crowd," which he defined as anyone "who regard religion as a superstition, good for the ignorant, but who think that one can outgrow the necessity for religion when he reaches a certain stage of intellectual development."

"Inventive genius has been exhausted to find new ways by which man can kill his fellowman!" Bryan thundered.

"The intellectuals have led civilization to the verge of a bottomless abyss," Bryan said after the war. "Learned men have built battleships; scientists have mixed poison gases and manufactured liquid fire; the putting of the mind above the heart has made war so hellish that civilization was about to commit suicide," he continued. "The world needs an international anthem, and there is none save the song that startled the shepherds at Bethlehem, 'On earth peace, good will toward men.' Darwinism can not save the world. It can only make the wreck of civilization complete."

Bryan hastened to add that he wasn't quarreling with science. The theory of evolution was not science. It was a guess, a fairy story, a fiction, just a theory and as such an intellectual delusion. People who laugh at the story of Jonah buy the far weirder story of the Darwinists. Bryan said he couldn't find a single syllable in the Bible that supported the theory of evolution, and since the Bible was the word of God, the theory had to be wrong. Not for him were theological discussions about the meaning of Genesis. Not for him were the discoveries of paleontologists and strange skeletal remains of species now extinct. Not for him were the geological discoveries in inorganic rocks that suggested the age of the Earth was far older than six thousand years, a number calculated by literalists counting the generations from Adam and Eve and Noah to the present.

"Why should the children be taught," Bryan wanted to know, "that it is more important to know the age of the rocks than to trust in the 'Rock of Ages'?"

The result of such teaching was to Bryan a jazz-besotted, flaming youth, like those characters in F. Scott Fitzgerald's *This Side of Paradise,* where men carried hip flasks and women were flappers who smoked and coeds kissed in the back seats of automobiles and didn't give a damn. Colleges were turning out atheists, and college teachers encouraged the worship of the intellect and a commensurate deadening of morals, driving reverence from the heart and, he said, "substituting the guesses of Darwin for the Word of God."

Bryan was told that the female students at Wellesley College no longer believed in the Bible. When a Bryn Mawr College teacher called for a vote, most of the class voted that there was no God. The same was true at Columbia University. Two professors at the University of Michigan had dared say that no thinking person could believe in the Bible, and at Yale, there was a professor who turned students into atheists. Edward Birge, president of the University of Wisconsin and a Congregationalist, had said the teaching of science posed no problem for him or the school. Bryan called him an atheist. Behind the scenes, President Birge said Bryan was crazy; publicly, that the Commoner was a publicity hound.

"I leave him to the taxpayers whom he insults," Bryan shot back.

He believed he could do something more. Bryan would take his battle into the halls of government, as he had with Prohibition.

ON JANUARY 20, 1922, a chilly winter's day in Frankfort, Kentucky, Governor Edwin Morrow escorted William Jennings Bryan, bald and portly, into the elegant Legislative Hall to address a joint session of the assembly. State Senator Frank Daugherty introduced the Commoner as a man "outstanding in the world for honesty of purpose." Bryan flashed his familiar smile from behind the mahogany speaker's stand. A crowd of several hundred visitors, including state employees, jumped to their feet.

Bryan was there to encourage them to pass a bill prohibiting the public schools from teaching "Darwinism, atheism, agnosticism, or the theory of evolution insofar as it pertains to the origins of life." Bryan urged the legislators to stop these enemies of the Bible (the title of a recent talk he'd been giving) and then reached out his hand and grabbed for one of the books he'd placed near the lectern. He began to read, ostensibly from a zoology textbook, to mock the idea that humans might be descended from apes.

He didn't know much about his great-grandparents, he said, pausing with a smile, but one of them was from Kentucky, so they were bound to be all right. The legislators laughed.

As for Darwin, "He doesn't even let us descend from a good American ape," Bryan teased. "He makes us come from an African brute."

He grew more serious. "No time is to be lost in missing links," Bryan concluded. "The great need of the world today is to get back to God."

The Kentucky bill failed by only one vote and only after several eminent people, including Dr. Lyman Abbott, the editor of *The Outlook* magazine, and the presidents of Yale and Harvard weighed in. So had others. Edwin Conklin, biology professor at Princeton, contemptuously remarked that "there is a widely prevalent view, especially in politics, that one man's opinion is as good as another's on any subject whatever. Mr. Bryan may as well discuss the cause and cure of infantile paralysis."

But Bryan wasn't finished, and he would not stop. Again and again, he said scientists and elitists and Nietzsche and the makers of liquid gas all pointed in the same direction, toward doom and denial and Darwin. Marshaling his considerable popularity and as talented as ever at stirring controversy, Bryan went seemingly everywhere, up and down and across the country in his alpaca coat and comfortable shoes. His eyes shone under his shaggy eyebrows. He ate plate after plate of sausages and hard-boiled eggs. He ate custard pie, more than one slice. His appetite gargantuan, his endurance astounding, his appeal indisputable, he held audiences spellbound. "Good for forty acres of parked Fords anytime and anywhere," he was teased.

"Speaking became his business," Senator William Borah commented.

Having transferred his legal residence from Nebraska to Florida, he had also been delivering Sunday morning Bible sermons at the First Presbyterian Church in Miami that drew enormous crowds, eager and happy crowds numbering as many as six thousand, many of them tourists. These Sunday sermons soon grew so popular that they had to be held outdoors at the Royal Palm Park, within sight of the royal-blue waters of Biscayne Bay. Bryan stood on a specially made dais in his shirtsleeves with a cooling cake of ice nearby. In his hand he held a big fan shaped like a palm leaf with red edges. Under the sheltering palms stood the man with the beatific smile who championed peace until there was war; the man of Main Street and the Midwest who distrusted learning and the learned and decried the Sodoms of the East as well as the gamblers of the West; the man who cherished love and goodness and disarmament. This man declared his faith in the real America, good and old-fashioned and reliable, plain and principled. Women in their gingham dresses, men in straw hats, the press: they loved the whole setup.

He arranged to have his weekly Bible class nationally syndicated so he could reach the largest audience possible—about four million.

"People often ask me why I can be a progressive in politics and a fundamentalist in religion," Bryan readily told reporters. "The answer is easy. Government is man-made and therefore imperfect. It can always be improved. But religion is not a man-made affair. If Christ is the final word, how may anyone be a progressive in religion? I am satisfied with the God we have, with the Bible and with Christ."

Bryan was running for office again although this time it was to be moderator of the General Assembly of the Presbyterian Church, which represented 301 dioceses in America. Though not an ordained minister, as the candidate of the conservatives, Bryan was campaigning hard. He very much wanted the position, which would provide even more visibility than he already had and would allow him, with the church behind him, to profess his faith while acting as a deliberative judge on all matters of faith. So he spoke on the radio. He collected his popular lectures in his volume *In His Image*. He wrote letters on his own behalf. And he attacked the popular preacher Harry Emerson Fosdick.

Fosdick was the beloved pastor at the First Presbyterian Church on Fifth Avenue in New York City. A Baptist and a professor at the Union Theological Seminary—a place that Bryan loathed for what he considered its theological laxness—Fosdick intended to create an interdenominational ministry, which would be a house of prayer for everyone. He despised lynching, antisemitism, and 100 percent Americanism, and would go on record saying Fundamentalists were blinkered and that the Bible was utterly compatible with science.

A muscular man with a ramrod spine, at five feet eight, Fosdick was boyish looking, with dark brown bushy hair and chubby cheeks. Ordained in 1903 as a Baptist preacher, he wore glasses which didn't hide his light eyes or the laugh lines around them, although in his younger days he wore a pince-nez. Warm and direct, he packed the church, and long lines of people waited, rain or shine, to hear him preach.

In the spring of 1922, he had delivered a soon-to-be-famous sermon, "Shall the Fundamentalists Win?" To him, the significance of Christianity lay in Jesus Christ, not in stories about miracles or in the tale of the Virgin birth, which resembled the origin stories of many other religions, such as in the Koran. His sermon outraged Fundamentalists by insisting their intolerance was one of the great failures of history. He detested what he called the Fundamentalists' cruel and ruinous regime of interracial hatred and hostility. "We are all made of one blood," he said.

Widely published, Fosdick's sermon set off a firestorm of protest and made Fosdick the face of liberal Christianity, which also made him a target of the conservatives. He was attacked as a blasphemer, an infidel, a modernist, an evolutionist, and a "baboon booster." Indifferent to the mudslinging, Fosdick wryly declared that "the millennium will come when the Ku Klux Klan and the Knights of Columbus play a baseball game with a negro umpire for the benefit of the Jewish employees of Henry Ford at Zion City."

To Bryan, liberals like Fosdick were dissenters, and all dissenters were Darwinists who were particularly reprehensible because they believed both in God and in evolution, or what was known as theistic evolution, defined by Fosdick as "the progressive unfolding of the character of God."

"Theistic evolution is an anesthetic," Bryan stormed. "It deadens the pain while the Christian's religion is being removed." Harry Emerson Fosdick was a heretic who should be expelled from the First Presbyterian Church.

"How can a church exist unless it stands for something?" Bryan continued. As for denying freedom of thought—which he was accused of doing—Bryan said anyone has a right to believe anything. But here was the difference: "No man has a right to substitute his conscience for the conscience of a church." The church has the final word, which was the word of God.

Fosdick struck back. He disputed Bryan's notion that the theory of evolution was guesswork. A guess: that's one thing the theory of evolution was not. Bryan was wrong. Patiently, Fosdick explained how science works. A theory is a hypothesis, which is itself a "seriously proffered explanation of a difficult problem ventured when careful investigation of facts points to it, retained as long as the discovered facts sustain it, and surrendered as soon as another hypothesis enters the field which better explains the phenomenon in question."

But Fosdick was interested in Bryan's theology—insofar as it could be called theology. He dismissed Bryan's idea that God was an occasional wonder-worker who set the world in motion and then went home. He accused Bryan of undermining the Bible's rich grandeur. "Instead of using it for what it is, the most noble, useful, inspiring and inspired book of spiritual life which we have, the record of God's progressive unfolding of his character and will from early primitive beginnings to the high noon in Christ," Fosdick declared, "he sets it up for what it is not and never was meant to be—a procrustean bed to whose infallible measurements all human thought must be forever trimmed."

So the fight was on. If Bryan plunges the nation's schools into "incredible folly," Fosdick warned, "we can promise him also that just as earnestly as the scientist will fight against him in the name of scientific freedom of investigation, so will multitudes of Christians fight against him in the name of their religion and their God."

Let the scientists hash out the problems of biological beginnings—but in the meantime, Fosdick begged Bryan, "Do not teach men that if God did not make us by fiat, then we have nothing but a bestial heritage." Fosdick was not a modernist, if modernism was defined as cynical materialism, which is how the orthodox church had defined the term since the end of the fifteenth century. Fosdick was a religious man firm in his conviction that Christianity's real enemies were people like Mr. Bryan—that is, those who would legislate a medieval Christianity and deny that God is divinely immanent in the world, revealing himself in all living things.

BRYAN TOOK HIS battle against "Apeism" to the nation's capital, where he gave an impromptu speech at the annual banquet of the Southern Society of Washington. Appealing to the white Southern constituency he'd been cultivating since moving permanently to Florida, Bryan praised segregation and voting restrictions. These restrictions were a matter of necessity, essential to the welfare of the (white) South. Without them, Bryan claimed, "the Government would be in danger of passion under the control of the blacks." And since the white race was more advanced— Bryan's old argument—"the blacks have the advantage of living under laws that the white man makes for himself as well as for the black man."

Sure, everyone, white and Black, deserved life, liberty, and the pursuit of happiness, but the "advanced race" (that is, white), as he patiently explained, had to remain in control to guide and protect those who were inferior to it. Why, if Massachusetts faced the same threats to its white population that South Carolina faced, he summarized, it would do the same thing.

"Bryan's passion for democracy always cooled at the color line," Michael Kazin, Bryan's most recent biographer, astutely observed.

"It did look as if Mr. Bryan had lost his reason," responded the eloquent Black evangelist Francis Grimké of the Fifteenth Street Presbyterian Church in Washington, D.C. Grimké, who had been born into slavery and, as a boy, served as valet for a Confederate soldier, said Jesus Christ would be ashamed. "Can this man be the great Commoner that he is represented to be?" Grimké wondered. "The great Christian that he would have others believe him to be?"

"Pray tell me what kind of Christianity is this you profess? Do you conceive God a discriminating God?" W. Thomas Soders, a Black lawyer, wrote to Bryan. "Were the Black man given a square deal in America for what he has done for America he would now be holding Congressional Representation in Congress, but in lieu of fair play and justice you democrats and

Southern hypocrites, robbed him of justice and the ballot in the South land."

Black nationalist Marcus Garvey pointed out that Bryan's position was no different from that of the Klan's—but unlike other politicians, Bryan was at least up-front about his bigotry.

As for the Klan, it praised Bryan, a man willing to step boldly on the thin ice of race.

WHEN, IN THE spring of 1923, the Presbyterian General Assembly met in Indianapolis, Bryan lost the moderatorship. Enraged, he claimed that a gang of college men as well as a Black cabal cost him the position. "I have had experience enough in politics to know a machine when I see it," he stormed. The "black vote" was against him: "The colored people," he complained, possess very "liberal tendencies," although that was not necessarily true. But while men like the Reverend Grimké were not liberal, they'd voted against Bryan on account of his bigotry. Though Bryan might say he was a Christian, Grimké wrote a friend, "this eloquent champion of Christianity" was nothing but a hypocrite. "There are ten million of Negroes, who are everywhere discriminated against, treated as if they were less than human beings, with no rights which white men are bound to respect," Grimké continued. "Not one word in public ever escaped his lips or appeared in print, that would indicate that he had any sympathy for them or felt the least indignant at the wrongs inflicted upon them."

There were whites too, moderates as well as church liberals, who cringed at Bryan's racism, his uninformed dogmatism, and the uncharitable way he demanded religious conformity. Liberal Christians deplored Bryan's Fundamentalism, which they called a "religious Ku Klux Klan." One of them, Reverend Horace Ferry, pastor of the First Presbyterian Church in Marquette,

Michigan, explained some theological points that Bryan did not seem to understand. Christ didn't come back in the very same body that he had when put in the grave. And the denial of the Virgin birth wasn't a denial of the deity.

But the real and main issue was evolution: "I do not feel a burning sense of shame which you seem to think I should in having an ancestry rooted in the brutes," Reverend Ferry declared with biting humor. "I value ancestry as much as any man, because I belong to a quite well-known and well-respected family, but if that ancestry can be traced back to the brutes, I know that yours can too."

Reverend Ferry continued in dry jest. "I am not nearly so much interested in how much brute there is back of me as in how much brute there may be in me."

Bryan's defeat for moderator was perhaps inevitable. No one in the General Assembly wanted the controversy that would come with Bryan and that Bryan seemed to cultivate. Even his conservative allies hesitated. They'd heard he'd be running for president again in 1924, and they didn't want Bryan to politicize the church, which was a kinder way of saying what others had said: he was not judicious, impartial, dispassionate, or even fair.

To Bryan, this was galling. "We have preachers in this audience who don't believe in the resurrection of Christ's body," he had shouted when he proposed that no federal or state funds should go to any school, college, university that accepted the theory of evolution. "There has never been a reform for twenty-five years that I did not support, and I am now engaged in the biggest reform of my life. I am trying to save the Christian Church from those who are trying to destroy her faith."

His proposal was defeated. At least the General Assembly had passed one resolution he strenuously supported. It would investigate Fosdick's preaching. The assembly would eventually demand that Harry Emerson Fosdick, the baboon booster, accept the strict Westminster Confession of Faith. Fosdick refused and offered to resign from his pulpit. His congregation would not accept the offer, though he was forced to leave the First Presbyterian in 1925. "I wouldn't live in a generation like this and be anything but a heretic," he said.

BRYAN TURNED BACK to the matter of government legislation, which he'd never really forgotten. Conjuring images of bomb-throwing revolutionaries and unbelievers, he warned John Hylan, the mayor of New York City, to beware the "oligarchy of professors—a sort of scientific soviet government that will collect taxes and pay themselves salaries but will not allow the taxpayers to decide what shall be taught," Bryan predicted.

In New York, the superintendent of schools had appointed a committee to review history books, noting that "truth is no defense to the charge of impropriety." A committee headed by a civic official who called himself "101 percent American" wanted to ban the standard history textbook written by David S. Muzzey, a distinguished Columbia University professor. Denouncing Muzzey's widely used and respected textbook as subversive, the official said there wasn't enough Nathan Hale, for instance, or praise for American patriots. (History books by Albert Bushnell Hart and Charles and Mary Beard also came under fire.) Jumping on the case, cartoonists for the Hearst newspapers depicted Muzzey as a rat gnawing at the schoolhouse. When Mayor Hylan joined in the censuring of Muzzey, Bryan applauded: ban these books. "If teachers are to be allowed to undermine the Bible," Bryan sarcastically noted, "why object to them undermining American history?"

"I think you are right in insisting that people who pay taxes have a right to decide what will be taught as history," Bryan wrote Mayor Hylan, "and on the same ground the people who pay taxes have a right to protest against the teaching of irreligion in public schools."

The National Library Association had recommended a list of children's books that included *Gulliver's Travels* and *Robinson Crusoe* and *Tom Sawyer* but not Bible stories. "The scientific soviet . . . seeks to discard the eternal truths and put a bad guess in their places," Bryan said, again calling up the specter of Bolshevism. "There is a scientific soviet in this country today that tries to act as the final arbiter of all knowledge, that tries to tell us what we shall teach our children."

Henry Mencken drily observed that Bryan the adroit politician had found in Darwin an excellent way to get votes.

"MR. BRYAN IS a typical democratic figure," the philosopher John Dewey declared.

That is, Bryan represented the conformity enforced in villages and small towns, where decent people respect their neighbors but fear or punish outsiders just because they seem different or strange or because they do not pray where and how their neighbors pray, if in fact they pray at all. In America, that kind of America, all Americans are evangelicals.

MARY BRYAN'S FRAGILE health was one of the reasons the Bryans had made Florida their permanent home. Another was political. Bryan had wanted a seat in the United States Senate. Of course since Park Trammell, the incumbent, was a well-liked white supremacist, Bryan did not want to appear too eager for his job, so he staged his candidacy by not staging it, as he had done so many times before, saying only that he was ready to serve, which many people had been urging him to do, although of course he was not actively seeking anything. Still, he spoke out about developing more of Florida, draining the Everglades, doubling the population, and cultivating croplands to appeal to the farm bloc. Florida voters showed little enthusiasm.

. . .

CRITICISM DIDN'T stop him. William Jennings Bryan knew what he was about.

He was about hope. For three decades, he'd battled lobbies and trusts and special interests that threatened to destroy the farmer, the worker, the women—anyone who had been pushed to the sidelines, ignored, and trampled while those predatory plutocrats greedily lined their pockets. He had lobbied for the direct election of senators, a graduated income tax, the abolition of the Electoral College, a bipartisan national newspaper, and international disarmament.

He was about peace. He was the Prince of Peace. He was the prince of stability, continuity, endurance. He'd promised peace before the war and peace after the war. He desired nothing more than the good of everyone, for their own good, and he was ready to explain to everyone what was good for them.

He was about comfort, for he possessed the smiling confidence and granite certainty of one who envisions a better and kinder and more stable life, especially now, when that life seems out of reach.

He was about religion, as he understood religion, and as he defined religion, his religion. He was about reassurance. Follow the text, keep the faith, follow the heart. "The heart of mankind is sound," he declared.

Otherwise, what do we have? Selfishness, futility, desolation, and savagery. "We are not progeny of the brute," he cried again and again, sounding desperate.

To Bryan, we cannot ever be linked to brutes precisely because we are made in God's image. We sit high above all other species, all of nature, at God's right hand. And we know right from wrong—a distinction, said Clarence Darrow, that's not always easy to determine.

Part 3

About My Father's Business
1924–1925

The democratic state, despite the contrary example of France,
almost always shows a strong tendency to be also a Puritan state.

—HENRY MENCKEN

Chapter Seven

Leopold and Loeb and the Book of Love

1924

"B RYAN CAN TELL WHAT IS right and what is wrong," Clarence Darrow chuckled, "but it's a puzzle for the intelligent man."

Clarence Darrow, famous lawyer and debater, with his ferocious intelligence and gentle manner, climbed onto stage after stage to talk about crime and its causes, about which, he said, we know very little. He talked about crime and its treatment and that we do not treat it, and about capital punishment, which he despised. So clear were his opinions and so firmly held were they that he put them in a book, *Crime: Its Causes and Treatment,* taking legislatures, lawyers, and evangelists to task.

The criminal justice system had merely institutionalized revenge, Darrow insisted, and in any case, it was silly to think that meting out punishment would deter crime.

"What we need in this world," he said, "is a little more humanity."

Darrow contributed an essay to Henry Mencken's new magazine, *The American Mercury,* which Mencken and George Nathan had launched in 1924. Mencken wanted to find and tell the truth—nothing new there—and hoped that the magazine might "introduce some novelty into the execution of an enterprise so old." That is, the editors provided no solutions to current problems. Instead, they would publish writing that was polished and aseptic, and thrash the Ku Klux Klan, the Anti-Saloon League, utopianism, despotism, sentimentality, moral uplift, and evangelism: Mencken's pet peeves. Though Nathan eventually left, the magazine continued to publish a range of authors, including W.E.B. Du Bois, composer Virgil Thomson, anthropologist Franz Boas, novelist William Faulkner, poet Countee Cullen, writer Mary Austin, social critic James Weldon Johnson, and of course Clarence Darrow.

No longer did Darrow want to be known as a labor lawyer, he told Mencken. He was a defender of civil rights and of human life. And he'd be known as a notorious defender of human life, in fact, when he argued that the lives of two teenage boys be spared even though they had murdered a third teenager, whom the killers chose at random and for no apparent reason.

RUBY DARROW ANSWERED the door when Jacob Loeb rang the bell. Darrow's phone number was unlisted, so Loeb had rushed to the Darrows' apartment, accompanied by three other men, hoping to hire the famous, and famously emotional, lawyer to represent his nephew Dickie and Dickie's friend Nathan Leopold, who'd been charged with first-degree murder.

Darrow was sixty-seven years old. He was the Old Lion, and he did feel old. During the trial of Benjamin Gitlow, a communist charged with criminal anarchy for his writing, Darrow was said to look "a bit bent, a bit scarred, a bit mutilated." He was tired. Still, not so very long before he had said, "It never occurs to me that I should refuse to defend anyone."

What had happened: On May 21, 1924, Nathan Leopold and Richard Loeb brutally killed fourteen-year-old Robert Franks. The murder was premeditated and without motive—not greed or passion, not jealousy or revenge or bigotry. It was simply and hideously a senseless crime and seemed specifically modern, a sensational case of children run amok. The two young men had "jazzed" through life, promiscuous, boozy, and bohemian, and then committed a "jazz murder," newspaper writers scolded, the young men fueled by "gasoline and gin and maybe a puff or so once in a while of marijuana, you never can tell, or perhaps a sniff of white joy powder."

And so it was as if the boys and their crime demonstrated that horrible things could happen, did happen, seemingly at random, especially if you were Bobby Franks, the murdered boy. This is exactly what Bryan had warned would take place if we lived for the intellect alone, godless and unguided and hollow at the core.

Evangelist Billy Sunday, the former baseball player who went to bat for God, said the world was fox-trotting to perdition. "Nowadays it is considered fashionable for higher education to scoff at God," he added. He sounded like William Jennings Bryan.

He too went after Darwinism, which, along with higher education, he and Bryan held responsible for the cold-blooded crimes of Leopold and Loeb. Darwin and Nietzsche.

A LONELY, RECLUSIVE, and brilliant child, Nathan Leopold had been a student at the University of Chicago, entering the freshman class at fifteen. He had recently been admitted to Harvard Law School, was fluent in eleven languages, and as a recognized amateur ornithologist, he had collected and cataloged about eight thousand species of birds, some thought to be extinct. He was also the son of a millionaire, who lived in the same wealthy Chicago neighborhood as his friend, Richard Loeb, the child of an even more prominent family. Loeb's father was vice president of the mail-order house Sears, Roebuck and Company.

Richard "Dickie" Loeb had entered the University of Michigan at the age of fourteen and would soon start graduate work at the University of Chicago. Far more popular than Nathan

Leopold, Dickie Loeb was good-looking, gregarious, and an avid reader of detective fiction. Together, young Leopold and Loeb shoplifted, stole cars, broke windows, and set fires. And craving more—a thrill, they later said—they concocted a kidnapping plan that, they decided, had to end in murder. Otherwise, their victim could identify them. So they lured the fourteen-year-old Robert (Bobby) Franks into their automobile on a sunny day in May as he was walking home from school. They hit him several times on the head with a chisel, stuffed a cloth soaked in hydrochloric acid into his mouth, stripped him naked, and then poured more acid on his face and his genitals but not before stopping to buy a sandwich at a lunch counter.

That night, they called the Franks home and said Bobby was alive and would stay alive if Mr. Franks paid ransom. Further details were to follow. The next morning, the Franks received a special-delivery typewritten letter asking for $10,000. But almost at the same time, the naked body of a boy had been discovered near Chicago's Wolf Lake, not far from the Indiana border. It had been shoved into a large drainpipe under the railroad tracks. Near his body, on the grass, lay a pair of horn-rimmed glasses. The glasses did not belong to the dead boy but to Nathan Leopold.

Taken to the LaSalle Hotel for questioning to avoid publicity, Nathan Leopold said yes, the glasses were his. He must have lost them near Wolf Lake, where he would often go to bird-watch. Nathan Leopold also said he'd spent May 21 with his friend Dickie, driving around in the Leopold family automobile. Dickie Loeb corroborated the story. The two young men had been motoring, drinking Scotch, and later they had dinner at the Coconut Grove restaurant.

But the Leopold family chauffeur said that the family automobile, a shiny red Willys-Knight, had not left the garage the day of the murder. Nathan Leopold confessed. Dickie Loeb confessed too but claimed Leopold had killed Bobby Franks. Leopold said the opposite. Dickie was the killer. Only in that did their stories differ. Detail by gory detail, they each recounted the unimaginable crime, almost boasting.

The *San Francisco Examiner* and *The Chicago Tribune* featured tawdry columns detailing the crime, every lurid aspect of it: the murder, the confessions and what the boys said, and how they bragged that they "did it for the experience." Any wealthy victim would do, for they also wanted ransom money. After the murder, Dickie Loeb collected newspaper articles about it and talked at length with reporters, even volunteering to accompany them to the drugstore where the kidnappers must have made the telephone call to Mr. Franks.

Later, Darrow would insist that the very fact Dick Loeb had grandly piloted reporters around the city was so very wacky, it had to be the action of a very sick person.

Though Leopold and Loeb confessed to a capital crime, because they were wealthy, they were put up in the Windermere Hotel before being transferred to jail, where their meals were delivered from a restaurant. Cigarettes too. They were beyond good and evil, they said; they were Nietzschean supermen.

DARROW HAD BEEN ambivalent about defending Leopold and Loeb. He knew that he'd be pilloried in the press, though that hadn't stopped him before. He would be accused of pocketing millions to get a couple of rich killers off the hook, though that had never stopped him either. With assistance from two lawyers, Benjamin Bachrach and his brother Walter, Darrow decided to take the case and received a $10,000 retainer. As for the rest of his fee, arrangements would be completed after the trial, but his clients understood it would be very high, given the work involved.

That, right now, was getting the boys life imprisonment and not the death penalty. "No client of mine had ever been put to death, and I felt that it would almost, if not quite, kill me if it should ever happen," Darrow later said. "I am strongly—call it morbidly—against killing." Horrified by the murder of Bobby Franks, he could not abide capital punishment, and he never would.

He was also battling what he called "the greatest enemy that ever confronted man—public opinion." The case dominated the news. *The Chicago Tribune* wanted to broadcast the proceedings, and the *Chicago Evening American* offered to hire the White Sox stadium to use as a courtroom. The press quickly convicted Leopold and Loeb, calling them diabolical young men without religion, without respect for humanity, and who sneer at the distinction between good and evil.

Pleading not guilty, Leopold and Loeb were arraigned on June 11 in the graying Criminal Courts Building so jammed that people were sitting on the windowsills. To enter, reporters or spectators had to show a pink ticket before being conducted to the fifth floor, where a row of police guarded the stairs. Up another flight, passing three more guards, they were finally allowed into the courtroom.

There Darrow stood. Nathan Leopold later remembered thinking he seemed a raggedy scarecrow, a bumpkin, even, dressed in a light seersucker jacket that looked as though he'd slept in it. The eggs he'd eaten at breakfast were on his wrinkled shirt.

But the Old Lion surprised the court when, more than a month after the arraignment, he changed Leopold and Loeb's plea to guilty. That meant there would be no jury trial. That meant Darrow could argue for a mitigating sentence in front of the judge alone. Hands in his pockets, hair falling over his forehead, in his nondescript and wrinkled suit, Darrow reminded the judge that in Illinois, not a single person under the age of twenty-three had ever been hanged after pleading guilty.

A twenty-four-year-old did hang probably because of the color of his skin, Darrow mordantly recalled.

It was a gamble.

Hearing the change in plea, the courtroom was stunned into silence for a moment. Darrow apologized to the judge. "We dislike to throw this burden upon the court," he said. But he had no choice.

"Should two boys of this age," Darrow softly explained, "be hanged by the neck until dead, it would in no way bring back Robert Franks or add to the ease and security of this community. I insist it would be without precedent, upon a plea of guilty."

State's attorney Robert Crowe was incensed. Formerly a judge in the Circuit Court of Cook County, the forty-five-year-old Crowe was a Yale-educated anti-prohibitionist Republican who had been considering a run for mayor. Characterized by the press as a panther, ready to pounce, Crowe believed in capital punishment as a deterrent, and he had assumed the verdict in the sensational case before him was a foregone conclusion. Leopold and Loeb were headed for the gallows, deservedly.

Darrow hadn't consulted him about the change in plea. Worse, Darrow wanted psychiatric testimony to mitigate the sentence. A guilty plea presupposes sanity, Crowe countered. That is, a sane person can choose between right and wrong, and hence knows they're responsible for their actions. But an insanity defense had to meet legal guidelines. A defendant claiming insanity can't know the difference between right and wrong and thus cannot choose between them. Clearly Leopold and Loeb could distinguish between right and wrong. They admitted the crime and should hang for it. Darrow was pulling a fast one.

"Are you people trying to plead these two insane and guilty both?" Crowe sneered. "If so, I ask Your Honor to call a jury."

Darrow calmly explained that although they might not be considered legally insane, Leopold and Loeb were nonetheless suffering from "derangements of their emotional life." Therefore he asked to introduce expert testimony so he could demonstrate that Leopold and Loeb were obviously disturbed even if they did choose to commit this heinous crime, which they knew was wrong. For the defendants were not normal boys. In fact, they sat in the courtroom, frequently smiling and chatting with each other and their attorneys, and they seemed to be at ease, which was chilling.

How could they be normal, Darrow continued.

He turned to Robert Crowe. "This will be tried like a lawsuit in spite of your desire to get blood," he said.

The gray-haired Judge John Caverly had already served as chief justice of the Cook County Criminal Court, and he had already sentenced five men to hang during his time on the bench. However he did allow expert testimony to be submitted in this case. William Randolph Hearst offered Sigmund Freud a half-million dollars, plus transportation, to testify. Freud declined. But eighteen psychologists and psychiatrists did examine Leopold and Loeb, four requested by the defense, the rest by the state.

During the weeks that followed, Darrow argued before Judge Caverly that Leopold and Loeb were precocious but troubled. Crowe would have none of it. Calling Darrow an atheist, Crowe described the defendants as rich, heartless Jewish boys, overeducated and without morals. Their Bible was Nietzsche, which they'd said taught them that the superior man was not bound by conventional morality. Cunning monsters, they had called their brutal killing of Bobby Franks merely a scientific experiment conducted "as easily" as sticking "a pin through the back of a beetle." Anything was acceptable in the interest of science, according to that monster Leopold. "A 6-year-old-boy is justified in pulling the wings from a fly," he had said, "if by so doing he learns that without wings the fly is helpless."

Were these the statements of a sane person, Darrow countered. Was the awful murder of Bobby Franks the act of sane persons? For clearly the murder of Franks was the weirdest, the most unprovoked, purposeless, and senseless action of two profoundly disturbed persons, both minors, both sick, who killed for nothing, who killed, Darrow said, "because somewhere in the finite processes that go to the making up of the boy or the man, something slipped."

Not that there was any excuse. "If to hang these two boys would bring him back to life, I would say let them go," Darrow continued. If hanging the boys would prevent future murders, he might well say fine, hang them.

But Darrow said he wanted the senseless murder of Bobby Franks to mean something. Let him not have died in vain. Let us not blindly and cruelly call for yet another death. Let us acknowledge that capital punishment grows out of our primitive need for vengeance, and let's acknowledge that our killing two defective, abnormal adolescents would not prevent other impaired boys or malevolent men or vicious women from committing murder.

Darrow intended not only to save the lives of Leopold and Loeb but to demonstrate how the administration of criminal law could and should be enlightened.

Clarence Darrow at the bar: modulating his voice, peppering his questions and his talk with slang, he was, as always, skilled, logical, and convincing. His closing address began on Friday, August 22, 1924, and stretched over three days while crowds swarmed outside, cordoned off by the police.

At first he spoke softly, but soon he was smashing his fist on the table. The books on it shifted. "I sometimes wonder whether I am dreaming, whether I am not living in centuries long gone by, when savagery roamed wild, and the world was wet with human blood!" Darrow exclaimed. He spoke of the public opinion that had already convicted Leopold and Loeb, and the way hatred and a desire for revenge had swept across the nation.

Crowe had accused the two cold-blooded "modernists" of reading Nietzsche, so Darrow then recited long extracts from Nietzsche and pointed out that while the German philosopher has many readers, including himself, those readers don't take Nietzsche literally. Nietzsche has no actual application to life, Darrow continued. But Leopold, who became obsessed with the idea of a superman, did not understand this.

And anyway, why did the boys kill another boy? "There are causes for this terrible crime," Darrow said. Surely there are reasons, many reasons: education, perhaps; and birth; and money; and—unquestionably—the war.

About the war, Darrow told the court, "I believed in it. I don't know whether I was crazy or not. Sometimes I think perhaps I was. I approved of it; I joined in the general cry of madness and despair."

The war: How could it not influence us? "We read of killing one hundred thousand men in a day. We read about it and we rejoiced in it—if it was the other fellows who were killed."

"Right or wrong, justifiable or unjustifiable—which I need not discuss today—it changed the world. For four long years the civilized world was engaged in killing men," Darrow said, persisting.

The war: "It was taught in every school, aye in the Sunday schools. The little children played at war. The toddling children on the street. Do you suppose this world has ever been the same since?"

The war: "We have preached it, we have worked for it, we have advised it, we have taught it to the young until the world has been drenched in blood. It has left its stains upon every human heart and every human mind, and has almost stifled the feelings of pity and charity that have their natural home in the human breast."

. . .

CALLED A PHILOSOPHER of infinite mercy, Darrow sought understanding where there is none: the mad act of two mad boys, motiveless, vicious, cruel. Yet Darrow's forensic analysis was lucid, his melancholy appeal plaintive and wholehearted. His eyes glistened with tears.

He directly addressed the bench. At times, the judge had pursed his lips, at times he brought a pencil to his mouth. "I know Your Honor stands between the future and the past," Darrow's voice was low. "I know the future is on my side."

"Your Honor stands between the past and the future," Darrow repeated. "You may hang these boys; you may hang them, by the neck until they are dead. But in doing it you will turn your face toward the past."

"I am pleading for the future," he explained. "I am pleading for a time when hatred and cruelty will not control the hearts of men. When we can learn by reason and judgment and understanding and faith that all life is worth saving, and that mercy is the highest attribute of man."

The courtroom was still while Clarence Darrow read a verse of the Persian poet Omar Khayyam: "So I be written in the Book of Love / I do not care about the Book above; / Erase my name, or write it as you will / So I will be written in the Book of Love."

He gathered his notes and papers. Hunched over, drained, the lines on his face deeper, sturdy if very tired, Clarence Darrow sat back down.

ACROSS THE STREET from the Loeb mansion, someone left a picture of a skull and crossbones on the porch of Frank Harris, the uncle of one of the boys Leopold and Loeb had considered killing before they settled on Bobby Franks.

Along with the note was an envelope addressed to "Chicago,

City of Crime." In it was a message, evidently meant to be reassuring.

"If the court don't hang them, we will. K. K. K."

AFTER FIVE WEEKS of courtroom drama, on September 10, 1924, Judge Caverly adjusted his glasses and handed down the verdict. Leopold and Loeb each received ninety-nine years for the kidnapping, and they received a sentence of imprisonment for life for the murder of Robert Franks. Judge Caverly said he had considered the age of the defendants. They would not be executed, but he urged no paroles be granted, ever.

THE FUTURE PULITZER PRIZE–WINNING playwright and Academy Award–winning screenwriter whose credits included an adaptation of Sinclair Lewis's novel *Arrowsmith*, Sydney Howard in 1924 published a series of scathingly satiric essays in *The New Republic*. In them, he pretended to interview a man he dubbed the professional patriot. The professional patriot was bent on eliminating from American schools all subjects, like Russian literature or evolution, that might be subversive.

After all, as this professional patriot told Sydney Howard, "There is nothing to be surprised at in Leopold and Loeb. With all this radicalism in the colleges, what do you expect?"

Chapter Eight

A Revival

1924

THERE WERE AS MANY JOURNALISTS at the trial of Leopold and Loeb in Chicago during that summer of 1924 as had been at the Democratic convention in New York, for the convention had promised to be as electrifying in its own way.

Among the presidential front-runners that year was the charismatic, blunt, and very affable New York governor Alfred E. Smith, a man of the urban streets. The son of immigrants, he symbolized the immigrant. Square-shouldered, the cigar-smoking and derby-wearing Smith was a self-educated Irish Catholic from Manhattan's Lower East Side. His ties to Tammany Hall didn't stop him from overhauling New York's labor laws or fighting for better public education. When he signed a bill basically banning the Klan in New York, the Klan notified him that "you have signed your own political death warrant so far as your aspirations for the Presidency are concerned." Four thousand hooded men and women celebrated the Fourth of July in New Jersey and burned Governor Smith in effigy.

Before he took on the defense of Leopold and Loeb, Clarence Darrow too planned to go to the convention as a Smith delegate. "He might help us get a drink," Darrow quipped. Smith was a "wet." William Jennings Bryan loathed Al Smith.

Al Smith stood for everything that Bryan opposed—and, in

particular, the repeal of Prohibition. For Smith had signed the repeal of the prohibition laws in New York. One of Smith's aides remembered watching Bryan fall to his knees, praying to defeat Smith and the anti-prohibitionists. The story is likely apocryphal though metaphorically accurate. "If the wets expect to obtain control of the Democratic Party and make it the mouthpiece of the underworld, they must prepare for such a struggle as they never had before," Bryan vowed.

The wrangling on the floor of Madison Square Garden spread out over a seemingly endless sixteen days of noisy static, rowdy and raw, tiresome and acrimonious. Fifteen thousand people had arrived, various bands played "The Sidewalks of New York"—a kind of Smith anthem—over and over, and the streets had been cleared of traffic. The Garden itself was lit by huge movie spotlights. Special press rooms had been arranged to accommodate the glut of reporters, and telegraph and telephone facilities had been installed with equipment set up for the radio broadcasts, so the expectant nation could learn in real time who might emerge as the party's favorite. This was the first national convention ever to be broadcast on radio.

Bunting of red, white, and blue decorated the speakers' stand, and huge canopies were suspended from the ceiling, but they could be moved to open the skylight, though this allowed the scorching sun to beat down on the delegates. The heat was terrible. Perspiring men took off their jackets. The place still stank from the circus animals that had romped around the Garden not long before the delegates came to town.

In the upper galleries, signs forbidding smoking and spitting had been printed in Italian as well as English. "Those bilingual signs told a real story," said Kansas journalist William Allen White, noting the large number of immigrants in the galleries: "A queer crowd," White continued, "for a Westerner to see." There were women too, women delegates; when Lena Jones

Wade Springs, chair of the committee on credentials, rose to make a speech, the band struck up "Oh, You Beautiful Doll."

The convention had opened on Tuesday, June 24, the day after *Time* magazine, founded just the year before, had placed the Ku Klux Klan Imperial Wizard Hiram Evans on its cover. Determined to stop Smith—a Catholic—Klan members roamed the convention floor. Red-cheeked from the heat, Henry Mencken ran into several of them. "They are wandering around half dazed and terrified," Mencken gloomily reported, "an armed Jesuit behind every post and eager to find a hero to save them from the Papal galleys and the Constitution from the wops."

Ridiculing the convention—all conventions—as nothing more than a conclave of professional job-seekers, grotesque and hypocritical, Mencken reported with disgust that the Democrats had invited former Attorney General A. Mitchell Palmer as its distinguished guest. The thing couldn't have been better staged by Aristophanes, Molière, or Buffalo Bill.

Bryan had come to the city he long regarded as Babylon, his secretary having driven him there in his Ford, and once at Madison Square Garden, he too strolled around the convention floor, shaking hands with everyone, relentlessly grinning, and wearing a huge pennant pinned to the front of his jacket with "Florida" emblazoned on it.

A churlish reporter dismissed Bryan as a walking dead man, but the Commoner had a purpose. He'd worked hard to become a delegate from Florida, telling would-be supporters that he fully intended to argue against what he considered the prejudice that for sixty years had excluded Southern men from the presidency. He therefore intended to nominate his friend, Dr. A. A. Murphree, president of the University of Florida. "In presenting the name of Dr. Murphree, I am going to make a plea for the South," Bryan explained. "I am in a position to do this because twenty-eight years ago I announced my willingness to have a Southern

man for my running mate, and twenty years ago I seconded the
nomination of an ex-Confederate soldier." He was referring to
the white supremacist from Georgia, Tom Watson, the Populist
Party choice for vice president in 1896, and to the ex-Confederate
general Francis Cockrell from Missouri, Bryan's choice for president in 1904.

Murphree of course didn't have a chance. Not only did he
have no experience, he didn't want to run. But Bryan may have
had other intentions. As he told a friend, in a somewhat garbled
way, "The only condition under which I feel I would be justified
in considering the question [of the nomination] from a personal
standpoint is the remote contingency, which cannot be brought
about by any plans of myself or my friends—if when the convention meets, no one had a preponderating influence and no one
else can lead our forces—note the number of 'if's'—and the party
should feel that it is my duty to my party and my country to be
a candidate the fourth time."

Lest he seem too ambitious, Bryan had told Alabama Representative George Huddleston, "I do not care to discuss the matter
on paper, further than to say that I have not felt that I should ever
make a fight for a Presidential nomination. My past nominations
have come to me without a contest, and it would be mortifying
to have to make a contest; and whenever a contest is necessary
there is a possibility of defeat, which would be still more mortifying." He did not want to end his career with a defeat. But a re-
cruitment: well, that might be a horse of a very different color.

Feigning disinterest, maneuvering strategically, avoiding embarrassment while staying available: that's what Bryan had been
doing since he failed to be elected moderator of the Presbyterian
General Assembly. And he was taking religion on the political
road—or his politics on a religious one. "Mr. Bryan's religious
convictions discourage him from drink or dancing," the columnist Heywood Broun coldly remarked, "and so he has gone in
for political conventions."

If his Murphree nomination went nowhere, Bryan said he'd support the other front-runner, William Gibbs McAdoo. Born in the South, McAdoo had moved to New York City and as head of the Democratic National Committee had worked on Woodrow Wilson's 1912 presidential campaign. In 1914 he married Wilson's daughter. Long and lean and patrician, this former Tennessee lawyer was an apparent progressive in matters of labor relations—even if he'd been director general of the United States Railroad Administration. But his reputation had been irreparably stained by the notorious oil scandals associated with the Harding administration and, specifically, the sleazy Teapot Dome bribery affair.

Former Interior Secretary Albert B. Fall had leased federal oil reserves to private corporations for an estimated and whopping $500,000 without competitive bidding. One of these private corporations was the Pan American Petroleum Company, run by Edward Doheny. Doheny, it turned out, had paid William McAdoo's private law practice a large retainer—$250,000 in all, it was first alleged—which seemed to implicate McAdoo in the scandal or at least smear his reputation.

McAdoo was also a segregationist who had introduced Jim Crow into the Treasury department—to remove friction, he said; the new policy cost many Blacks their jobs. That didn't disqualify him with many Democrats, particularly in the South. In fact McAdoo was presumed to be an open supporter of the Klan, which was not true, although he was widely regarded as the Klan's candidate.

It was the Klan, not Teapot Dome or Prohibition, that was the most contentious issue on the floor. The Republicans had sidestepped mentioning the Klan at their convention, but here the Klan was out in the open. One of the delegates was the Klan senator from Texas, and circulating were other Klan members such as Georgia Grand Dragon Nathan Bedford Forrest III, the great-grandson of Confederate General Nathan Bedford Forrest, the Klan's first Grand Wizard and infamous for his slaughter of Black soldiers during the Civil War. Several delegates were running up and down the aisles shouting, "Get up, you Kleagles!," referring to Klan officers, while the galleries, loaded with rowdy Smith delegates, hissed and booed.

The question of whether to condemn the Klan by name was hotly debated by the Democratic Party's Committee on Resolutions when it met at the Waldorf-Astoria. Everyone was angry, though not William Jennings Bryan, who, as a member of the committee, insisted that the robed and hooded order need not be explicitly censured. He did not want to pit one group of people— one group of Christians, that is—against another.

The members of the Resolutions Committee were worn-out. At six A.M., Bryan asked them to recite the Lord's Prayer to help settle their differences.

The differences were hardly settled. The majority report fudged the issue by merely affirming the Constitution's protection of religious liberty and equality without mentioning the Klan. The minority report also condemned all secret societies and any attempt on their part—and, more to the point, on the part of the Ku Klux Klan, which it did name—to limit the civil rights of persons or groups because of religion, place of birth, or racial origin.

William Pattangall, a Yankee from Maine, declared, "I hate bigotry." The sweaty audience roared its approval. "When we went to war, did we draft only white Protestants and native born boys?" he shouted. "If the Klan or any other secret society discriminates against Jews and Catholics and negroes in civil life," Pattangall continued, "I'll oppose them everywhere and all the time."

Women too wanted to censure the Klan by name. Women's rights activist Emma Guffey Miller, who had seconded New York governor Al Smith's nomination, said that women should fight this guerrilla organization out in the open. Tall and brave,

Andrew C. Erwin of Georgia jumped up. A descendent of Confederates, he too vehemently condemned the Klan, and in the name of Judah Benjamin, a Confederate Jew, Erwin begged the delegates to purge prejudice from their hearts and the stigma on his state, where the Klan was strong. Delegates from several states ran over to shake Erwin's hand. The applause grew louder and more boisterous as well-wishers lifted him on their shoulders to parade around the Garden.

There were more than two hundred Klansmen delegates waiting for the last speaker of the evening—none other than the Commoner himself. Just before midnight, William Jennings Bryan made his way to the speaker's podium. Bryan wore his signature black alpaca coat and baggy trousers. He looked ratty and moth-eaten, Mencken reported. But Bryan was cheered for twelve minutes. Soon he lifted his hand, gesturing for quiet. His eyes were harder than they had been, his voice not quite as melodious although it was still rich and warm.

Bryan began with self-assurance but within minutes he had offended the gallery, which was packed with Smith supporters. They hooted and heckled when he said that putting those "three magic and mystic words"—the Ku Klux Klan—into a Democratic Party platform wasn't at all necessary.

"Yes, it is," shouted the gallery. More boos. The chair rapped for order.

Momentarily hushed, Bryan carried on, earnest and apparently nonplussed. Calling the Klan out by name would give it free advertising and "start a prairie fire and carry the Klan into every Congressional district." More boos and catcalls. Bryan soldiered forward.

"The Catholic Church," Bryan shouted, "does not need a great party to protect it from a million Klansmen." Cheers and applause.

"The Jews do not need this resolution," he said, referring to the minority report that boldly condemned the Klan. "They have

Moses. They have Elijah." No one needed the minority resolution. There was no need to condemn the Klan. Cheers. Hisses.

The Klan is "misguided," he said. That's all.

He swerved into a lecture on religion. "Much as I owe to my
party," Bryan said, "I owe more to the Christian religion. If
my party has given me the foundations of my political faith, my
Bible has given me the foundations of a faith that has enabled me
to stand for the right." Applause and cheers.

Digressing further, he spoke of war and the fact that neither
education nor science could prevent war and, in fact, science had
invented poison gas and a hellishness so horrid that civilization
can barely survive it. The world needed the Prince of Peace. He
circled back to the Klan.

"We can exterminate Ku Kluxism better by recognizing their
honesty and teaching them they're wrong." Their honesty? The
jeering began again. It almost seemed as though he was saying
the Democrats couldn't afford to alienate the Klan.

Hisses, now louder than ever, filled the Garden. But applause
too. The band played "America."

Bryan was exhausted. The hair on the back of his neck was
wet.

Jane Loretto West, president of the Federation of Democratic
Women, said that she had very much wanted to hear the famous
William Jennings Bryan; but after she heard what he had to say,
she no longer wanted anything to do with him. For Bryan seemed
either afraid of the Klan or perhaps in sympathy with it. Not to
denounce the Klan was to tolerate it. Or condone it. "Calling on
God," a critic observed, "Bryan counseled compromise with
evil."

Everyone knew, too, that the Klan was intensely "dry," as
was Bryan, who was courting white Southern Democrats. Bryan
would not therefore rebuff the Klan. Still, he admitted that it
"combines about all the race prejudices we have in this country." But, as he confidently added, "in the south it rests largely

upon the doctrine of white supremacy, a doctrine absolutely essential to the welfare of the south." He could therefore rationalize that since white supremacy in the South was not in jeopardy, there was no reason to protest the Klan's existence there. Or anywhere? For many in the convention hall, the logic was confusing, self-serving, even sad.

Unsurprisingly, Black nationalist Marcus Garvey again pointed out that he considered Bryan to be the Klan's defender. "William Jennings Bryan is as big a Klansman as the Imperial Wizard himself," he said.

At nearly two A.M. the committee's minority report condemning the Klan was defeated by only one vote. The Klan praised the majority report, and it praised Bryan, whom it considered its author.

"Democrats catered to Klan's race hatred and midnight murder, itself a threat to democracy," W.E.B. Du Bois said.

And Will Rogers joked, though not in jest, that "Saturday will always remain burned in my memory as long as I live, as being the day when I heard the most religion preached, and the least practiced."

IT WAS THE charismatic Franklin D. Roosevelt who had nominated Al Smith for president. This was Roosevelt's first public appearance since the onset of the polio that had paralyzed him from the waist down. Assisted by one of his sons and leaning on his crutches, he walked carefully and with courageous dignity to the speaker's rostrum. The cheers finally died down, and smiling, Roosevelt spoke warmly of Smith and, quoting William Wordsworth, he named Smith the " 'Happy Warrior' of the political battlefield." The crowd went wild.

But the convention deadlocked—neither McAdoo nor Smith had enough votes for the nomination—and Bryan asked to speak again. Granted permission, he walked to the convention's rostrum as the galleries screamed, "Sit down Bryan." Undaunted, he sang the praises of several candidates from the South, like Murphree. Someone yelled, "Never heard of him." Bryan praised ex-Confederates and Southern Democrats. Someone else shouted, "What is the matter with Underwood?" but Bryan would not name Oscar Underwood of Alabama, a vocal opponent of the Klan and no fan of Prohibition. Instead, Bryan backed William Gibbs McAdoo as the progressive candidate. Now the gallery chanted "Oil," "Oil," "Oil," referring to McAdoo's proximity to the Harding scandals, and others yelled out, "Hurrah for Al Smith."

Bryan had not even mentioned the New York governor.

Delegates complained Bryan had gone over his time. Disoriented by the racket, he retreated and spoke of the familiar, if real, objections he had to long-standing issues, like illicit campaign contributions. He began to ramble on about the New York millionaires. Bryan looked up at the galleries that had jeered and hooted him. "You do not represent the future of the country," he told them.

Smiling, Franklin Roosevelt leaned over to a friend. "Mr. Bryan has killed poor McAdoo and he hasn't done himself any good."

A reporter covering the convention noted without sympathy that Bryan was the main act of the Bungling Brothers Circus. The balloting continued in the heat and dirt while hot dog wrappers and tired streamers littered the convention hall. It wasn't until the afternoon of July 9 that exhausted delegates abandoned both Al Smith and William McAdoo on the 103rd ballot. "The two factions lost everything that they had fought over," Mencken drily observed. "It was as if Germany and France had fought over Alsace-Lorraine for centuries, then handed it over to England."

Their nominee was John W. Davis, a lawyer from West Virginia and former ambassador to England; his hair white; handsome and elegant and neither wet nor dry. Bryan had vigorously opposed Davis, declaring Davis was the Wall Street tool of J. Pierpont Morgan. But twelve hours after Davis's nomination, Bryan's brother Charles, governor of Nebraska, was placed on the ticket as the vice-presidential nominee. It was widely believed that since the Commoner had messed up the convention, party leaders figured "a member of his family should be in on the beating."

Bryan peering at a solar eclipse, reminding Democrats
the sun will soon shine again
COURTESY LIBRARY OF CONGRESS

Bryan was now forced to support Davis. "If monkeys had votes, Mr. Bryan would be champion of evolution," a journalist bitterly observed.

"There is something about a national convention that makes it as fascinating as a revival or a hanging. It is vulgar, it is ugly, it is stupid, it is tedious," Mencken wrote after the Democrats went home. "Yet it is somehow charming. One sits through long sessions wishing heartily that all the delegates and alternates were dead and in hell—and then suddenly there comes a show so

gaudy and hilarious, so melodramatic and obscene, unimagin-
ably exhilarating and preposterous that one lives a gorgeous
year in an hour."

That show had been William Jennings Bryan.

THE ISSUES WERE not preposterous. Hatred and fear had been
funneled into the convention, and the very debate over the Klan
laid bare the anxiety of delegates from the rural regions who did
not understand, or could not face the fact, that Black men and
women and immigrants and Catholics and Jews, particularly on
the two coasts, were growing in numbers and power. The recently passed immigration restriction act had tried to stop them,
and where it failed to stop them, the Klan was ready with torch
and tar.

Yet there was no stopping any of it. The country contained
multitudes still, always had, and now the radio and the newsreel
and recordings and movies, celebrities, scandals, and spectacles,
magnified the difference among peoples. At the convention, days
and days of deadlock reflected this, as in a funhouse mirror, just
as the trial of Leopold and Loeb reflected in a crueler mirror the
underworld of violence that also was America.

The Democrats would lose the presidential election in a land-
slide to the incumbent Republican stalwart Calvin Coolidge.
Davis and Charles Bryan did, however, carry the eleven states of
the former Confederacy, as well as Oklahoma.

Bryan had dutifully campaigned for the ticket and promised
his fans—there still were many—that he would stay in politics
till death did them part. Even so, just before the Commoner
walked out of Madison Square Garden for the very last time,
recalling the hooting and hissing and catcalls, he plaintively confided to Alabama Senator J. Thomas Heflin that he'd never been
so humiliated in his life.

Chapter Nine

The Man Everybody Knew

1925

BRUCE BARTON'S *The Man Nobody Knows,* a huge bestseller in 1925, the year of the Scopes trial, promised its readers both God and Mammon, both spiritual salvation and material riches. Barton's Jesus Christ was a muscle-bound, amiable publicist with nerves of steel who had plucked twelve men out of nowhere and launched a global corporation.

"Wist ye not that I am about my Father's *business*?" Barton's book begins. The word "business" was italicized.

Barton offered a modernized Christianity fit for the times. Here was a vision of a messiah who just happened to be the most sought-after dinner guest in all Jerusalem, a positive thinker and manly outdoors man who was the world's greatest salesman, rather like Barton himself. The son of a well-known pastor's son, Barton had attended Amherst College, was elected to Phi Beta Kappa, and planned to earn a PhD in history when, despite a fellowship, he left academe and began writing about religion for the Chicago *Home Herald*.

Barton sincerely wanted people to care about religion, but he also understood a great deal about psychology, advertising, and the times in which he lived. Working as the assistant sales manager for the publisher P. F. Collier and Son, he wrote successful copy for Harvard president Charles Eliot's "Five-Foot

Shelf" of classics, which promised a liberal education in just fifteen minutes a day. By 1919, he was a prolific sloganeer—"A man is down, but he's never out," he wrote—and with two friends he opened an advertising agency, Barton, Durstine, and Osborn. Their clients soon included General Electric, General Mills, and Calvin Coolidge. They helped invent and market the character Betty Crocker. Barton became quite rich—the power of positive thinking. "What I am you can be," says his Jesus Christ. "What I do, you can do."

William Jennings Bryan dismissed Barton as nothing more than an unbelieving hack. He preferred his evangelism straight, serious, savvy, and orthodox, like that of the Reverend William Bell Riley, militant Baptist preacher and head of the ultraconservative World's Christian Fundamentals Association, which he'd organized in 1919. Good-looking and somewhat stern, witty and productive, Riley published the magazine *The Christian Fundamentalist* and ran the Anti-Evolution League in Minnesota, where he was the pastor at the First Baptist Church. He loathed theological liberalism, dancing, drinking, Jews, and communists. He thought capital punishment a fine idea. Riley was zealous, unflinching, and intent on building a vast network of Fundamentalists, which he did.

Bryan was slightly more modern than Riley. To Bryan the world wasn't quite as fallen and hopeless as Riley insisted. And Bryan didn't object to a little spectacle in his religion. For that, there was Aimee Semple McPherson. She was not threatening. She was not a flapper. She was modern but not a suffragette even though McPherson's very presence suggested that a woman had a right, even a duty, to take to the stage as long as she was tending the soul. Aimee McPherson seemed to care about people's hunger and their sense of alienation, much as Bryan did.

A self-made evangelical healer, at seventeen Aimee had bolted from the confines of a small family farm in Ontario, Canada, having been born again under the wing of the Pentecostal

preacher Robert Semple, whom she married in 1908 in a ceremony managed by the Salvation Army. Her mother had worked
in their soup kitchens during Aimee's youth, and Aimee was
keeping up the tradition, in her own way. In 1910, she and Semple sailed to China, where they planned to work as missionaries.

Aimee Semple McPherson
COURTESY LIBRARY OF CONGRESS

Robert Semple contracted malaria and died in Hong Kong
just before their daughter, Roberta, was born. Aimee telegraphed
her mother, who cabled money so Aimee and Roberta could

come to New York, where her mother was living. There, Aimee met and married an accountant, Harold McPherson. After giving birth to a son, she sank so profoundly low that when she was hospitalized with appendicitis, she heard a voice. It told her she had two choices: either die or enter the ministry. She chose the ministry.

Aimee Semple McPherson left Harold and with her children took to the road, where, as an itinerant preacher, she conducted so many successful camp meetings that she was able to buy a Packard, which she called her Gospel Car. On its side, she posted such signs as "Jesus is Coming—Get Ready." Touring up and down the East Coast, she preached in tents and churches to audiences that grew larger and larger until they numbered in the thousands.

In 1918 she arrived in Los Angeles with nothing more, she said, than "ten dollars and a tambourine." Calling herself Sister Aimee, she published a paper, *The Bridal Call*. She spoke in tongues, and by the laying on of hands—she was said to cure eczema—she rivaled the megastar Billy Sunday, the professional athlete turned celebrity evangelist. But unlike Sunday or Riley, who warned of brimstone and agony, Sister Aimee talked more in the manner of William Jennings Bryan. She delivered a popular sermon, the "Foursquare Gospel": the four sides were baptism, healing, the savior, and the Second Coming, though she often added God, home, school, and government. She spoke of love and kindness.

A self-made woman born in the nineteenth century, she adapted to the twentieth, marketing herself as the people's preacher. A thoroughly modern revivalist, gifted in the art of publicity, in 1920 she flew over San Diego in a biplane to drop her handbills direct from heaven. In San Francisco she filled the old Coliseum, where she preached to more than ten thousand people. In Los Angeles, Aimee opened a dazzling Angelus Temple that accommodated as many as five thousand worshippers.

On its peak was an enormous revolving cross visible for fifty miles, and inside there was a lovely sky-blue dome decorated with fluffy clouds of silver.

When he first entered the building, William Jennings Bryan said that he felt "the spirit of God."

An actress and a good one, she was like the stars of the silver screen. She piled her chestnut hair high and outfitted herself in a long white dress, which she covered with a long, dark blue, military-style cape. The signature costume made her look like a matronly nurse, comforting, unthreatening. She was slightly plump, she carried a bouquet, and she stood under gleaming lights of purple and red and blue. She delivered an unbeatable set of shows: sacred skits and biblical reenactments accompanied by a big brass band. She often wrote the music and designed the costumes. Sister Aimee dressed as a traffic cop and rode to the altar on a motorcycle. She borrowed a camel from the Barnes Zoo to reassure the crowd that the animal couldn't possibly pass through the eye of a needle. It was hocus-pocus, hardly spontaneous or intimate, but infectious; she worked hard, and she made a fortune. Religion sold, in book form, or on the stage. Bryan knew that.

And she knew how to use technology. "Now, the crowning blessing, the most golden opportunity, the most miraculous conveyance for the Message has come—The Radio!" The first woman to receive a broadcast license, she aired her sermons from her own station, KFSG (Kall Four Square Gospel). Her 500-watt transmitter reached as far as Hawaii. Dorothy Parker called her "Our Lady of the Loudspeaker."

"You can't laugh Aimee McPherson off. Once you come beneath the spell of her personality you're lost," a reporter noted. The poor and the forgotten, the outcast and the pariah faithfully flocked to the Temple and to the ministrations of this sunshiny healer. "The Cathedral of the Air am I," she declared in her magazine, "the church with no boundary line. And under my broad, canopied expanse, I house the sons of men—the black, the white, the yellow, the brown and red man, too. Brothers all sit side by side, in the church with no color line."

She welcomed Blacks to the Temple as well as Mexican residents, whether in the country legally or not. She also accepted gifts from the Ku Klux Klan, which offered her protection along with a bouquet of snowy-white flowers. She did warn them, though, that God could see right under their hoods. Mostly she preferred to denounce modernism, which to her meant jazz, booze, dance halls, and Leopold and Loeb.

She believed that evolution was "the triumph of Satanic intelligence," remarked a journalist. When William Jennings Bryan preached for the second time at the Angelus Temple, he said that if all ministers believed what Sister Aimee believed, that the Bible was true, they too would have mighty congregations. She returned the favor. During the Scopes trial, she telegraphed Bryan that the "ten thousand members of Angelus Temple, with its millions of radio church membership send grateful appreciation of your lion hearted championship of the Bible against evolution and throw our hats in the ring with you." Then she arranged an all-night prayer service, a parade, and a rally, which, she said, would be crowned by another spectacle—the "hanging and burial of monkey teachers" in effigy.

THE TABLE-BANGING, CHEST-WHACKING, no-holds-barred Billy Sunday said he never heard Mrs. McPherson preach though he gathered she told the truth, mainly. But he didn't need special effects or klieg lights. He was for real, he said, though he too was a performer, a real go-getter for Jesus and a crowd-pleaser who, as he boasted, "number my friends by the millions." But his preaching came to him "as naturally as a bird flies," he said, as he jumped up and down and punched the air. He lacerated his audience, he exhorted, he soothed. More a promoter than a theologian, he cheerfully admitted he knew as little about theology "as a jack-rabbit knows about ping-pong."

Carl Sandburg called him a "bughouse peddler of second-hand gospel."

Born in Iowa during the Civil War, Billy Sunday (William Ashley Sunday Jr.) was sent to the Civil War Soldiers' Orphans Home by his widowed mother. He and his brother ran away and worked at various odd jobs while they began to play for a local baseball team in Marshalltown, Iowa. Billy helped make the team one of the best in the state—and before long was offered a position on the Chicago White Stockings. He played five years for Chicago, then for the Pittsburgh Alleghenies and the Philadelphia Phillies.

Billy Sunday
COURTESY LIBRARY OF CONGRESS

His days as an outfielder came to an end after he heard a street evangelist, or so he said. He began preaching himself, and he preached even better than he played baseball. Newspapers loved to show Billy Sunday pitching a baseball at the devil.

Ordained by the Presbyterian Church in 1903, he brought to his revivals a muscular Christianity—clearly Bruce Barton was influenced by it, though Bryan less so. Begging his audience to accept Jesus Christ as their Lord, he threatened them with eternal damnation and hellfire if they did not. Billy Sunday electrified listeners as he smote thieves, bootleggers, and liars and said that anyone who puts politics above the pulpit could go straight to hell—though like Bryan, he was a politician and tried to run for president in 1920 on the Republican ticket.

In the winter of 1925, Billy Sunday went to Memphis to preach at the magnificent new auditorium conveniently located near several streetcar lines so the audience could leave their Fords at home and avoid the parking problems. "It is an honor to welcome you," the city mayor grandly greeted Sunday. Billy Sunday had promised the American Legion that he'd show its members how to fight the devil as vigorously and successfully as they fought the enemy in the World War. And Billy Sunday delivered. Wearing gray spats that matched his gray suit and a showy tie with blue diagonal stripes on a red background, he launched into his sermon. The liberal church was a dead church. He climbed on a chair. He swung at the devil with a left hook and bit him before lying facedown on the stage and lapping water from an imaginary brook. Breathless, he hollered that the recent war, which he'd supported, had been needless and "the most useless war ever fought." He yelled capital punishment was just fine. "I'd give him the juice," he howled.

As for evolution, that was a favorite topic these days. "If anyone wants to teach that God-forsaken, hell-born bastard theory of evolution," Billy Sunday warned, "then let him go out and let him be supported by men who believe that bastard theory and not expect Christian people of this country to pay for the teaching of a rotten, stinking professor who gets up there and teaches our children to forsake God and make our schools a clearing house for their God-forsaken dirty politics."

He'd knock the tar out of those atheistic scoundrels. "Darwin was a rotten old infidel."

As it was with Bryan, though with a far more colorful performance, Sunday fused together religion and politics.

Billy Sunday then went on to Nashville to deliver his sermon "The Three Krosses."

"Attention, KKK!" the Exalted Cyclops advertised Sunday's appearance.

Thousands of Klansmen marched into the auditorium to hear him. Mostly they were without costume, having left their bedsheets and pointy bonnets at home, as the reporter Ridley Wills noted, though a dozen of them were decked out in long snowy robes and elaborate headpieces.

"You could hear the dragons flap their wings when Billy Sunday's words soared high," Wills wrote, "and you could sense the kleagles rising on stately pinons with the gilt notes of the swelling klorus."

After the sermon, twelve of the robed Klansmen paraded to the stage, eleven in starch white and one arrayed in ruby red. They handed a flowery cross to Reverend Sunday as Klan members cheered, and one of them read their statement aloud, swearing the Klan's loyalty to Billy Sunday and his one-hundred-percent crusade for Jesus Christ.

IN KNOXVILLE, BILLY Sunday insisted on keeping his audience segregated. Local Black ministers refused to attend.

. . .

REVEREND FRANCIS GRIMKÉ said Billy Sunday was "astonish-
ingly dumb" on the subject of race. "He either doesn't know, or
knowing, for some reason doesn't care to say."

"So far as Mr. Sunday's preaching is concerned, and so far as
the preaching of all white evangelists in this country to whom I
have listened is concerned," Grimké continued, "he may give
himself wholly to God, and yet be chock full of this nasty, hateful race prejudice."

But to the Reverend Grimké, as to Bryan and Billy Sunday,
evolution left God out of creation. It also raised to him other
questions. Does God evolve? How could that be? Aren't humans
immortal, which is to say made as God wished them?

As for Clarence Darrow, he might be "saying some good
things on behalf of the rights of the race," Grimké conceded, but
"Beware, beware," he would warn. "It will be a sad day for the
race when it turns away from Jesus Christ . . . to the vaporings
of Mr. Darrow!" Yet Grimké's discrediting of evolution was not
necessarily shared by other Black clergy. Black evangelicals, like
white evangelicals, were divided. In 1922, Bishop Randall Carter
of Chicago at the African Methodist Episcopal Church General
Conference explained that "recent science declares that all humanity came up by evolution from the slime pools of long forgotten eons, and Holy Writ declares: 'Of one blood hath God
made all the nations to dwell on the face of the earth together.'
One race is not superior to another."

WITH SO MUCH competition, Bryan feared he was losing his audience. Newspapers no longer wanted to carry his syndicated
Bible Talks. They were too controversial, particularly about evolution. "Sunday school teachers say they are of little value to
them, being more Mr. Bryan's opinions than light on the lessons," explained the owners of the Republic Syndicate, agents
for his weekly columns.

"I really believe we could both get further with the Talks, both as to selling and as to their influence, if the controversial and the quasi-controversial were rigidly cut out."

SENSING THE GROWING opposition to the theory of evolution from those Fundamentalists who, based on no scientific knowledge whatsoever, would prevent the theory of evolution from being taught in the schools, the science writer Maynard Shipley organized the Science League of America to argue on behalf of science education. The League's constitution declared "the time is ripe for organized opposition to this reactionary movement." Membership was open to anyone who believed in academic freedom.

WILLIAM JENNINGS BRYAN ostentatiously sent a five-dollar check to a different organization, the far older American Association for the Advancement of Science, founded in 1848, which promoted dialogue among the scientists as well as the integration of science and religion. Membership was open to anyone. Though Bryan forgot to sign the check, he said he was pleased to take his place among those distinguished citizens who promoted science— science, that is, which was part and parcel of God and God's divine plan.

IN EARLY JANUARY 1925, William Jennings Bryan appeared at Nashville's Ryman Auditorium and again denounced the theory of evolution. He also talked about his role the year before in the presidential campaign. As he'd say to a reporter, "If you would be entirely accurate, you should represent me as using a double-barreled shotgun, firing one barrel at the elephant as he tried to enter the treasury and another at Darwinism—the monkey—as he tried to enter the schoolroom."

There was still lots of speculation about Bryan's political plans. Before he left Tennessee, he made sure that copies of his speech were distributed at the state house when it opened its legislative session later that month. When a reporter asked him if he planned to run for the United States Senate, Bryan smiled like the Cheshire cat and, affecting nonchalance, basked in the attention. "Simply say for me that I have nothing to say," he said.

Behind the scenes, he was testing his candidacy. "I regard the Senate as the highest legislative body in the world," he confidentially told one editor in March 1925. "The chance for serving the State of Florida and the nation is the thing that makes the office appeal to me." Pleased to have the matter discussed openly, Bryan then contacted the editor of Florida's *Sanford Herald*. "I can render the party more service than any other person now in the Senate," he said, referring to the incumbent Florida senator, Duncan Fletcher. "If this matter strikes you favorably and you have an editorial along those lines, I wish you would send me a number of copies of the paper so I can send them to other papers that are friendly."

"I dread the thought of adding anything to my already heavy burdens," he then demurred, while careful not to appear too hesitant. He outlined his qualifications. "My acquaintance with politics and the confidence of many people in me would enable me to defend the people's rights in our highest legislative body," he said, finally dropping the mask.

He sent this letter to well-positioned editors and friends.

Yet reports that he was a millionaire were embarrassing him. He was no millionaire. He'd made only $500,000 in his real estate dealings.

In fact, Bryan had been hired by the Coral Gables Miami Riviera company, a giant real estate developer that had just purchased more than six thousand acres in Florida. For the enormous sum of $100 per twenty-minute talk, Bryan promoted balmy Florida as a paradise of opportunity. He decided to sell his Villa Serena estate and bought property in nearby Coconut Grove overlooking the bay on a cliff that sloped down from a height of about eighteen feet. He planned to subdivide part of the area and sell the lots to friends who wanted to build there— "so we can have a pleasant little community"—and he wanted only one-tenth of the purchase price up front, with the remainder in annual installments at a fixed rate of interest. "It may be The Commoner will become The Realtor," *The New Yorker* ribbed him.

He saw nothing wrong with earning his living this way— honorably, he added. He'd never damned capitalism per se, just the predatory corporations and the bankers who financed war.

He was like Bruce Barton, Aimee Semple McPherson, and Billy Sunday. He too was making money. But the journalist Mark Sullivan assumed Bryan wasn't hawking real estate merely to line his own pockets. If the Florida bubble didn't burst, the Florida voter would adore him in 1928. That, and the anti-evolution campaign, were savvy investments in his political future.

Bryan aspired to be the man everybody knew.

DURING THE FIRST few weeks of the year 1925, in the stately old Capitol building in Nashville, there was debate over House Bill 185, which banned the teaching of evolution in the public schools and colleges of Tennessee.

Representative John Washington Butler, of Lafayette, Tennessee, was the bill's sponsor. A six-foot-tall farmer who grew corn and tobacco and wheat, Butler, who had had fewer than three years of schooling, was also clerk of the Round Lick Association of Primitive Baptists. A preacher who came once a month to his church told him an evolutionist cannot be a Christian, and that evolution turns Jesus Christ into a modernist faker.

Butler decided to run for office on the sole promise of legislating against this diabolical theory.

"Ninety-nine people out of a hundred thought just like I did, too," Butler would tell the writer Marcet Haldeman-Julius. "I say ninety-nine out of a hundred because there may be some hold different from what I think they do, but so far as I know there isn't a one in the whole district that thinks evolution—of man, that is—can be the way scientists tell it." Butler was a thoughtful man, and though he believed that the Bible and the theory of evolution conflicted, he would soon admit that many good Baptists believed in both.

"I reckon it's a good deal like politics," he told Haldeman-Julius.

The time was propitious. Butler conceived of a bill that would ban the teaching of the theory of evolution in the state's public schools. He wrote it out by hand before breakfast and brought it with him to Nashville. State Senator John Shelton, who had already introduced a similar bill, had contacted William Jennings Bryan for advice. Bryan was happy to oblige but warned not to attach a fine to the bill, at least not yet.

Introduced on January 21, 1925, the House passed Butler's bill, called House Bill 185, just a few days later, in a 71 to 5 vote. Richard Owenby, pastor of the First Methodist Church in Columbia, Tennessee, said that the legislators were "making monkeys of themselves at the rate of 71 to 5." One of the five representatives who voted against the bill bitterly observed that anyone looking for a "missing link"—the popular term used for some link between humans and an earlier, mythical half-ape creature—could find it in the Tennessee House.

The bill now went to the senate chamber, where the debate grew nasty. Senator Lew Hill poignantly pleaded for the bill's passage, as did Senator Shelton, who said that to claim we have a "blood relation with animals of a lower order" destroyed the happiness and hope of mankind.

Senator Bennett replied that his colleagues might just as well offer an amendment proclaiming the earth "flat as a fritter." Senator Hill ruled him out of order.

Senator Giles Evans explained that the Butler bill was unconstitutional, both in terms of state and federal law, but leaving that aside, he suspected that the defenders of the bill had no problem with evolution itself. What they objected to was the idea that people originated from monkeys. (Someone joked that the monkeys should be invited to speak for themselves.) And all that monkey talk, Evans also said, was more William Jennings Bryan hogwash. It had nothing to do with Darwin. "The true evolutionist has a conception of our God as greater and bigger and broader than that of the literal text of orthodoxy and dogmatism," Evans said.

He got nowhere.

Proclaiming himself a member in good standing of the Baptist church, Senator Trice opposed the Butler bill. Wasn't Jesus Christ an evolutionist? Didn't Christ teach the Pharisees to evolve to a higher plane?

On March 13, the bill passed in the Senate, 24 to 6. "The earth still revolves around the sun," a Tennessee physician had grimly joked, "despite the frantic efforts of the Tennessee Legislature to stop it."

The North Carolina legislature had voted down a similar bill just weeks earlier, making Tennessee the first state in the country to pass such a bill. "Be it enacted by the General Assembly of the State of Tennessee," the law would read, "that it shall be unlawful for any teacher in any of the Universities, Normals and all other public schools of the State which are supported in whole or in part by the public funds of the State, to teach any theory that denies the story of the Divine Creation of man as taught in the Bible, and to teach instead that man has descended from a lower order of animals."

The second section provided fines of one hundred to five hundred dollars for anyone convicted of violating the law.

"They've got their nerve to pass the buck to me when they know I want to be United States Senator," Governor Austin Peay grumbled. A delegation of Nashville citizens knocked on his door and begged him to veto the Butler bill. Others showed up at his office and begged him to sign it.

Deluged with mail for and against the bill, on Saturday, March 21, 1925, Governor Peay signed it into law. He said he definitely opposed the "irreligious tendency to exalt *so-called* science and deny the Bible."

William Jennings Bryan wired his congratulations.

A GROUP OF university students in Tennessee petitioned the legislature to consider a few more bills to promote the welfare of Tennessee's children: amend the law of gravity, for instance, and do something about the excessive speed of light.

But Billy Sunday praised the Tennessee legislature for outlawing that "Godforsaken gang of evolutionary cutthroats." He and Billy Bryan had led the way.

The conservative, controversial, and charismatic John Roach Straton, pastor of the Calvary Baptist Church in New York City, also praised the new Tennessee law. Straton regarded evolution as a cult that barely camouflaged its atheism, and William Jennings Bryan "the outstanding intellect of the age." As for anyone he considered a "modernist," Straton called them cuckoo birds and would declare that the fight against evolution "is not merely religious, but is patriotic."

It would be better to wipe out all schools rather than undermine the Bible.

Raised and educated in the South, Straton had moved to New York in 1918, believing a "real preacher," namely himself, was the best person to combat the moral rot he saw all around him— the indifference, the sloth, the illicit sexuality, yellow journalism, and those "modernist botanical baboon boosters." For he too was a performer, with a radio station installed in the Calvary Baptist Church enabling him to broadcast the word of God, as spoken by God. "Our radio system will be so efficient that when I twist the devil's tail here in New York his squawk will be heard across the continent," he had promised in 1923. He would thus redeem the fallen and the depraved of the city in which he lived; he vowed to fight any inclusion of Darwin in the schools.

"Keep politics out of the pulpit," Charles Francis Potter replied. A theological liberal and minister of New York's West Side Unitarian Church, he too considered both Straton and Bryan a danger to church and country. He too took to radio. Raised a conservative Baptist who switched to Unitarianism—but would find even that too confining—Potter debated Straton over the airwaves about the Virgin birth, biblical infallibility, Thomas Paine, capital punishment, and of course evolution. Straton would win a debate, then Potter would win one. They were sensations and invited to take their show on the road. They declined. They were not Barnum and Bailey, they said, though each of them willingly addressed the new Tennessee law.

"It will be very interesting to see how this law works out," Potter remarked. "Bootlegging evolution ought to be pretty profitable in Tennessee from now on."

BISHOP WILLIAM MONTGOMERY Brown, head of the Episcopal diocese of Ohio, read Marx and Engels and Darwin, and in his book *Communism and Christianity* criticized supernatural interpretations of religion: "All living species of animal and vegetable life exist as the natural results of evolutionary processes, not as the supernatural results of creative acts."

He was seventy years old; he was garrulous and mischievous and lovable. The top of his head was bald, but he wore what hair he had long and white. He walked with a bit of a wobble. The Episcopal Church called him crazy, and when he asked what made the church think that, the elders pointed to what they said were his blasphemies. He said he wasn't crazy. It was just that no influential preacher in any church believed that the world was made six thousand years ago or that God really formed Eve out of a rib.

"If you ask whether I am still a professing Christian," Bishop Brown said, "I will answer: Yes, yet the Brother Jesus of the New Testament, catholic creed and protestant confessions, is not for me an historical personage, but only a symbol of all that is for the good of the world, even as the Uncle Sam of American literature is not an historical personage but only a symbol."

What would be left, then, if we didn't believe in these things, he was asked. Ethics, he replied. He wanted peoples of all colors to unite and remove all gods from the skies, all capitalists from the earth. As for evolution, the Bad Bishop said that the dear, good, gifted Bryan "believes it is not right to think, and he has quit thinking."

"Mr. Bryan wants to call a halt in the science of biology," the bishop continued. "Of course he cannot do it. For nobody can call a halt to anything, especially to the advance of human consciousness."

Also called the bishop of atheists and Bolsheviks, Bishop Brown was tried three times for heresy and found guilty, he said, of being innocent.

LIBERAL CHRISTIANS BELIEVED that the fainthearted clergy and their moral cowardice were to blame for the Butler Act. But there was blame enough to go around. A Tennessee state senator who voted for it said he felt pressured by the fanatics. It was hard to combat the likes of a Straton or a Bryan or a Billy Sunday. Harcourt A. Morgan, president of the University of Tennessee, told journalist Joseph Wood Krutch, a Tennessee native, that he needed the state legislature on his side. They held the purse strings, and Morgan wanted to expand the university. He'd already rid the school of faculty he'd considered troublemakers, like John Randolph Neal, the popular and eccentric forty-six-year-old law professor who seldom showed up for class on time.

John Randolph Neal Jr., Tennessee lawyer
defending Scopes

COURTESY W. C. ROBINSON COLLECTION
OF SCOPES TRIAL PHOTOGRAPHS, MS-1091,
UNIVERSITY OF TENNESSEE, KNOXVILLE—LIBRARIES

John Neal would soon defend John Scopes.

Morgan also told Krutch that he considered the Butler Act unconstitutional. He figured, though, it wouldn't be enforced, so it would be like Prohibition: play along in public and drink in private.

"Every time one man turns fundamentalist out of fear of a second," Krutch wearily concluded, "a third turns fundamentalist out of fear of him."

Part 4

The Hand That Writes the Paycheck
1925

The contest between evolution and Christianity is a duel to the
death. It has been in the past a death grapple in the dark; from
this time it will be a death grapple in the light.

—WILLIAM JENNINGS BRYAN

Chapter Ten

The Hand That Writes the Paycheck

IN HER OFFICE IN NEW York City, Lucille Milner combed the newspapers every day. Executive Secretary of the American Civil Liberties Union, she was on the alert for stories about civil rights violations. They'd give the ACLU a chance to offer its services and publicize its work.

One article grabbed her. The Tennessee legislature had just passed a law called the Butler Act. She clipped the piece. "Here's something that ought to have our attention," she informed Roger Baldwin, the director of the ACLU.

A longtime women's rights activist, Milner, originally from Saint Louis, had gone East to enroll in the New York School of Philanthropy, and after graduation, she returned to Saint Louis as a progressive suffragette without a day job until one day in 1916 she received a call from Roger Nash Baldwin, the head of the nonpartisan Saint Louis Civic League. "We have a tailor-made job for you," Baldwin told her. "We want you to administer the Children's Code Commission," which meant lobbying politicians to pass child labor laws. She accepted, and the two of them remained friends for a lifetime.

Boston-bred, Mayflower-descended, and Harvard-educated, by the time Baldwin met Milner, he had already been a social worker, a probation officer, an instructor in sociology at Washington University, and the joint author of the book *Juvenile Courts and Probation*. Part radical, part idealist, part pragmatic political operator who loved to cook and would watch birds from a cabin near the Hackensack River, he'd become frustrated by the slow pace of reform, particularly after he heard a lecture by Emma Goldman on the stupidity of violence. He was also a pacifist.

He left Saint Louis for New York to work with the American Union Against Militarism, an organization that hoped to prevent the United States from entering the war in Europe. After the United States did enter the war, Baldwin, along with the socialist Norman Thomas and the activist lawyer and editor Crystal Eastman, established the National Civil Liberties Bureau, with Baldwin as its director. Harnessing about 150 volunteer lawyers, they were able to provide legal aid to anyone who thought their civil rights had been violated before, and then during, the war years. "No economic or political question has been too delicate to merit their examination," A. Philip Randolph and Chandler Owen, editors of *The Messenger*, said, praising the Bureau.

In 1918 Baldwin himself flouted the Conscription Act when he refused to appear before the local draft board to register. "I seek no martyrdom, no publicity," he told the judge at his trial. "I merely meet as squarely as I can the moral issue before me, regardless of consequences." He was sent to jail.

After the war, the National Civil Liberties Bureau was reorganized as the American Civil Liberties Union. With some of the same goals and some of the original NCLB members, the ACLU offered counsel to any individual or organization whose constitutional rights had been threatened or in any way disregarded or contravened. Its offices were in Manhattan on the first floor of a red brick townhouse on West Thirteenth Street. On the second floor were the offices of the magazine *The Liberator*, which, like the new organization, mixed Village bohemia and politics.

The organization believed, as had the nineteenth-century abolitionist Wendell Phillips, that "no matter whose lips would speak, they must be free and ungagged." When Mayor James Michael Curley of Boston outlawed a Klan parade, Baldwin wrote the mayor to say every American citizen is guaranteed the right of assembly. As Lucille Milner recalled, "The future of democracy, we thought, was at stake."

"The American Civil Liberties Union *is* Roger Baldwin," said Arthur Garfield Hays, the organization's general counsel. Everyone who knew him praised Baldwin's courage, sincerity, intelligence, and judgment, even those who thought he wasn't progressive enough, like the brilliant Black radical A. Philip Randolph and the socialist Joseph Freeman.

And he was shrewd. Baldwin understood that not all people understood what their civil liberties were, so, as a way of both educating the public and bringing attention to the ACLU, he was always looking for apparent violations of civil or constitutional rights that could serve as "test cases." So when he saw the article about the new Tennessee law that Milner had clipped, he told her, "Take it to the Board on Monday."

On Monday the board agreed with him. The stakes here were high. Free speech and religious freedom were in play. The ACLU board decided it would take the case, if necessary, all the way to the Supreme Court. This would be a test of academic freedom, at the very least.

ON SUNDAY, MAY 3, the ACLU placed a small article in the *Knoxville Journal*. Because the Butler Act had struck a serious blow "at scientific teaching," the article read, the organization was seeking a Tennessee teacher willing to test the new law in the courts. "By this test we hope to render a real service to freedom of teaching throughout the country, for we do not believe the law will be sustained."

It would be a "friendly" test case—that is, the teacher wouldn't necessarily lose his or her job. And the distinguished lawyers of the ACLU were ready to defend the teacher at no charge. All the ACLU needed was a volunteer.

The next day, on Monday, May 4, the same article appeared in another Knoxville paper under the banner, "Any Professor at UT Feel Like Making a Fight?" The local superintendent of schools huffed. "Man from monkey," he exclaimed, "has no place in the curriculum."

William Jennings Bryan got right to the point. "The hand that writes the paycheck," he said, gesturing to the taxpayer, "rules the school."

THINGS ESCALATED QUICKLY. In Dayton, Tennessee, George Washington Rappleyea, the manager of the Cumberland Coal and Iron Company, was reading one of the Knoxville papers while eating lunch at his desk. Coal and iron were no longer Dayton's great industry, and the company was insolvent though it still owned some abandoned mines and old furnaces, which Rappleyea had been hired to sell off. As much a custodian as an engineer, Rappleyea insisted he was the latter. That was his way: self-promoting, slightly brash, fanciful.

While reading the paper during lunch, he happened to see that the American Civil Liberties Union was looking for a volunteer to test the validity of the Tennessee anti-evolution law. He immediately picked up the telephone.

Rappleyea would soon be asked repeatedly why he was so interested in testing this law. When he was a young boy, he explained, he'd gone to the funeral of another boy who'd been killed in a factory accident and overheard the minister telling the boy's mother that her son was now in hell because he'd never been baptized. Rappleyea instantly decided he'd have nothing to do with that kind of religious orthodoxy.

George W. Rappleyea, Scopes trial impresario
COURTESY SCIENCE SERVICE RECORDS, SMITHSONIAN
INSTITUTION ARCHIVES

It was a good story. More to the point, it represented Rappleyea as both the local impresario and the local religious liberal.
Originally from New York, the thirty-one-year-old son of a
Catholic mother and Baptist father, he said he'd learned a great
deal about intolerance from each of them. He'd attended Ohio
Northern University, a Methodist institution, and in 1917 joined
the army as a lieutenant in the engineering corps. He told people
in Dayton he'd taken a correspondence course in civil engineering. After the war, he was hired by the Cumberland Coal and
Iron Company, in Dayton, where he met his wife, Ora, a nurse,
while being treated for a snakebite. In nice weather, they could

be seen together riding horseback through the hills outside of town. "Everybody liked Rappleyea," one of the Scopes prosecutors would recall, "except they knew he was kind of a screwball."

From Rappleyea's earliest years, he liked to say, his study of nature had convinced him of the presence of God. "I don't believe in evangelic Christianity," he declared. "Crying on your knees today, forgotten tomorrow." In Dayton, he taught a Bible class in the Methodist Sunday school and didn't think science conflicted with religion. "I believe if the young people were taught more science and studied nature, they would be genuinely converted through these, God's best means of letting men know of his greatness."

When the Tennessee legislature passed the Butler bill and the ACLU offered its services to test it, Rappleyea decided he would take charge.

He claimed that he picked up the telephone and called Frank Robinson, who owned the local drugstore, and asked him to contact Walter White, the superintendent of schools, and for him to call John Thomas Scopes, who taught science at the local high school. Scopes might be willing to test the law. But the schools were already closed for the summer, White uncertainly replied.

Another story had it that Superintendent White, worried that he'd now have to replace all the biology textbooks, called on his friend the young lawyer Sue K. Hicks (so named for his mother, who had died in childbirth), and the case began there, with Superintendent White and lawyer Hicks, not Rappleyea at all.

Whatever exactly happened, Rappleyea evidently joined Hicks and Superintendent White together at Robinson's drugstore, where people—almost always men—congregated, as if it was a club room. White sat in the back drinking Coca-Cola laced with cherry syrup. Several others had gathered there too, sipping their soft drinks at a glass-topped table. They started talking. In his account, Rappleyea mentioned the article in the newspaper he'd read and convinced White to test the law if they could get the young biology teacher Scopes to say that he had, in fact, taught the theory of evolution.

John Thomas Scopes
COURTESY SCIENCE SERVICE RECORDS, SMITHSONIAN
INSTITUTION ARCHIVES

Either someone then sent for John Scopes, or Scopes happened to drop by, and in the next day or two everyone seemed to show up at Robinson's drugstore.

And then there was John Thomas Scopes himself. He was soft-spoken, slender, twenty-four, and single. He wore owl-shaped glasses that resembled Rappleyea's but otherwise the two men were quite different. Rappleyea was not too tall—about five feet six—and wore his thicket of dark brown hair in a somewhat disheveled way, unlike Scopes. At almost six feet, Scopes was well-combed, diffident, and definitely more reserved.

He too was new in town. Fresh out of the University of Kentucky, Scopes had arrived in Dayton just that year to teach physics and math and to coach the raggedy football team, which he whipped into shape even though he allowed them to smoke while in training. When the regular biology teacher fell ill, an obliging Scopes took over his class. He taught it from George William Hunter's *A Civic Biology*, which the state textbook commission had officially adopted in 1919 for use in its public schools.

Robinson's drugstore, the Dayton gathering place
COURTESY W. C. ROBINSON COLLECTION OF SCOPES TRIAL
PHOTOGRAPHS, MS-1091, UNIVERSITY OF TENNESSEE,
KNOXVILLE—LIBRARIES

Of course the textbook included a short section on evolution but also emphasized that studying biology was a patriotic act, which showed "boys and girls living in an urban community how they may best live within their own environment and how they may cooperate with the civic authorities for the betterment of their environment."

Though Scopes didn't like public attention, after Robinson called him to the drugstore—he'd been playing tennis—the young teacher did say, "I don't see how any one can teach biology without bringing in the theory of evolution." Rappleyea claimed he worked hard to convince Scopes to test the law. Hicks recalled that Scopes was willing because he wouldn't have to pay for the defense.

Rappleyea wrote out a telegram for the ACLU on a piece of yellow wrapping paper and walked over to the Western Union office. He explained that though the school was closed, he would get someone to swear a warrant against Scopes, who would be indicted for teaching evolution in the high school. Local businessmen would put up his bond, should that be necessary. Wire me collect if you wish to cooperate, the telegram read in part, and Scopes's arrest will follow.

The ACLU replied quickly, guaranteeing financial and legal assistance as well as publicity. "Have you a competent local attorney?" the ACLU wanted to know. "Has he considered getting federal injunction or otherwise raising federal issue?"

Like the ACLU, Rappleyea assumed that Scopes would be found guilty. The decision could then be appealed, and the case would come before the Tennessee supreme court, and maybe even the Supreme Court.

JUST TWO DAYS after the ACLU article first appeared, George Rappleyea, sitting at the drugstore table, was ready to swear out a warrant for the arrest of John Scopes, or "Scoaps" as the teacher was first named in the newspaper.

.   .   .

SUE K. HICKS was again there at Robinson's. Knowing Hicks was a Fundamentalist, Rappleyea asked him to prosecute Scopes. Years later, Hicks disputed Rappleyea's account. Rappleyea, Hicks said, did not know anyone's religious convictions and certainly not Hicks's own. Wanting to separate himself from the way Dayton citizens were already being characterized in print, Rappleyea made himself out as the Yankee evolutionist who'd organized the whole affair. Hicks and his brother Herbert, also a lawyer, would have none of that.

Sue K. Hicks, Scopes prosecutor
COURTESY SUE K. HICKS PAPERS, MPA.0137. UNIVERSITY OF
TENNESSEE, KNOXVILLE—LIBRARIES

A justice of the peace happened to walk into the drugstore, with some blank warrants that Sue Hicks filled out. Rappleyea signed the warrant as a witness. Deputy Sheriff Perry Swafford arrested Scopes. Charged with violating the law banning the teaching of evolution in the public schools, Scopes would be defended by local lawyers, who intended to argue that the Butler law was unconstitutional. Judge Godsey, a lawyer for the board of education, would be one of them. "In that way I felt there would be no ill feeling between Mr. Scopes and members of the school board," Rappleyea told the newspapers. Rappleyea also contacted John Randolph

Neal in Knoxville—the man who had recently lost his job at the university—and asked him to join Judge John Godsey in the defense of Scopes. Neal consented to assist in defending Scopes. Sue Hicks would prosecute with the assistance of his brother Herbert.

Everything was in place. News of Scopes's arrest rocked the community. According to John Moutoux, a young Knoxville reporter, the citizens of Dayton hadn't even heard of the Butler law. Once they did, it seemed inconceivable to them that such a nice young man as John Scopes would be up to such "evil, devil-inspired ideas."

But young Scopes had been taught to think for himself, said his father, Thomas Scopes, an Englishman with a slight cockney accent who'd come to America in 1883. Though the elder Scopes had originally planned to return to London, he had married and found work as a railroad mechanic for the Illinois Central. He ran twice for public office as a socialist. When he arrived in Dayton to support his son, he was criticized as a "rank socialist"—that is, a follower of Eugene Debs, which meant that Mr. Scopes talked "long and loud against the political and religious systems of America." He had to be an infidel. "His influence was all against God, the Bible, Society and the United States Government," a concerned citizen wrote.

It was no wonder, then, that his son, young John Scopes, the lean and modest science teacher, should embrace evolution. "Socialists, as a rule, have little regard for the laws of our country," claimed a preacher in Chattanooga. Ditto the ACLU, a disreputable organization that supports all subversive movements. No matter. Thomas Scopes was pleased about his son's stand. "He's a chip o' the old block, and I'm proud of him," Scopes said. Besides, he and his son were good Christians.

Embarrassed by all this buzz, John Scopes wanted to stay in the background and at times wanted to drop the whole thing. Rappleyea was again persuasive.

·   ·   ·

THE PRELIMINARY HEARING took place on May 9, a Saturday, when three justices of the peace heard the case. John Neal and John Godsey, arguing for the defense, said that since the Tennessee constitution stipulated "no preference shall ever be given to any religious establishment," and that the duty of the government was to "cherish literature and science," the Tennessee anti-evolution law was therefore unconstitutional.

Prosecutors Sue Hicks and Wallace C. Haggard replied that the constitutionality of the law wasn't at issue. Scopes's violation of the law was. They read from the textbook, *A Civic Biology,* that Scopes used to make their point.

> We have now learned that animal forms may be arranged so as to begin with very simple one-celled forms and culminate with a group that contains man himself. This arrangement is called the evolutionary series. Evolution means change, and these groups are believed by scientists to represent stages in complexity of development of life on the earth. Geology teaches that millions of years ago, life upon the earth was very simple, and that gradually more and more complex forms of life appeared, as the rocks formed latest in time show the most highly developed forms of animal life.

They continued to read from another section of the textbook.

> The great English scientist, Charles Darwin, from this and other evidence, explained the theory of evolution. This is the belief that simple forms of life on the earth slowly and gradually gave rise to those more complex and that thus ultimately the most complex forms came into existence.

The hearing lasted three hours. Scopes was told to appear before the Rhea County grand jury. The grand jury hearing was scheduled for the first Monday in August.

His bond set at $1,000, Scopes was released on his own recognizance. He went to Paducah, Kentucky, to visit his parents.

PUBLISHING A SURVEY of the regulations imposed on teaching in schools and colleges, the ACLU demonstrated that more restrictive laws had been passed in the previous six months than at any time before—laws that included, for instance, a rider to a 1925 appropriations bill for the District of Columbia that forbade any educational director to permit "the teaching of partisan politics, disrespect of the Holy Bible, or that ours is an inferior form of government."

What happened to the constitutional guarantee of the separation of church and state? What to make of mandatory Bible reading prescribed in the schools of Pennsylvania, Ohio, Delaware, or South Dakota? What about that resolution demanding the investigation of faculty members of the state university in Ohio who seemed to be radicals—or atheists? "The efforts to impose majority dogma by law and intimidation have shifted from the industrial arena to the field of education," the ACLU would report.

"The chief sources of inspiration for this new and unprecedented crop of gag laws on teaching are the Ku-Klux Klan, the fundamentalists and the professional patriotic societies," the ACLU concluded. "The Klan is back of the compulsory Bible reading and antiparochial school laws, the fundamentalists back of the antievolution bills and the professional patriots back of the antiradical and antipacifist measures."

The time had come to do something, Roger Baldwin, the head of the ACLU, said. He was not the only one who thought so.

· · ·

WILLIAM JENNINGS BRYAN went to Memphis to address the thousands who had come for the Southern Baptist Convention. On Sunday, May 10, an overcast day, Bryan spoke four times to deafening applause. He described the South as the bulwark of Fundamentalism and praised the Tennessee legislature for passing the Butler bill. He hailed Governor Peay for courageously signing it into law. Teaching evolution is equivalent to murder, murdering a child's belief in God, Bryan cried. Evolution is nuts.

Two days later, the Reverend William Bell Riley of the World's Christian Fundamentals Association wired Bryan on behalf of his organization: Help prosecute the case against Scopes.

Who better? "Mr. Bryan could do nothing else than see in this battle for the faith the best opportunity that had ever opened before him," Riley later reminisced.

Bryan formally announced he was joining the team prosecuting Scopes to preserve the church. "It's a fight to the finish," he cried at the next Presbyterian General Assembly. To Bryan, this was another opportunity to fight the good fight and to return to the limelight as the righteous, religious democrat he knew he was. In 1920, he had been ignored at the Democratic National Convention. In 1923, he had been passed over as the moderator of the Presbyterian General Assembly. In 1924, he had been belittled at the Democratic National Convention. It didn't look as though he could unseat the incumbent senator from Florida. The Dayton trial could offer Bryan another chance at the brass ring.

That he hadn't worked as a lawyer in decades didn't matter. He was a crusader and now about to take up the lance and sally forth to combat a foe as part of a holy mission, a moral mission, as meaningful and important, even more important, than silver and Prohibition and rapacious Wall Street had been. "There's no compromise possible," he bellowed.

. . .

"THE SCOPES TRIAL was weird," the reporter Russell Owen later noted, "and so was Mr. Bryan."

But William Jennings Bryan was not weird, not really. According to the liberal *New Republic,* Bryan represented "the same group of ideas and desires which was responsible for the extraordinary success of the Ku Klux Klan in all parts of the country, North and South."

That is, "if Bryan could succeed in making the religious issue the central one in a national political campaign," the magazine predicted, "he might succeed in breaking party lines and securing a majority of the popular vote in a large number of states." The goal: the presidency.

William Jennings Bryan and John Washington Butler
COURTESY W. C. ROBINSON COLLECTION OF SCOPES TRIAL
PHOTOGRAPHS, MS-1091. UNIVERSITY OF TENNESSEE,
KNOXVILLE—LIBRARIES

Speculation blew around the nation. Bryan could have the Butler law or something like it written into the Democratic Party platform of 1928. He might lure independent and Republican

Fundamentalists to unite under a new and formidable Democratic banner. He might propose a constitutional amendment, like the Prohibition amendment, which would outlaw any mention of evolution or Darwin in all public schools. He might turn a secular country into a theocracy. "Bryan is a clever demagogue," the editor Negley Cochran observed. "He is either ignorant or is deliberately playing upon the ignorance of the great mass of the people—for he deliberately misrepresents the theory of evolution."

Bryan wasn't deliberately misrepresenting the theory of evolution. He believed what he said. He was telling the truth and dubbed people who supported the theory of evolution—whether in the church or the academy or the laboratory—as dishonest scoundrels. "We cannot afford to have a system of education that destroys the religious faith of 75 per cent of our children," he cried.

To friends, including John Roach Straton, he outlined the plan he had in mind in joining the prosecution of Scopes. He would indict evolution on four counts. First, evolution denied the miracle of creation—that God created Adam and Eve. "The Bible rests upon the miraculous," he explained. Second, "evolution, by denying the need or possibility of spiritual regeneration, discourages all reforms," Bryan further explained, "for reform is always based upon the regeneration of the individual. It is through the regeneration of the individual that the nation can be regenerated." Third, "evolution would carry us back to the law of the jungle—the killing of the weak by the strong—the law by which man is supposed to have come up from lower forms of life."

Fourth and finally, evolution "diverts attention from the great practical problems of life to useless speculation as to the distant past and the distant future."

If Bryan did not understand evolution, he was nonetheless adept at attacking it, and he was preparing. "We cannot be caught napping," he declared.

·   ·   ·

BACK IN DAYTON, Sue Hicks couldn't have been more excited. "We will consider it a great honor to have you," he said, welcoming Bryan to the prosecution.

George Rappleyea was delighted too. "I am glad that William Jennings Bryan has offered to handle the prosecution of J. T. Scopes," he said. "This is a fight not only for the freedom of teaching, but for the freedom of both science and religion and the separation of church and state."

THAT SAME MAY, Clarence Darrow was in Richmond, Virginia, preparing to address the American Psychiatric Association and talk about "Sane Treatment for Criminals." Before the banquet, he was sitting in the large, ornate lobby of the Jefferson Hotel and chatting with a cub reporter. "Evening clothes are a nuisance," Darrow jovially complained. "They take away all individuality from a man."

Perhaps the reporter might write something about men's dinner jackets, Darrow teased the young man, who was hoping for a big story. Write about conformity in men's clothes and work up to conformity—standardization—in their thinking. Darrow paused. His smile disappeared. Standardization. "Anybody ought to know it leads to idiotic action like the Tennessee matter forbidding libel against monkeys."

After Richmond, Darrow went to New York, where he learned that Bryan was joining the prosecution team in Dayton. There and then, he knew he had to offer to defend Scopes. Though he'd announced his retirement, as he often did, he later noted, "I realized that there was no limit to the mischief that might be accomplished unless the country was roused to the evil at hand." He had to go. He had to stop Bryan.

On Saturday, May 16, Darrow and his friend Dudley Field

Malone wired John Neal, the Tennessee lawyer representing Scopes. "We are certain you need no assistance in your defense of Prof. Scopes," the telegram read. "But we have read the report that William J. Bryan has volunteered to aid the prosecution. And in view of the fact that scientists are so much interested in the pursuit of knowledge that they cannot make the money that lecturers and Florida real estate agents command, in case you should need us we are willing without fees or expenses, to help the Defense of Prof Scopes in any way you may suggest or direct."

Accepting their offer, John Neal wired back. "As we see it, the great question is whether the Tennessee legislature has the power to prevent the young minds of Tennessee from knowing what has been thought and said by the world's greatest scientists and thus prevent them from forming their own judgment in regard to questions of life and science," he wrote, somewhat sententiously.

"We regard equally un-American and therefore unconstitutional," Neal concluded, "any attempt to limit the human mind in its inquiry after truth." That would be the point.

AS ALWAYS, DARROW'S motives were complicated. Certainly he wanted to wake the country to "the evil at hand," but then the country already knew about the evolution controversy, which did not affect the daily lives of most people or their forms of worship. And to the cognoscenti and self-styled modernist, the controversy was just another instance of foolish ignorance that could be lampooned and patronized.

Darrow, of course, understood the need for religion. "I am inclined to think that life is so hard and insoluble that the race must needs have some religion," he said. But taking issue with evolution, as Bryan was doing? That was different. To him, demanding that the Bible be read literally, as if each word were written with the hand of God, fostered a dogmatism that in turn abrogated "liberty of conscience and speech." To him, the handwriting was on the wall: this controversy was about the abridg-ment of the rights to think, to speak, and even to worship.

To Darrow, then, belief in God per se was not the issue in Ten-nessee. Rather, a Fundamentalist reading of the Bible mandated by a state legislature would easily lead to a devastating loss of civil liberties. Church and state must remain separate. Freedom of speech must remain free. Freedom of thought must remain free. And Bryan was a dangerous man, a demagogue on the loose.

To William Jennings Bryan, Darrow was an infidel of the most contemptible kind but not worthy of too much notice. Back in the spring of 1923, Bryan had sent a long letter to *The Chicago Tribune* affirming his conviction that the Bible was the word of God and that teaching the theory of evolution should be banned in public schools. Darrow couldn't resist replying and sent a series of questions to the *Tribune* that Mr. Bryan might kindly answer. To Darrow, Bryan's ignorance did nothing but inspire hate. And having known Bryan, he sensed danger.

He therefore asked Bryan if the earth had been made in six literal days.

Was Eve literally made from Adam's rib?

How did Noah gather all the animals of the earth from all the continents and islands of the earth?

The questions tumbled out, one after another. He was joking, for sure, and in deadly earnest. Can't one be a Christian without believing in the literal truth of the Bible?

Darrow's questions ran in the paper, aptly, on the Fourth of July.

An imperturbable Bryan responded by not responding. He dismissed Darrow. But if Darrow couldn't help himself, Bryan couldn't either. "My controversy is not with atheists like Mr. Darrow," Bryan announced, with hauteur, "but with those who claim to be Christians and who substitute the guesses of evolution for the word of God."

Bryan would have to reply to Darrow sooner than he thought.

Chapter Eleven

The Great Race

How long are we Americans to be so careful for the pedigree of our pigs and chickens and cattle—and then leave the ancestry of our children to chance, or to "blind" sentiment?
—AMERICAN EUGENICS SOCIETY

The horrors of the war, the disappointment of the peace, the terror of Bolshevism, and the rising tide of color have knocked a good deal of the nonsense out of us, and have given multitudes a hunger for realities. . . .
—LOTHROP STODDARD, *THE RISING TIDE OF COLOR*

T HE DEDICATED FORREST BAILEY, ASSOCIATE director of the ACLU, had been a high school English teacher who used the novels of Joseph Conrad as textbooks. A graduate of Stanford University and a California native, after the armistice, Bailey sailed to Europe to help naval officers stationed in France adjust to civilian life. A handsome man, blond, with a high forehead, he had joined the ACLU shortly after he returned to America. The Scopes case was one of the first he handled.

The ACLU had asked the former presidential candidate John W. Davis if he would be interested in taking the case. Should

Davis decline, they were also considering Secretary of State Charles Evans Hughes, former associate justice on the Supreme Court, former governor of New York, and an upright constitutionalist with a conservative bent. He would be perfect. But George Rappleyea had told the press that John Neal of Tennessee had accepted Clarence Darrow as a member of the defense team, which "spoiled our chances" to secure Hughes, Bailey complained. Unlike Hughes, Darrow had no conservative inclinations.

Bailey contacted the Academic Freedom Committee of the ACLU. "Messrs. Darrow and Malone, it should be understood," Bailey somewhat sheepishly explained, "acted on their own initiative and not on any suggestion from this organization."

Clarence Darrow knew that the ACLU had other far less radical lawyers in mind. Soon he announced he was not part of the defense team after all. "If Mr. Scopes wants me to help him," he demurred, "I shall be mightily pleased to give my services."

In Dayton as well as New York there was some consternation about John Neal having jumped too fast to accept Darrow and Malone. George Rappleyea was slightly nettled. He didn't want any association with a socialist, which Dudley Malone was rumored to be.

A FEW DAYS LATER, in New York City, at the June 1 executive board meeting of the ACLU, Clarence Darrow was elected to the organization's National Committee. At that same meeting, the ACLU board reiterated its support of John Scopes and the need to protect academic freedom in primary and secondary schools. No one disagreed with that.

But the board was divided about the nature of the defense. Some members felt that since the case was about constitutional issues, like the separation of church and state, constitutional lawyers should argue it. As others pointed out, with Bryan as part of the prosecution, and Darrow and Malone volunteering to defend Scopes, the nature of the case had changed. It would be a showdown between God and monkeys—as Bryan would have it—locked in a duel for the soul of the young.

Dudley Field Malone, John R. Neal, and
Clarence Darrow strategizing
COURTESY CHICAGO HISTORY MUSEUM, DN-0079177

Nothing was decided. Instead, the board voted to pay the traveling expenses of Messrs. Rappleyea, Scopes, and Neal to come to New York to confer. It also authorized Forrest Bailey, as associate director of the ACLU, to invite Clarence Darrow to that conference.

"IF YOU WANT this case to be tested only on its constitutional grounds; if you want it respectable and dull so that it won't command a column of newspaper publicity; if you want to overlook the opportunity of making this a universal education in evolution then take Hughes," the *Chattanooga Daily Times* sneered. "If you want it jazzed, take Darrow and Malone."

Scopes and Rappleyea arrived at New York City's Pennsylvania Station, a bustling riot of a place after the peaceful pace of Dayton. They were soon driven off to a series of meetings with the ACLU. The first one took place on Monday, June 8. Scopes later said the meeting seemed like a briefing or a play in which he was the spectator though the drama was about him, and the real stars were people like Felix Frankfurter, then a Harvard Law School professor, and the aristocratic Bainbridge Colby, Secretary of State under Wilson after Bryan resigned. A Wilson loyalist whose eminent clients, earlier in his legal career, had included Mark Twain, Bainbridge Colby spoke with a faint British accent though he was born in Saint Louis. Said to strut while sitting down, he wore his mustache elegantly trimmed, he backed Governor Al Smith at the Democratic convention in 1924, he denounced the Ku Klux Klan there, and he loathed Prohibition.

Scopes, George Rappleyea, and John Neal then attended a lunch sponsored by the ACLU at the Civic Club in a brownstone at 14 West Twelfth Street with about twenty other men and women. Father John A. Ryan, the Catholic progressive and later staunch New Dealer, was there, as was Dudley Malone, who sat next to Scopes.

Malone lobbied for Darrow all through the lunch and when the meal ended jumped to his feet and again offered his and Darrow's services. Some members of the group, like Forrest Bailey, didn't think that a good idea. There was Darrow's atheism to consider. And remember that thanks to Darrow, Leopold and Loeb escaped the death penalty, which not everyone appreciated. Someone called Darrow a "headline hunter." One of the ACLU lawyers helping to finance the case, Walter Nelles, a prominent civil liberties attorney, strongly opposed Darrow. Frankfurter preferred Charles Evans Hughes, who would limit the case to the question of its constitutionality. With Darrow, he said, the case would never get into the federal courts—a point of view that Neal courteously rebuffed. Federal judges weren't likely to move the case out of Tennessee's jurisdiction anyway, now that Bryan was one of the prosecutors. Only Father Ryan seemed to support Darrow.

Roger Baldwin rose. Turning to Scopes, Baldwin, as head of the ACLU, said the defendant should voice his opinion. "I want Darrow," Scopes declared. Scopes may have seemed bashful and boyish but on the question of Darrow, he wouldn't budge. He'd already told John Neal, back in Tennessee, that he wanted Darrow. Now, in New York, he firmly said Darrow was an *agnostic*, not an atheist, and besides, Scopes too was an agnostic in his own religious way.

The trial was being made into a circus, some of the lawyers objected. "It's a circus already; it has been ever since Bryan came into the case," Scopes replied. "And, if it's going to be a gutter fight, I'd rather have a good gutter fighter."

Someone said Malone was all right, just not Darrow. Too flamboyant. Malone jumped up again. Without Darrow, he would not take the case.

It was decided. Darrow and Malone.

And John Neal, of course.

The lawyer Arthur Garfield Hays, formerly a manager of the Robert La Follette presidential campaign, would represent the ACLU, and if he was willing, Charles Evans Hughes would join the ACLU for the appeal. And former Secretary of State Bainbridge Colby would also go to Dayton. He'd been included for his highborn looks and trim mustache.

SOMEONE ASKED DARROW if there'd be monkeys in Dayton. "No," he replied, with a grin. "But there will be a lot of lawyers."

Would the trial be vital for the progress of science? Darrow again smiled. He referred to the early pope who had issued a bull against a comet. "The comet came along just the same," Darrow noted, amused. "It hadn't heard of the bull."

Scopes too was in a good mood. He visited the Museum of Natural History and met with its president, Henry Fairfield Osborn, who warned the young man not to be tarred with a radical brush. Scopes said nothing. Osborn asked him about life in Appalachia. Scopes calmly replied that in Dayton these days no one used squirrel guns on humans.

Malone's spirits weren't as high. Frankfurter and some of the others at the ACLU said Malone should remain in New York to dig up related case files. Malone would not be treated like a clerk, he said, just because he was Catholic, had been divorced, and was Irish. He'd be an active participant in the trial or wouldn't bother with it at all. It was decided he'd go to Dayton after all.

BRYAN SHOUTED FROM the shores of Florida that "religion and education are the two greatest subjects known to man."

He wrote Sue Hicks that he'd been explaining the case to his audiences. "It is the *easiest* case I have ever found," Bryan crowed. "While I am perfectly willing to go into the question of evolution," he added, "I am not sure that it is involved. The right of the people speaking through the legislature, to control the schools which they create and support is the real issue as I see it. If not the people, who? A few scientists?" he scoffed.

"No such oligarchy would be permitted. Who then controls? The teachers? That too is absurd."

He sounded like his father all those years ago. Back then, the issue was popular sovereignty and, by extension, states' rights. Now, it was more or less the same issue, and a winning one, Bryan believed. To him, popular sovereignty and states' rights were the foundation of democracy. But the issue would also be evolution, an emotional issue, and the issue would seem to be God; and both would rile the people Bryan wanted to rile. He did not or could not imagine that an entity called "the people" could ever vote to support the theory of evolution.

The prosecutor Sue Hicks agreed with Bryan. Coming to Dayton, the heart of the country, populated with the purest of the Anglo-Saxons, Hicks said, the defense lawyers were a menagerie of agnostics, socialists, and communists, all working together to tear down America.

FOR ALL THEIR differences and animosity, William Jennings Bryan and Clarence Darrow were more alike in some ways than either of them would admit. The journalist William Allen White, who knew both men, characterized them as equally ardent, emotional, and committed to the ideal of a better world. For Darrow did not despair as much as he said he did. Although cruelty and human folly infuriated and often depressed him, his trenchant wit, often mistaken for cynicism, masked an old-fashioned romanticism. He believed if he simply refused to give up, he really could make, for an instant, the world a kinder and perhaps more just place.

Recently, Darrow's target had been the sham science of eugenics, which Bryan also detested. To a large extent eugenics was the brainchild of the English anthropologist Sir Francis Galton (a cousin of Charles Darwin), who suggested that people were not created equal. Galton argued that certain populations, called races, possessed different inherent characteristics. And since certain diseases were presumed to be congenital, and other traits—like intelligence, criminality, drunkenness, and even poverty—were also presumed to be hereditary, eugenicists planned to eliminate, through breeding, these "bad" aspects of human character in order to generate a utopia populated by the "better" sort of humans.

"Do we really know that we can make it what is called 'better'?" Darrow sniffed. "If so, better for what?"

Mixing together sociology, economics, anthropology, politics, snobbery, antisemitism, and white supremacy into a brew of cruelty, propaganda, violence, and xenophobia, eugenicists assumed humans could be regulated so that they would "improve" more rapidly and with more purpose than if left alone. This was natural selection and survival of the fittest, as social Darwinists understood them, with a vengeance. Or as the noted eugenicist and former president of Stanford, David Starr Jordan, noted years earlier when responding to the "Man with the Hoe" poem, certain "alien" races and ethnic groups—such as but not limited to Filipinos, Mexicans, Africans, Chinese, the Indigenous of Australia—were "unfit" and thus inferior to the blond people of Europe.

The American Eugenics Society, founded in 1921, called for the sterilization of 10 percent of the American population to prevent "the suicide of the white race." Six years later, in *Buck vs. Bell,* Supreme Court Justice Oliver Wendell Holmes Jr. presented one of the most famous and famously foul explanations of eugenics when the Court upheld the sterilization of a woman supposedly incapable of taking care of herself or her infant daughter. "It is better for all the world if, instead of waiting to execute degenerate offspring for crime or to let them starve for their imbecility, society can prevent those who are manifestly unfit from continuing their kind," Holmes declared. His unnerving conclusion: "Three generations of imbeciles are enough."

Eugenics had caught on. The biologist Charles B. Davenport had opened an influential, privately funded research center called the Eugenics Record Office, near New York City at Cold Spring Harbor Laboratory. There was a Galton Society at the Museum of Natural History in New York City. Birth control advocate Margaret Sanger was a eugenicist. (As the non-eugenicist Henry Mencken pointed out, the right to have or not have children is one of the most basic rights of human beings.) The corn flake king John Harvey Kellogg, who ran the Battle Creek Sanitarium, set up something called a Race Betterment Foundation and then went so far as to set up a "pedigree registry" so that the affianced could check out their prospective partner and make sure the line was good. From Massachusetts to Texas, "Fitter Families" and "Better Babies" contests were held at state fairs, often in the "human stock" section, and the winners of the 1925 Kansas competition were paraded in automobiles that advertised them as "Kansas' Best Crop."

The eugenicist Madison Grant, in his volume of prejudices *The Passing of the Great Race*, decided that the geniuses Leonardo and Michelangelo couldn't possibly be Italian because Italians were inferior to "Nordics," or people from northern Europe, so Leonardo and Michelangelo had to have been Nordic. It sounded crazy, but many liberal or progressive scientists jumped on the eugenics movement with its quixotic promise of paradise on earth, even if manufactured and exclusive. Eugenics often appealed to progressives and conservatives alike, all of them bent on improving humankind. The Reverend Harry Emerson Fosdick served as an adviser for the American Eugenics Society. The president of the American Museum of Natural History, paleontologist Henry Fairfield Osborn, formerly a student of Thomas Huxley, wrote a laudatory preface to Madison Grant's diatribe. "Conservation of that race which has given us the true spirit of Americanism is not a matter of either racial pride or of racial prejudice," Osborn claimed, "it is a matter of love of country."

"America must be kept American," President Calvin Coolidge said. There were too many immigrants, too many foreign-language speakers and foreign-language newspapers, and too much miscegenation. The melting pot was a false theory. You can't melt the tainted, grubby, the squalid. And since the war had slaughtered too many of the best of the best, the Nordic families who founded the country were disappearing. Science must do something; it must "enlighten government as to the prevention of the spread of worthless members of society."

"The bigoted and the ignorant are very sure of themselves," Clarence Darrow drily observed.

The "unfit" and so-called mongrel races should be kept from taking over white America. In F. Scott Fitzgerald's *The Great Gatsby,* published at the same time Scopes was arrested, the character Tom Buchanan fully agrees, having read something called *The Rise of the Colored Empires.* "The idea is if we don't look out the white race will be—will be utterly submerged," Buchanan sputters. "We're Nordics," he proudly boasts. "We've produced all the things that go to make civilization—oh, science, and art, and all that."

The textbook used in the Tennessee schools, *A Civic Biology,* told the same story, fusing eugenics and evolution with the social Darwinism that so deeply offended Bryan. "If the stock of domesticated animals can be improved, it is not unfair to ask if the health and vigor of the future generations of men and women on the earth might be improved by applying to them the laws of selection," the textbook explained. Too many people were infirm, immoral, or syphilitic, and "if such people were lower animals, we would probably kill them off to prevent them from spreading. Humanity will not allow this, but we do have the remedy of separating the sexes in asylums or other places and in various ways preventing intermarriage and the possibilities of perpetuating such a low and degenerate race."

"The science of being well-born is called eugenics," the textbook creepily concluded.

Anthropologist Franz Boas took unequivocal exception to eugenics: every classification of mankind was basically artificial— and phony—and the so-called Negro problem was for Boas only

a "problem" for white people, who denied Blacks equal opportunity and justice. Black newspapers called these eugenics theories "racial baloney."

Yes, the whole thing was absurd, Darrow noted. If eugenicists really looked far enough into their supposedly lustrous lin-
eage, he jested, they'd know "that the line should have ended
before it began." But sham science wasn't funny. Neither Darrow nor Bryan thought it funny, so while they were not agreeing
on much else, and while they were avowed antagonists, they
both did everything they could to counter the horror that eugenics portended. For, as Darrow said, "those in power would inevitably direct human breeding in their own interests."

"At the present time it would mean that big business would
create a race in its own image."

And though Bryan agreed, to him, eugenics and Darwin and
social Darwinism were all of a piece: Darwin's theory of make-
believe allowed the strong to exploit the weak, and in the name
of perfecting humans created humans without God but who
think of themselves as gods when they propose "a system of
breeding under which a few supposedly superior intellects, self-
appointed, would direct the mating and the movement of the
mass of mankind—an impossible system!" And a horrific one,
Bryan would write, over and over, duly horrified.

Chapter Twelve

Dayton

Causes stir the world.

—WILLIAM JENNINGS BRYAN

L IKE JOHN SCOPES, THE TOWN of Dayton had been indifferent
to publicity. Initially. Though drugstore owner Frank Robinson may have had his eye on the kind of exposure, good for
business, that the trial would bring, he hadn't engineered the
trial as a publicity stunt. Dayton had always been content to stay
as it was, tucked away in a valley in East Tennessee.

The town was something of an anomaly in the South. It
wasn't part of the Solid South. It generally voted Republican,
and back in 1860 it differed from the other Southern states on
the question of secession from the Union. Many of its boys
fought in the Union army. Tennessee's former governor and future American president Andrew Johnson was an anti-secessionist
from East Tennessee. The area around Dayton was mountainous
and the people in the mountains owned few, if any, slaves.

Prosperous after the Civil War, it had been home to two but-
ton factories, an ice plant, and the Dayton Coal and Iron Company. The apple and peach orchards and those lush strawberry
beds were known far and wide, much to the pride of local grow-

ers. About one thousand carloads of strawberries left Dayton each spring. But in the first decade of the twentieth century, the coal mines started to close, and by 1914, the furnaces of the Coal and Iron Company were ice-cold.

The town had three hotels (though two were closed), two drugstores, two banks, two blacksmith shops, a pool hall, a railroad station, five churches, one Jewish family, and three Catholic families. Five percent of the population was Black. Mostly the town was Protestant and white, but without a chapter of the Klan.

Now Dayton was known around the world. And since publicity can be intoxicating and there was talk of thirty thousand visitors with money to spend coming to town, the citizens of Dayton had worried that Chattanooga was trying to upstage them. Chattanooga teachers might be arrested for violating the Butler law, and a trial might be held here.

There was a town meeting, the courthouse bell clanging to urge citizens to attend to discuss their options. George Rappleyea was cheered when he said that Chattanooga was "aping" Dayton. He and the barber Thurlow Reed staged a fight. Rappleyea shouted there were more monkeys in Dayton than in the Chattanooga zoo, and Reed yelled, "You can't call my ancestors monkeys," before he pretended to punch Rappleyea in the face. Reed was fined. The whole performance was meant to attract the press, which it did.

Then there was the matter of the regular grand jury, which hadn't been scheduled to convene until August. A group of local Dayton citizens was dispatched to ask Judge John T. Raulston of the judicial circuit to call a special session of the Rhea County Grand Jury as soon as possible. Which the judge did, using his power to convene the grand jury to a special session in the case of emergency. Though he was supposed to give a thirty-day notice, Judge Raulston waived it.

For Judge Raulston also wanted to keep the trial in Dayton.

He would be presiding, after all. "I'm perfectly willing to hold court in the ballpark or in a big tent," he declared. "Everyone is entitled to hear the trial." He joined the faction that wanted to build an outdoor stadium, but the proposal was defeated. As one citizen said, "We have a fine chance here to put Dayton before the world in a favorable light, and we don't want to lose it by doing anything that might cheapen the town."

Fifty-six years old, with a wide forehead and thinning hair, Judge Raulston was born in a place nicknamed Gizzard Cove, in Marion County. As he explained to amused reporters, back in the day, after a wild turkey was killed, one of the pioneers who had settled the place burned his fingers while cooking it and yelped, "Darn this fiery gizzard." Hence the name Gizzard Cove.

Judge Raulston's father was a poor farmer; his mother, Comfort Raulston, rode muleback six miles every day to the local school to earn enough money to support her nine children after her husband died. Young Raulston too taught for a while and saved enough to attend U. S. Grant University. He studied law in a Chattanooga law office, passing the bar in 1896, the year Bryan first ran for president. A proud Fundamentalist, he was a lay preacher in the Methodist Episcopal Church and ran unsuccessfully for the United States House of Representatives in 1908. He'd been elected judge in Tennessee's Eighteenth District and was up for reelection in 1926. So a little publicity never hurt. During the Scopes trial, he often paused the proceedings to let photographers snap his picture. "He was a good man and meant well," the lawyer Sue Hicks said years later. "But he was too easy-going. Out of his depth."

On Monday, May 25, Judge Raulston, his dictionary under one arm and his Bible under the other, entered the red brick courthouse just before nine A.M. to meet with the grand jury. Inside, there were thirteen men on the jury, farmers and merchants. There were no women. The judge read from Genesis. He reminded the jury that Scopes had in fact broken the law.

The grand jury swiftly returned an indictment, and Judge Raulston set the trial date as July 10. It would occur during a special term of the court, he said, because he didn't want the trial to interfere with the opening of schools.

NEWSPAPERS GLEEFULLY REPORTED that the defense had invited H. G. Wells, but Wells said he'd never heard of Dayton—they must mean some other Wells. Asked about the upcoming trial, George Bernard Shaw observed that the churches got themselves "connected with an extremely tiresome lot of people," particularly William Jennings Bryan, a man, Shaw said, "with no discoverable brains of any kind."

Anticipating the hordes that would soon arrive, the local impresario George Rappleyea organized a committee to raise money to beautify the town. Drinking fountains were installed every fifty feet around the town square, arc lights were strung from the maple trees to accommodate nighttime prayer meetings, and newly painted benches were placed near the courthouse. The interior of the courthouse was repainted pale yellow, the windows were washed until they sparkled, and for the press, three long teak tables were placed on the second floor, where the trial would be held. The tables stretched across the front of the railed enclosure. The stage was set.

Though that second-floor courtroom could hold about a thousand people, the expectation was that there would be many more than that seated or milling about on the courthouse lawn, listening to what was happening inside, thanks to the forty-five loudspeakers that were sent to Dayton. *The Chicago Tribune* would broadcast the trial over the radio so anyone could tune in.

George Rappleyea also put himself in charge of accommodations for the defense and anyone they brought to testify. It was a place locally and somewhat sarcastically called the Mansion, an eighteen-room ramshackle house with brown trim about a mile outside of town, set on a hill and accessed by a long gravel road. In its heyday, it had been the residence of the Dayton Coal and Iron Company's managing director and principal stockholder, Peter Donaldson, where he'd entertained guests when he came to town from Scotland, home of the parent company. But when the company declared bankruptcy, Donaldson tied one dumbbell round his neck and another to his leg and jumped off a bridge into the Clyde River.

The Mansion hadn't been used in years. People said it might be haunted. Not to Rappleyea, who set about renting furniture as well as linens, pots and pans, and dishes. He made sure the plumbing worked, though it often didn't, and he hired people to do the cooking. It would be a good, secluded place for the defense team to work or to relax on the wide veranda. It was called the Monkey House.

Reporters had reserved rooms at the Aqua Hotel, with or without a private bath. In the dining room, there were no flies, the coffee was strong, and breakfast was served at seven, after a clerk knocked on doors to announce it. The Western Union telegraph company took up residence in the large ballroom on the first floor. Reporters not fortunate enough to book the Aqua rented rooms in local homes, where they were often asked not to smoke, and United States Representative Cordell Hull of Tennessee, later Franklin Roosevelt's Secretary of State, suggested the War Department lend the town its tents and army cots just in case there was a shortage of space.

"Dayton was more like a town prepared for a Billy Sunday revival than a court trial," said one of the visiting scientists. But if the trial promised to be a cross between a revival and a sleazy, commercial spectacle, it was also the inevitable upshot of an America already obsessed with celebrity and advertising and prosperity—and an America anxious about change, the unfamiliar, the unknown, and the seemingly incomprehensible. "The trial," wrote Luther Burbank, "appears to be a great joke, but one which will educate the public and thus reduce the number of bigots."

FARMERS HITCHED THEIR mules near the maples of the town square, and a large crowd had gathered in front of Robinson's drugstore to greet Clarence Darrow when he opened the door of George Rappleyea's car. Boys holding telegrams ran over to him, and after he read one, he smiled. "That's from some poor soul interested in my soul," he said a bit ruefully.

He soon met the former district attorney general, Ben McKenzie, a member of the prosecution team. "Good morning, General," McKenzie said as he put out his hand. "Glad to see you wear suspenders."

With his slightly stooped shoulders and rumpled face, Clarence Darrow wasn't the man most Dayton people had assumed he would be. He did not put on any airs, his eyes looked kind, and it seemed as though he'd come to Dayton only to make friends. He did not want to be regarded as a "furriner" or a radical come to blow up the place. Not at all; he even had a sense of humor. When a reporter teased him about his wrinkly clothes, he charmed them. "I buy just as good clothes as you boys do," he said, "only I sleep in mine."

A woman in the group asked him if he believed in God. "What is God, ma'am?" Darrow replied in his mild-mannered and pleasant way. She said, God is love. He stopped for a moment. "Yes," he reflected. "Then, I believe in God."

Darrow's visit to Dayton would be brief. He'd come mainly to confer with John Neal and Judge John Godsey, the Tennessee lawyers on the defense team. But the trip was also something of a public relations tour. "I voted for William Jennings Bryan two times but sidestepped the third," Darrow told a group of about seventy-five members of the Dayton Progressive Club that evening. "I even made speeches for him both times, and maybe that's what helped defeat him," Darrow said, again smiling, "but I wasn't guilty the last time."

"Square ahead of me lies the end," he added more seriously, referring to his own mortality. "No one realizes this more than me.

"I have been an agnostic to all creeds that have come before me, but am still seeking with an open mind, and I hope I may still find an answer.

"We all live on hope," he added. "If anybody can grab any hope, let him have it."

When Darrow finished his speech, a few of the men there said they'd never heard a better sermon.

ALONG WITH NEAL, Scopes, and Bainbridge Colby, who'd also arrived in Dayton for a short visit, Darrow drove to Knoxville the next day. The road was slippery, and on the way the editor of the *Knoxville News,* who was with them, said if they were interested, they might see a case being tried in a mountain court. So on the way to Knoxville, they stopped the car in Kingston and walked inside the courtroom there. Colby was uncomfortable, especially when he saw the unshaven men, revolvers in holsters, standing in the back of the room.

Darrow wasn't uncomfortable. He was angry. The defendant didn't seem to understand what was happening, and his even more pathetic lawyer was allowing him to be browbeaten, Scopes later remembered. To help the hapless defendant, Darrow started to rush over to the defense table, but Neal and Scopes, realizing what Darrow was up to, ran after him and were able to grab his arm and usher him out the door and back into the car before he could say anything. Colby was already sitting there, upset by what he'd seen: the guns, the confused defendant, the incompetent lawyer. "Those poor, poor unfortunate people!" he muttered.

Darrow was silent.

That evening, in Knoxville, pulling on his suspenders and shoving his hands deep into his pockets, he spoke at a high school auditorium packed with lawyers, students, and curiosity-seekers. It was the first commencement ceremony of the small law school that Neal had recently founded there.

"Race, color, poverty have everything to do with what happens to an individual," Darrow declared as he had so many times before and as he would again and again. "The way to cure crime is to find the cause." He shrugged his big shoulders but not because he was indifferent.

As a young man, he continued, he'd started out with great ideas, but he'd learned that life isn't all that long, that we aren't all captains of our fate—unexpected things happen to everyone— and we need to treat each other with compassion and maybe bring peace and some measure of joy into the world, not pain and more misery.

"NO PART OF freedom is more essential than the freedom of instruction and the freedom to learn," Bainbridge Colby said. "It is one of the essential elements in our constitutional right to pursue liberty and happiness."

The festivities at Dayton—the hot dog and lemonade stands, the placards reminding you of your sins—also unsettled Colby. To him, the issues at stake were serious, not lurid. And it was this uneasiness that prompted him to seek a temporary federal injunction against the state court in Dayton. Because the state would appeal, an injunction would provide the most direct route to the Supreme Court. That way, there would be no trial in Dayton at all.

If the Supreme Court sustained the injunction, declaring the Tennessee anti-evolution law incompatible with guarantees of freedom of religion and speech, Scopes couldn't be prosecuted.

Darrow agreed with Colby, and they filed for the federal injunction. "Darrow is disgusted with the way some of the newspapers seem determined to make a monkey show of the Scopes trial instead of treating it seriously. That's why he wanted to get it into the federal courts if possible and sidetrack the Dayton trial," a friend of Darrow's remarked. Declaring Tennessee's anti-evolution law unconstitutional had been Darrow's goal all along. "Unless we land it in the federal courts," Darrow explained, "the whole matter of evolution, pro and con, may be ruled out of the testimony in Dayton." Otherwise the case might hinge on the simple matter of whether or not Scopes had taught evolution in his classes. He had, and he admitted he was guilty. But, as Darrow continued, "this is an increasingly serious matter, and it is, indeed, unfortunate that many do not realize the significance of the question involved," he explained. "Tennessee is not the only State that has this law."

He'd withdraw from the case if John Neal insisted on keeping the trial in Dayton.

The federal injunction argued that Scopes could not responsibly teach science without the theory of evolution. The defense was therefore seeking the protection of the Fourteenth Amendment, arguing that the Tennessee law unreasonably deprived Scopes of his liberty and therefore denied his privileges as a citizen.

Judge John J. Gore of the United States District Court, vacationing in Cookeville, Tennessee, read the petition and three hours later refused to grant the injunction. He said he had no power to interfere with the state courts except in bankruptcy proceedings. He did not talk about the merits of the case. He went back to fishing.

Hearing the news, Robinson put a sign in the window of his drugstore: "Dayton Keeps It."

Darrow announced he wouldn't resign from the case after all, but Colby withdrew in a matter of days, pleading that some confusion in New York municipal affairs required him to stay in New York. Not eager to confront the folks of Dayton, whom he knew well, Judge John Godsey also withdrew.

Arthur Garfield Hays

THERE WAS ANOTHER attorney involved in the case, one who had helped found the ACLU and would become its general counsel. That man was Arthur Garfield Hays, so named for three presidents by his German-Jewish parents. (The surname had originally been Haas.)

Born in Rochester in 1881, raised in New York City, a graduate of Columbia University and its law school where he was an editor of the *Columbia Law Review,* Hays was now in his midforties. A stocky man, not too tall, rather good-looking, and considered a "Red Jew"—or the "brilliant Jew with the good

name and face which does not harmonize with it"—he was
smart, witty, and walked with a slight limp, one leg being shorter
than the other. Specializing in international corporate law, he
was prosperous and well-regarded but equally distinguished for
his defense of workers and unions and dissenters. He also worked
occasionally with Dudley Field Malone, a friend, on international divorce cases and, like Malone, Hays despised Woodrow
Wilson for allowing Attorney General Palmer to violate the
rights of pacifists, conscientious objectors, socialists, and
women—and for ignoring the Spanish flu epidemic that had
killed his brother.

He greatly admired Roger Baldwin's courageous refusal to
register for the draft. As for himself, he would say he wasn't
quite sure how he became so passionately interested in civil liberties: maybe he hated authority, or maybe he just enjoyed fighting it.

As he told Baldwin, "My general view on these civil liberties
cases is that sometimes we win, but we never lose."

Bryan called him "some Jewish lawyer from New York" and
Bryan's daughter Grace later said Hays was "never heard of before nor since" the Scopes trial. That was not true. After the
election of 1920, Hays joined the newly established "Committee
of 48" (named for the 48 states) to form a third political party,
and in 1924 he served as the progressive campaign manager in
New York for Robert La Follette's presidential bid. He would
assist Felix Frankfurter in the defense of Sacco and Vanzetti, the
two anarchist immigrants accused of robbery and murder, and
along with Darrow had been asked by the NAACP to work on
the Scottsboro case, where nine black boys from Alabama, ages
twelve to nineteen, were accused of raping two white women. In
1933, Hays appeared at the Reichstag fire trial in Germany on
behalf of the four defendants, all communists, accused of starting the fire, though the Nazis wouldn't let him speak since he
was Jewish.

In the spring of 1925, a Nashville newspaper asked the prosecutors and the Scopes defense team what church they belonged to, whether they believed in God, whether they believed in the divinity of Christ and the authority of the Bible, and whether they favored or opposed teaching the Bible in public schools and universities.

The prosecution supplied their church affiliations and affirmed their belief in the divinity of Christ and the authority of the Bible. Sue Hicks went on to say that the United States is a Christian nation.

Arthur Hays took offense at the newspaper's questions. "This is the first time in my professional experience that the views of lawyers on religious and other questions have been regarded as important in connection with any law case," he sharply replied.

"Any attempt to support either side of the case by public opinion concerning the views of lawyers on social, economic or religious questions is regarded by me as quite as un-American and pernicious as is the law which we are about to test."

WHEN WILLIAM JENNINGS Bryan stepped off the Palmetto Special on Tuesday morning, July 7, a hot summer's day in the valley, he was wearing a shiny white pith helmet to protect him from the sun and which he seldom removed as he went about town.

After he shook a few hands and posed for a few pictures, the smiling Bryan was driven to the place where he and his wife would be staying, a small white house with striped awnings and a veranda that was owned by a clerk in Robinson's drugstore. By now confined to a wheelchair for her arthritis, Mary Bryan would arrive in Dayton later by car. In the meantime, Bryan gladly spoke to reporters, still smiling even as he explained that evolution was trash and that the people of Tennessee would give up their schools before they gave up their Bibles. But they would keep both, he promised. Although he'd like to see every child

educated, he declared, "I believe religion is greater than education."

William Jennings Bryan steps off the train in Dayton
COURTESY W. C. ROBINSON COLLECTION OF SCOPES TRIAL
PHOTOGRAPHS MS. 1091, UNIVERSITY OF TENNESSEE,
KNOXVILLE—LIBRARIES

Shedding his coat—the heat was oppressive—Bryan went
over to Robinson's where he had a strawberry ice cream soda,
despite his concern—or his wife's—about his diabetes. That
night at the Aqua Hotel there was a banquet for Bryan sponsored by the Dayton Progressive Club, which had also greeted

Darrow. Seated across from John Scopes, Bryan asked him if he was going to finish his corn and potatoes, and if not, he would. Scopes later said that Bryan had sworn off white bread because of his diabetes but didn't seem to know potatoes and corn contained starch. He heaped them onto his plate and dumped several spoonfuls of sugar into his iced tea. "The incident was a good tip-off to Bryan's scientific knowledge," Scopes drolly remembered.

But Scopes had been impressed by Bryan's friendliness, especially when Bryan said he remembered Scopes from the commencement address Bryan had delivered at the high school in Salem, Illinois, the year Scopes graduated.

After dessert, Bryan spoke at the banquet, again declaring that the people should decide what is taught in their schools. The room was hot and stuffy. He'd already said he would rather have his son unable to read and write and be an honest man rather than what he called an educated scoundrel. Maybe the heat affected him, for he began to digress. He claimed that the American South had a right to teach its students that the Confederate army was justified, and the North had a right to teach that the Union army was justified. What Southerners decided for the South was true, and what Northerners decided for the North was true. That was popular sovereignty. The majority decides what's true. But the real issue wasn't the Civil War. It was the Bible. And only the Bible contained the truth. Besides, he would add, the South was going to defend the faith. It was going to lead the country back to Christianity, where it belonged.

HE WOULDN'T HAVE taken the case, Bryan concluded, if there wasn't so much at stake. He hadn't practiced law in almost thirty years. The trial would be a duel to the death, a duel to the very death, he said, Christianity pitted not just against evolution, but against the vast conspiracy determined to destroy it.

When Darrow returned briefly to Chicago, he sat at his desk in his law office, and surrounded by a mound of mail, he spoke to a reporter. No one was safe, he said, if the prosecution won in Dayton. People like Bryan, undoubtedly honest people, who nonetheless think they are crusaders, with God on their side, cannot stomach doubt, and they open the door to intolerance and bigotry. Fanatics are dangerous.

"One man's liberty cannot be protected without protecting all men's liberties," Darrow insisted.

"Nothing will satisfy us but a broad victory," Darrow concluded, "to prove that America is founded on liberty and not on narrow, mean, intolerable and brainless prejudice of soulless religo-maniacs."

THE EXPECTED HORDES hadn't materialized, except for the reporters, and the town crawled with them—about 160, many of whom were women.

They were the best the papers had to offer, and many became quite well-known. There was Nunnally Johnson, later an Academy Award–winning screenwriter (*The Grapes of Wrath*). There were the progressives Marcet and Emanuel Haldeman-Julius, who published the first inexpensive little paperbacks known as the Blue Books. There was George Fort Milton, then editor of the *The Chattanooga News,* who would write a laudatory biography of the impeached president Andrew Johnson. There were Washington journalists Frank R. Kent and the esteemed Raymond Clapper (who would be killed in World War II), and Hearst journalists Arthur Brisbane and Mildred Seydell (who interviewed Mussolini in 1927). There was the Tennessee reporter Nellie Kenyon, who would later cover the trial of Jimmy Hoffa, and the science writer Watson Davis. Westbrook Pegler of *The Chicago Tribune* was in Dayton briefly but was soon pulled off the job because his dispatches were considered abusive.

(Pegler would come to despise FDR and join the conservative John Birch Society but won a Pulitzer for exposing a crime syndicate.) Also in Dayton was the literary-minded writer Joseph Wood Krutch for *The Nation*.

Marcet and Emanuel Haldeman-Julius, publishers of the little Blue Books, who covered the Dayton trial

Henry Mencken was also sent to Dayton along with two other journalists from the Baltimore *Sun* and the noted cartoonist Edmund Duffy. To his surprise, Mencken found the town rather lovely, the streets wide and shady, the people friendly and without rancor—which they might well have been because Mencken had been bashing the South, to him the home of boobs and yokels, for a very long time. But he also noted that no one there seemed to suffer from much self-doubt. "To call a man a doubter in these parts is equal to accusing him of cannibalism," Mencken observed. When he ran into Bryan on the street, the two were cordial. Bryan liked the sage of Baltimore because he was honest. Mencken didn't return the compliment. He had not forgotten the jailing of conscientious objectors or the arrest of German Americans before and during the war, or after it, the "Red Scare," the deportations and harassments, all of which he associated with prohibitionists, fanatics, the Daughters of the American Revolution, Ku Kluxers—and William Jennings Bryan.

BRYAN TALKED TO Mencken. He talked to anyone who would listen, Dudley Malone said with a laugh. The trial must be over since he'd already heard Bryan deliver his closing argument at least three times before it began. John Neal wasn't amused. He thought Bryan was out of line and obviously trying to sway the prospective jury.

Bryan ignored him. He would prevail, he said, and he'd lead the campaign to put the Bible in the United States Constitution. Dayton was the lion's den, and he was Daniel, spoiling for the fight, which would begin on Friday.

Part 5

The Trial: Flying Banners and Beating Drums

1925

Yes, I am the devil, and I have a very great interest in this case.
You see, I have arranged many of the details so far, and it's going
to be a clear case of "Heads, I win—tails, you lose."

—"DEVIL DISCUSSES THE SCOPES CASE,"
THE LOS ANGELES TIMES, 1925

Day One

O<small>N FRIDAY, JULY 10, THE</small> morning temperature was already high and Dayton sticky. Outside the Rhea County Courthouse, extra police from Chattanooga in lively blue uniforms were directing traffic. People had come down from the mountains in anticipation of the trial—"tall, gaunt, thin, underfed, sad," Mary Bryan would note—in a sea of calico and denim, the men's blue shirts under their blue overalls and on their heads, high-crown felt hats.

Just before nine A.M., a slightly flushed Judge Raulston, again carrying his dictionary and his Bible, entered the courtroom. He arranged himself at the bench, a raised platform, where a large bouquet of rhododendrons had been placed. His wife and daughter were already there. The paint still smelled fresh and slightly acrid. He fumbled a bit, having broken his glasses.

There were at least fifty cameramen in the place, and it seemed as though all of them had been setting up their tripods in every corner of the stifling room until William Jennings Bryan appeared. All eyes were on Bryan, who seemed to enjoy the attention. The spectators erupted in cheers. Women waved their sunbonnets. Bryan ambled over to the defense table where Clarence Darrow was already seated, rumpled as usual, his shirt a mess from the heat.

Malone and Hays had also arrived. Malone had put on a little weight but looked rather dapper in his elegant silk shirt, sky blue. No one took much notice of Arthur Hays. The three defense lawyers—Hays, Malone, Darrow—chatted quietly with Bryan, who returned to his table, which, like that of the defense, had been placed in front of the raised platform where Judge Raulston sat. Bryan removed his jacket, as Darrow had. Darrow wore lavender or faded blue suspenders (it was hard to tell) over his pale yellow shirt, and Bryan didn't wear suspenders but, instead, a silver-buckled belt. That seemed odd. Men in these parts wore suspenders.

Judge Raulston banged the desk with his gavel.

During a prayer that lasted a full fifteen minutes, the Reverend William M. Cartwright, pastor of the Dayton Methodist Episcopal Church, South, asked God to bless the judge, the jury, the counsel, and the case. Then the trial stopped for a moment so that the photographers could take pictures.

Right away the prosecuting attorney, Arthur Thomas (Tom) Stewart, jumped up.

District Attorney General for the Eighteenth Circuit, comprising the seven counties that Raulston also presided over, Stewart was prepared, eager, and aggressive. Thirty-three years old and a member of the bar since 1913, he was known, in Bryan-like fashion, as the handsome, fair, and freckle-faced "boy orator of the South." Some years later, in 1938, Stewart would be elected to the United States Senate as a Democrat and during the war made a name for himself railing against Japanese Americans.

Today, Friday morning, Stewart asked that the Scopes indictment be quashed and a new grand jury called. He feared the original indictment had been too loosely drawn. An appellate court might throw it out on a technicality.

The defense didn't object. But first, before a new grand jury was to be seated, John Neal asked that counsel from out of state be introduced to the court.

Arthur Thomas (Tom) Stewart, district attorney general
and Scopes prosecutor

COURTESY W. C. ROBINSON COLLECTION OF SCOPES TRIAL
PHOTOGRAPHS MS.1091. UNIVERSITY OF TENNESSEE,
KNOXVILLE—LIBRARIES

Stewart replied that William Jennings Bryan and his son, who
had come to assist him, needed no introduction.

John Neal then introduced Darrow, Hays, Malone, and the
silver-haired lawyer, William O. Thompson, Darrow's partner,
who would for a short while assist them.

"I desire to assure you that we are glad to have you," Judge
Raulston welcomed them all. "The foreign lawyers for both the
state and the defendant."

The foreign lawyers on the defense team took notice of their
foreignness.

Without apparent irony, the judge addressed Clarence Darrow as "Colonel."

The spectators mopped their brows. It was time for a boy,

about four years old, to draw slips of paper from a hat on the judge's desk. That was how the men for the grand jury were chosen. Their names were called, and once they were seated, the prosecution addressed them, saying John Scopes had violated the Tennessee law forbidding the teaching of any theory that denies the story of divine creation of man as taught in the Bible in any of the state-sponsored universities, and normal (the contemporary term for a teachers' college) or public schools.

Judge Raulston read the Tennessee statute out loud. The grand jury heard testimony from one of the children that Scopes taught, and they listened to District Attorney General Stewart read from the textbook that Scopes used in order to teach. He also read aloud the first chapter from the Book of Genesis.

A recess was called so that the grand jury could confer. At eleven A.M., the grand jury returned a new, airtight indictment that was accepted by the court. The earlier one was quashed.

Jury selection for the actual trial would take place that afternoon, after another recess.

CLARENCE DARROW KNEW it would be best to select jurors who were like his client. That was impossible. There was no one in town like John Scopes. So Darrow was hoping to find jurors who were humane and instinctively kind and able to put themselves in someone else's shoes. It wouldn't hurt if they had a sense of humor.

Bryan's job was easier. His jury pool would consist of local folks eager to meet him or those who'd come down from the mountains to hear him, on the courthouse lawn, defend the Bible. "There were many among them, who believed that Bryan was no longer merely human," Henry Mencken later reflected. "I saw plenty of his customers approach him stealthily to touch his garments, to wit, his shirt and pants."

Mencken was exaggerating, which he often did, but he did have a point. Bryan was both preacher and politician: the preacher in Bryan was a politician, and the politician, a preacher. He'd consistently denounced plutocracy, or what he regarded, often rightly, as the government by the few for the few. He had long been the voice of distressed farmers, miners, and small business owners hard put to make a living, the people abused and disgusted by government indifference and corporate profiteering, the people who had been squeezed and ignored by what Bryan called special privilege–hunters, whether the J. Pierpont Morgans or the liquor interests that destroyed both morals and lives. He seemed to be one of those wounded, angry people himself. He wanted to help them by taxing the rich, controlling the trusts, allowing women and men to vote directly for their senators. But now, in the exhilarating, addled, materialistic 1920s, which he did not completely grasp, he detected that underneath the brittle excitement of the moment, with its glitter and glamour, lay anxiety and exhaustion. It was what the political commentator Walter Lippmann called a "feeling of unrest," which Bryan so successfully combated with "the traditional language of prophecy."

Though Bryan did not understand the exuberance that an Al Smith or an NAACP or an immigrant population brought to politics, he saw the unrest. He felt it, especially in the aftermath of a catastrophic war that had produced neither peace nor certainty. And since he was a moralist, and since he had been courageous and radical in many of his political views, he combined that former radicalism with a religious orthodoxy that, as he aged, led to a close-minded arrogance. "Democracy to him was just a matter of voting, and not a matter of what the people were voting for," Edgar Lee Masters remarked. Into the pasture where politics and religion converged Bryan would take his renewed campaign. There, he was utterly self-confident. "I have always been right," he claimed.

"The new front is the religious front," the author McAlister Coleman wrote, "and there will be no peace until every last girl and boy in every last public school is taught to believe, with no mental equivocation, that the Fundamentalist whale swallowed a white, Nordic, Protestant Jonah."

The democratic masses whom Bryan adored and sought to represent were generally rural, white, and often Protestant of a Fundamentalist stripe. "Therein lies their difficulty," observed *The Chicago Defender,* the popular Black newspaper. If Bryan's followers admitted even the possibility that the theory of evolution could be valid, the columnist continued, "they will have to admit that there is no fundamental difference between themselves and the race they pretend to despise."

William Pickens was more direct: "The law of evolution

William Pickens, educator, author,
Field Director of the NAACP
COURTESY LIBRARY OF CONGRESS

cannot be overthrown by the wisdom of a state where they burn men alive."

A DAYTON CITIZEN identified as merely "Richard, the Georgia Negro," said he found the town comparatively liberal. "Look at this Mr. Scopes," he observed. "He is still walking the streets, and nobody does anything to him. Now in Georgia where I come from, if a gentleman said he didn't believe in the Bible he would done have been lynched a long time ago." Of course, Scopes never said he didn't believe in the Bible, but no matter.

NOT UNTIL AFTER lunch, at one-thirty on Friday afternoon, July 10—the twenty-ninth anniversary of Bryan's "Cross of Gold" speech—did jury selection begin. There were sixteen men summoned.

His thumbs hooked on his suspenders, Darrow asked if they belonged to a church. Did they read the Bible? Do you know Mr. Scopes? Would they be fair?

And what had they read about evolution, if anything? "I can't read, sir," said Jim Riley, a farmer. He clutched his hat in his hands.

Pointing to Riley's dark blue spectacles, Darrow asked why Riley was unable to read. "Is that due to your eyes?"

"No, sir. I am uneducated."

"That is because of your eyes?" Darrow seemed slightly confused.

"I say I am uneducated."

But he was not prejudiced, Riley added. His unabashed candor impressed Darrow, who accepted him. Darrow excused only Reverend J. P. Massingill, a Fundamentalist who proudly said he'd preached against evolution—"Of course!" The courtroom broke out in applause. To Mencken, the trial had the air of a religious orgy.

Darrow looked up at the judge. "Your Honor, I am going to ask to have anybody excluded that applauds."

Judge Raulston instructed the spectators to refrain from clapping.

Of the twelve jurors finally selected, nine were farmers. The youngest, W. F. Robertson, was the only man not affiliated with a church. The rest belonged to the Baptist or Methodist congregations, and three of them said the only book they read was the Bible. The oldest was Captain Jack Thompson, formerly a United States marshal under President Wilson and now a fruit grower with icy white hair, a goatee, and a gold watch chain. He looked a bit like Buffalo Bill, and he addressed Darrow politely as Colonel Darrow, much as Judge Raulston had. All of them said they sincerely wanted to give Scopes a fair trial. Fair did not mean impartial, Mencken noted.

None of the lawyers except the dapper Malone kept his jacket on. The rest sat in their shirtsleeves, as did the men in the gallery. And as did Bryan, who fanned himself with his large palm leaf–shaped fan, the one with red borders. Newspaper photographers and men cranking movie cameras stood shoulder to shoulder, heavily perspiring, and a rosy-cheeked Judge Raulston, his glasses resting on his nose, chewed gum. Behind his cherry-stained bench stood a hefty policeman in his blue uniform. He too waved a fan over the judge.

Once the jury was selected, Darrow expected the men to be sworn in, but Judge Raulston explained that in Tennessee, the jury must first hear the indictment read and both sides must present their opening argument. The prosecution and defense then argued about whether to permit the expert testimony from scientists or biblical scholars that the defense was bringing to Dayton. They agreed to postpone their debate on the issue until Monday. It was growing late. The court recessed.

Bryan had been quiet during jury selection, but as he walked out of the courtroom, he said with satisfaction, "We have a beautiful jury."

"It is as we expected," said Darrow.

THE FRIENDLINESS IN court on the first day, if that's what it was, evaporated over the weekend. On Saturday, District Attorney General Stewart decided that testimony by scientists wasn't relevant to the case and would be "offensive" besides.

The prosecution was revealing its strategy. The Tennessee statute was straightforward. The statute forbade the teaching of evolution in a public school. In teaching the theory of evolution, according to the prosecution, Scopes had implicitly denied the truth of the biblical record of creation. So he had broken the law. No testimony by scientists would be needed.

Reporters rushed to the tumbledown Mansion to interview Darrow. He too revealed his strategy. If you don't explain evolution, how is a Tennessee jury supposed to understand, never mind deliberate. The jurors had admitted they knew nothing much about evolution. Not only that, Darrow continued, how are the jurors even to know what the Bible teaches about creation since there are so many versions of it, "some thousand different religions and 500 sects of Christians," he went on. "Naturally there is some difference of opinion as to the divine account as taught in the Bible."

What's more, how is the jury to learn that the theory of evolution and the Bible do not conflict? Millions of competent people, religious people, God-fearing and pious people are Christians and evolutionists, both at the same time. So you need to give the jury evidence. Darrow wanted to bring geologists from Harvard, biologists from Yale, and theologians from Chicago, fifteen in all.

Bryan would have none of it. "Foreign scientists should be

barred from Dayton," he declared, emphasizing the "foreign." Anybody coming to defend Scopes, whether lawyers or scientists, were a new form of carpetbagger, alien invaders aiming to uproot a way of life and take away a state's rights to determine what's best for its citizens.

As the lawyers sparred, so too did the town. The Reverend Charles Francis Potter of New York's West Side Unitarian Church had arrived in Dayton with his wife. After his debates with the Fundamentalist John Roach Straton, Potter had become increasingly alarmed by the growing number of Fundamentalists and their well-trained lobbyists, who were pressuring school committees, college boards, and legislatures, like the one in Tennessee. He simply had to go to Dayton.

After learning that Bryan was scheduled to speak at Dayton's Methodist Episcopal Church, South, the Reverend Howard Byrd of Dayton's Methodist Episcopal, North, invited Potter to speak to his congregation. Reverend Byrd believed parishioners should hear several points of views. But when the announcement of Potter's upcoming appearance was posted at Robinson's drugstore, a committee of women from the church walked over to Reverend Byrd's house to inform him that his congregation would walk out if Potter were allowed to preach at their church. A group of men followed, saying basically the same thing. "I've been here three years," the mild-mannered Byrd told the reporters gathered on his lawn, where he sat with his twenty-two-year-old wife and their three children, the youngest an infant in her arms. "This is the first conflict I have ever had."

Potter didn't wish to be the cause of more unpleasantness, so he canceled his talk. Reverend Byrd felt he had no choice but to resign. A group of sympathetic reporters raised $50 for Byrd and his family.

That Sunday, Bryan successfully addressed the congregants of the other Methodist church, with Judge Raulston beaming in the front row.

"I fear the aristocracy of wealth," Bryan cried yet again. "I respect the aristocracy of learning, but I thank God for the democracy of the heart."

Aristocracy opposed to democracy; head opposed to heart. "While God does not despise the learned," Bryan continued, "neither does he give them a monopoly of his attention. The unlearned are much more numerous." According to Bryan, it seemed God was partial to the side with the greatest number. "A religion that didn't appeal to any but college graduates would be over the head or under the feet of 99 percent of our people. The God I worship is the God of the ignorant as well as the learned man." He sipped a glass of water. Lawyers, the educated, the elite: they were "a little oligarchy of intellectuals, attempting to force their views upon the people through the public schools," he declared.

That afternoon, Bryan continued his sermon. Addressing a crowd estimated at three thousand, far more than the population of Dayton, Bryan talked of Jesus Christ, "a great Physician who has never lost a case," he shouted. "The Christian church should wake up and carry the gospel until everyone shall know the truth."

Curious about Bryan, Reverend Potter sat in the audience. "The once great and silver-tongued Bryan of old had all but vanished. I heard a dignified but worn-out old man repeating worn-out ideas in sentences themselves meaningless for much repetition," Potter later commented.

But William Jennings Bryan reveled in repetition, as if he was talking to his children. And he especially reveled in recounting the horrors of the recent war. "How many more wars will it take for the white race to kill itself off," Bryan asked, "leaving the world to the darker races until they imitate the white races?"

Evolution and race: they had merged.

Mencken heard that too. Do not make the mistake of laughing at Bryan or at the trial, he advised. "You probably laughed at the prohibitionists, say, back in 1914," he said. "Well, don't make the same error twice."

EMANUEL HALDEMAN-JULIUS SAID the trial was not about right and wrong or truth and error. "It is purely a question of power. He who has the power makes Right. And power can remake the Constitution." Bryan suggested that if courts or constitutions interfered with the popular will, then the constitutions themselves should be changed by popular vote. He also hinted that Christianity should become the country's religion.

But Bryan indignantly denied that he intended to propose a constitutional amendment to ban the teaching of evolution. He insisted that he wanted only to make sure public schools taught the good and the true and the right—and by the good and the true and the right, he meant the Bible.

Chapter Fourteen

And It Was Good

MONDAY MORNING, DAYTON, TENNESSEE, JULY 13. It was going to be another hot and humid day. A few electric fans were now whirring, creating a small damp breeze that cooled nothing. William Jennings Bryan arrived wearing his white pith helmet and carrying his palm-leaf fan. To his right sat his son, a lawyer with a dark mustache and carefully dressed in gray striped trousers. Mrs. Bryan had arrived too and was carried up the stairs to the second floor, where the courtroom was located, in her wheelchair. Her nurse placed the chair not far from Bryan.

Because they were climbing over each other, the cameramen and newspaper photographers caused the opening prayer to be delayed. Despite the heat, Malone still did not remove the jacket of his chocolate-colored double-breasted suit. Scopes sat patiently next to his father. "A grinning, long-jawed, mountain product with pale blue eyes and yellow hair," Mary Bryan described Scopes. "He carries himself wretchedly, letting his head drop forward between his shoulders. His whole appearance is simpering, weak and gauky [*sic*]."

After the opening prayer, prosecutor Tom Stewart asked to question one of the jurors again. Darrow's objection was overruled because the jury had not yet been sworn in.

Had Mr. Gentry an opinion on the guilt or innocence of Scopes, Stewart asked.

Not at all.

John Neal and Arthur Hays spoke but not about the admissibility of expert testimony, as everyone expected. Instead, they moved to quash the indictment against John Scopes. They would show that the indictment violated the Tennessee constitution as well as the United States Constitution. Though they knew their motion would certainly fail—Judge Raulston would never agree—their larger strategy was to be sure arguments against the indictment's constitutionality went into the record for any later appeal.

Prosecutor Stewart had asked that the jury be removed during the argument. He didn't want them to hear anything, as he said, that "might handicap them in rendering a verdict."

What's the harm? Neal replied. The jury is the judge of the law and the facts.

"Oh, that is all foolishness," Stewart said, brushing him off.

Raulston sent the jury out of the room.

Neal spoke first. He reminded the court that in the Tennessee constitution, it was written that "knowledge, learning and virtue" were "essential to the preservation of republican institutions," and, further, quoting from that constitution, he read that "it shall be the duty of the general assembly in all future periods of this Government to cherish literature and science." Therefore, Neal argued, as he had during the preliminary hearing, that to mandate a school's curriculum along specific religious lines violated the state's constitution, which provided that "no preference shall ever be given by law to any religious establishment" and no preference to one religion over another.

In addition, Tennessee's anti-evolution law violated the United States Constitution's protection of due process, as embodied in the Fourteenth Amendment. For what exactly was forbidden to teach, Neal asked. It wasn't clear. Was it unlawful to teach anything but the story of creation as outlined in the Bible, or to teach the idea that humankind is descended from lower animals?

Also, the law did not specify what was meant by "teach." To deliver information? To illustrate? To take as fact? Thus, no law is sound if you didn't know what it takes to break it. And if the law is vague, it's not enforceable. And if vague and unenforceable, it cannot fall within the police powers of the state.

Arthur Garfield Hays took over. In his shirtsleeves, his dark, thick hair looking as though it stood at attention, he came across as if he'd read all the books that Reverend Potter had lugged to Dayton. He also displayed a mastery of the law and spoke without theatrics or appearing arrogant, although Mary Bryan reported to her family that Hays was "as forward and self-asserting as the New York Jew can be."

Leaving his pipe on the table, Hays reiterated that the Tennessee anti-evolution law is so vague no one can tell when it's being violated, especially not a teacher. As a matter of fact, if the current Tennessee law were to be strictly enforced, then it might also be against the law to teach that the sun was the center of the solar system since that contradicts what is "taught by the Bible"—namely, that the earth is the center of the universe.

"The chief point against the constitutionality of this law," Hays concluded, "is that it extends the police power of the state unreasonably and is a restriction upon the liberty of the individuals."

Ben McKenzie, the eldest member of the prosecution, now rose. "The old war horse of the Tennessee Bar," as Hays called him, McKenzie was a plainspoken lawyer practiced in the art of unctuous condescension. Standing in his crinkled seersucker suit with his glasses perched on his nose, he enjoyed pouring contempt on the sweaty city slickers and their sophistries. Hays's hypothetical example was "no more kin," McKenzie drawled, to the indictment "than he claims we are to monkeys." The spectators laughed.

Benjamin McKenzie, Scopes prosecutor

"This is not a statute that requires outside assistance to define," McKenzie continued. The construction of the Tennessee law was clear as day. "We don't have to send out and get some fellow to construe it for us," he said, playing to the room. A sixteen-year-old boy in our schools could understand the law.

"I don't know what they do up in his country," McKenzie slowly said, with a smile, pointing to the defense.

"If these gentlemen have any laws in the great metropolitan city of New York or in the great white city of the northwest that will throw any light on it"—he again gestured amicably toward the defense—"we will be glad to hear about it." The typewriters at the press table clacked away.

Dudley Malone stiffened. "I would like to say here," he said, "that I do not consider further allusion to geographical parts of the country as particularly necessary, such as reference to New Yorkers and to citizens of Illinois."

Malone tersely added, "We are here, rightfully, as American citizens."

Judge Raulston waved Malone aside. "Colonel Malone" didn't understand that "General McKenzie" was joshing. McKenzie smiled and said he loved the distinguished gentlemen from New York. He just had no respect for their legal position.

Raulston continued with a friendly twang. "I want you gentlemen from New York or any other foreign state to always remember you are our guests." Foreign states. Guests.

Malone courteously thanked the court and the people of Tennessee for their hospitality—he could play the same game—smoothly adding, "But we want it understood that while we are in this courtroom we are here as lawyers, not as guests."

AFTER A RECESS for lunch, District Attorney General Tom Stewart addressed the Tennessee constitution's directive to "cherish science and literature." It was not binding, he stressed. It was merely a suggestion.

He went on. The Tennessee law does not interfere with religious worship. You can attend any church you wish. The law merely addresses itself to the public school system.

Darrow interrupted. The defense had been referring to the

constitution's stipulation that "no preference shall ever be given, by law, to any religious establishment or mode of worship." The Tennessee anti-evolution law gave preference to the Fundamentalist interpretation of the Bible.

Stewart seemed puzzled. Darrow explained that the law was partial to the Bible over all other sacred books. Stewart coldly replied, "The laws of the land recognize the law of God and Christianity as part of the common law."

Malone and Neal pressed Stewart again, repeating that this anti-evolution law, the Butler law, favored the Bible over, say, the Koran.

"We are not living in a heathen country," Stewart exploded, "so how could it prefer the Koran to the Bible?"

Malone persisted. "If there be in the state of Tennessee a single child or young man or young woman in your school who is a Jew," he calmly replied, "to impose on any course of science a particular view of creation from the Bible is interfering, from our point of view, with his civil rights."

Darrow leaned over to Arthur Hays to ask, as if with a sigh, "Isn't it difficult to realize that a trial of this kind is possible in the twentieth century in the United States of America?"

NOT UNTIL THREE that afternoon did Darrow address the court, pacing beneath the judge's bench, tugging at his suspenders, pointing his finger, and delivering a broadside against not just the technical aspects of the Tennessee anti-evolution law that Neal and Hays had enumerated but the spirit of that law, a spirit that to him was compounded of bigotry, fanaticism, and error.

He began by thanking the entire community for its hospitality, and the judge for bestowing on him the great honor of being called "Colonel." He nodded toward the prosecutor Ben McKenzie, and said he knew Mr. McKenzie didn't intend to be rude when he referred to the defense lawyers as out-of-towners.

Then he began, firm, eloquent, dramatic, and "with a transition too quick to be noticed," a reporter marveled.

The only sound in the room was the click of the typewriters and the unavailing whir of the electric fans.

Darrow addressing the court
COURTESY GETTY IMAGES

Darrow spoke with gentleness and with indignation. If some of the spectators thought he looked frail or old or even like one of the Holy Rollers come down from the hills, he was unmistakably Clarence Darrow, clear-eyed, shrewd, experienced, utterly prepared. Here was a man pulling no punches. He spoke for two hours.

He began by noting that the people of Tennessee had adopted a constitution that declared they should always enjoy religious freedom. But what if the legislature said that children could read only *The Pilgrim's Progress* and Bryan's *In His Image*? Would that be constitutional? "If it is, the Constitution is a lie and a snare," Darrow declared, "and the people have forgot what liberty means."

"It is a travesty upon language, a travesty upon justice and a travesty upon the constitution to say that any citizen of Tennessee can be deprived of his rights by a legislative body in the face of the constitution."

Repeating the phrase "religious bigotry" over and over, raising his voice, lowering his voice, pacing, standing still, thrusting his hands deep in his pockets, Darrow was sarcastic one minute, he was friendly the next, and sometimes he seemed more like the local farmer who lived down the road than some big-city lawyer. The hole in his shirt expanded into a huge tear, and his sleeves slapped around his wrist. There was nothing pretentious, uncertain, unfelt in what he said.

He coldly faced the prosecution table, where Bryan sat. Bulky, unsmiling, collarless, his thin lips pressed together, Bryan suspiciously studied his opponent. "Unless there is left enough of the spirit of freedom in the state of Tennessee and the United States," Darrow pointedly went on, "there is not a single line of any constitution that can withstand bigotry and ignorance when it seeks to destroy the rights of the individual; and bigotry and ignorance are ever active.

"Here we find today as brazen and bold an attempt to destroy learning as was ever made in the Middle Ages," Darrow continued, "and the only difference is that we have not provided that they shall be burned at the stake, but there is time for that, Your Honor. We have to approach these things gradually.

"If this proceeding, both in form and substance, can prevail in any court, then no law, no matter how foolish, wicked, ambiguous or ancient, can but come back to Tennessee," Darrow explained. "All the guarantees go for nothing. All the past has gone and will be forgotten if this can succeed."

Darrow picked apart the law. The law says that it is a crime in Tennessee to teach any theory—not just evolution, but any theory that differs from the divine account of creation as recorded in the Bible. But Tennessee has no more right, Darrow insisted, to teach the Bible as a divine book than to teach the Koran or the Book of Mormon or Confucius or Emerson. These too are books "to which human souls have read for consolation and aid."

In his easygoing way, Darrow then said he hadn't come to Tennessee, nor would he go anywhere, to undermine the faith of those who revere the Bible. "I know there are millions of people in the world who look on it being a divine book, and I have not the slightest objection to it," he allowed. "I feel just exactly the same toward the religious creed of every human being who lives."

"If anybody finds anything in this life that brings them consolation and health and happiness, I think they ought to have it."

But the Bible is not one book, he reminded the courtroom. "The Bible is made up of sixty-six books written over a period of about one thousand years, some of them very early and some of them comparatively late." And what is the Bible? "It is a book primarily of religion and morals. It is not a book of science. Never was and was never meant to be," he explained.

It cannot tell you how to build a railroad. It is not a text on chemistry or on geology or astronomy. It can't be. "It was written by men who thought the earth was flat and that the sun moves round it to give us light."

The Bible is a book of hope and faith, not science.

Yet this law says you can't teach anything that conflicts with the Bible. Whatever does that mean? This law is indefinite and uncertain, no one can obey it, no court can enforce it. A law must be plain and simple so that someone can understand what it means. Not to mention that there are five hundred warring sects of Christianity, all debating how to interpret the Bible.

So the law masks an ingenious attack upon the religious freedom of people.

If you were to ask why John Scopes is on trial, Darrow warmly continued, answering his own question, "he is here because the Fundamentalists are after him. Ignorance and bigotry are combined against him. That is a mighty strong combination. It makes me fearful."

Still unsmiling, still fanning himself with his palm-leaf fan, Bryan listened. His wife thought he looked tired. District Attorney General Stewart sat transfixed. Drama had returned to the courtroom, despite the blasting heat, despite the nit-picking, despite everything. Stooped-over Darrow had come to Dayton to fight against intolerance, against ignorance, against prejudice. True, Darrow was an agnostic. But he was a dreamer and a believer in an ideal—of charity for all, of freedom of thought, of tolerance.

Darrow finished his soliloquy with the plea that touched the many who heard him on that hot July day:

> Ignorance and fanaticism is ever busy and needs feeding. Always it is feeding and gloating for more. Today, it is the public school teachers, tomorrow the private. The next day the preachers and the lecturers, the magazines, the books, the newspapers. After a while, Your Honor, it is the setting of man against man and creed against creed until with flying banners and beating drums we are marching backward to the glorious ages of the sixteenth century when bigots lighted fagots to burn the men who dared to bring any intelligence and enlightenment and culture to the human mind.

"NO SUBJECT POSSESSES the minds of men like religious bigotry and hate," Clarence Darrow said, "and these fires are being lighted today in America."

Sweating in that airless Tennessee courtroom, hair parted in the middle and clinging to his head, Mencken heard every syllable of Darrow's speech, which he said, "rose like a wind and ended with a flourish of bugles." Even Judge Raulston seemed touched, and when back out on the street, Ben McKenzie stepped out of his Ford, threw his arm around Darrow and exclaimed, "It was the greatest speech I ever heard in my life on any subject."

Though there were some faint hisses when Darrow concluded, as the crowd filed out of the courtroom, the overwhelming response was one of downright admiration, except of course for those who called his soliloquy bitter and vitriolic—if admittedly brilliant. To the extent that the speech was aimed at Bryan, who sat solemn and implacable and patient, it made little difference.

And the Scopes jurors had still not taken their oath. Excused from the courtroom, they'd heard not one iota of Clarence Darrow's two-hour speech, not a word of the soliloquy that many considered one of the best of his career. But newspapers across the nation printed it.

THAT NIGHT, A violent thunderstorm caused the power to fail. A water main broke. Arthur Hays later recalled that "the denizens commented, with furtive-looks Darrow-ward, upon the miracle that the water had ceased to flow, the lights had ceased to burn, and some suggested that the rivers flowed with blood!"

Hays was tickled. "We looked upon the day's work," he said, "and found it good."

Chapter Fifteen

Render Unto Caesar

ENCKEN'S DEPICTION OF BRYAN AS mangy and flea-bitten might have led readers to believe that Mencken wasn't worried, but he was very worried. "The fellow is full of such bitter, implacable hatreds that they radiate from him like heat from a stove," Mencken said of Bryan. "He hates the learning he cannot grasp. He hates those who sneer at him. He hates, in general, all who stand apart from his own pathetic commonness."

But be forewarned, Mencken concluded. This clown is in the saddle, fully armed.

TUESDAY, JULY 14, Dayton, Tennessee, and another day of sweltering heat. Under the shady trees in front of the lemonade and hot dog stands, Seventh-day Adventists, Baptists, and itinerant evangelists were arguing with each other, all of them standing pat "on the common ground of complete faith," Mencken observed. A man handed out his calling card: "100 per cent American. N.B., Yes, We have No Monkeys in Our Family Tree." A chimpanzee from a nearby circus paraded through town wearing a felt hat, a suit, and spats, and he carried a walking stick. Bryan posed for a picture in front of a real estate advertisement, "Ask Us About Tampa, Florida."

Inside the courtroom, the fans circulated clammy air. It was packed again, doorways blocked and people lined up against the walls. Dressed in their blue uniforms and uncomplaining, the police were trying to keep the aisles clear. Ruby Darrow had arrived. Wearing a dark dress and a hat trimmed in wine-colored chiffon, she sat behind her husband.

Everyone seemed jittery.

Just as Judge Raulston asked Reverend A. C. Stribling to deliver the morning prayer, Clarence Darrow leaped up. No one expected him to say what he said. "I object to prayer," he announced, "and I object to the jury being present when the court rules on the objection."

The gasps were audible. If the hundreds of people inside the courthouse listening to his soliloquy the day before, or the hundreds more listening on the courthouse lawn, had decided that the city lawyer may not have had horns and a tail after all, they were no longer so sure. Prayer cut to the heart of their world, and Darrow had the nerve to object to it.

"The nature of this case being one where it is claimed by the state that there is a conflict between science and religion," Darrow said, "there should be no part taken outside of the evidence in this case and no attempt by means of prayer or in another way to influence the deliberation and consideration of the jury of the facts in this case."

He asked that reporters write down every single word of his objection.

Sitting at the prosecution table, Ben McKenzie was shocked. He protested.

"I do not object to anyone praying in private," Darrow replied, "but I do object to this court being turned into a meeting house."

The lead prosecutor, District Attorney General Stewart, fumed at such an outrage from the "agnostic counsel for the defense."

Hays now raised his voice to object to Stewart. "May I ask to enter an exception to the statement 'agnostic counsel for the defense.'"

Dudley Malone sprang forward. "I respect Mr. Darrow's right to his unbelief, which is as sincere as my belief," he said, just as sharply. "As one of the members of counsel who is not an agnostic, I desire to file my objection from my point of view," Malone emphatically continued. "Those prayers we have already heard, having been duly argumentative, help to increase the atmosphere of hostility to our point of view, which already exists in this community by widespread propaganda."

"So far as creating an atmosphere of hostility is concerned," Tom Stewart sourly observed, "I would advise Mr. Malone this is a God fearing country."

"It is no more a God fearing country than that from which I came," Malone replied, referring to New York.

Judge Raulston, a devout Fundamentalist, overruled Darrow's objection to the opening prayer, finding it unthinkable. "I believe in prayer myself," the judge said. "I constantly invoke divine guidance myself when I am on the bench and off the bench; I see no reason why I should not continue to do this."

It seemed a religious war had come to court.

The Reverend Stribling blessed the proceeding. Bryan bowed his head. Darrow stated he wished his objection to prayer be read into the record every morning. Judge Raulston agreed, adding that the objection would be overruled every morning. Then he ordered a court recess until the afternoon so he could finish preparing his opinion on the defense's motion, made the day before, to quash the indictment.

Before he left the courtroom, Judge Raulston amiably asked the photographers if they wanted to take pictures, which they did.

After lunch, Arthur Hays presented a petition from Unitarians, Jews, and Congregationalists asking the court to rotate the

clergy who offered opening prayers. The signers were Reverend
Potter along with Rabbi Jerome Mark of Tennessee, Reverend
D. M. Welch of the Knoxville Unitarian Church, and the Reverend Fred W. Hagan of the First Congregational Church in Huntington, West Virginia.

"His honor has passed on this," Stewart asserted, as if to say
enough was enough.

Hays placidly repeated that he had made a motion about ro-
tating the clergy who were to offer the opening prayer.

Stewart turned on him in a fury. "Please shut your mouth,"
Stewart lashed out.

"I insist on courtesy," Hays stonily replied.

To mollify everyone, Judge Raulston said he'd refer the petition to the town's association of pastors. The courtroom loudly
applauded and laughed. The pastors' association was a Fundamentalist group.

Judge Raulston then said he needed more time to deliberate
on the motion to quash the indictment. His term of office would
soon expire, and he wanted to get everything right. Marcet
Haldeman-Julius scrutinized the judge. "The plain fact was that
he sincerely longed to appear before the world as a great and
nobly generous judge. But even more than he wished this," she
wrote, "he wanted to be re-elected. As the crude phrase has it,
he well knew on which side his bread was buttered"—that of the
Fundamentalists.

JUDGE RAULSTON DID not reappear until almost four o'clock
that afternoon. His smile had vanished. He'd heard that the International News Service had leaked his decision about whether
to grant the defense's motion to quash the indictment. He said he
would withhold his ruling until the next day, Wednesday the
fifteenth. In fact, he was delaying the trial until he learned how
his decision got leaked.

Marcet Haldeman-Julius and Ruby Darrow

COURTESY HALDEMAN-JULIUS COLLECTION,
LEONARD H. AXE LIBRARY, SPECIAL COLLECTIONS AND
UNIVERSITY ARCHIVES, PITTSBURG STATE UNIVERSITY

Several reporters in the courtroom affected outrage. Was there any actual proof that the INS was the source of the leak? Perhaps, said the judge. The reporters offered to conduct their own investigation to restore honor to their profession. The judge assigned five of them to look into the crime. Court adjourned.

.   .   .

"I CAME ALL the way from New York," Doris Stevens declared, "to find what? That the defendant was a man, the prosecutor a man, the judge a man, the jury all men, the attorneys on both sides men, the witnesses for the prosecution boys and men, and the witnesses for the defense carefully selected men of intelligence."

"One would think there weren't any women in this world, or that they didn't do any thinking."

Newspaper reporters feigned shock at her daring to introduce herself as Doris Stevens and not as "Mrs. Dudley Malone." They rushed to interview her. She wore no wedding ring.

"But I suppose this is one-time, when an equally great cause is at stake," Stevens conceded. "Of course, if this same trial were held several years later, there would be women among the principals and the cause would be just as great."

ON THE FOURTH day of the trial, July 15, Wednesday morning, the person chosen to deliver the opening prayer was none other than Unitarian Reverend Charles Francis Potter of New York. He was as surprised as everyone.

There were other gestures toward conciliation. Tom Stewart apologized to Arthur Hays, saying he was ashamed for having lost his temper, and he'd not meant to be discourteous, especially since Hays himself had been nothing but considerate. Hays replied that he admired anyone who was both human and courteous. Stewart's outburst showed he was human; his apology, that he was courteous.

But when John Neal asked Stewart to apologize to Darrow, Stewart snarled, "So long as I speak what I conceive to be the truth, I apologize to no man."

The spectators cheered.

Darrow curled his thumbs around his suspenders and nod-ded. He needed no apology. Being called an agnostic was a com-pliment, not an insult, and he took no offense. "I do not pretend to know where many ignorant men are sure," he said, gener-ously smiling. "That is all 'agnostic' means."

As for the word "infidel," it has no meaning. "Everybody is an infidel that does not believe in the prevailing religion; among the Saracens, everyone is an infidel that does not believe with them," Darrow easily explained, "and in a Mohammedan coun-try, everybody that is not a Mohammedan is an infidel."

"I think we are wasting a lot of valuable time, Your Honor," Stewart complained in response.

Judge Raulston cared only about learning what the investiga-tion into the leak had turned up.

Richard J. Beamish of *The Philadelphia Inquirer*, a plump man, well-respected in his profession, had led the investigation, which amounted to little more than a group of reporters playing poker until the wee hours of the morning. They all knew what had happened the other day. When young William K. Hutchin-son of the International News Service walked out of the court-room with the judge, Hutchinson had asked Raulston if he planned to deliver his decision that afternoon. A talkative man, happy to be in the company of reporters, Raulston told Hutchin-son he would, and when Hutchinson followed up and asked if the court would then adjourn until the next day, Judge Raulston again said yes. So Hutchinson concluded that Judge Raulston wasn't going to grant the defense motion to quash the indict-ment. If it had been granted, there wouldn't be any need to meet the next day, for the trial would be over: two and two made four.

The leak, Beamish told Judge Raulston, had inadvertently come from the judge himself. Satisfied, Raulston motioned to the photographers. They might take some pictures before he read his decision.

As was expected, Raulston denied the defense motion to quash the indictment. Since a teacher could teach evolution in private schools, if that teacher wanted, no one's rights had been infringed upon. The teacher could still teach evolution, just not in public schools, for the anti-evolution law pertained only to public schools. As for the law's imposing religious beliefs: not at all. Anyone could worship whatever they wanted. As for the indictment being vague: not at all. The indictment was based on the anti-evolution law, which had been passed by the legislature.

Judge Raulston mopped his brow and sipped his ice water. The policeman standing behind him kept fanning.

Having read his decision aloud for forty-five minutes, Judge Raulston was exhausted. The court would take a recess.

Swearing in of jury. Reporters in foreground; Hays leaning to talk with Neal; defense table on the right.

. . .

SCOPES'S PLEA OF not guilty was entered into the record, and District Attorney General Stewart got right to the point. Mr. Scopes had violated the new Tennessee law by teaching evolution. That was it. A simple, obvious misdemeanor.

But the defense was headed in a far different direction. The case must go down in history as a constitutional issue involving the separation of church and state and freedom of thought. As Arthur Hays would say, a legislature may dictate what subjects can be taught, but if science is to be taught, it cannot be taught falsely.

It was Dudley Field Malone's turn. Considered the dandy of the defense, debonair and dashing, today he was wearing a dark blue double-breasted jacket over a gray shirt. Perching himself at times on the corner of the defense table, he contended that it wasn't enough to say that Scopes broke the law by teaching evolution. The prosecution had to prove that Scopes taught the theory of evolution while at the same time denying the theory of creation as set forth in the Bible.

To do that, the prosecution had to define evolution, which is not, as they seemed to suggest, a theory that says humans are descended from monkeys, or, as Bryan liked to say, from jungle animals. "No scientist of any pre-eminent standing today holds such a view," Malone declared. "The most that science says today is that there is an order of men-like mammals which are more capable of walking erect than other animals, and more capable than other animals in the use of the forefeet as hands."

In addition, the defense would show that there was more than one theory of creation set forth in the Bible and that those different versions conflict. Finally, Malone said, the defense maintained that scientific truth is not contained in the Bible. "Moses never heard about steam, electricity, the telegraph, the telephone, the radio, the aeroplane, farming machinery," Malone said in all seriousness. Today we enjoy the fruits of technological progress, which are the result of science. The Bible is not a book of science; it's a work of religious aspiration and moral conduct. Science and religion are two disparate fields of thought and learning and need not, should not, be confused.

The purpose of the defense is twofold, Malone began to summarize. Narrowly, it intends to prove Scopes innocent. More broadly, it would demonstrate that the Bible is a religious work whose proper sphere is theology.

Malone finished with a biblical flourish. "We remember that Jesus said: 'Render unto Caesar the things that are Caesar's and unto God the things that are God's.'"

THOUGH DISTRICT ATTORNEY General Stewart had objected over and over, Raulston had allowed Malone to proceed. Reading from Bryan's introduction to Thomas Jefferson's "Statute of Religious Freedom," Malone used Bryan's own words against him. "The regulation of the opinions of men on religious questions by law is contrary to the laws of God," Bryan had written.

Whatever would Bryan the modernist of twenty years ago have to say to Bryan the prosecutorial Fundamentalist of today, Malone rhetorically wondered.

Bryan's name should not be dragged into anything, Stewart yelled out, and should be omitted from the defense's opening statement.

Coolly indifferent, Malone replied, "I don't think Mr. Bryan is the least sensitive about it, Your Honor."

"Not a bit," Bryan piped up at last, his voice shaking with suppressed anger. Beads of perspiration dropped from his forehead. "I ask no protection from the court," he declared, "and when the proper time comes, I shall show the gentleman that I stand exactly where I stood then and that these things have nothing to do with the case at bar."

Noisy applause filled the courtroom. The policemen from Chattanooga rapped their night sticks on the bench.

AFTER THE JURY was called into the courtroom, the foreman, Captain Jack Thompson, requested that they too be provided with electric fans. "This heat is fearful," he said.

Ben McKenzie replied that the state didn't have enough money for fans. Dudley Malone offered to pay for some out of his own pocket, and Judge Raulston intervened before there could be another quarrel. He offered to share the fan on his desk with the jury. On his desk was also a vase of gladiolas brought by a small child during the recess.

At last, now, the jury took their oaths. So too the four witnesses for the prosecution. Walter White, the superintendent of schools, wearing a white tie, affirmed that John Scopes taught from Hunter's biology textbook, *A Civic Biology*. A copy of the green-bound book was placed into evidence, as was a copy of the King James Bible.

Arthur Hays objected. The Tennessee statute said nothing about the King James Version of the Bible, and certainly there are other versions. Why not enter Thomas Jefferson's rewritten version of Scripture? Or the Catholic Bible? There are sixty-six Protestant Bibles. How could Mr. Stewart know he was offering the right version?

Objection firmly overruled by the judge, but with a smile.

As for the textbook *A Civic Biology*, Darrow made certain the jury knew it was the state's official and authorized textbook.

Then came the young boys from the Rhea Central High School, students from Scopes's class. They'd been at the nearby swimming hole, and the bailiffs had to fetch them while the judge amiably waited, chatting with well-wishers.

Howard Morgan, a serious and shy fourteen-year-old wearing white trousers, took the stand. He said Mr. Scopes had explained that man evolved from a one-celled organism. And man was a mammal.

Darrow cross-examined the boy. "Scopes didn't tell you a cat was the same as a man, did he?"

"No, sir; he said a man had reasoning powers these animals didn't have."

"Well," Darrow replied with a grin, "there's doubt about that, but we'll let it pass."

The jurors and spectators laughed. Bryan did not.

Another student in the class, Harry Shelton, affirmed that he learned life came from a single cell.

Darrow asked if the boy left the church after he'd heard about this. No, Harry Shelton said, he still attended church.

The last state's witness, the druggist Frank Robinson, who was chairman of the school board, recounted a conversation with Scopes. Scopes had said any teacher who taught science from Hunter's biology textbook would be breaking the law.

During Darrow's cross-examination, Robinson said he'd been selling Hunter's textbook in his drugstore for the past six or seven years. His drugstore was the designated book depository.

It was not against the law to sell the book, Tom Stewart interrupted, just to teach from it. Laughter in the courtroom.

When Darrow asked if Mr. Robinson had seen any moral deterioration during all that time, Stewart objected. Judge Raulston sustained the objection.

Darrow read a page from Hunter's textbook on evolution. At first, he read the same passage that the prosecution had used during the preliminary hearing: "We have now learned that animal forms may be arranged so as to begin with very simple one-celled forms and culminate with a group which contains man himself," Darrow recited. "This arrangement is called the evolutionary series. Evolution means change."

Hunter's book said there were five hundred thousand species of animals known in existence, and of them, humans were classified with mammals. "Mammals are considered the highest of vertebrate animals, not only because of their complicated structure, but because their instincts are so well developed," Darrow continued. "Monkeys certainly seem to have many of the mental attributes of man."

Darrow read on. "Professor Thorndike, of Columbia University, sums up their habits of learning as follows: 'In their method of learning, although monkeys do not reach the human stage of a rich life of ideas, yet they carry the animal method of learning, by the selection of impulses and association of them with different sense-impressions, to a point beyond that reached by any other of the lower animals. In this, too they resemble man; for he differs from the lower animals not only in the possession of a new sort of intelligence, but also in the tremendous extension of that sort which he has in common with them. A fish learns slowly a few simple habits. Man learns quickly an infinitude of habits that may be highly complex.'"

Annoyed, Stewart asked to read from the first two chapters of Genesis. "In the beginning God created the heaven and the earth," Stewart began. Darrow listened, half smiling.

When Stewart finished, the prosecution rested. There was nothing more to say. It was, as they said from the start, a simple case.

DURING THE RECESS, a reporter rushed over to Robinson's drugstore to buy the biology textbook. The woman at the counter told him in a whisper that they'd sold out. The reporter left and once outside the store, a man beckoned to him. "I know where you can get a copy," the man furtively whispered, "if you are willing to pay the price." The reporter laughed and told his readers he'd been ambushed by the local literary bootlegger.

.   .   .

MENCKEN FIDGETED IN the heat, slightly surprised that the prosecution kept jumping up, contesting almost everything that the defense had said. "In view of the fact that everyone here looks for the jury to bring in a verdict of guilty," Mencken commented, "it might be expected that the prosecution would show a considerable amiability."

When it was time to call witnesses for the defense and Darrow called the eminent Professor Maynard Metcalf, Stewart was on his feet again reminding the court that in Tennessee the defendant, John Scopes, was required to be the first defense witness or would not be able to testify later.

The defense confirmed that Mr. Scopes would not be taking the stand, so Metcalf was called.

Formerly at Oberlin College, Metcalf would be conducting research at Johns Hopkins University after he completed a zoological expedition in South America that was underwritten by the National Academy of Sciences. He was also a Congregationalist who had taught Bible classes at Oberlin and in Baltimore. He was round-faced, bald, fifty-seven, and he wore glasses.

"Are you an evolutionist?" Darrow asked him.

"Certainly," Professor Metcalf said, nodding. Darrow asked the witness if he knew any other scientists who were evolutionists.

Stewart objected. That was hearsay. Judge Raulston sustained the objection. Hays took exception. "Hearsay testimony is allowed in cases where it is a question of how a scientific theory is substantiated," Hays stated. "Our whole case depends upon proving that evolution is a reasonable scientific theory."

Judge Raulston suggested a compromise. He instructed the professor to answer softly so that the jury, court stenographers, and the press couldn't hear him.

Darrow asked Professor Metcalf to define evolution. District Attorney General Stewart objected. That testimony would be out of bounds.

Darrow responded. The jury needed to know what evolution was before they could rule on whether Scopes taught a theory that conflicted with any divine story of creation, he explained. Stewart emphatically disagreed. The sole issue in the trial was whether Scopes had broken the law. Pure and simple. Stewart insisted that the jurors should not hear any testimony about evolution.

Judge Raulston said he'd like to listen to Professor Metcalf so that he could be better qualified to rule on the admissibility of expert evidence but, agreeing with Stewart, he asked the jury to leave the courtroom. He also asked them not to linger outside within earshot of the testimony being broadcast through the loudspeakers. Captain Jack Thompson, the jury foreman who had asked for electric fans, assured the judge that none of them had been listening to anything.

With the jury gone, Darrow guided Professor Metcalf's testimony through a series of questions that, together, would put a basic definition of evolution into the record.

Metcalf explained that evolution generally meant the change of an organism with one set of characteristics to another organism with a different set of characteristics.

As for whether the scientific community accepted the theory of evolution, Metcalf said, "I am absolutely convinced from personal knowledge that any one of these men"—the zoologists, botanists, and geologists of this country who have materially contributed to those fields—"feel and believe, as a matter of course, that evolution is a fact."

Of course, Metcalf added, he doubted that any two scientists could completely agree on the exact method by which evolution was brought about.

Bryan leaned forward in his seat. "It would be entirely impossible, for any human being," Metcalf concluded, "to have even for a moment the least doubt even for the fact of evolution, but he might have tremendous doubt as to the truth of any hypothesis—as to the methods of the evolution which this or that or the other man—even great men of science—might bring up."

Darrow asked Metcalf when life first appeared. Alluding to the number that the biblical literalists used, Darrow prompted, perhaps six thousand years ago? Bryan leaned forward again.

Darrow understood, just as Stewart and McKenzie understood, that the mere fact of Bryan's presence in the courtroom, his public statements outside the courtroom before and during the trial, and his insistence that the trial would be a duel to the death contradicted the prosecution's claim that this was a simple case of John Scopes breaking a Tennessee law. The more than one hundred journalists in Dayton and the photographers and cartoonists and cameramen knew that William Jennings Bryan, the Prince of Peace, had come to Tennessee as the "Fundamentalist pope" (or so Mencken dubbed him) with a larger purpose in mind: that duel to the death during which he would vanquish atheists and agnostics and wishy-washy church liberals, all of them, and reaffirm Christianity as he understood and practiced it, as a biblical literalism that brooked no other interpretation and which he declared superior to all other faiths.

Professor Metcalf returned to Darrow's question: When did he estimate that life first appeared? Metcalf said he figured more than six hundred million years ago, not a mere six thousand.

Bryan was not pleased. His face was drawn, his mouth set. But he bided his time.

Mencken watched him closely. "It is a tragedy indeed to begin life as a hero and to end it as a buffoon," he observed. But underestimate the Prince of Peace at your peril. "In Tennessee he is drilling his army," Mencken cannily noted. "The big battles, he believes, will be fought elsewhere." Likely, in the halls of the United States Congress.

Chapter Sixteen

The Fear

INSIDE THE COURTROOM, CLARENCE DARROW sat at the defense table drinking some kind of red soda pop while he opened the mail that a postal clerk had dumped there, piles and piles of it, on the morning of Thursday, July 16. He wore a small blue lapel pin engraved with the letters "L.L.L." They stood for "live and let live," he told a reporter.

Darrow wanted to continue questioning Professor Metcalf, but when District Attorney General Stewart had objected, again the jury was asked to leave the room. After some wrangling over technical matters, Judge Raulston sententiously reminded Darrow and the defense team that the court sought only "light and truth." He certainly didn't want the counsel "from foreign states" to feel mistreated.

The real issue at hand was the admissibility of the scientific evidence, and Bryan's son, not Bryan, was to lead the argument against allowing any of it. Tall like his father, William Jennings Bryan Jr. did not look like a leader of the common folk. With his striped flannel pants, blue coat, horn-rimmed glasses, and razor-thin mustache, he belonged in a glossy fashion magazine, not a broiling Tennessee courtroom. And he had a soft speaking voice, made more inaudible by a head cold. Bryan Jr. would not be running for president.

Bryan Jr. maintained that Scopes had broken the law. No one needed an expert to demonstrate that. Permitting expert testimony would "announce to the world Your Honor's belief that this jury is too stupid to determine a simple question of fact."

Scientists who volunteered to testify, Dayton. BACK ROW, LEFT TO RIGHT: Horatio Hackett Newman, Maynard Mayo Metcalf, Fay-Cooper Cole, Jacob Goodale Lipman FRONT ROW, LEFT TO RIGHT: Winterton Conway Curtis, Wilbur A. Nelson, William Marion Goldsmith
COURTESY SCIENCE SERVICE, RECORDS, SMITHSONIAN INSTITUTION ARCHIVES

After a fifteen-minute recess, Hays answered Bryan Jr. These are expert witnesses who have traveled to Dayton, Tennessee, in the interest of science to speak about science. How can it be dangerous to admit the opinions of scientific men? There aren't two sides to the scientific questions posed, and the witnesses were not coming to this court to provide opinions. They would supply facts. "Who is afraid of a statement of facts?" Hays asked, disingenuously.

Hays distinguished between evolution, meaning change in species over time, and natural selection, the way this change may have occurred—the occurrence, say, of random mutations that allowed a species to prosper and then the passing on of that mutation through successive generations. That is, natural selection might have been the mechanism by which evolution occurred, or it might not have. In other words, natural selection could be discredited without in the least undermining the legitimacy of evolution.

This is what Professor Metcalf had said. Unfortunately, though, Hays pointed out that people who don't believe in evolution are confused and don't understand the difference between evolution and the way it may have come about.

Why wouldn't the court want to know that? It would be the same if an engineer came to testify how an elevator works—its mechanism—and not whether that elevator happened to crash because of negligence.

As for the prosecution's claim that any boy of sixteen can understand the anti-evolution law, it's also true that no one here seems to understand it.

And let's not forget William Jennings Bryan had said this was to be a duel to the death, which suggested that he would refute the scientists. So let the scientists have their say.

MORE WRANGLING. The prosecution contended that the experts didn't believe in God. Malone sharply asked how the prosecution knew what the experts believed.

Speaking on behalf of the prosecution, Herbert Hicks, the brother of Sue Hicks, claimed that scientific experts would usurp the role of the jury. "The issue of fact for the jury to determine is whether or not Professor Scopes taught man descended from the lower order of animals. Now, if Your Honor is going to permit [the defense] to make a special issue of these experts, if you are going to permit them to come in here as a secondary jury, which they are endeavoring to do, that is an unheard of procedure in the courts of Tennessee." This is a court of law. He sarcastically added that if the defense wanted to "make a school down here in Tennessee to educate our poor ignorant people, let them establish a school."

The prosecution's hostility was on full display especially because they believed, and weren't entirely wrong, that they were disrespected by "these foreign gentlemen" from the North. "The most ignorant man of Tennessee is a highly educated, polished gentleman compared to the most ignorant man in some of our northern states," Hicks indignantly exclaimed. "The ignorant man of Tennessee is a man without an opportunity, but the men in our northern states, the northern man in some of our larger northern cities, have the opportunity without the brain."

Loud laughter.

"We have done crossed the Rubicon," Ben McKenzie was yelling. Round-shouldered McKenzie had come to act the part of the gray-haired, down-home Tennessee lawyer, sharp and unpretentious. But he too was losing his down-home temper. The court had ruled the Tennessee law constitutional. There was nothing to add.

Plus, God created Adam first as a complete man, McKenzie reminded the court: "The cell of life" didn't develop over time. McKenzie thumped the table with his fist. "Man did not descend from a lower order of animals that originated in the sea and then turned from one animal to another and finally man's head shot up."

And what did the defense want to do, these foreigners who'd invaded Tennessee? Well, they wanted to "prove by the mouth of their scientist," McKenzie raged, motioning toward the defense, "they want to put words into God's mouth, and have Him to say that He issued some sort of protoplasm, or soft dish rag, and put it in the ocean and said, " 'Old boy, if you wait around 6,000 years, I will make something out of you.' "

More loud laughter.

Darrow interrupted. "When it said, 'in His own image,' did you think that meant the physical man?"

He sure did, answered McKenzie. "'He is like unto me.'"

"I say they are seeking to put words into the mouth of God," McKenzie said, turning back to the judge, "and substitute another story, entirely different to God's word."

With that, it seemed that now Ben McKenzie himself was going beyond the question of whether Scopes broke the law.

The quarrel went on, but Judge Raulston wanted to recess because ceiling fans were to be installed during the lunch hour.

THE REVEREND Thomas W. Callaway of the Baptist Tabernacle in Chattanooga arrived in Dayton, where he saw a woman pushing a monkey on a little tricycle down Main Street. The monkey was dressed up as a little boy. "What a travesty upon true womanhood and motherhood," the horrified pastor exclaimed in horrified disgust.

"Giant intellectuals of the north," Reverend Callaway angrily added, "can come south, suggesting entire revolutions in our educational system, shed their crocodile tears over the poor ignorant southerner, preach their doctrine of universal brotherhood of man with social equality for the down-trodden negro, and then humiliate both the white and black races of the south by bringing into its midst a little black monkey to show its kinship to the bushman of Africa."

Callaway was so upset that he contacted the Reverend George Washington Sandefur, a Black minister, of the Memorial Baptist Church, who was attending the trial. How did Sandefur's Black congregation feel about all this nonsense, these carpetbaggers, these humiliations, Callaway asked. Don't worry, Sandefur soothingly replied. "These evolutionists try to make us believe that the whites not only have negro blood in their veins coming from the bushmen of Africa, but even down to the ape and tad-pole of the cesspool. It's too much for me."

The Reverend Calloway took comfort. "The Christian edu-cated negroes of the south are getting their eyes open," Reverend Sandefur continued to reassure him. "The thinking negro knows that it is Christ of Christianity that has emancipated him from human and spiritual bondage." Then he added, "The negro commends William Jennings Bryan for his solid stand."

But, as yet, during the trial Bryan had not broken his silence. Spectators had sat, day after sultry day, often with a Bible open on their laps, waiting for William Jennings Bryan, the former Secretary of State, the former Boy Orator, to vanquish his op-ponents with the good book and his silvery voice. It was in fact rumored he might speak on Thursday.

Bryan had dressed that morning in a white shirt and soft col-lar although many, and not just Mencken, had noticed a hard-ness in his dark eyes and a grimness to the set of his mouth. "It is anything but a weak face," Marcet Haldeman-Julius observed. "But it is a face from which one could expect neither under-standing nor pity."

Bryan flapped his red-bordered palm-leaf fan to provide a bit of relief. In front of him sat a large granite jug of water. He took a long drink before walking to the center of the courtroom, in front of the judge's bench and between the two long tables where opposing lawyers hunched over their papers.

"We are now approaching the end, and I have not thought it proper to take part in the discussion up to this time," Bryan modestly began. After all, he was not well versed in the state laws that were being discussed.

Still, the issue was clear. If the court ruled against allowing expert testimony, the trial would soon be over, and as far as he was concerned, it should be.

The people of Tennessee understood the danger of evolution

and passed a law to protect their children, and experts had no right to come to Tennessee and say this law should never have been passed. How dare they? He appealed to local pride.

And to the democratic majority. Can a minority force a teacher to teach that the Bible is not true and take religion out of the hearts of children? Are we supposed to believe that humans come "from below"? Christians believe that humans come from above, which is to say God. Bryan seized Hunter's *A Civic Biology*, opened it, and displayed a table illustrating the number of types in each species.

"There's the book they're teaching your children," Bryan said, raising his voice. "Find him among the mammals with thirty-four hundred and ninety-nine other mammals." Laughter and applause.

"How dare those scientists put man in a little ring like that—with lions and tigers and everything that is bad!" he shouted. "These animals that have an odor."

Man was no malodorous mammal.

Laughter, lots of it. Malone's mouth fell open. Stewart looked uneasy.

What were experts, anyway? Referring to Professor Metcalf, with his "number of degrees," Bryan said, with an odd defensiveness, "he did not shame me, for I have more than he has, but I can understand how my friends felt when he unrolled degree after degree."

But, and here was the point, with all those fancy degrees, "Did he tell you how life began? Not a word."

"An expert cannot be permitted to come in here and try to defeat the enforcement of a law," Bryan continued. Of course that was not what the defense had maintained, nor was it the purpose of expert testimony, but to Bryan the desire to challenge the law had come from New York and Chicago, and it was those big-city lawyers who dared to tell the people of Tennessee how to live. What if Tennessee had sent lawyers and witnesses to New

York to block the repeal of Prohibition? Wouldn't this kind of interference be regarded as an insult?

He called on mothers and fathers. "Tell me the parents of this day have not any right to declare that children are not to be taught this doctrine." He was shouting again, perspiration speckling his brow.

He stirred up anxiety and a sense of dislocation. "Shall he be detached from the throne of God and be compelled to link their ancestors with the jungle?" He appealed to white nationalism. To think that man is supposedly linked to monkeys—he was still waving Hunter's *A Civic Biology*—"not even from American monkeys, but from old world monkeys." Appreciative laughter.

"They want to come in with their little padded up evolution that commences with nothing and ends nowhere," Bryan charged. "They do not dare to tell you that it ended with God."

"They shut God out of the world," he said, stifling a sob. He was inspired, inspiring, evangelistic, and wholly moved by his own oratory.

Judge Raulston interrupted. He had a question. Wouldn't evolution be "reconcilable" with the Bible if it was "admitted that God created the cell?" It was a good question.

Bryan dodged. "There would be no contention about that, but our contention is, even if they put God back there, it does not make it harmonious with the Bible."

He insisted that half the scientists in America didn't believe in God or immortality. Evolution disputes the principle of the Virgin birth. It disputes miracles. It robs children of their savior and of heaven. It robs them of moral standards. "It is this doctrine that gives us Nietzsche," Bryan declared, "who tried to carry this to its logical conclusion."

That brought Bryan to Nathan Leopold and Richard Loeb's vicious murder of Bobby Franks. Pointing a finger at Darrow, their defense attorney, Bryan held up a copy of the speech that Darrow had delivered at their trial. "We have the testimony of my distinguished friend from Chicago," Bryan continued, "pleading that because Leopold read Nietzsche and adopted Nietzsche's philosophy of the superman, that he is not responsible for the taking of human life."

Darrow objected.

But Bryan read from Darrow's speech. " 'Is there any blame attached because somebody took Nietzsche's philosophy seriously and fashioned his life on it?' " Bryan quoted Darrow. " 'Who is to blame? The university would be more to blame than he is. The scholars of the world would be more to blame than he is. The publishers of the world—and Nietzsche's books are published by one of the biggest publishers in the world—are more to blame than he.' "

Darrow shook his head and again objected. "These two people," Darrow explained, "were insane." Besides, Bryan was not reading the whole of what Darrow argued in that Chicago trial, and anyway the argument from another case had been introduced merely to prejudice the judge.

"No, sir," replied Judge Raulston. "It does not prejudice me."

"Then it does not do any good," Darrow countered with a half smile. The courtroom tittered.

Darrow then added Nietzsche was not connected to a university and did not preach any doctrine of evolution. He had merely said that Darwin had a great mind. Darrow read the parts of his speech at the Leopold and Loeb trial that Bryan had ignored.

Bryan was unperturbed. Nietzsche had died insane, and he drove others insane, and his supermen were the logical outgrowth of the survival of the fittest, which was the logical outcome of evolution, Bryan added, as if to settle the matter.

"He didn't make half as many insane men as Jonathan Edwards, your great theologian," Darrow retorted.

Bryan returned to his argument. "The Bible is the Word of God," he plaintively cried. "The Bible is the only expression of man's hope of salvation."

Neither the Bible nor the Word of God should be driven from the court by experts who have come from afar to humiliate the great state of Tennessee and its great, God-fearing people.

Bryan's arms were outstretched as he delivered his summary. He mopped his brow. "I never saw him quite so agitated," Mary Bryan told her children. "He trembled when he stood up."

Something was missing. "Once the voice had in it the qualities of brazen trumpets, but the resonance had gone from the brass," a reporter eulogized. "Once it had the booming note of the drum, but today the drum showed that it had been punctured in many places and its hollowness was evident."

Still, there was warm applause and an occasional "amen," which Darrow, laughing, asked reporters to make sure they put in the record.

"I DEFY ANYBODY, after Mr. Bryan's speech, to believe that this was not a religious question."

Dudley Field Malone was now speaking. He had finally succumbed to the heat and removed his suit jacket, which he carefully folded and deliberately placed on the table. He was the surprise of the trial, this proud Irish Catholic urbanite in the double-breasted suit, immaculate day after day no matter the heat and humidity, his blue eyes twinkling, his manners exemplary. His voice rang as true as Bryan's, with as much force, fire, and fluency—and as much simplicity. Those who heard Malone that day admitted that he outshone, outspoke, outclassed Bryan, his former boss, not just in volume but in eloquence and fervor.

He started to talk in almost hushed tones but, before long, as Mencken recalled, "with his own naked voice he filled the big room with so vast and terrifying a din that it seemed almost to bulge the wall."

"What is the issue that has gained the attention not only of the American people, but people everywhere?" Malone asked.

"Is it a mere technical question as to whether the defendant Scopes taught the paragraph in the book of science?" Of course it was not. The matter at hand was not the brainchild of some so-called foreigners come to Tennessee to interfere with its citizens. If that was the case, then William Jennings Bryan of Florida had no more right to be in Tennessee than he had.

No, the issue was America. And we are American citizens. Our freedom is at stake.

"This issue is as wide as Mr. Bryan has made it," Malone adding, more in sorrow than anger, that once a fearless man, Mr. Bryan seems suddenly afraid. Mr. Bryan is afraid to face facts. "Whether Mr. Bryan knows it or not," Malone said, half laughing, "he is a mammal, he is an animal, and he is a man."

But why be afraid? "Why the fear?" Malone asked again. "My old chief—I never saw him back away from a great issue before."

Malone knew what the fear had to be. It was the fear of the new, the different, the fear that if you admit knowledge or information, the world as you know it would turn unrecognizable, alien, and terrifying. Malone spoke of the war, which had also been terrifying, with its twenty million dead. "Civilization is not so proud of the world of the adults."

We should provide the youth of this generation information—data, theories, learning—so that they might make a better world of this one than the hash we've made of it.

So let the jury hear evidence. Wasn't it their right to hear evidence? "We want everything we have to say on religion and on science told."

"I believe that if they withdrew their objection," Malone then said of the prosecution, "and hear the evidence of our experts, their minds would not only be improved but their souls would be purified." There was nothing to fear.

He himself was in front of the court, he said, his very presence offering proof that one could believe in both God and science. He did.

He said he firmly believed that neither teachers nor scientists in America sought to destroy the morals of children, children to whom they'd dedicated their lives. It is in poor taste, Malone continued, for the leader of the prosecution to cast aspersions on teachers—the poorest-paid professionals in America—or anyone who has given their whole lives to teaching or to God.

But the Bible was not to be taken literally as science. Let the youth of the country then have science and theology; let them have both; let them love both, let them revere both.

Malone continued, adding that the defense has a right to call witnesses to show that there's more than one theory of creation in the Bible.

"Mr. Bryan is not the only one who has spoken for the Bible," Malone observed. "McKenzie is not the only defender of the word of God."

And, Malone added, Bryan was a politician, not a preacher. "Mr. Bryan, to my knowledge, with a very passionate spirit and enthusiasm, has given most of his life to politics," Malone pointedly said.

As far as any "duel to the death" was concerned, Malone said, half in jest, he knew very little about dueling; it's against the law of God and the church and of Tennessee.

He turned very serious. "There is never a duel with the truth," Malone said, raising his voice.

"The truth always wins, and we are not afraid of it. The truth is no coward. The truth does not need the law."

"The truth does not need Mr. Bryan."

Bryan glowered.

"The truth is imperishable, eternal, and immortal and needs no human agency to support it." Malone again raised the volume.

"We are ready. We are ready. We feel we stand with progress. We feel we stand with science. We feel we stand with intelligence. We feel we stand with fundamental freedom in America. We are not afraid.

"Where is the fear? We meet it. Where is the fear? We defy it," he finished. "We ask Your Honor to admit the evidence of the scientists as a matter of correct law, and a matter of sound procedure, and as a matter of justice to the defense in this case."

AFTER AN INSTANT of spellbound silence, applause rocked the courtroom. Men leaped from their seats. Dudley Field Malone was no longer the Paris and New York divorce lawyer, no longer the foppish materialist of the East in a silk shirt. The bailiff rapped a stick on the judge's desk, but the bailiff was cheering too. Men and women rushed forward to shake Malone's hand, not just supporters but those who had come to jeer. They had been dazzled. One reporter put it best: "The speech of Dudley Field Malone was a wow."

"Great God!" Darrow whispered to Mencken, who was sitting nearby. "The scoundrel will hang the jury!" Malone had been so good, he feared, that there'd be no verdict.

John Scopes saw tragedy written all over Bryan's face.

"Dudley," Bryan said, turning to Malone, "that was the greatest speech I have ever heard!"

"Thank you, Mr. Bryan," Malone replied, subdued. "I am sorry it was I who had to make it."

Malone left the defense table to pick his way through the crowd. He kissed the hand of Doris Stevens, who had extended it. She and Malone had been on the verge of divorce just before the trial, and they would divorce by the end of the decade. In Dayton, though, there was no sign of a rift. Evenings they were together at the Mansion, where the scientists were staying. And she'd been delighted by Malone's great speech. Malone had been wonderful, instructive, stirring. Mencken thought so too. "These Tennessee mountaineers are not more stupid than the city proletariat; they are only less informed," he decided.

"If Darrow, Malone, and Hays could make a month's stumping tour," Mencken observed, "fully a fourth of the population would repudiate fundamentalism."

COURT WOULD NOT be adjourned until District Attorney General A. Thomas Stewart refuted Malone and the entire defense.

"I don't believe that I came from the same cell with the monkey and the ass," Stewart began. He was then ready to leap into the literal reading of the law in much the same way Bryan had offered a literal reading of the Bible. As far as he was concerned, the Tennessee legislature knew precisely what it was doing when it passed the anti-evolution law. Slapping a fist on the table where the reporters furiously scribbled shorthand, Stewart insisted that the legislature was sovereign, that Tennessee was sovereign; that the state could interpret the Bible as it saw fit; and if there was a battle between religion and science, he stood four-square with religion.

"I want to know beyond this world that there may be an eternal happiness for me and for all," he bellowed.

"I say, bar the door, and not allow science to enter. That would deprive us of all the hope we have in the future to come. And I say it without any bitterness." He turned to Darrow. "Mr. Darrow says he is an agnostic. He is the greatest criminal lawyer in America today. His courtesy is noticeable—his ability is known—and it is a shame, in my mind, in the sight of a great God, that a mentality like his has strayed so far from the natural goal that it should follow—great God, the good that a man of his ability could have done if he had aligned himself with the forces of right instead of aligning himself with that which strikes its fangs at the very bosom of Christianity."

Science had fangs, Stewart continued. Science is the serpent come to tempt us, to lure us into nothingness. If you admit scientific evidence, the next thing you know is that someone will raise some objection to the idea that Jesus Christ was the son of God or that there was a Virgin birth. And if you object to that, you will soon object to the right to teach the resurrection, and after that, you will let the Bible be taken away from us.

"The great general of the southern Confederacy, Robert E. Lee," Stewart concluded with a flourish, "prayed to God before each battle and yet here we have a test by science that challenges the right to open the court with a prayer to God." His arms and face pointed heavenward, as if to call down battalions of Confederates to repel the invaders and save Tennessee—or the entire South—from the great serpent.

What had begun in a legal argument ended in a sectional sermon.

As if he'd heard nothing, Arthur Hays politely interrupted, asking if the defense shouldn't have a chance to present their scientific evidence. Stewart responded curtly. "If Your Honor please, that charge strikes at the very vitals of civilization and of Christianity, and is not entitled to a chance."

Spectators heartily applauded, Bryan flapped his palm-leaf fan, but it was Dudley Field Malone who had carried the day.

Chapter Seventeen

It Is In

CLARENCE DARROW HEADED BACK TO the Mansion that Thursday afternoon to remind the scientists that "today we have won, but by tomorrow the judge will have recovered and will rule against us. I want each one of you to go to the stenographer's room the first thing in the morning and prepare a statement for the press, saying what you would have said if allowed to testify in court."

THE NEXT MORNING, Friday, July 17, was cloudless and warm when Judge Raulston delivered his ruling on the admissibility of expert scientific witnesses.

Darrow had been right. Judge Raulston would not allow the scientists to take the stand. Metcalf had been enough. The Tennessee law was unambiguous, Raulston announced. He read from the first section of the statute. "The ordinary, no-expert mind can comprehend the simple language, 'descended from a lower order of animals,'" Judge Raulston declared, referring to the language of the law.

Irrelevantly, he added that "I believe evolutionists should at least show man the consideration to substitute the word 'ascend' for the word 'descend.'"

"This is the end of our attempt to have a trial," John Neal muttered.

Mary Bryan was pleased. "As matters now stand," she told her family, "the case is clearly lost by the defense, and the trial will probably end Monday or Tuesday."

Bryan too was satisfied.

Hays took predictable exception to Judge Raulston's ruling. The court was assuming knowledge about science that it couldn't possibly have.

Stewart took exception to the exception, as if defending the honor of the court.

Darrow was furious. "The state of Tennessee don't rule the world yet," he barked. With barely controlled contempt, he noted that he rather doubted the scientists would "correct" the word "descent." "I want to explain what descent means, as starting with a low form of life and finally reaching man."

"We all have dictionaries," Stewart replied with bite.

Judge Raulston also bristled. "I think the court understands some things as well as the scientists."

Arthur Hays intervened to mollify the judge. He praised Raulston's open mind. He said that the defense wished merely to put into the record the scientific evidence that the experts would have offered. That way, a higher court, should an appeal go there, might decide if Judge Raulston had ruled correctly. And of course Judge Raulston would want that.

That seemed to calm Stewart too, who consented to let the testimony of scientists be admitted by affidavit. Raulston agreed.

But Bryan asked if the prosecution could cross-examine. You don't cross-examine evidence, Darrow impatiently replied, and you don't cross-examine anything with the jury absent. All the defense wanted to do was enlighten the court, and if that doesn't enlighten the court, no cross-examination by Bryan would do that.

Judge Raulston asked if the purpose of cross-examination wasn't an effort to ascertain truth.

"No," Darrow shot back. "It is an effort to show prejudice." The spectators in the large room laughed.

As Hays later admitted, allowing the prosecution to cross-examine the expert witnesses might have proved dangerous. The scientists were religious, to be sure, but they may have admitted they didn't believe in such miracles as the Virgin birth. The defense did not want to go there. "It was felt by us that if the cause of free education was ever to be won," he later recalled, "it would need the support of millions of intelligent churchgoing people who didn't question theological miracles."

Raulston agreed to the affidavits. He would decide about how exactly they might be entered into the record later. But he was reluctant to allow the defense the rest of the day to prepare their statements. Darrow lost his temper again. "I don't understand why every request of the state is granted and our merest suggestion overruled."

Raulston seemed taken aback. He considered himself a fair man. "I hope you don't mean to reflect on the court," he replied.

Darrow rocked on his heels. "Your Honor has a right to hope," he growled.

An arctic chill passed through the hot, tense courtroom.

"The court has a right to do something else, too," Judge Raulston snapped. His florid face lost its color.

"All right; all right," Darrow answered. He pulled at his suspenders. Raulston backed off and gave the defense witnesses the day to prepare their affidavits.

"I hate to lose the time," Raulston said, "but justice is more important than time."

Court had been in session only an hour.

.   .   .

JOHN WASHINGTON BUTLER, the state representative who had first proposed the anti-evolution law, was disappointed that the testimony of scientific experts had been excluded. "I'd like to have heard the evidence," he said. "It would have been right smart of an education to hear those fellows who have studied the subject."

Despite the ruling, Scopes was hopeful. "People who have never thought before are now beginning to think," he told reporters.

Science writer Watson Davis was hopeful too but to a lesser extent. He'd come to Dayton assuming that the trial would be a kind of sideshow, and though it was clearly not, he felt that scientists and political progressives should heed it well. "Just as a World War seemed impossible in 1913," Davis warned, "so Fundamentalism by law, stifling freedom of thought, may seem impossible now."

But Malone was fuming. He who had spoken passionately about the freedom to learn noted that the jury had been consistently excluded from the courtroom. They hadn't heard the arguments. They'd been excused, time after time, when the lawyers argued about procedure or about whether to admit the testimony of experts or whether to hear the defense explain the Bible. They'd been in the courtroom for about three hours, total, and for the rest, they had access to the case only through newspapers, radio, and the loudspeakers on the lawn. So if Bryan and the prosecution were ultimately to win, it would be a technical victory, based on legal wrangling, and not a moral one.

Darrow was frustrated too. Testimony from expert witnesses would have been allowed if Mr. Bryan had not done everything in his power to prevent it. It was one thing to preach against evolution. It was another to stand up against eminent scientists and theologians. Anyone coming to Dayton to see a knockdown fight—a duel—between Bryan and the evolutionists had to be sorely disappointed. For Bryan had ducked. "Bryan, who blew loud trumpet calls for a 'battle to the death' has fled from the field, his forces disorganized, and his pretentions exposed," Darrow told the press.

No doubt about it, Bryan had damaged his prestige. Many of the spectators were frustrated not to have heard the scientists testify—though not because they'd have believed them. "They expect Bryan to eat the scientists alive," a reporter remarked. "Now it looks to them like he is running away."

Bryan disagreed. He saw himself, still, at the vanguard of a movement that "uncovered the conspiracy against Biblical Christianity."

Mencken agreed with Mary Bryan. To him, the judge's decision to exclude the testimony of the scientists meant the trial was basically over. "Holy Church is everywhere triumphant," Mencken confided to his fiancée. Shrugging, he packed up his portable typewriter and decided to leave town the next day. "All that remains of the great cause of the State of Tennessee against the infidel Scopes," he said in print, "is the formal business of bumping off the defendant."

DORIS STEVENS WAS curious about Bryan: Why had he come to Dayton, what was he up to, what was he planning to do next, she wondered. She sought him out for an interview. He greeted her with one of his electric smiles, and when she asked if he was the one who'd initiated the anti-evolution law in Tennessee, he humbly said that his Nashville speech, "Is the Bible True?" may have had an influence. It had been widely distributed.

He was of course interested in the Scopes case. "Nearly twenty-five years ago," he explained, "after my first nomination, I spoke often at colleges throughout the United States and became increasingly impressed with the chilling influence on students." He was referring to what he called the "fundamental theory of evolution" which, he said, claimed "man had reached his present position by a cruel law under which the strong kill off the weak."

"How did this chilling influence manifest?" Stevens asked.

"In talking with them I found lessened spiritual enthusiasm," Bryan replied. Then there was the war. And Nietzsche. "During the war I became more and more impressed with the idea that Nietzsche's philosophy had something to do with the war. I purchased several of his books, five, I think, and read them. So convinced was I that his philosophy had an important part in bringing on the war, that in January 1919, I delivered an address, 'Back to God,' in which I spoke more extensively than I had before. From that time on I enlarged upon my criticism of evolution."

But Stevens wanted to know how and when the Commoner came to advocate *legislation* banning the teaching of evolution. He didn't quite answer. "Naturally I have advocated legislation forbidding the teaching of evolution as fact in schools supported by taxation," he said, "and I have also advocated elimination of teaching of evolution as a fact in religious schools."

Stevens pressed him. The Tennessee law prevented teaching of evolution as a theory, not as a fact, she said.

"I wish you would not stress that point," Bryan said, growing irritable. "I would not have the people think I did not support this law."

She changed the subject. "Do you think the time will come, Mr. Bryan, when fundamentalist belief will be the issue put to candidates as was the wet and dry issue in recent campaigns?"

"I prefer to let the opposition prophesy," Bryan said, sidestepping the question.

"But it can hardly now be kept out of politics," she pointed out.

The broad smile returned. "It is in," he vowed.

. . .

"HE COULD HAVE answered my question with a flat 'no,'" Stevens said. "Or he could have said he would lament such a situation. He did neither. He left me with no doubt that he intends to try to use it politically."

There was no doubt at all. "It is in."

Bryan may not be able to swing his own nomination for president, but at the next Democratic National Convention, Stevens wagered, this evangelical power broker could fuse church and partisan politics into a gigantic national revival, with the campaign managers recruited from firebrands like Reverend John Roach Straton and Billy Sunday.

Chapter Eighteen

Come Unto Me

THE PENTECOSTAL RELIGIOUS SECT POPULARLY known as Holy Rollers met out in the open, beneath the arc of heaven, where they worshipped God directly through singing and dancing, speaking in tongues, and falling to the ground in a kind of trance.

Learning they were encamped not far from town, Henry Mencken and a few other reporters had driven there about four miles from Dayton and quietly walked over to the huge tree where, under the glow of torchlights, they saw women and men seated on a series of crude benches arranged in a circle near two huge elms. There were about one hundred of them.

Their preacher was Joe Leffew, lean and long and sandy-haired, who looked a bit like Abraham Lincoln except for his light blue eyes. During the war Leffew had been a conscientious objector, and ever since he had been denouncing violence and bloodshed and government.

There would be no lawyers, doctors, courts, newspapers, or presidents in heaven, Leffew cried. The Lord took care of him—and all people—he said, for he knew that for salvation, you had only to know God's word, which would be revealed to anyone who sought it.

A tall woman stood. Everything she needed to know was in

the Bible, she said. It was the one true book. Education was a snare, Leffew agreed. That way lay damnation. "I ain't got no learnin's an' never had none." He paced back and forth, swinging his arms. "Glory be to the Lamb! Some folks work their hands off'n up 'n the elbows to give their young-uns education, and all they do is send their young-uns to hell."

The men and women sang, and when the singing ended, a young girl with bobbed blond hair came forward. "This sinner has asked for prayers," said Brother Leffew. Everyone huddled around, praying and dropping to their knees until Leffew too knelt, falling into a kind of trance while unintelligible words "spouted from his lips," Mencken said, "like bullets from a machine gun."

With some disgust, Mencken described the "barbaric grotesquerie," by which he meant the singing, convulsing, and shrieking of the group that said their belief had no name. More sympathetic, Darrow too visited their encampment. He and his wife, Ruby; Dudley Malone and Doris Stevens; two reporters; and three of the scientists staying at the Mansion found them in that same grove of trees. Under the spreading branches of the huge elm, some sixty men and women sat illumined by the glow of barn lanterns and miners' lamps. The women rocked back and forth cradling their babies in their arms, their hands gnarled, their faces leathery.

Joe Leffew came forward, his voice robust and strong. "Out of the Fourteenth Psalm of David, I read: 'The fool hath said in his heart, there is no God.' How many within the hearing of my voice hath said that?"

"I have never said that," Darrow whispered to his wife.

There would be no lawyers in heaven, Leffew said again.

Women jumped and screamed, seeming to be in a state of self-hypnosis, and as Darrow watched them sing and stamp their feet, he murmured again and again, "It is all they have. It is all they have." These were among the poorest people in the state.

They shared their food, they hated war, they taught brotherly love. "These people are sincere," he remarked. "They seek no money, no fame. Bryan should come here instead of I. He would learn much.

"They are better than Bryan," Darrow continued. "They at least don't demand that anyone join them. They leave other people alone and their church is free."

"Take heed of hypocrites," another one of the group shouted. "There are some among ye who talk of the Bible who in their hearts are enemies of God."

"True, eternally true," Darrow said.

A reporter turned to Darrow and asked if he'd ever seen a performance like the one before him. "Yes," he softly replied, a gleam in his eye, "in the courtroom."

It started to rain. The worshippers didn't care. They continued to pray. Darrow and his friends rushed to their cars and, during the ride back to town, none of them spoke. Russell Owen, the reporter from *The New York Times*, said there was nothing to say. "We had been looking at the release of emotions that we could not understand."

THERE WERE TWO different worlds, the one huddled under the spreading branches of the elm trees, and the other at the Mansion where, over the weekend, Darrow had brought in stenographers, typewriters, and an old mimeograph machine at his own expense. The scientists were preparing their statements, with copies for the press.

In addition to that of Professor Maynard Metcalf, who had already testified, there were seven other sworn statements: from Horatio Hackett Newman (University of Chicago, dean, embryologist); Fay-Cooper Cole (University of Chicago, anthropology); Winterton Curtis (University of Missouri, invertebrate zoology); Jacob Lipman (Rutgers College, agricultural chemist);

Charles Hubbard Judd (University of Chicago, former president of the American Psychological Association); Wilbur A. Nelson (state geologist, Tennessee); and Kirtley Mather, head of the geology department at Harvard University.

These statements were intended to provide a definition of the theory of evolution and its significance from the vantage point of their respective fields. Yet before they could be entered into evidence, there was another scrimmage between the prosecution and the defense. Despite District Attorney General Stewart's objection, Hays read from a new biology textbook, *Biology and Human Welfare,* which had recently been authorized by the state. As Hays pointed out, the textbook praised Darwin's *Origin of Species* as "epoch-making" and even displayed a picture of Charles Darwin. His point: you can't teach biology without teaching something about Darwin and evolution, as Scopes had said. And he repeated his claim that the Tennessee anti-evolution law was therefore at the very least unreasonable—if not unconstitutional.

Hays wasn't finished. He'd learned that evidence could be entered into the record in a Tennessee court in three different ways: by calling a witness; by telling the court what you intend to prove; or by composing an affidavit and presenting it to the opposing counsel. Since it was up to the defense to decide which method it preferred, Hays said they had chosen the third option: to read from the sworn statements, which would define evolution and demonstrate that it did not conflict with Genesis. "I don't say that will be convincing to Your Honor, but I suggest we want to prove it," Hays noted, "on the ground that after hearing the evidence, Your Honor might change your opinion as to the reasonableness of this law."

Stewart, livid, did not want the statements from the scientists read in open court, even if the jury wasn't present. Just put them in the record. No reason to read anything aloud.

"I like to try my case in open court," Hays countered.

Stewart knew what the defense was trying to do. The defense would stage a performance directed at the press and the radio audience. "There could be no purpose in reading the sworn statements, or making the statement in open court to this crowd, the people here, except for the purpose of furthering its educational campaign as they call it, or spreading propaganda, as I call it," he protested.

Stewart didn't quite persuade Judge Raulston since Raulston had to admit that reading the statements aloud would "relieve the court of a great amount of work." That is, he could simply listen to them.

Stewart pointed out it would take two or three days to read the statements.

"Justice is more important than time," Hays helpfully added.

Raulston was flummoxed. "In my practice we have not had a big case like this," he said.

Bryan interjected. He wanted to rebut the scientific statements if they were read out loud. That was too much for Darrow, who said no lawyer would ever think that proper—to rebut sworn evidence that was being entered into the record. He was insinuating that Bryan was not a lawyer, though he was.

The courtroom was silent; the atmosphere, frosty. More than an hour had already passed since court had convened that Monday morning, July 20. The prosecution was exasperated, the defense persistent.

Raulston finally granted Hays one hour to read and summarize the various statements by the scientists. Of course it took Hays much longer.

"IT IS NOT true that men came from monkeys, but that men, monkeys and apes all came from a common ancestry millions of years ago," Winterton Curtis, the zoologist from the University of Missouri, patiently explained in his statement.

This was the heart of the issue. Evolution meant to many—and most important to Bryan—that humans were directly descended from monkeys, which was an incorrect understanding of Darwin. "Tell me that I come from the cell of the ass and the monkey? No," Tom Stewart had bellowed, the tears welling up in his eyes. But why was this misconception so prevalent—and so troubling? "If the origin of man were not involved, there would be presumably little serious opposition from nonscientific sources of the present day," Curtis said. Few doubted the concept of change over time; geologists could explain how rivers changed course, astronomers how the universe was expanding. It was biological evolution that Christian Fundamentalists, particularly but not exclusively in the South, singled out for attack. They insisted that men and women were created by God, as the Bible stated. Period.

Underlying this anxiety about the origins of humankind was of course another anxiety: that the vaunted superiority of the so-called Nordics may be a fiction. Those monkey jokes and cartoons and the monkey trinkets and dressed-up chimps strolling on the sidewalks of Dayton suggested a racism implicit in much of the furor that evolution inspired. "Maybe Bryan and the Solid South would have felt better about everything if Darwin had said 'donkey' instead of 'monkey,'" the *New Yorker* magazine wisecracked. Comparing Black people to monkeys and other animals was one of the many ways white people dehumanized Blacks and rationalized slavery, as Darrow understood, and after slavery was abolished, it helped justify discrimination, never mind violence, against anyone not considered "white."

But the theory of evolution helped make indefensible the notion that racial hierarchies could be fixed, separate, and consigned to hierarchies of superior and inferior. There was no hierarchy. The Harvard geologist Kirtley Mather demonstrated that the discovery of bones, to give one example, link together "the white, yellow, brown and red races."

"It is not true that men came from monkeys," Winterton

Curtis had said, "but that men, monkeys and apes all came from a common ancestry." But Bryan deplored what he called "the hypothesis that links man to the lower forms of life and makes him a lineal descendent of the brute," which made his "chief concern in protecting man from the demoralization involved in accepting a brute ancestry."

"Shall [schoolchildren] be detached from the throne of God and be compelled to link their ancestors with the jungle?" Bryan had been asking. Again, these were terms used to disparage or humiliate Black men and women, and Black men and women, whether they supported the teaching of evolution or not, knew this.

Certainly the savvy satirist George Schuyler did. Pretending to rush to the Bronx Zoological Garden to interview a Mr. G. Orilla, "dean of the Simians," the Black writer learned that Mr. G. Orilla didn't appreciate the evolutionists' contention that monkeys were related to people. "Nobody had ever seen us carry on war, lynching each other, filling up jails, or working our little children," Mr. G. Orilla fumed. "Did you ever see monkeys straightening their hair or whitening their skins? Did you ever hear of monkeys allowing one of their race to appropriate all of the trees in the jungle, and then pay rent to him?" he asked. "Did you ever hear of the Ku Klux and the Rotarians among monkeys?"

"Well, then," he continued. "It must be evident that we are more intelligent than the humans." And Mr. G. Orilla's champion was none other than William Jennings Bryan, who "saw that there was no comparison between us and his people. So he became a fundamentalist and fought our battle.

"Bryan from the pulpit preaches the domination of Christ; in politics he practices Ku Kluxism and white domination, the bulwarks of which are lynching, murder, rape, arson, theft, and concubinage," the Jamaican American journalist Joel A. Rogers wrote in The Messenger.

Evolution was on trial in Dayton, The Chicago Defender

concluded, precisely because it supposes that the human race can be traced to a common origin, which "conflicts with the South's idea of her own importance. Anything which tends to break down her doctrine of white superiority she fights."

THE SCIENTISTS WHOSE sworn statements went into the record all came to the same conclusion: that the theory of evolution was universally believed to be true, even if there wasn't agreement about how or even why it occurred. "It stands in the strength of demonstrated facts and invites you to view the evidence," Winterton Curtis affirmed.

Unquestionably, the causes of evolution are difficult to figure out, Curtis added, which is why he showed the letter he'd received from William Bateson. Bateson was the well-established British geneticist whose belief that species don't evolve gradually but in big leaps was often cited by anti-evolutionists to prove that the theory of evolution was nothing more than guesswork. "Let us then proclaim in precise and unmistakable language," Bateson wrote to Curtis, "that our faith in evolution is unshaken."

Whatever doubts he may have expressed about how evolution works should not trouble the layperson, Bateson further explained. He had merely been disagreeing about how evolution may have occurred, not whether it had. Curtis explained that scientists widely accept evolution as a plausible theory "to give meaning to so many phenomena that would be meaningless without such a hypothesis." Yet there is an ongoing debate about whether natural selection adequately explains how adaptation occurs. But that debate doesn't mean evolution has been rejected. Not at all. And Curtis added, as if with a sigh, "there are many, even today, who rejoice at anything that appears to weaken this major generalization of biology." He was gesturing toward Bryan.

"The past history of events, whether of human or animal

origins, is subject matter for scientific inquiry," Curtis further stated, "and the answer of science is evolution." He illustrated what he meant with concrete examples such as the Grand Canyon, which was produced not by a miraculous creation or a catastrophe but by running water acting on the rocks through "innumerable centuries." He quoted the Darwin popularizer Herbert Spencer, who said that "those who cavalierly reject the theory of evolution as not adequately supported by facts seem quite to forget that their own theory is supported by no facts at all. Like the majority of men who are born to a given belief, they demand the most rigorous proof of any adverse belief, but assume that their own needs none."

So, simply stated, the universe is not static. Evolution is the theory of how things have changed and are changing. Similarly, the embryologist from the University of Chicago, Horatio Hackett Newman, wrote in his affidavit that "evolution is merely the philosophy of change as opposed to fixity and unchangeability." Newman understood, by implication, why there was resistance to the theory of evolution. "Once admit a changing world," he wrote, "and you admit the essence of evolution."

But change doesn't have to be terrifying, not at all. It can imply continuance and development. And there is evidence to demonstrate the development of life proceeded from simple to more complex forms. Life forms that exist today, in other words, have evolved over time, immense periods of time, from earlier forms. Jacob Lipman, the authority on agriculture and soil and director of the New Jersey Agricultural Experimental Station, added in his statement that even "the change of rocks into soils is a slow and gradual process," he wrote. "Like plants and animals, our soils had to pass through a long period of change to support the varied forms of life on earth. A direct relation may be traced between soils, plants and animals in the evolution of organic life."

Wilbur A. Nelson, Tennessee's state geologist, stated that

"different layers of rock which form the surface of the earth unfold the remarkable story of evolution. These rock layers may be read as clearly as the leaves of a book. The buried remains of animal and plant life which they contain show the rise of life and its development on this earth. It would be impossible to study or teach geology in Tennessee without using the theory of evolution."

Further, the age of the earth has been estimated as a billion years from the time it attained its present diameter, but life on earth seems to have existed not more than 50 million years, so the development of humankind represents a very short time, compared to the life of the earth. As Newman acknowledged, "There are no living eye-witnesses of events so far removed from the present and there are no documentary records written in human language." But evidence of evolution still exists indirectly, circumstantially, almost poetically. "Records of past events are written, however, for him who has learned the language, in the rocks, in the anatomical details of modern species, in the development of animals and plants, in their classification, and in the geographical distribution, past and present."

And like all the scientists who offered statements, Newman documented those various languages of change, even the kind written into humans themselves, which make them a "veritable walking museum of antiquities." Take vestigial organs, for instance, which are organs now obsolete, like the tail used by animals, birds, or fish, "which can be reasonably interpreted as evidence that man has descended from ancestors in which these organs were functional," Newton explained. "Man has never completely lost these characteristics; he continues to inherit them, though he no longer has use for them. Heredity is stubborn and tenacious, clinging persistently to vestiges of all that the race has once possessed."

Similarly, Fay-Cooper Cole stated that anthropology "reveals the fact that man closely resembles certain members of animal worlds in every bone and organ of his body. There are differences, but they are differences of degree rather than kind."

Evidence of evolution thus exists in several of the sciences, and no one biological discovery is incompatible with the theory of evolution. "Without evolution as a guiding principle, comparative anatomy would be a hopeless mass of meaningless and disconnected facts," Newman wrote.

And it could easily be said that God was behind these facts, connecting them and making them meaningful. Evolution could be God's method of "ever-growing revelation of Himself to the human soul," Maynard Metcalf suggested. "Knowledge and mystery exist side by side; mystery does not invalidate the fact."

The geologist Kirtley Mather, who taught Sunday school every week in his Massachusetts hometown, explained that "natural science deals with physical laws and material results." But it is not at odds with moral laws or spiritual truths. "Although it is possible to construct a mechanistic, evolutionary hypothesis which rules God out of the world," he said, "the theories of theistic evolution held by millions of scientifically trained Christian men and women lead inevitably to a better knowledge of God and a firmer faith in his effective presence in the world.

"Science has not even a guess as to the original sources of matter," Mather wrote. The Bible is a "textbook of religion, not a textbook of biology or astronomy or geology," yet science is utterly consistent with its spiritual truth, "which rings clearly and unmistakably through every theory of theistic evolution."

He went on. "To say that one must choose between evolution and Christianity is exactly like telling the child as he starts for school that he must choose between spelling and arithmetic." There is no moral dilemma; you can read the Bible and read evolution in the rocks, in animals, and in humans without fear that the world is founded cruelly and without pity or in conflict with Christianity.

"The survival of the 'fit' does not necessarily mean either survival of the 'fittest' or 'fightingest,'" Mather continued. "It has meant in the past, and I believe it means today and tomorrow, the survival of those who serve others most unselfishly."

But Mather said he knew why many Christians distrusted evolution: too many people hadn't really read the Bible. "The Bible does not state that the world was made about six thousand years ago," Mather said. "The date 4004 B.C. set opposite Genesis 1:1 in many versions of the Bible was placed there by Archbishop Ussher only a few centuries ago. It is man's interpretation of the Bible."

One man's literal interpretation "is not only puerile," Maynard Metcalf had pointed out, "it is insulting, both to God and to human intelligence."

Kirtley Mather concluded by quoting the preacher Henry Ward Beecher: "The theory of evolution is the working theory of every department of physical science all over the world. Withdraw this theory, and every department of physical research would fall back into heaps of hopelessly dislocated facts, with no more order or reason or philosophical coherence than exists in a basket of marbles, or in the juxtaposition of the multitudinous sands of the seashore. We should go back into chaos if we took out of the laboratories, out of the dissecting rooms, out of the field of investigation, this great doctrine of evolution."

WINTERTON CURTIS HAD also entered into the record a letter he'd received from Woodrow Wilson, Bryan's former boss. "Like every other man of intelligence and education," Wilson wrote, "I do believe in organic evolution. It surprises me that at this late date such questions should be raised."

This seemed aimed right at Bryan, who had remained silent during the entire presentation.

. . .

THE PROSECUTION HAD objected to what it called an educational program. It was irrelevant, they said. But an educational program is what they now had. Still, the jury heard none of it. Again, the jury had been excluded. The expert testimony was being read into the record and, according to the prosecution, had no real bearing on the case.

Regardless, across America, newspapers printed verbatim long excerpts from the scientific evidence. That was the defense's plan: to educate the public. The prosecution had been right about this.

THAT HAD OCCURRED on Monday, or most of it, a day when the old brick building was crowded to overflowing with men and women eager to know what Judge Raulston would do about Darrow's insolence the previous Friday, when the judge had said he hoped that Darrow didn't mean to reflect on the court, and Darrow had answered, snidely, "Your Honor has a right to hope."

That Monday, the opening prayer didn't bode well. "Sometimes we have been stupid enough to match our human minds with revelations of the infinite and eternal," the presiding reverend declared. Then an unusually stern Judge Raulston picked up a sheet of paper and cited Clarence Darrow for contempt. He set bond for $5,000, which a Chattanooga attorney, Frank Spurlock, was ready to post.

But before the jury was allowed back into the courtroom that afternoon, Darrow apologized. "I have many a case where I have had to do what I have been doing here—fighting the public opinion of the people, in the community where I was trying the case," he said, "and I never yet have in all my time had any criticism by the court for anything I have done in court."

"I do think, however, Your Honor, that I went further than I should have gone," Darrow continued. "So far as its having been premeditated or made for the purpose of insult to the court I had not the slightest thought of that. I had not the slightest thought of that." He'd spoken ill-advisedly and in anger. "I haven't the slightest fault to find with the court."

"I don't think it constitutes contempt," he added, "but I am quite certain that the remark should not have been made and the court could not help taking notice of it."

It was the judge's moment to shine and rescue the honor of his state, a state that had produced such great men as presidents James K. Polk and Andy Johnson, he said. His sternness disappeared. As the representative of that state in the courtroom, he had no choice but to cite Colonel Darrow for contempt, he said almost apologetically. But he was equally proud to represent the state of Tennessee's reliance on Christ and his infinite mercy.

Grandly, Judge Raulston reminded the court that he was the faithful servant of "the Man that I believe came into the world to save man from sin." With his savior's example in mind, he would practice Christian forbearance.

Clarence Darrow seated with Judge John F. Raulston
LIBRARY OF CONGRESS, LC-USZ62-95411

But he recommended that Colonel Darrow "learn in his heart the words of the Man who said, 'If you thirst, come unto Me.'"

Judge Raulston dropped the contempt charge.

Spectators clapped with joy, some cheering.

Darrow and the judge shook hands and posed for photographs.

AFTER THE LONG recitation of scientific testimony, after lunch, and after Darrow's apology, Judge Raulston said he feared that the sagging floor of the courthouse might collapse. The huge number of spectators standing in the back of the room had ignored the order to leave and were spilling out into the corridors while powdery white plaster was falling from cracks in the ceiling onto the floor below.

Raulston announced that as a result court would reconvene outdoors, on the courthouse lawn. Cameramen packed up their cameras and reporters their typewriters, and they and the defense and prosecution teams and the court attendants, along with the spectators, all trudged downstairs into the open air. A rough plank platform had already been built to accommodate the various religious services that were being routinely held in front of the building. Bryan had preached there, and, in the evenings, the anti-evolution revivalists took the stage. Now Judge Raulston would rule from it.

Some of the spectators sat on the courthouse window ledges while others found seats on the pinewood sawhorse benches. A few climbed onto the tops of the automobiles parked nearby, and some of the cameramen stood in the windows of the courthouse, pointing their equipment at the long tables that had been set up on the lawn for the lawyers and the reporters. Shaded by the maple trees, Judge Raulston sat at a smallish wooden table on the makeshift dais and placed his water pitcher near his elbow. The defense sat before him, on his right; the prosecution, on his left. Mrs. Bryan, in her wheelchair, had been carried down the stairs and placed near her husband.

Picking up where he'd left off, Arthur Hays introduced the statement of Shailer Mathews, dean of the Divinity School at the University of Chicago. Mathews flatly stated that evolutionists don't deny Genesis any more than the laws of light, gravitation, or electricity deny it. "God is in the creative process: Genesis and evolution are complementary to each other," he wrote, "Genesis emphasizing the divine first cause; and science the details of the process through which God works."

Hays also read a statement from the Reverend W. C. Whitaker, rector of Saint John's Episcopal Church. "A man can be a Christian without taking every word of the Bible literally; not only so, but the man has never lived who took every word of the Bible literally." He continued. "When St. Paul said, 'I am crucified with Christ,' and when David said, 'the little hills skipped like rams,' neither expected that what he wrote would be taken literally."

Hays then submitted the sworn statement of Rabbi Herman Rosenwasser, a multilingual Hebrew Bible scholar come all the way from San Francisco to identify the various translation errors in the King James Bible.

For instance, in the King James Version there appears in Genesis the word "created," which should have been translated from the Hebrew as "set in motion." "If the Hebrew Bible were properly translated and understood," Rabbi Rosenwasser testified, "one would not find any conflict with the theory of evolution which would prevent him from accepting both."

In sum, the defense intended to prove that the Bible has been interpreted in many ways. "There is nothing necessarily inconsistent between one's understanding of the Bible and evolution," Hays claimed, wrapping up the presentation. The Bible is concerned with the ethical and spiritual—the soul—he continued, and "the means of self development or self-expression of that soul."

Hebrew lesson at the Mansion. Arthur Hays, with pipe,
to left of facsimile; next to him, John Neal, John Scopes,
and Dudley Malone. George Rappleyea, on left,
embraces the rabbi.

COURTESY W. C. ROBINSON COLLECTION OF SCOPES TRIAL
PHOTOGRAPHS MS.1091. UNIVERSITY OF TENNESSEE,
KNOXVILLE—LIBRARIES

Certainly the Bible says that God created the human body—
not *how* God created it, Hays explained. By contrast, natural
science is concerned with the "developmental history, the structure and the functions of all living bodies, and not with any religious or ethical questions."

The various testimonies submitted then tell a straightforward
story, each consistent with all the others, and each illuminating
the others. "The evolution principle is thus a great unifying and
integrating scientific conception," Hays concluded. "Any conception that is so far-reaching, so consistent, and that has led to
so much advance in the understanding of nature, is at least an
extremely valuable idea and one not lightly to be cast aside if it
fails to agree with one's prejudices."

Perhaps Hays would have been convincing—if anyone had
been listening. Or if the real issue had been science, not prejudice
or fear. No scientific information, however well argued and co-
gently presented, could allay fear or eliminate prejudice. It could
not address the longings of those Holy Rollers under the large

trees or the aspirations of the judge who toted a Bible into the courtroom every day or the real anxiety of people who believed that Clarence Darrow, whom they liked, would burn in hell. It could not speak to the indignation of those who resented invaders from the big cities and the Northeast telling them what to think.

But they all knew that something big was at stake: a way of life, a set of beliefs that made life tolerable and livable, a set of beliefs that gave their lives purpose.

Part 6

The Trial:
A Duel to the Death
1925

I thought it was terribly raw in him,
But he said to Bryan, there, in a group:
"You'd better go back to Lincoln and study
Science, history, philosophy,
And read Flaubert's Madam something-or-other,
And quit this village religious stuff.
You're head of the party before you are ready
And a leader should lead with thought."
And Bryan turned to the others and said:
"Darrow's the only man in the world
Who looks down on me for believing in God."
"Your kind of a God," snapped Darrow.

—EDGAR LEE MASTERS, "THE COCKED HAT"

Chapter Nineteen

The Witness

IT WAS STILL MONDAY AFTERNOON; it remained hot and sticky, even outdoors under the shade trees. Judge Raulston was about to send for the jury when Clarence Darrow interrupted him.

"I think it my duty to make this motion," Darrow began. "Off to the left of where the jury sits is a large sign about ten feet long reading, 'Read Your Bible,' and a hand pointing to it. The word 'Bible' is in large letters, perhaps a foot and a half long."

Bewildered, Judge Raulston said that sign didn't measure a foot and a half. Darrow conceded it might be a foot. Someone yelled out, fourteen inches.

"I move that it be removed," Darrow repeated, ignoring the digression about size.

Ben McKenzie's son Gordon, also a member of the prosecution, approved. Remove the sign, he said, since it obviously offends the defense, who don't want to be reminded that they should be reading their Bible.

"We are trying a case here which we believe has very definite issues," Malone spoke up. "Everything that might possibly prejudice the jury along religious lines, for or against the defense, should be removed.

"The opinions of the members of the counsel for the defense, our religious beliefs, or Mr. Darrow's nonbelief, are none of the business of counsel for the prosecution," Malone briskly added. "We do not wish that referred to again. The counsel for the defense is not on trial here.

Spectators outside courthouse, "Read Your Bible" on left
COURTESY W. C. ROBINSON COLLECTION OF SCOPES TRIAL
PHOTOGRAPHS MS.1091. UNIVERSITY OF TENNESSEE,
KNOXVILLE—LIBRARIES

"We are merely asking this court to remove anything of a prejudicial nature that we may try these issues." Applause for Malone.

The younger McKenzie, annoyed, changed his mind and decided he wanted to keep the sign after all. "I have never seen the time in the history of this country when any man should be afraid to be reminded of the fact that he should read his Bible, and if they should represent a force that is aligned with the devil and his satellites—" McKenzie broke off. The applause was too loud for him to continue.

The devil and his satellites? Aghast, Malone tried to interrupt. McKenzie paid no attention. "I say when that time comes that then is time for us to tear up all the Bibles, throw them in the fire and let the country go to hell," he yelled.

His face scarlet, Malone objected again. Judge Raulston swiftly expunged the part of McKenzie's statement that referred to devils and satellites.

Still fuming, Malone persisted. "I think it is all right for the individual members of the prosecution to make up their minds as to what forces we represent. I have a right to assume I have as much chance of heaven as they have, to reach it by my own goal, and my understanding of the Bible and of Christianity, and I'll be a pretty poor Christian when I get any Biblical or Christian or religious views from any member of the prosecution," he sniffed. More applause.

Officer Kelso Rice pounded the table. "People! This is no circus. There are no monkeys up here. This is a lawsuit. Let us have order!"

Bryan chimed in. If the sign offended the defense, take it down, he said charitably.

Darrow walked forward, his folksy self, hands in his pockets, with a clever suggestion. "We might agree to get up a sign of equal size on the other side and in the same position reading 'Hunter's Biology,' or 'Read Your Evolution.' Why not place another sign, on the other side of the courthouse, telling people to 'Read Your Evolution.'" He had made his point.

"This sign is not here for no purpose, and it can have no effect but to influence this case, and I read the Bible myself—more or less—and it is pretty good reading in places."

Judge Raulston sighed. He ordered the sign taken down. "I have no purpose except to give both sides a fair trial," he almost groaned.

Time to call the jury? Not so fast, said Hays. He wanted submitted into evidence a copy of the King James Bible; a volume of the Vulgate (or Catholic) Bible; and the Hebrew Bible, in Hebrew. There was more back and forth, but a weary Raulston finally agreed to admit the Bibles into evidence, which is when Malone whispered to Scopes, seated not far from him, "Hell is going to pop now!"

John Scopes wasn't sure what Malone meant until Arthur Garfield Hays rose once more.

In a deep voice, Hays declared, "The defense desires to call Mr. Bryan as a witness."

Chapter Twenty

Salt of the Earth

THE REVEREND CHARLES FRANCIS POTTER remembered that he and Clarence Darrow were walking up the hill to the Mansion house when Darrow turned to him. "I'm going to put a Bible expert on the stand," Darrow said.

Potter was startled. "No, not you," Darrow said, smiling. "A greater expert than you—greatest in the world—he thinks."

"You mean Bryan?" Potter replied. "That would be a master stroke."

"Never mind the master stuff," Darrow said, ignoring the compliment. "And don't talk so loud." Darrow wanted to keep the plan secret. He asked Potter to find in the Bible the "unscientific parts—about hares chewing the cud," Darrow suggested, "and daylight before the sun was created, and all that."

He handed Potter a sheaf of telegrams that he'd been receiving since the trial began. "Go through them and see if there are any good ideas we can use. Probably not," he said, laughing. "I notice one says, 'Have found missing link. Wire instructions.'"

Putting Bryan on the stand was a bold, sly strategy inadvertently suggested by Bryan himself. When Judge Raulston excluded the scientific testimony, Darrow wasn't just peeved at the judge, he was furious at Bryan, who'd prevented any real discussion about the issues and didn't "test his views in open court under oath," as Darrow told reporters. But if the Bible itself were to be examined, the defense could call Bryan as an expert and expose him for the fraud they believed he was.

That is what Arthur Hays had reasoned. "Like lightning, you thought of calling Bryan," Darrow later reminisced with Hays. "Had we stopped to think about such an audacious thing, calling a member of the prosecution, we probably wouldn't have done so." That summer in Dayton, they didn't care.

"How in blazes do you expect to get Bryan on the witness stand," an incredulous Kirtley Mather asked the lawyers. "That's our job," they replied. "Just leave that part to us."

Over that weekend, then, before the evidence had been read into the record, Mather played the part of Bryan in a two-hour practice session at the Mansion.

Darrow and Hays would throw questions at him not unlike the questions that Darrow had put before Bryan two years earlier, in the summer of 1923, when he couldn't resist needling him in the pages of *The Chicago Tribune:* Was the earth made in six literal days? Did Mr. Bryan believe in the literal interpretation of the whole Bible? Were there no ships in the days of Noah, except the ark, and how did Noah gather all the pairs of animals on the earth, never mind the food and water necessary to preserve them? Did God really tell Eve that he'd multiply the sorrows of all women and that their husbands should rule over them?

Isn't history full of proof that all colors and kinds of people lived over large and remote parts of the earth within fifty years after the time of Noah? Not to mention, doesn't geology show by fossil remains, and by the erosion of rocks that became riverbeds, and by mineral deposits of all sorts, that the earth is much more than a million years old and probably many millions of years old?

Can't someone be a Christian without believing in the literal truth of the stories in the Bible?

Bryan had refused to answer these questions back in 1923. Now he would have no choice. He'd been ambushed.

BRYAN SAT OUTDOORS in the sultry summer heat, sweating under a bright sun, as men in overalls and women in their summer dresses eagerly gathered near the courthouse, more and more of them once the word was out: Darrow would put self-proclaimed Bible expert William Jennings Bryan on the stand. Eating ice cream and sipping the soda pop that little boys were selling, all of them waited in the hot sun for the duel to the death to occur at last.

Bryan and Darrow would face each other with nothing between them—no other lawyers, no judge, not even the whirring of the fans in a stuffy courtroom.

Only three years apart in age, they both had grown up before the invention of the telephone, before the radio or moving pictures, before the automobile. Bryan and Darrow grew up during a time when miners worked sixteen-hour days, a time of strikes and labor riots and deportations and, more recently, during a time of world war when Americans had died in faraway places—a war buoyed up for a while with platitudes, though not for Bryan, about making the world safe.

Now in Dayton it was Bryan who was saving the world—for Genesis, some pundits teased. And Darrow, who was Satan's satellite, was sure to let all hell break loose.

Yet there was something valiant about each of them: grand old men fighting for causes in which they wholly believed, even though Darrow might pretend he didn't believe in much beyond the need for compassion.

During the trial, Bryan had been resolute but often silent and irate. And he wasn't entirely well. He was looking drawn, if not gaunt, and though diabetic, he seldom watched his diet. He was not producing enough insulin, which meant that no matter how much he ate, he stayed hungry. Consulting a specialist in Chicago about his diabetes since earlier that year and likely before, he was placed on a strict regimen, though he didn't always follow it.

His voice wasn't as musical as it had been, his mood not as serene. Quick to anger, he occasionally jumped to his feet, beads of sweat dripping down his forehead, to shout "atheist" at Clarence Darrow. Tom Stewart tried to prevent Bryan from taking the stand, but Bryan pushed him away. If he did not consent, he'd be called a coward. "It will go out to the world that I am afraid to let these atheists and enemies of God's Word question me," he almost pleaded.

So it began.

Clarence Darrow interrogating William Jennings Bryan,
seated on left

SEATED ON A swivel chair on a makeshift platform in the glare of the July sun, Bryan calmly told Clarence Darrow that he'd been studying the Bible for more than fifty years and that everything in the Bible "should be accepted as it is given there."

Of course, he added, there was room for what he called the illustrative. "For instance," Bryan clarified, " 'Ye are the salt of the earth.' I would not insist that man was actually salt, or that he had flesh of salt, but it is used in the sense of salt as saving God's people."

Darrow pounced. "But when you read that Jonah swallowed the whale—or that the whale swallowed Jonah—excuse me please—how do you literally interpret that?"

"I believe it, and I believe in a God who can make a whale and can make a man and make both do what he pleases."

After some back and forth about whether the Bible said whale or big fish, Darrow continued. "You believe that the big fish was made to swallow Jonah?"

"I am not prepared to say that; the Bible merely says that it was done."

Darrow affected bewilderment. "You are not prepared to say whether that fish was made specially to swallow a man or not?"

"The Bible doesn't say, so I am not prepared to say."

Then Bryan suggested it was a miracle. "A miracle is a thing performed beyond what man can perform," Bryan explained. "When you get beyond what man can do, you get within the realm of miracles, and it is just as easy to believe the miracle of Jonah as any miracle in the Bible."

"Do you consider the story of Jonah and the whale a miracle?"

When Bryan said yes, Darrow turned to the story of Joshua. "Do you believe Joshua made the sun stand still?" he asked.

"I believe what the Bible says," Bryan said. "I accept the Bible absolutely."

"The Bible says Joshua commanded the sun to stand still for the purpose of lengthening the day, doesn't it, and you believe it?"

"I do."

"Do you believe at that time the entire sun went around the earth?"

"No, I believe that the earth goes around the sun."

"Do you believe that the men who wrote it thought that the day could be lengthened or that the sun could be stopped?"

"I don't know what they thought." Testy, Bryan sensed a trap.

"You don't know?"

"I think they wrote the fact without expressing their own thoughts."

Tom Stewart could not stand it. He begged Judge Raulston to stop the proceedings, but Judge Raulston wanted to hear what his hero had to say.

"I believe that the Bible is inspired, an inspired author, whether one who wrote as he was directed to write understood the things he was writing about, I don't know."

"Whoever inspired it?" Darrow eagerly asked. "Do you think whoever inspired it believed that the sun went around the earth?"

"I believe it was inspired by the Almighty, and He may have used language that could be understood at that time. Instead of using language that could not be understood until Darrow was born."

The men and women on the courthouse lawn cheered. Bryan was their hero too.

"Now, Mr. Bryan," Darrow coolly continued, "have you ever pondered what would have happened to the earth if it had stood still suddenly?" Bryan had not. He did not need to ponder the question, because God would have taken care of whatever was needed. And in any case, Bryan loftily added, "I have been too busy on things that I thought were of more importance than that."

"Haven't you ever wondered, Mr. Bryan, what would happen to the earth if the sun had stood still?" Darrow lunged. "Don't you know that it would become a molten mass?"

"When you go on the stand"—Bryan was losing patience— "you can testify to that."

"Don't you believe it?" Darrow pursued.

"I would want to hear expert testimony on that."

"You have never investigated the subject?"

Bryan had regained his composure. "I have been too busy on things that I thought were of more importance," Bryan answered somewhat haughtily.

Darrow turned to the story of Noah and the Flood. When did it occur?

Bryan repeated that it was not his concern. "I do not think about things I don't think about."

"Do you think about things you do think about?" Darrow was sarcastic.

"Well, sometimes." The spectators laughed. Officer Rice called for order.

Stewart interrupted again, objecting to Darrow cross-examining his own witness.

"He is a hostile witness," Darrow replied. Judge Raulston was not inclined to halt the proceeding.

Bryan was not inclined to stop either but, turning crimson, he defended himself angrily.

"These gentlemen have not come here to try this case." Bryan pointed to Darrow. "They came here to try revealed religion. I am here to defend it, and they can ask me any question they please." The crowd erupted in applause.

"Great applause from the bleachers," Darrow noted drily.

"From those whom you call 'yokels,'" Bryan pressed, seething.

"I have never called them yokels."

"That is the ignorance of Tennessee, the bigotry."

Darrow laughed mirthlessly. "You mean who are applauding you?" Applause again, but it wasn't clear for whom.

"Those are the people whom you insult." Bryan was their defender, and he knew they were listening.

Darrow would have none of it. "You insult every man of science and learning in the world because he does not believe in your fool religion." He had lost his temper. He too could not stay serene.

"I will not stand for that," Judge Raulston declared.

"For what he is doing?" Darrow would not budge.

"I am talking to both of you," Raulston answered gravely.

"This has gone beyond the pale of a lawsuit," Stewart said, raising his voice in exasperation. "I have a public duty to perform, under my oath, and I ask the court to stop it."

Raulston disagreed. He said to stop the proceedings would be unfair to Bryan. "He wants to ask the other gentlemen questions along the same line." Bryan was silent. Raulston allowed the questioning to continue. Stewart muttered his objection. Bryan wanted to continue.

Darrow returned to the subject of Noah. When did the Flood take place? Were all living things that weren't in the ark destroyed by the Flood?

Maybe not the fish, came the answer, though Bryan said he was kidding, as if to regain an upper hand.

When did the Flood take place? Darrow pointed out that there were civilizations whose existence could be traced back five thousand years. Bryan demurred. He had no evidence of that, he said, and he would not accept opinions of anyone against what he believed to be the inspired word of God.

"Let me make this definite," Darrow said. "You believe that every civilization on the earth, and every living thing, except possibly the fishes, that came out of the ark, were wiped out by the Flood?"

"At that time."

"At that time. And then, whatever human beings, including all the tribes, that inhabited the world and have inhabited the world; and who run their pedigree straight back, and all the animals, have come onto the earth since the Flood?"

"Yes."

"Within 4,200 years?"

Bryan cited the computations of Archbishop James Ussher. According to Archbishop Ussher, Noah's Flood occurred 4,262 years ago.

"Do you know a scientific man on the face of the earth that believes any such thing?" Darrow asked.

Bryan did not. He did not think it an important question. He'd been more interested in present-day Christians than any speculation about the past.

"You have never had any interest in the age of the various races and people and civilization and animals that exist upon the earth today? Is that right?" Darrow was incredulous.

"I have never felt a great deal of interest in the effort that had been made to dispute the Bible by the speculations of men, nor the investigations of men," Bryan placidly answered, though he was very angry.

"Are you the only human being on earth who knows what the Bible means?" Darrow was on a roll.

Stewart objected. Judge Raulston sustained him. But Darrow made it obvious that Bryan did not know that the "ancient civilizations of China" were more than six thousand years old. Bryan said they could not be older than the creation story in the Bible. The age of civilizations was calculated by the speculations of men. He believed the Bible.

Nor did Bryan know how old Egyptian civilization might be.

Nor did Bryan know that there were other ancient religions, in addition to the Jewish religion, that described the Flood. Bryan said he had not examined other religions or read much about them. "The Christian religion has satisfied me," he said.

What about the religions of Confucius or Buddha?

"I think they are very inferior. Would you like for me to tell you what I know?" Bryan asked.

"No."

"Well, I shall insist on giving it to you."

"You won't talk about free silver, will you?" Darrow teased.

Stewart was panicky. He objected. Darrow said again it was his right to examine a hostile witness.

"The attorney is also hostile," Bryan interjected.

"I am not hostile to you," Darrow replied smoothly, as he hunched over. "I am hostile to your views."

Bryan was allowed to tell what he knew about Confucianism. He had learned something about it when he went to China and met a follower of Confucius. Bryan asked the man if there was one word that expressed, as Bryan put it, "all that was necessary to know in the relations of life." The follower answered, "reciprocity."

"I know of no better illustration of the difference between Christianity and Confucianism than the contrast that is brought out there," Bryan explained. "Reciprocity is a calculating selfishness. If a person does something for you, you do something for him and keep it even. That is the basis of the philosophy of Confucius. Christ's doctrine was not reciprocity."

"I haven't asked you that." Darrow was indifferent to Bryan's speech. "Do you know how old the Confucian religion is?"

Bryan did not. Nor did he know the age of the "religion of Zoroaster," and when he was asked again if he knew they were religions older than Christianity, he fiercely replied, "I am not willing to take the opinion of people who are trying to find excuses for rejecting the Christian religion." He couldn't care less about the number of people who may have lived in ancient civilizations, and Clarence Darrow was the first man he'd ever heard of who was interested in the subject.

"You mean to say," Darrow demanded, "that I am the first man you ever heard of who has been interested in human society and primitive man? Where have you lived all your life?"

"Not near you," Bryan replied crossly. There was laughter.

"Not near anybody of learning? . . . Do you know there are thousands of books in our libraries on all those subjects I have been asking you about?" Darrow pressed.

"I have been so well satisfied with the Christian religion that I have spent no time trying to find arguments against it," Bryan repeated. To Bryan, history and anthropology and comparative religion were veiled arguments against Christianity. And as far as he was concerned, he said, "I have all the information I want to live by and to die by."

"And that's all you're interested in?"

"I'm not looking for any more on religion."

"You don't care how old the earth is, how old man is and how long the animals have been here?" Darrow asked again.

But Bryan wanted to continue talking about Confucianism and how it differed from the teachings of Jesus, and then he insisted on talking about Buddhism. Darrow sighed but didn't object.

"Buddhism is an agnostic religion," Bryan began. He described his visit to Rangoon where he met a man from England who said that the most important aspect of Buddhism is that you didn't have to believe.

Darrow was exasperated. It was hot, and Bryan was making speeches. Judge Raulston said Darrow should proceed.

Darrow brought up the Tower of Babel. Again, he and Bryan sparred about the date it was built, which Bryan calculated as a little more than four thousand years ago.

"Up to 4,155 years ago, every human being on earth spoke the same language?" Darrow raised his eyebrow. "Do you know how many languages are spoken on the face of the earth?" Bryan did not.

Pointing out that Bryan was uninterested, by his own account, in philology and the history of languages, Darrow changed his focus and asked Bryan if he thought the earth was made in six days.

"Not six days of twenty-four hours" came the reply that would stun Fundamentalists, who clung to the literal interpretation of the Bible that Bryan had championed. A few gasps could be heard from the lawn.

Bryan fidgeted on his swivel chair. "Doesn't it say so?" Darrow smiled.

"No."

Stewart immediately grasped what had happened. Bryan had
walked into a trap. Stewart sprang to his feet. "What's the purpose of this examination?" he cried.

Also grasping what happened—that he had just contradicted
his own literal interpretation of the Bible—Bryan returned to his
attack on Darrow. Darrow's agnosticism threatened the church
and everyone who embraced its spiritual and moral teaching.
"The purpose is to cast ridicule on everybody who believes in the
Bible." Bryan shook his fist. He was perspiring. He was appealing to the Fundamentalists whose faith in him he depended upon.

No, Darrow irately replied, his voice loud. He was shouting.
"We have the purpose of preventing bigots and ignoramuses
from controlling the education of the United States and you
know it." He could barely control himself.

Bryan was sweating profusely. "I am simply trying to protect
the word of God against the greatest atheist or agnostic in the
United States," Bryan too was shouting, his face flushed. Rising
from the swivel chair, he cried, "I want the papers to know I am
not afraid to get on the stand in front of him and let him do his
worst." He was a martyr, a twentieth-century Christian martyr.
"I want the world to know." He was screaming.

The applause was loud and long.

Seated on camp stools and chairs, the crowd remained sympathetic to Bryan, but the prosecution was nervous and both
sides were enraged. Stewart pleaded with the judge to restore
order. "Your Honor," he begged, "I respectfully except to it and
call on Your Honor in the name of all that is legal to stop this
examination and stop it here."

Arthur Hays promptly answered. Bryan was a witness because he was an expert on the Bible and the court was entitled to
the interpretation of the Bible from such an expert.

"This is resulting in a harangue, and nothing else," Stewart shot back.

"I didn't do any of the haranguing," Darrow calmly said.

Malone called out, "Mr. Bryan doesn't need any support." Everyone was talking at once.

"I don't need any advice, if you please," Stewart snarled. Prosecutor Sue Hicks entered the fray, asking the court to intervene and stop the proceedings in the name of the taxpayers. Judge Raulston remained firm.

The lawyers continued to brawl until Judge Raulston advised Darrow to hurry up, and he told the prosecution that he was allowing the examination to continue for the sake of the appellate court.

Bryan protested. "The reason I am answering is not for the benefit of the superior court," he lectured the judge and the lawyers. "It is to keep these gentlemen from saying I was afraid to meet them and let them question me, and I want the Christian world to know that any atheist, agnostic, unbeliever, can question me any time as to my belief in God."

"I want to take an exception to this conduct of this witness," Darrow objected.

More argument. Stewart was desperate to have the interrogation stopped. The Supreme Court would not care what Bryan had to say. Ben McKenzie spoke. "These gentlemen would no more file the testimony of Colonel Bryan as part of the record in this case than they would file a rattlesnake and handle it themselves," he said, again with a drawl.

"We will file it," Darrow, Malone, and Hays answered in unison.

Ever since the question about whether the earth was created in six days, Bryan could not contain himself. Red in the face, perspiring, he yelled, "The only reason they have asked any question is for the purpose, as the question about Jonah was asked, for a chance to give this agnostic an opportunity to criticize a believer in the word of God; and I answered the question in order to shut his mouth"—Bryan was still screaming—"so that he cannot go out and tell his atheistic friends that I would not answer his question."

Malone had to speak. "I would have asked Mr. Bryan—and I consider myself as good a Christian as he is—every question that Mr. Darrow has asked him." His own temperature rising, Malone added, "I hope for the last time no further attempt will be made by counsel on the other side of the case, or Mr. Bryan, to say the defense is concerned at all with Mr. Darrow's particular religious views or lack of religious views. We are here as lawyers with the same right to our views." There was great applause.

Malone took care never to mention that Arthur Hays was Jewish.

Darrow was permitted to continue. "Mr. Bryan, do you believe that the first woman was Eve?"

"Yes."

"Do you believe she was literally made out of Adam's rib?" Darrow asked.

"Yes." Bryan's voice was low.

"Did you ever discover where Cain got his wife?" Some spectators were giggling.

"I leave the agnostics to hunt for her." Bryan fanned himself, growing red again.

"You have never found out?"

"I have never tried."

Darrow pursued. Having ascertained that Bryan did not know or care if there were other people on earth at the same time, Darrow went back to the question of the creation of the earth in six days, asking what Bryan thought "the morning and the evening were the second day" might mean.

"I do not think it necessarily means a twenty-four-hour day," Bryan replied, explaining, "I do not see that there is any necessity for constructing the words 'the evening and the morning' as meaning necessarily a twenty-four-hour day, 'in the day when the Lord made the heaven and the earth.' "

Darrow dug in. "You think those were not literal days?"

"I do not think they were twenty-four-hour days."

Bryan then added, "I think it would be just as easy for the kind of God we believe in to make the earth in six days as in six years or in 6,000,000 years or in 600,000,000 years. I do not think it important whether we believe one or the other."

"Do you think those were literal days?" Darrow prodded.

"My impression is they were periods, but I would not attempt to argue as against anybody who wanted to believe in literal days."

"Have you any idea of the length of the periods?" Darrow asked.

"No, I don't."

"Do you think the sun was made on the fourth day?"

"Yes."

"And they had evening and morning without the sun?" Darrow quizzed him.

"I am simply saying it is a period."

"They had evening and morning for four periods without the sun, do you think?" Darrow feigned nonchalance.

"I believe in creation as there told, and if I am not able to explain it, I will accept it. Then you can explain it to suit yourself." Bryan sensed what was happening, and the two men fenced until Darrow was completely satisfied that he'd made his point plain. "And they had the evening and the morning before that time for three days or three periods," Darrow said. "All right, that settles it. Now, if you call those periods, they may have been a very long time."

Bryan agreed, glumly. "They might have been." He was cornered.

"The creation might have been going on for a very long time?" Darrow emphasized the contradiction.

"It might have continued for millions of years," Bryan answered. He couldn't extricate himself. He was not the literalist he pretended to be.

That was that.

Darrow shifted course. Was Eve tempted by the serpent, and for that reason, because she ate the apple, were women condemned to the pain of childbirth and the serpent condemned to slither on his belly?

Growing tired and increasingly distressed, Bryan said yes.

Darrow asked how the serpent crawled around before that. Perhaps on his tail?

The spectators were laughing.

Darrow changed the subject again. "You refer to the cloud that was put in the Flood, the rainbow. Do you believe in that?"

Bryan was trembling. Rising from his chair, he yelled out that Clarence Darrow was an atheist who was trying to slur the Tennessee court.

Darrow cut him off. "I object to your statement," he said, flaring. "I am exempting you on your fool ideas that no intelligent Christian on earth believes."

The crowd hissed, while men jumped to their feet, ready to fight—but Bryan was broken, crushed, and bone-tired. Judge Raulston pounded the table with his gavel as he stood and adjourned the court, which would meet again the next day.

He may have prevented a riot. Mary Bryan heard that there were armed men in the audience, one of whom had his hand ready to shoot Darrow dead.

No wonder the judge, the next day, was relieved that a cold rain, come at last, had forced everyone back inside, sagging floors notwithstanding.

The Verdict

B RYAN HAD WANTED THE NEWSPAPERS to know he wasn't afraid to take the stand, but their account of his testimony was far from what he wished. True, he had been courageous, sometimes nimble, always passionate. True, his declaration of faith was unshakable. But by and large reporters and spectators were aghast. The interrogation had been sad and ridiculous, operatic and futile. The Tennessee papers detailed Bryan's painful lack of knowledge even of the Bible. The man's ignorance was so pitiful he himself was virtually "allied with the powers of darkness," they said. It appeared that Bryan didn't want to know about anything that disagreed with him, and he was described as "near hysterics" and "intellectually butchered."

RUNNING FOR COVER, he was reduced to accusing Darrow of waging a war against Christianity. William Jennings Bryan had been no match for Clarence Darrow.

But Darrow did not escape unscathed. The Chicago lawyer had metamorphosed into a bird of prey poised over an opponent whom he gleefully humiliated. He was a heckler who, though perhaps an honest man, had stubbornly refused to acknowledge the "innate goodness of Mr. Bryan's heart." He had spared Bryan

nothing; he was sarcastic, merciless, mocking, cold and contemptuous. Clarence Darrow was nothing but "the grim, deft,
sneering man."

LEFT: William Jennings Bryan, Dayton, 1925
RIGHT: Clarence S. Darrow, Dayton, 1925
COURTESY W. C. ROBINSON COLLECTION OF SCOPES TRIAL
PHOTOGRAPHS MS.1091. UNIVERSITY OF TENNESSEE,
KNOXVILLE—LIBRARIES

Unfazed by such criticism, Darrow did say he felt sorry for
Bryan, a little bit anyway, "for being obliged to show his gross
ignorance by simple and competent questions I asked him on the
witness stand."

When Bryan walked into the courtroom the next day, Tuesday, he seemed smaller and sadder, and though Bryan protested,
Tom Stewart simply had to take Bryan off the stand. Enough was
enough. Stewart had allowed a rumor to circulate that he would
walk away, right now, from the case, should these extralegal
shenanigans continue.

Bryan, however, wanted to answer the charges, as he called
them, made by Darrow regarding his ignorance and bigotry. His
pride was at stake. Bryan said that the defense had made his
views on religion public while it hid behind a "dark lantern that
throws light on other people but conceal themselves." He would

not be robbed of his chance to shine his own light on these atheists and villains.

"The attorneys for the defense are hiding behind no screen,"
Dudley Malone replied. Darrow and Stewart approached the
bench. Let's not waste more time, Darrow suggested. Stewart
quickly agreed. "I feel that the testimony of Mr. Bryan can shed
no light upon any issues that will be pending before the higher
courts," Stewart said.

Concurring, the judge struck from the record Bryan's testimony of the day before.

The defense entered an exception to the judge's decision but
asked that the court now call the jury and instruct it to find John
Scopes guilty. That was unusual, of course, but as Darrow explained, arms folded across his chest, "We came down here to
offer evidence in this case, and the court has held under the law
that the evidence we had is not admissible. So all we can do is
take an exception and carry it to a higher court to see whether
the evidence is admissible or not."

There would be no summation from either side. Darrow had
waived his right to offer a closing argument for the defense,
which, under Tennessee law, meant there would be none from
the prosecution. That made it impossible for Bryan to deliver the
closing speech he'd been preparing.

Raulston called for the jury, which returned to the courtroom
and filed into their seats, one by one.

"It is charged that the accused violated what is commonly
known as the anti-evolution statute," Judge Raulston read aloud
a little after eleven A.M., "the statute providing that it shall be
unlawful for any person to teach in any of the universities, normals, or other public schools of the state any theory that denies
the story of the divine creation of man, as taught in the Bible,
and teach instead thereof that man is descended from a lower
order of animals."

He went on. "The court calls the attention of the jury to the

wording of the indictment, wherein it is charged that this defendant taught a certain theory or theories that denied the story of
the divine creation of man as taught in the Bible and taught instead thereof that man descended from a lower order of animals."

He explained how the law should be construed. "The court,
after due consideration, had held that the proper construction of
the statute is that it is made an offense thereby to teach in the
public schools of the state of Tennessee which are supported in
whole or in part by the public school fund or the state, that man
descended from a lower order of animals. In other words, the
second clause is explanatory of the first, and interprets the meaning of the legislature; and the court charges you that in order to
prove its case the state does not have to specifically prove that
the defendant taught a theory that denied the story of the divine
creation of man as taught in the Bible, other than to prove that
he taught that man descended from a lower order of animals."

That was it. Bryan's eyes were closed though he'd been nodding in assent.

It took the jury just nine minutes to deliver a verdict of guilty.
John Scopes had violated the Tennessee anti-evolution law,
which prohibited the teaching of the theory of evolution in the
state's public schools. Malone placed his hand on Scopes's shoulder.

Judge Raulston asked John Scopes if he wished to say anything. "I feel that I have been convicted of violating an unjust
statute," Scopes said, speaking for the first time and with composure. "I will continue in the future, as I have in the past, to
oppose this law in any way I can. Any other action would be in
violation of my ideal of academic freedom—that is, to teach the
truth, as guaranteed in our Constitution, of personal and religious freedom."

Mary Bryan thought he'd been coached.

Judge Raulston imposed the minimum fine, which was $100.

Bond was set at $500, which the Baltimore *Evening Sun* offered to pay.

Judge Raulston then gave the defense team thirty days to prepare the appeal for the Tennessee Supreme Court, which would convene in Knoxville in September. From there, it would be possible to bring the case before the United States Supreme Court.

Malone thanked the people of Tennessee. And again, Malone received a great deal of applause.

Ben McKenzie's son, a member of the prosecution, also addressed the court, damning the defense with faint praise while saluting the maligned citizens of Tennessee. "While much has been said and much has been written about the narrow-minded people of Tennessee, we do not feel hard toward you for having said that, because that is your idea," McKenzie announced. "We people here want to be more broad-minded than some have given us credit for, and we appreciate your coming, and we have been greatly elevated, edified and educated by your presence."

Bryan too had to speak. "Causes stir the world," he said. "Here has been fought out a little case of little consequence as a case, but the world is interested because it raises an issue, and that issue will some day be settled right, whether it is settled on our side, or the other side."

He was correct about causes stirring the world.

"And we who participated may be congratulated that we have attached ourselves to a mighty issue." That was true too. He said that right would prevail, whether his or someone else's, though he was sure it would be his.

Darrow responded, his sleeves rolled up to his elbows. He too appreciated the courtesy of the counsel and the hospitality of the citizens. And of the court, which did not send him to jail. (Laughter.)

He turned to Bryan. "Events come along as they come along," Darrow observed. "I think this case will be remembered because it is the first case of this story since we stopped trying people in

America for witchcraft because here we have done our best to turn back the tide that has sought to force itself upon this—upon this modern world, of testing every fact in science by a religious dictum."

Darrow had chosen his words with care. The press jumped on his comparison of this trial to the witchcraft trials, which was his intention. For him, the issue was not even the rightness or wrongness of science, which science alone could determine, but openness to diverse points of view—not subservience to one of them. He was referring to Bryan's desire to subordinate everyone and everything to what Bryan believed was the one and only true church.

Judge Raulston was worn out, but he too made a little speech. He thanked everyone, adding that not only was truth indestructible but so was the eternal Word of God, which would never perish from this earth.

Arthur Garfield Hays had the last word. He asked if he might send Judge Raulston *Origin of Species*. There was grateful laughter in the courtroom. The Reverend Charles R. Jones, of the Methodist Episcopal Church, South, offered a closing prayer. "May the grace of our Lord Jesus Christ, the love of God and the communion and fellowship of the Holy Ghost abide with you all. Amen." Court was adjourned.

Many of the spectators rushed over to Bryan. Still others swarmed around Clarence Darrow and Malone and Hays and Neal to shake their hands. Outdoors, it had started to rain a little, putting an end to the terrible heat.

CAPTAIN JACK THOMPSON, the jury foreman, said of the verdict that "there was nothing else we could do." Raulston's instruction had been simple: Had Scopes violated the Tennessee law? "I do not want to state any views about the constitutionality of the law," Thompson added. "But I do want to say that I personally have an open mind on the question whether the evolutionary theory is in conflict with the Bible."

Another member of the jury, R. L. Gentry, told Darrow that the jury was sorry they hadn't gotten a chance to hear him make a closing argument. "We all wanted to hear what you had to say." Darrow smiled, almost shyly.

IT WAS SAID that a Fundamentalist college, with Bryan as president, would be erected in Dayton. It was said that Congressman William Upshaw, an outspoken supporter of the Ku Klux Klan, had been chosen by Bryan to sponsor a bill in the United States Congress that would cut off federal funds to institutions that taught the theory of evolution. Upshaw resisted, citing states' rights. There was still talk about a constitutional amendment banning the theory of evolution from being taught in public schools and colleges.

To many, it seemed obvious that Bryan was hoping to establish a theocracy in the country, and that, to them, was the real issue, not whether evolution was itself true, or how true. The issue was not science itself, or the religion of science, or even Darrow's vaunted agnosticism. It was freedom: freedom to worship and to reason and to learn. "Mr. Bryan has been organizing through political and church organizations a campaign to control the educational system of the country by dogmatic religion," Dudley Field Malone declared, "and to organize sufficient church and political power to create a state religion in America." That way lay tyranny, not tolerance, and government rule by fear, not freedom.

THE BATTLE WAS not over. Demeaned, his pride more deeply wounded than he could admit, Bryan sought to repair his reputation, to insist he was no fool, to show he was no bigot. For it was William Jennings Bryan, the Prince of Peace, the Commoner, the three-time presidential candidate, whom Darrow had humiliated. Bryan wanted to turn the tables, to quiz Darrow and unmask him as the very embodiment of all that is cruel and heartless and as the hater of all things or people identified as Christian. "The attack upon the authority of the Bible is organized, deliberate and malignant and had only to be uncovered to be understood," Bryan declared.

"Mr. Bryan's convulsions seem due to the fact that I placed him upon the witness stand," Darrow impassively remarked. "It is very likely that we were wrong in this, as he probably is not an expert. . . . How much Mr. Bryan knows about the Bible, or anything else, can be best judged by his answers."

Though the trial was over, Darrow said he'd be happy to answer any of the questions Bryan wanted to ask. "Of course I speak for myself and myself alone, and I speak of my present opinions, which I am always ready to change," he added. He had never tried to impose his view of religion on anyone, he said, and he'd fight as hard to protect anyone's right to their views. Shrewdly, he also emphasized Bryan's blunder on the stand, which to Darrow was no blunder at all. That is, Bryan had admitted that the days of creation were not literally days of twenty-four hours each, which is exactly what the defense had wanted to prove: that other interpretations of Genesis were possible. But though he said he was sorry that Bryan had to reveal his ignorance, he wanted only to show that the Bible ought not to be taken literally, and that people who profess knowledge about science or geology—or religion—should know something about science or geology or religion.

As to Bryan's question to him about the origin of the universe and whatever had caused it, Darrow said, "I do not pretend to know. I have not the intimate acquaintance with it that Mr. Bryan has."

Asked if Darrow believed the Bible was the revealed word of

God, reliable and trustworthy, Darrow replied that to him, the Bible should be read like any other great book. Portions of it are sublime and inspired. Bryan asked him if he believed in miracles as recorded in the Bible, or in any of them, like the Virgin birth. "I believe that the universe acts and always has acted in accordance with immutable laws and that, whatever may be back of the universe, it has never violated these laws."

Bryan wondered if Darrow believed in the immortality of the soul.

"I have been searching for the truth of this all my life with the same desire to find it that is evident in every living thing," Darrow answered. He was a seeker, not a finder, and he never minded asking or answering questions, even if the answer was that he didn't know.

Bryan then quizzed Darrow on evolution. "At what point in man's descent from the brute is he endowed with hope and promise of a life beyond the grave?" Bryan asked.

"I have no knowledge on the question of when man first believed in a life beyond the grave. I am not at all sure whether some other animals have not the same hope of future life that man has," Darrow replied.

"The origin may have arisen in vivid dreams concerning the return of the dead, or, for all I know from actual evidence of the return of the dead."

Keeping the Faith

JUST OVER TWO WEEKS AFTER the Scopes trial ended, forty-six special railroad cars chartered by the Ku Klux Klan arrived in Washington, D.C., carrying its delegations to the Klan's first national parade. Considered by some a publicity stunt to boost membership, which seemed to be falling off, men and women, with their children, poured into the city—somewhere between 25,000 and 50,000 of them. The Pennsylvania Klan alone had sent more than 15,000 members, and President Coolidge had been invited to speak. The taciturn president had discreetly left town for a vacation in Swampscott, Massachusetts. Not that it mattered. The show would go on.

At three o'clock on Saturday, August 8, in blazing sunlight, after a blast of trumpets, the Klan began its march. Down Pennsylvania Avenue, the Klansmen and women came, from the Capitol to the Treasury Department, dressed in those now familiar long white sheets and wearing on their heads those big white cones. But they marched unmasked and arms akimbo; they stretched four, five, six across, some of them with big badges pinned to their white sheets that identified them as "100 per cent American."

A Klan color guard riding sleek black horses raised the first of the six hundred American flags on display, fluttering in the wind.

A police detail riding motorcycles roared behind the color guard, and fifty bands struck up favorite tunes like "Keep the Home Fires Burning" or "Onward Christian Soldiers." The band members wearing Scottish kilts drew the most cheers from the crowd. The men carrying open Bibles also received hearty applause. Banners waved. "Keep Kongress Klean" read one. A delegation of cowboys in sombreros had arrived from Beaumont, Texas, but they weren't allowed to march because they weren't properly gowned, the Klan insignia appearing only on their hatbands. But Imperial Wizard Hiram Wesley Evans was richly swathed in an elaborate purple nightshirt trimmed in gold that was tied just below his bulging belly.

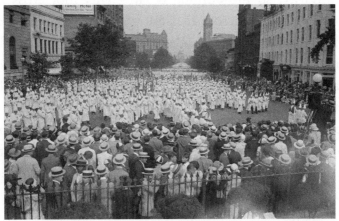

Ku Klux Klan's first national parade, with Capitol in background, Washington, D.C., August 8, 1925
COURTESY LIBRARY OF CONGRESS

It was "grander and gaudier," Mencken wrote, "than anything the wizards had prophesied." Mencken had rushed to Washington. He wouldn't have missed this performance for the world.

Spectators leaned out of the windows of office buildings, homes, or hotels while Klan sentinels prowled the sidewalks scouting for protesters or troublemakers. There were none. And it was no surprise that Washington's Black population avoided the city's main streets. Only one Black person, a man, took part in the parade. He posed as the driver of an old-timey horse-drawn coach in which sat women wearing Dolley Madison and Martha Washington costumes.

"We have long looked forward to when it would be possible for white, native-born, Gentile, Protestant citizens to march down Pennsylvania Avenue unmolested and unharmed," one of the Klan leaders exclaimed, though it was not at all clear whom he thought might be molesting them.

Dark clouds and loud rumbles of thunder threatened rain, but the Klan's Grand Kleagle, Washington division, shouted through the loudspeakers that it never rained on the Klan. It rained anyway, so the burning of an eighty-foot cross at the horse show grounds across the Potomac had to be postponed. When it was finally lit, on Sunday, under the glow of the flames and standing at the base of the cross, the leaders blasted bootleggers, gamblers, Catholics, Jews, scientists, evolutionists, Blacks, and newspapers.

The Reverend A. H. Gulledge, a Klansman from Ohio, finished his speech with a flourish. "I cannot conclude without paying a tribute of love to the man who always championed the cause of righteousness—William Jennings Bryan."

BRYAN WAS FREQUENTLY at pains to prove he was not an ignorant man. He often itemized his college and law degrees to bored reporters and boasted that in his three presidential campaigns he'd received more votes than any Democratic presidential candidate before 1896. He listed the political issues he'd backed when he'd been a congressman: the monetary question, the extension of suffrage, the nationalization of utilities. As Secretary of State, he'd negotiated fifty-two treaties. And in addition to publishing a paper devoted to political and economic questions, he wrote for innumerable magazines, he'd been the guest of emperors and kings, he'd addressed students at countless universities and colleges, and he'd sermonized at many synagogues, by invitation. No ignoramus, he.

In fact no one, he added, had ever called him ignorant or an ignoramus except evolutionists, and even they hadn't mocked him until, as he said, he "found it necessary to protect my family from the family tree by which evolutionists connect themselves with the jungle." But he told reporters that he wasn't going to debate any more atheists.

Far less anxious to prove anything—except that he didn't believe in much—after the trial, Clarence Darrow sipped iced tea while he planned a little vacation with his wife in the Smoky Mountains. Arthur Garfield Hays and Dudley Malone and Doris Stevens returned to New York, with Malone putting the best face on the verdict, calling it a "victorious defeat." Watson Davis, representing the Science Service, formed a committee to raise funds to send John Scopes to graduate school to study geology. Scopes would enroll at the University of Chicago but in the meantime could be found at the swimming hole near town.

Ben McKenzie delivered his parting shot at the defense lawyers. "They had better go back to their homes, the seat of thugs, thieves and Haymarket voters," he growled, "and educate their criminals rather than to try to proselytize here in the south, where people believe in the Christian religion and know that Genesis tells the full and complete story of the creation." But just a month later, he told Darrow, "I love you & did from the time I first met you. I don't agree with you, but what of that? I would get up at the midnight's unholy hour to do you a favor." The next year McKenzie would be arrested for disorderly conduct, and when the police found a half-full pint bottle of whiskey in his pocket, he was charged with transporting an alcoholic beverage. Grateful, he nonetheless turned down Darrow's offer to defend him.

Judge Raulston headed a hundred miles west to his home in Winchester, where Tom Stewart also lived.

In Dayton, flocks of reporters were no longer congregating on the sidewalks, and the drugstore where reporters had passed the time was almost empty. In the courtroom the extra tables and chairs and benches brought there for the reporters remained for a little while. As did Bryan, who was staying on for a few days with his wife. He intended to recoup his reputation and make sure his legacy was intact. For if Bryan had felt humiliated by Darrow, if he had in any way felt defeated in Dayton, he was still eager to prove he could be relevant and the crusader of old.

He traveled back and forth from Dayton to Chattanooga and to Winchester—about two hundred miles in all—continuing to inveigh against modernism and, in particular, evolution, pernicious evolution, which made people callous and cruel and that had brought on the Great War. In Chattanooga, he consulted with his friend George Fort Milton, editor of *The Chattanooga News*, about publishing nationwide the closing speech he'd not been able to deliver at the trial. Bryan had tasted "red meat," a journalist speculated, and was aiming to get anti-evolution laws passed nationwide.

In Chattanooga, to satisfy his wife, who had been concerned about his health, Bryan also saw a physician, who diagnosed a slight dilation of the heart and arrhythmia. The next day, Saturday, Bryan and Mary were driven to Winchester and en route stopped in the small town of Jasper where Bryan gave a short speech, reminding his audience that the world needed Christ now more than ever.

Bryan's goal was therefore clear: establish the right of taxpayers to decide what can be taught in public schools. According to Mary Bryan, she and her husband both believed this work was vital as well as constitutionally defensible. It did not bear at all on religious freedom. Bryan merely wanted to protect the "Christian faith," she claimed, "from influences which tended to undermine it."

"No religious zeal should invade this sacred domain and become intolerance," she insisted. Darrow's accusation of bigotry had evidently troubled her.

"Well, Mamma," Bryan reportedly soothed his wife when she seemed nervous about those accusations. "I have not made that mistake yet, have I?"

"You are all right so far, but will you be able to keep to this narrow path?" she remembered nervously asking.

Bryan smiled and said he could. She wasn't satisfied. "Can you control your followers?"

"I think I can," he said, the smile fading.

The closing speech he'd have given before the Scopes jury, had he been allowed to deliver it, did appear in newspapers across the nation, and many of them printed it in full, thanks to George Fort Milton. *The New York Times* placed it on its front page, and though readers were deprived of Bryan's magical voice, they could regardless follow his argument.

It was of course the same argument they'd heard now since the war. That was his intention, a cautionary and, as it happened, valedictory summation. "I feel that this is the mountain peak of my life's efforts," he had confided to George Milton.

First, he praised the Christian men and women of Tennessee "who come into daily contact with the earth, who, living near to nature, worship nature's God, and who, dealing with the myriad mysteries of earth and air, seek to learn from revelation about the Bible's wonder-working God." These are not the people living in cramped quarters in urban squalor. These are not city slickers but the good people, the salt of the earth, who outlawed the godless theory of evolution that would, if permitted in their schools, ensnare their children and lead them far astray. "No more repulsive doctrine was ever proclaimed by man; if all the biologists of the world teach this doctrine—as Mr. Darrow says they do—then may heaven defend the youth of our land from their impious babblings."

And thus a state legislature—the Tennessee legislature—had

every right to determine what could be taught in state-funded schools. The legislature was merely carrying out the wishes of the people.

He then repeated his main points. By lumping humans together with other mammals like the wolf and the skunk—creatures without a soul—the theory of evolution drags humans "down to the brute level." And anyway the theory was never anything more than speculation. There was no more reason to believe that we're "descended from some inferior animal than there is to believe that a stately mansion has descended from a small cottage." As Bryan once explained to an admirer, "if morality rests on religion as I believe it does then the entire absence of religion destroys the foundation upon which civilization rests." Without religion, in Bryan's understanding, there's nothing but greed, predation, and of course demon rum and decadence.

And neither unions nor the labor movement could fulfill the promise of a compassionate, more perfect world. "Capitalism, supported by force, cannot save civilization," Bryan had earlier declared. "Neither can government by any class assure the justice that makes for permanence in government. Only brotherly love can make employers willing to pay fair compensation for work done and employees anxious to give fair work for their wages." In other words, Bryan was a Christian utopianist, not a unionist or a theologian but a pious man appealing to the piety of others. He never stopped believing in social reformation—doing good—for and with the common people. He wanted to alleviate their suffering, to provide hope and the promise of something better. And he remained committed to democracy, or to the idea of it, and to expanding democratic participation in government.

But he also believed in strong governmental regulation, as paradoxical as that could sometimes seem: his commitment to the religious life bridged, for him, the apparent gap between an expanded electorate and a strong central government. For it was religion that made life better—and religious leaders, who inspire us "to noble deeds." These leaders were not adherents of just any religion; they were Fundamentalists. They were people like him. They were people he could lead. They were him. And if that meant religious uniformity and racial hierarchies, so be it. And if this made Bryan a supremacist in religion and race, so be it. He did not think so.

As his biographer Michael Kazin points out, Bryan was a contradictory man who brooked no ambiguities and thus he kept the faith, his faith, his promise to the people he loved.

And, again, Bryan mistook biological evolution for social Darwinism so imagined that Scopes the teacher was approving a dog-eat-dog way of life where the strong crowd out or kill off the weak. Again, he confused the sham science of eugenics with the theory of evolution and mixed it up with a little Nietzsche. Evolution, he claimed, would lead to "a system under which a few supposedly superior intellects, self-appointed, would direct the mating and movements of the mass of mankind—an impossible system!"

Yet he said, as he had said before, that he did not begrudge what he called "scientific truth" and the services science had rendered humankind, from photography to the ice machine to remedies for arthritis. But while the physical sciences are important, even more important was the question of how to live. It is more important to know the Rock of Ages than the ages of rocks, he liked to say, as he had so many times. "Science needs religion," Bryan explained, "to direct its energies and to inspire with lofty purpose those who employ the forces that are unloosed by science."

"Now we are told that newly discovered instruments of destruction will make the cruelties of the late war seem trivial in comparison with the cruelties of war that may come in the future," he again warned. About that, he wasn't entirely wrong.

It was thus to this dislocated, modern, anxious world that Bryan addressed himself. He finished the speech that would be published, the speech he would have given to the jury, reminding the jury—who stood for all Americans—that the trial in Dayton, Tennessee, represented nothing less than a confrontation between unbelief and Christianity—nothing less than a contest between the raw, ugly power of a Pontius Pilate and the loving goodness of Jesus Christ.

To allow the Pilates of evolution to crucify love and goodness must not be tolerated. "That cannot be the answer of this jury representing a Christian State," Bryan pleaded with the Dayton jury, the reader, the citizen at large. That jury of good Christians—that jury of Americans—must choose love, embrace love, fight for love, in the way that Bryan defined love. He had kept the faith.

Part 7

A Little Learning
1925–1926

And if I could do something, which I can't, to make the world
better, I would try to have it more tolerant, more kindly, more
understanding; could I do that and nothing else, I would be glad.

—CLARENCE DARROW, SUMMATION IN THE TRIAL OF
HENRY SWEET, 1926

I Have Finished the Race

S UNDAY, JULY 26, WOULD BE yet another day of baking heat in Dayton. That morning Bryan took his palm-leaf fan to the Methodist Episcopal Church, South, whose congregation had so enthusiastically welcomed him when he first arrived in Dayton. At noon, he consumed a typically large meal and afterward placed a call to George Fort Milton to discuss the proofs of the speech that would soon appear nationwide.

He decided to nap before climbing back into the pulpit that evening. Later that afternoon, Mrs. Bryan asked the family chauffeur, William McCartney, to wake her husband. She wanted him to be refreshed. McCartney tried to wake the Commoner. He didn't move and he seemed not to be breathing. A doctor was called, and soon after he arrived pronounced William Jennings Bryan dead. He'd most likely had a stroke.

Though some of his fans had figured Bryan could be swept up to heaven in a chariot of fire at any time, the news still came as a shock. The Commoner was just sixty-five years old—three years younger than Clarence Darrow—and he had so much left to do. No one, least of all Bryan, would have thought that his best days were behind him.

Six men from the local post of the American Legion were called as an honor guard and were soon standing on the front porch and in the parlor of the Richard Rogers home, where the Bryans had been staying. In Dayton, the flags flew at half-staff, and people of Rhea County, hearing the news, made a pilgrimage to the house. They came in droves, women gripping the hands of little children and holding their babies in their arms; merchants and farmers, their hats clutched in their fists, the young, the old with their hickory walking sticks, heads solemnly bowed. They climbed up the stairs of the front porch and passed into the front room of the Rogers home. The curtains were drawn, and in the dim light they saw a bronze casket wreathed in flowers. Kelso Rice, the Chattanooga officer who had policed the trial, paced up and down in front of the house as the grieving people filed silently by.

The Reverend Charles R. Jones spoke on the lawn in the shade of the maple trees. "I firmly believe that William J. Bryan went to an untimely death as a martyr fallen in the defense of the Son of God," he said. A slight breeze cooled the mourners.

"Today, my friends, there is a greater fear than ever among the disciples of agnosticism, atheism, pantheism, and every other damnable ism known to the devil and his cohorts," the reverend warned.

"We who have followed the great fundamentalist shall arise, a mighty unit, millions of God-fearing and God-loving men and women of this country," he promised, "and we shall meet the enemies of the word of God."

"Amen," came the reply. "Amen."

Mary Bryan wanted no fuss. We are simple people, she said. On Wednesday she and her family boarded a funeral train, which consisted of two cars, one for newspaper correspondents and newsreel cameramen, the other for Bryan's relatives and Kelso Rice, who insisted that he accompany them on the long trek from Tennessee to Washington, D.C. The Prince of Peace would be buried at Arlington National Cemetery, as he had wished.

On the way, whenever that train stopped, as it often did,

Mary Bryan watched from the railway window the surges of people at the platform, who waited patiently for the observation car to open so they could enter in single file and bid the Commoner farewell, gazing sadly at his large bronze coffin, draped in the flag of the country that he so dearly loved and surrounded by a mountain of red roses, double sweet peas, white snapdragons, and yellow tea roses.

"This last journey," Mary Bryan later recollected, "was like the early campaigns, except that now there was sorrow on the faces."

"GOD AIMED AT Darrow, missed him, and hit Bryan instead," Mencken remarked. Mencken notwithstanding, Bryan was now spared more of the satire and scorn heaped on the Scopes trial. Magazines like *Life* swiftly revised or destroyed the issues ready to lampoon him, and in New York, theaters canceled anything that depicted him as a buffoon. In death, Bryan loomed heroic, noble, and a sacrificial victim, having dramatically died right after he'd fallen apart under questioning.

"He died within the borders of our state," Governor Austin Peay stated, "a martyr to the faith of our fathers and the sacred word of God."

Among the large packets of telegrams that Mary Bryan received was one from Chief Justice William Howard Taft, who had run against Bryan in 1908. President Coolidge courteously wrote—loquacious for once—and on the day of the funeral, he ordered the flags on all federal buildings lowered to half-staff. In Oklahoma, Arkansas, and Arizona, civic offices closed at the hour of the burial.

Standing for hours in a drenching rain, and then filing by, one by one, the flag-draped casket, men and women paid their respects at Washington's New York Avenue Presbyterian Church, where the funeral took place. Near the casket were baskets of gladiolas and lilies and pink and white asters. A large cross of flaming red roses came from the Ohio branch of the Ku Klux Klan.

The funeral was broadcast over the radio. Thousands tuned in at 3:45 P.M.

From the church, just as the cortege entered the cemetery grounds, the drenching rain finally stopped. Taps were played against a background of muffled drums, and the pacifist was solemnly laid to rest on a knoll and among the rows and rows of white headstones marking the graves of veterans of the Civil War, the Spanish-American War, and the Great War—wars that had been fought during Bryan's lifetime.

Once again, from his knoll, he was in view of the White House.

To many of his fans, Bryan's death in Dayton was nothing less than stark tragedy, the death of a great and good man who suffered, unflinching, "a death from an ordeal of faith," as George Fort Milton put it. "No Christian martyr ever went to the stake with a firmer tread," *The Nebraska State Journal* celebrated its son. Similarly, in *Commonweal,* the reform-minded Catholic magazine, its founder and editor Michael Williams also insisted that Bryan died for his faith, giving his life "that others might live freed from the dangers against which he fought."

Or, if not exactly hailed a martyr, Bryan was celebrated for his causes and concerns: a humanitarian and true progressive, he was a remarkable man whose power came not from the prestige of office but from the people, ordinary people, working people, whose lives he strove tirelessly to improve. He backed an income tax law. He worked hard for the passage of such revolutionary constitutional amendments as women's suffrage and Prohibition, whatever one thought of the latter. He worked hard for the election of senators by direct vote of the people instead of their appointment by legislatures. "He was the golden voice of the Middle West beginning to feel that eastern capitalism was exploiting it," Felix Frankfurter later recalled. "It was all so fresh and romantic and the voice of hope." Bryan cared.

Much of the praise was well-deserved, for Bryan had for more than thirty years channeled the dreams and fears and needs of the many, many Americans whom he reassured as he always had, even while he traveled far from the political progressivism of his youth. Despite his sentimentality, his confusions, lack of clarity, and his almost purposeful misreading of science, he did respect whatever innovations made living easier. Even adversaries seemed kind and often more than kind, contributing in part to his canonization. As the philosopher John Dewey noted, almost regretfully, when speaking of Bryan and evolution, "The forces which are embodied in the present crusade would not be so dangerous were they not bound up with so much that is necessary and good."

Or, as the British journalist Sydney Brooks had once observed, Bryan's career was typically American: he was the type of man who can ruin countries from the best of motives.

Bryan wasn't petty, he was generous; he was sincere, empathetic, kind. He was one of the last of the major figures of the Populist movement. Putting it another way, Kansas journalist William Allen White, who knew Bryan fairly well, sharply and almost ruefully observed Bryan was a great political diagnostician: "Mr. Bryan never has been wrong in a single diagnosis or right in a single prescription." John Scopes said he respected Bryan "for his fearless stand on issues that he thought were right." And Clarence Darrow had been one of the first to offer a public tribute to the Commoner. "I am pained to hear of the death of William Jennings Bryan," Darrow announced. "I have known Mr. Bryan since 1896 and supported him twice for the presidency. He was a man of strong convictions and always espoused his cause with ability and courage. I differed with him on many questions, but always respected his sincerity and devotion."

What else could he say, especially if he or any of the defense felt as if they bore some responsibility for Bryan's death? Privately, though, when some reporter told Darrow that Bryan had died of a broken heart, Darrow grimaced. "Broken heart nothing," he said. "He died of a busted belly."

Whatever his personal opinion, Dudley Malone too fell into public line, calling Bryan a generous foe. "After our debate he was the first to come to me with his affectionate congratulations," Malone reminisced. "Mr. Bryan will always be affectionately remembered by his countrymen for the valor and the gallantry with which he fought for his causes." Arthur Garfield Hays seemed genuinely saddened. "Defense counsel left Dayton happy in the thought that they had won a moral victory," Hays admitted, "but the taste is bitter when followed by such a tragic ending."

This was all "apology, not praise," Mencken wryly noted. "The truth is that even Bryan's sincerity will probably yield to what is called, in other fields, definitive criticism. Was he sincere when he opposed imperialism in the Philippines, or when he fed it with deserving Democrats in Santo Domingo?" Though Bryan's sudden death had largely paralyzed the critics and carpers, shrewd analysis of the Commoner began to appear, particularly from those who knew him over the years. To some, Bryan fell from Democratic grace as early as 1912, after he engineered the defeat of presidential front-runner Champ Clark, once his friend. "He was crafty as a Talleyrand and as ambitious as a Caesar," said the political reporter Hugh Nugent Fitzgerald, who'd been acquainted with Bryan for at least two decades.

The *Nation* damned Bryan as a leader who meant well but who, as Secretary of State, lacked any talent for administration or statesmanship, and though he negotiated arbitration treaties, he'd said nothing during the armed and ruthless invasions of Veracruz and Haiti. Good intentions and grape juice do not a diplomat make. "It is pathetic to think of the hero of such crusades spending his last years selling real estate and attempting to keep science out of the schools," the editors concluded with some aspersion.

The German-born author George Sylvester Viereck remembered visiting Bryan in Miami in 1920 to thank the former Secretary of State for exempting German Americans from military service. "How did they thank me for it?" a petulant Bryan exclaimed. "Did they support me in Nebraska? No. They did not. They voted for beer." Suddenly Bryan seemed nothing but a griping, grasping politician, the kind who hoped to exact a price for every good deed.

If Bryan inspired conflicting emotions, it was in part because he was a contradiction. "Hate of his fellowman and love for humanity," Viereck said, "a fine spirit of self-sacrifice and shrewd self calculation." He was the peddler of real estate and an evangelist, a man who cared for the people, especially the poor, and loathed the plutocrats yet yearned to be one. After his death, his estate was worth about a million dollars. Yet while his syndicated columns from the Democratic and Republican conventions in 1912 and 1916 presumably netted him at least $20,000, the columnist James Morgan, who had faithfully followed him, speculated that "the riches that came to him left him feeling poor in the denial of his earlier and higher ambition."

Hypocritical eulogies coming from those who despised Bryan turned the stomach of Eugene Debs, five-time socialist candidate for president. "The cause of human progress had sustained no loss in his death," Debs declared. Like Darrow and many others, Debs had been an avid supporter of Bryan's presidential bid back in 1896 and delivered some seventy-seven speeches on his behalf. But when Debs was sent to prison for violating the Sedition Act of 1918, Bryan said not a word in his defense nor in defense of those many others who had been hounded, arrested, or deported. Taking Bryan's measure soon after his death, Debs was unusually, if understandably, bitter. "Had Bryan possessed the power he would have muzzled free thought and free speech; he would have re-enacted the blue laws and made them even more stringent; he would have made the state and church one with the church at the top; he would have compelled reading of the Bible and church attendance just as the Puritans did in Massachusetts colony two centuries ago, and he would have finally converted the whole country into a first class penitentiary."

The evolution trial wasn't the first time Bryan had displayed jingoistic bigotry. In 1901, citing "the yellow peril," he backed the Chinese exclusion law to preserve "the unity and homogeneousness of our nation." As Bryan explained several years later, after traveling round the world, "if every American could visit China, the question of Chinese immigration would soon be settled upon a permanent basis, for no one can become acquainted with the Chinese coolie without recognizing the impossibility of opening the doors of our country to him without injustice to our own laboring men, demoralization to our social ideals." He added that Japanese and Filipino immigration should be prevented as well.

"One race problem is enough," Bryan had declared. Democratic rule meant little after all, with Bryan claiming again and again that white people, with their "more advanced civilization," would be "more apt to deal justly with the blacks than the blacks would be." Over the years, those views did not change.

Yet conservative Black ministers often sided with Bryan's scriptural literalism, regardless of his racial views. "Thousands refuse to believe that man is descended from an ape, and we are one of them. We stand with the Commoner and the Bible," the Black columnist Floyd Calvin wrote in *The Pittsburgh Courier*, although just a week earlier, its editor had reminded readers that "Negroes have nothing to treasure out of the life of Bryan."

Such ambivalence was not unusual. Sure, Bryan was sincere, a sincerely religious bigot and liar. Bryan was the scourge of Wall Street speculators yet cheerfully hawked Florida real estate—"a sort of speculating and dealing in fictitious values," Black writer

Chandler Owen observed, "which in anybody else would have been termed by the prolific phrase-making commoner, 'a shell game.'" A white supremacist, Bryan did nothing to stop the Ku Klux Klan or help its victims, and he never once lifted his voice against its crusade of terror. And, Owen concluded, during the Scopes trial, Bryan happily pandered to the prejudices of the multitude when he referred to the "foreign lawyers from the Godless cities of New York and Chicago who come into Tennessee to impose upon its people their brand of religion."

"Bryan at his best was simply a magnificent job-seeker," Mencken observed, "deluded by a childish theology, full of an almost pathological hatred of all learning, all human dignity, all beauty, and fine and noble things." Reliably provocative, Mencken would not sentimentalize the Commoner. "This talk of sincerity, I confess, fatigues me," he scoffed. "If the fellow was sincere, so was P. T. Barnum."

"The job before democracy, is to get rid of such figures," Mencken incisively concluded. "If it fails, they will devour it."

ON A DRIZZLY spring afternoon in Washington, nine years later, in 1934, President Franklin Roosevelt accepted on behalf of the nation a twelve-foot-high bronze statue of William Jennings Bryan.

Arm upraised and wearing a cape that resembled a Roman toga, the heroic-sized bronze Bryan by Gutzon Borglum, the sculptor of Mt. Rushmore, was later removed from its spot overlooking the Potomac and carted off to Salem, Illinois, Bryan's birthplace, to allow for the construction of a highway.

But in 1934, Roosevelt had come to praise Bryan, whom he said he'd been lucky enough to know when they both served in the Woodrow Wilson administration, Roosevelt as a very young man. "No man of his time was or could have been more constantly in the limelight than he," Roosevelt said, speaking from

the covered grandstand where the dignitaries had gathered in a
rain that had begun to fall steadily. "Yet we can look back and
scan his record without being able to point to any instance where
he took a position that did not accord with his conscience or his
belief."

Unveiling of statue of William Jennings Bryan,
Washington, D.C., 1934
COURTESY LIBRARY OF CONGRESS

Those who stood there, like Bryan's friend Ambassador Josephus Daniels, and those across the nation who listened on the

radio, heard Roosevelt say that he loved Bryan, a real progressive Democrat, as he'd called him back in the day. "Bryan was a force for good in his own generation and today, keeps alive the ancient faiths on which we build," Roosevelt now declared.

"He did not have to dare to do what to him seemed right; he could not do otherwise," Roosevelt added. And he quoted from Bryan: "I respect the aristocracy of learning. I deplore the plutocracy of wealth, but I thank God for the democracy of the heart."

The United States Marine Band played the national anthem.

A Little Learning Is a Dangerous Thing

WHEN THE DAYTON JURY ANNOUNCED its guilty verdict in the matter of John Scopes, and Judge John T. Raulston determined what fine the young schoolteacher would pay, many of the spectators, particularly the younger ones, clustered around Clarence Darrow to shake his hand and clap him on the back. That evening they threw a dance in his honor, which he attended with great pleasure. He danced a little too. But though the stage was dark and the lawyers soon to depart, the reporters to vanish, and William Jennings Bryan soon gone to meet his maker, the trial was not quite over. There was still the appeal.

Bryan's sudden death had complicated matters. The same liberal journals that had been ridiculing Bryan, according to the reporter McAlister Coleman, were now suddenly raising "pained eyebrows in protest at the 'tawdry' methods pursued by the defense." It appeared as if Darrow the agnostic destroyer had single-handedly transformed Bryan from laughingstock to hapless victim. Worse yet, it seemed that Darrow had attacked Christianity.

Thus the defense's strategy, and even more particularly, its last theatrical act of calling Bryan to the stand, left the intelligentsia frustrated and embarrassed.

The main issue, these reproaches often began, should have

been the separation of church and state, as fixed in the Constitution. That is, the sole question for the trial should have been religious liberty. This was also Walter Lippmann's influential point of view in the liberal New York *World,* where he was editorial director. Not that Lippmann admired Bryan. "Apostle of the Morons" and "the Great Realtor of Miami," the *World* had called him. "A national politician has started a religious crusade among the ignorant and illiterate which aims to arm Fundamentalism with the police power of the state," the *World* lamented. But now Lippmann tacked in a different direction. The defense should have stayed on course. The Tennessee anti-evolution law had violated the constitutional separation of church and state. Darrow had thus blundered badly, having turned the trial into a referendum on whether one was "for or against the Christian religion."

Already widely known as an idealist, a socialist, a progressive, a gifted writer and a columnist as well as editor for *The New Republic* since its start in 1914, the intellectually agile Lippmann had graduated from Harvard just four years earlier in the same class as the socialist John Reed, the poet T. S. Eliot, and the columnist Heywood Broun.

Once the secretary of the socialist mayor of an upstate New York city and later a confidant of Woodrow Wilson, Lippmann gave Wilson, through his editorials, such slogans as "Peace Without Victory." Lippmann left *The New Republic,* joined the *World,* and would soon be considered one of the most powerful journalists of his generation.

"Lippmann evidently has not any sense," Darrow responded. "Scopes was indicted and it either had to go by default or somebody had to make a fuss about it. I was interested in waking the country up as to what they had to meet," Darrow continued. "They will never pull off anything else without a fight in the first instance and I think science should lead and I think will. However, life is nothing else but a fight, if you believe in any kind of freedom and they will edge in on us somewhere all the time. Prohibition was the first thing that caused all the difficulty, and I knew it would, but although I can get along without booze myself, I look on it as an outside fortification of freedom."

Walter Lippmann, journalist and author
COURTESY LIBRARY OF CONGRESS

Arthur Garfield Hays agreed, but he couldn't ignore Lippmann. Replying to him in *The Nation*, Hays insisted that the defense correctly wanted "to show that such laws result in hate and intolerance, that they are conceived in bigotry and born in ignorance—ignorance of the Bible, of religion, of history, and of science." As a result, the defense had based its argument on three propositions: The law was unconstitutional in that it tried to make the Bible the yardstick to measure truth, as Darrow's motion to quash the indictment had eloquently demonstrated; the law was unreasonable and therefore unconstitutional, based on the current definitions of evolution, as scientists would testify; and millions of Christians who accept the Bible find no conflict between it and evolution, which would further demonstrate that the law was both vague and unreasonable.

"This led to evidence what the Bible is, its history, meaning, translation, application, and interpretation," Hays explained. "Mr. Bryan was called as an expert."

The ACLU distributed copies of Hays's article but knew, as Hays did, that Clarence Darrow had been the real target. He was an easy mark. As Lippmann admitted, he had "no sympathy at all for the manner in which Mr. Darrow heckled Mr. Bryan." Darrow could be blamed for feeding the hungry press with the greatest show on earth. He could be blamed for putting Bryan on the stand and staging a debate that devolved into a travesty. And he was to blame for not emphasizing the important and constitutional issues at the heart of the case.

Nor was Lippmann alone. *The New Republic* criticized the defense lawyers for allowing the Fundamentalists to choose the terms of the battle. Worse yet, the whole thing seemed a pretext for publicizing evolution in the kind of melodrama that newspapers gobble up, with Judge Raulston and William Jennings Bryan cast as country clowns. There's no education in that, the editors wrote, and education was necessary, particularly the education of clerics. Christianity cannot be brought into the modern world without demonstrating how science complements religion and speaks to its socially responsible and tolerant heart.

The editors also maintained that the courts should never in-

tervene even when a legislature passes a foolish act, which the
Tennessee legislature had obviously done. To intervene is overreach, and so, if it wanted to do anything, the ACLU should
have shown the people of Tennessee, through its local lawyers
and liberal clergy, how "it would be disastrous for the Christian
church to confuse the truth of Christianity with either the truth
or falsity of any scientific theory." Sure, this method would have
taken much longer, but it would have been far preferable to
"staging a public trial and raising a hullabaloo about the Bible
and evolution."

Unpersuaded, Hays was adamant that whatever the trial may
have lacked in dignity, it gained in democracy.

The lawyer Walter Nelles, long associated with the ACLU,
also disagreed with *The New Republic,* suggesting that its editors seemed more offended by Darrow's suspenders—meaning
his plainspoken style—than by Tennessee's bigoted statute. And
because the statute was so absurd, it deserved the bluntness—
and theatrics—that incited interest, which was itself educational.
If, then, the trial was conducted to inspire chatter at the corner
drugstore or dinner table debate, so much the better.

The irrepressible Henry Mencken too hit back. The *New Republic* writers were nothing but a bunch of "kept idealists" (the
wealthy Dorothy and Willard Straight subsidized the magazine).
And should Clarence Darrow have addressed himself solely to
Tennesseans and not the whole country? Mencken waspishly
asked. As for educating the people of Tennessee, "Darrow did
more for them in two weeks," Mencken claimed, "than all their
pastors and politicians had done since the Civil War." But the
real point, Mencken concluded, was that a sixty-eight-year-old
Clarence Darrow, rugged and scarred and battle-weary but
showing no sign of wear, and without an iota of condescending
elitism, had magnificently conducted the Scopes case with fi-
nesse, intelligence, and downright good judgment.

. . .

"COLD FEET," DARROW surmised after learning that his colleague John Neal, the Tennessee lawyer in charge of the Scopes defense, seemed to vanish. "It is possible he had got cold feet with all the rest."

He was right. The ACLU had been backing away, at least from him. When its executive board met in early August, on the agenda was "the problem of counsel for the appeal." The problem was Darrow and how to get rid of him, Darrow the celebrity, Darrow in his disheveled shirt, Darrow stooped and sarcastic, Darrow the unruly radical unceremoniously squeezing the very life out of William Jennings Bryan. Behind closed doors, the prominent ACLU lawyer Walter Nelles said he wanted Darrow gone. Nelles wasn't alone. When Raymond Fosdick, head of the Rockefeller Foundation, complained that the case had been handled poorly, Roger Baldwin replied, "I guess we all feel as you do." Those ill feelings centered on Darrow.

So the executive board "recommended urging Dr. Neal to control the case in such a way as to preserve priority for the Tennessee counsel."

The associate director of the ACLU, Forrest Bailey, rushed out after the meeting to contact Neal. The ACLU, Bailey told Neal, had recently been "besieged with criticism of the spectacularity of the trial, its informality, and particularly the putting forward of the Darrow personality into a place of emphasis." Liberal Christians complained that they were being lumped together with Fundamentalists and, even worse, that despite his brilliance, Darrow's "baiting of Mr. Bryan seemed to us to be stirring up the dregs of the worst sort of bitterness," Bailey explained.

Bailey also admitted that "there seemed to be difficulty in the way of our taking any step to insure his disappearance." They wouldn't want to seem ungrateful, of course. Yet despite the ACLU's appreciation for Darrow's enormous gifts and superb achievement in Dayton, if the case were to get to the Supreme Court, "there ought to be more of Neal and less of Darrow," Bailey proposed. "We believe that the time has passed for the playing up of the Darrow personality."

Bailey was even more frank in his next letter to Neal. "If there is any graceful way in which it may be pointed out to Darrow that his personality and his court style might be an embarrassment in the dignified proceedings of an appellate court, that point ought to be made and that Darrow would be the first to appreciate it," he hinted broadly. He had already flattered Neal, calling him "quiet, modest, scholarly." Perhaps then the modest and scholarly Neal would speak to Darrow.

"The last thing in the world that we should want to do would be to give him the slightest offense or any suggestion of ingratitude," Bailey reiterated, protesting a bit too much. He knew the Dayton impresario George Rappleyea was also targeting Darrow. If the famous Chicago attorney appeared before the Tennessee Supreme court in Knoxville, Rappleyea told Bailey, it wouldn't be John Scopes who was on trial; it would be Clarence Darrow, "the man who spiritually and literally crucified Bryan on the cross examination." The Tennessee justices would consider Darrow crude. "Blue shirts and galluses [suspenders] harmonize perfectly with the Circuit Court of Rhea County," Rappleyea continued, "but they would be sadly out of place alongside the dignified robes of the Supreme Court." Rappleyea added, preposterously, that he was sure Malone would agree with him about dumping Darrow.

Rappleyea then assured Bailey that he admired Darrow and had no "personal feelings" against him. He just didn't want to run afoul of Arthur Garfield Hays, who found all this lobbying distasteful and inappropriate. Still, Rappleyea continued to push, even after he learned that Malone utterly disagreed with him. "It must be understood that neither Hayes [*sic*] nor Malone is running this case," Rappleyea implored Bailey, "and that Dr Neal is still Chief Counsel, and I believe that it is proper that Dr. Neal should not be questioned when he suggests who should or should not appear before the Supreme Court."

Though it's possible that Bailey or Neal had solicited Rappleyea's opinion, the wonder is why he was so determined to remove Darrow. But Bailey again insisted that the ACLU would do nothing to offend Darrow or Malone, which was to say that the ACLU would not do anything more than support John Neal, and if Neal was really taking the position that Darrow should be removed, Neal should inform Darrow as soon as possible. Bailey restated the ACLU's "deepest appreciation of Darrow's big achievement," although "whenever we think of him in Knoxville, we have chills and fever."

Bailey asked Felix Frankfurter to urge Darrow, courteously of course, to withdraw from the case. Bailey told former Stanford president and noted ichthyologist (and eugenicist) David Starr Jordan that while Darrow had been useful in "meeting the prosecution on their own ground of intolerance," that strategy had unfortunately "involved thrusting forward of Darrow's agnosticism." Since the case would now enter a new phase, Jordan might write John Neal and suggest that he speak to Darrow about withdrawing. Bailey also communicated with the liberal church leaders who were disappointed in Darrow, suggesting that they too might sway John Neal.

It was an all-out campaign.

Anticipating the question of why the ACLU didn't speak directly to Darrow themselves, Bailey continued to allude to "delicate factors in the situation." Fortunately, for the ACLU, Brewer Eddy of the American Board of Commissioners for Foreign Missions, the missionary arm of several major church denominations, took up Bailey's suggestion and wrote to John Neal. "You employed a man who was an avowed skeptic, a clear and cold agnostic; and whenever the reports have been read in the small churches of this land, you have lost the approval of Christian people," Eddy admonished Neal.

"It would seem to us obvious that lawyers of great national prominence, who are avowedly Christian, who give money and time in Christian obedience, and who stand for Missions and Christian service and a rich belief in the Bible, should be employed as leaders in the case," Eddy concluded.

Of course nothing and no one could persuade Darrow to walk away. But neither did he wish to advertise himself as critical of all Christianity. That had never been his position. Often invited to lecture on evolution or whether science is the enemy of the church, Darrow just as often refused. "I am not at all sure that religion is an enemy of science," he explained to Oswald Garrison Villard, editor of *The Nation*. The recent experience in Dayton, "where I saw the dense ignorance of what we call Fundamentalists," Darrow continued, "caused me to draw nearer to those who are fighting bigotry from the inside of some church organizations, and with some church organizations.

"I believe a large part of the church is very rapidly aligning itself with scientific thought, and personally I do not feel like doing anything to drive them away." Besides, he added, as he always did, people need some kind of faith.

That was of no moment to the ACLU.

Neal finally acted. Asking Darrow to step aside, he evidently told Darrow he was speaking on behalf of the ACLU.

Darrow was angry. "I never at any time asked that you be invited to withdraw," Bailey countered, trying to smooth things over. "I merely wished to put [Neal] in a position where he could act on his own responsibility in any way that he saw fit," Bailey continued half-truthfully. "I cannot believe that he actually committed the error of asking you to withdraw on our authority." Bailey did admit, however, "It did seem to us that you ought to be made aware that a problem existed."

"Of course we have to expect criticism if we do what we think we should do, and I get used to it," Darrow deftly replied. "I thoroughly understand the situation." In fact, he'd already recommended that Neal enlist a good Tennessee lawyer—he had suggested Frank Spurlock—not because he, Darrow, considered resigning from the case but because Neal was not quite the right person to lead such an important appeal. "He is a fine man and an able man and could have been a good lawyer if he had given his time to it," Darrow said, regretting that he felt "a little mean" saying this.

Darrow remained friendly, if miffed, but Hays was irritated, if not offended. Insisting that the ACLU owed Darrow a huge debt of gratitude for his splendid contribution to the case and for alerting the public to the gravity of the issues, Hays categorically declared that "I am not willing to have conservative lawyers and conservative organizations reap the benefit of work done by liberals or radicals.

"I think the whole idea is wrong. I never yet found any conservative lawyer who, at the beginning, wanted to undertake a case which *might* reflect discredit on him. When it turns out differently and there seems publicity or honor to be had, then offers of assistance come." Not to mention, Hays added, conservatives wouldn't really be passionate about the case. He clearly was. Darrow clearly was.

John Neal went dark. Perhaps he was evading the ACLU and Darrow and Hays. Perhaps he was on the stump, planning to run for governor. No one knew. "Dr. Neal is neither communicative nor particularly alert when it comes to action," Bailey complained to John Scopes.

Exasperated, Darrow told Hays that the "absolutely hopeless" Neal seemed not to be on top of the appeal. He apparently hadn't filed the "bill of exceptions," which was necessary for the appeal, since it included the detailed objections that Darrow, Hays, and Malone had made during the trial when they disputed some of Judge Raulston's rulings, like his decision to quash the indictment, his decision to allow prayer at the opening of each session, and his refusal to allow the testimony of the scientists. The bill of exceptions also included an objection against Judge Raulston's expunging the testimony, heard on the courthouse lawn, of William Jennings Bryan.

There was another wrinkle. Although Raulston had allowed the defense thirty days to file the bill of exceptions, someone had written sixty days on the document, just above the thirty days. Because the change had no legal weight, when the state moved to exclude the exceptions because of what it claimed was a late filing, the Tennessee Supreme Court upheld the state's motion. The scientific testimony, Bryan's testimony, the objections about quashing the indictment were all stricken from the record. Nothing was left of the Scopes appeal but the constitutional issue—that is, the constitutional validity of the anti-evolution law.

SINCE THE APPEAL now had to be argued solely on constitutional grounds, Bailey and the ACLU were even more determined to drop Darrow. Bailey turned to John Scopes, who had already enrolled at the University of Chicago, to enlist his support. "It would be a grave mistake for Mr. Darrow to continue as counsel after the Tennessee phase," Bailey wrote the younger man. But Scopes was friendly with the Darrows and visited them fairly often in Chicago. Bailey had put him in an awkward position.

Bailey nonetheless explained to Scopes the ACLU's new proposal. They would create a committee of "eminent lawyers" to act "in an advisory capacity in shaping future policies and selection of counsel." This committee would be essential if the case were to be heard before the United States Supreme Court.

Scopes didn't answer Bailey's letter.

Bailey wrote again. The executive committee had decided unanimously to exercise their authority and replace Darrow with that proposed advisory committee—but only if Scopes approved.

Scopes hedged. Mr. Darrow was out of town, and he couldn't speak for him but was sure Mr. Hays could make a satisfactory arrangement with Mr. Darrow. Scopes suspected, then and later, that Darrow was much too militant for the ACLU. And he knew that Darrow would never withdraw.

Scopes was stalling. Darrow was in Detroit, working with Hays on a case there. Bailey already knew that. In fact, he asked Hays to make sure that no one connected the ACLU to their Detroit case. Hays replied evenly, telling Bailey not to worry. The Detroit case wasn't an ACLU issue. It was a racial one.

The same day that Bailey was pressing Scopes to cut Darrow loose, Clarence Darrow was at the Detroit Court of Records registering as chief counsel for the family of Dr. Ossian Sweet and his friends. They'd been accused of killing one white man and wounding another in defense of their home when, on September 9, 1925, just thirty-one days after that Klan parade in Washington, a mob composed in part of Klan members attempted to drive the Sweets out of the white residential neighborhood where they, a Black family, had recently purchased a house.

The celebrated, radical, and unruly Clarence Darrow had been hired by the National Association of Colored People to defend the Sweets and their friends.

"This case is a cross-section of human history," Darrow would tell the court. "It involves the future."

The Lost Cause

THREE MONTHS LATER, IN EARLY January 1926, the defense's appeal—more than a hundred pages—was filed at the Tennessee Supreme Court. It had been signed by two Tennessee lawyers, Robert Keebler of Memphis and Frank Spurlock of Chattanooga, and Frank McElwee, once John Neal's student. Signing the appeal were also the so-called foreign lawyers, Darrow and Hays (Malone was back in Paris) along with ACLU lawyers Samuel J. Rosensohn and Walter H. Pollak. But only Hays and Darrow, of the foreigners, would appear in Tennessee when the time came.

Regardless, there were those in the ACLU who wanted even more Tennessee lawyers involved. Hays disagreed and so did Keebler, who pointed out that adding more lawyers might look desperate. Forrest Bailey backed off. "If any other suggestions are to be passed on to you, somebody else will have to do it," Bailey told Hays. "The pressure upon me has been so strong."

Whatever pressure Bailey felt, Hays was optimistically proud of the appeal. It enumerated what the defense considered to be errors, like excluding the scientific testimony, and it alleged that neither the Butler Act nor the indictment clearly defined the crime that Scopes was said to commit. "If the indictment is invalid or the Act is invalid," the appeal declared, "the sentence pronounced upon the defendant Scopes is likewise invalid."

Darrow had little to do with the appeal at this juncture. As chief counsel in the Sweet murder case, he was dealing with bigotry yet again, though this time his target was racial bigotry. For during the Sweet trial, Darrow turned the tables on the jury, asking whether they, an all-white body of men, really thought it possible to give Black men a fair shake.

The jury having failed to agree on a verdict, the presiding judge, Frank Murphy, had to declare a mistrial. But Darrow wasn't finished, and he wasn't dealing with the Scopes appeal, not yet. He went from Detroit to New York to speak with Hays at the annual meeting of the NAACP and then returned to Detroit to collaborate with a local Black lawyer, Julian Perry, as well as a white lawyer, Thomas Chawke, in the defense of Dr. Sweet's brother Henry, who was being tried separately.

At the trial, Darrow delivered yet another poignant summation, without notes as usual. "Now, gentlemen, I am not saying that the white people of Detroit are different from the white people of any other city," Darrow coaxed the jury. "I know what has been done in Chicago. I know what prejudice growing out of race and religion has done the world over, and all through time.

"Make yourselves colored for a little while. It won't hurt, you can wash it off," he sharply added. "They can't, but you can; just make yourselves black men for a little while; long enough, gentlemen, to judge them, and before any of you would want to be judged, you would want your juror to put himself in your place. That is all I ask in this case, gentlemen. They were black, and they knew the history of the black." The Sweets and their friends were acting in tragic self-defense; and the tragedy is what they were forced to face, as Black women and men.

"It tore our hearts," recalled Marcet Haldeman-Julius, who

wrote about the trial for the *Haldeman-Julius* paper. Almost no one else in the white press had.

Henry Sweet was acquitted, and eventually the state dropped the murder charges against his brother, Ossian, and all the other defendants.

ON MAY 9, 1926, just a few days before the acquittal of Henry Sweet, the state of Tennessee filed its response to the defense's appellate brief. The response ran to four hundred pages.

It duplicated much of what Bryan had already said or written—but with far more vitriol.

Labeling the defense arguments on behalf of Scopes as specious, captious, and quibbling, the authors of the brief—mainly Edward Seay and K. T. McConnico—began by commending the state legislature for remembering that "A Little Learning Is a Dangerous Thing." Contemptuous and patronizing, they went on to mock the theory of evolution as a "*pseudo*-science," italicizing "pseudo."

Writing as if no scientist of any merit had traveled to Dayton, they also declared that "no really great and outstanding scientist, none except (1) the little group of superficialists and those who are very desirous and enthusiastic to be regarded as sublimated 'intellectuals,' (2) some well-intentioned would-be rescuers of religion who have been unduly alarmed by the clamor of these superficialists, and (3) some others who belong to the forces of unrest—have ever *claimed* that it has ever been, or, by the nature of things, can ever be, demonstrated or established 'that man has descended from a lower order of animals.'"

Less concerned with legal arguments than with ridiculing the defense team, the prosecutors accused Darrow and Hays and Malone of flying under a "soiled or even red banner" and desiring to "overthrow the existing order and established government." Tossing around such words as "pathetic," "perverted," "hysterical," and "repulsive," the state attorneys charged the defense with denigrating religion, "which is the safeguard of constitutional government in our state." The prosecutors also warned that once you allow the theory of evolution into the classroom, you'll soon have to permit "the doctrine of communism, of the 'left wing' of socialism, of Bolshevism, of 'Free Love' or 'Free Thought' or 'Free Property.'"

Whether the state's attorneys really believed this, their arguments were an admission that the issues involved in this unusual and celebrated case were not narrow, simple, or specific, as they'd originally claimed, but broad, complex, and cultural.

THE APPEAL WOULD be argued before the Tennessee Supreme Court in the elegant state capitol of Nashville on May 31, with two days allotted for oral arguments.

Five justices would hear arguments: Chief Justice Grafton Green and Associate Justice Colin P. McKinney, both Presbyterians, along with Justices W. L. Cook and Frank Hall, Methodists. Judge Alexander Chambliss, a Baptist, was not only a descendant of French Huguenots but of the dissident minister Roger Williams, the founder of colonial Rhode Island who fought for the separation of church and state.

For the defense, Darrow and Hays would be joined by the lawyer Charles Strong, speaking on behalf of the Unitarian Laymen's League. Representing the Tennessee Academy of Science would be the lawyer Henry Colton, who'd filed an amicus curiae ("friend of the court") on behalf of Scopes. Also filing an amicus curiae was Thomas H. Malone, special judge of the Tennessee Supreme Court, and no relation to Dudley Field Malone. Judge Thomas Malone too would speak.

Countering them would be K. T. McConnico and Edward T. Seay, who had signed the reply brief. Though he too had signed it, Bryan's son William Jennings Bryan Jr. did not appear in

Nashville, though he offered an argument for public control of education, as against "scientific infidelity."

Courteous and subdued, though still fatigued from the Sweet trial, Darrow arrived in Nashville wearing his blue suspenders under his vest. His jacket was crisp and spotless. His clothes and manner had changed with the venue. Though not scheduled to speak until the second day, when he would deliver the closing argument, on the first day of the hearings, people who wanted to see him flocked to the state house more than an hour before the doors to the building officially opened. The chamber quickly filled, and near the doors and the windows, people jostled and then stood on chairs and tables for a better view.

But this time, national newspapers did not send two hundred correspondents. There would be no newsreel cameras or flashing bulbs, and the clicking of whatever telegraph equipment had been allowed had to be muffled.

There would be no John Scopes, who had stayed in Chicago, and of course there'd be no William Jennings Bryan.

John Randolph Neal opened by introducing members of the defense from out of state. He proceeded to outline the case as he had in Dayton: the law violated both the state's constitution and the Fourteenth Amendment's guarantee of due process. Arthur Garfield Hays elaborated some of Neal's argument, insisting again that the law was indefinite, its interpretations vague. He'd said all this before, but concluded with a vehement plea for "the freedom of education, for the liberty to teach and the liberty to learn."

Charles Strong claimed that many Christians didn't think evolution weakened the faith of their youth, and speaking for science, Henry Colton said that evolution doesn't deny the divine nor does the Bible conflict with the theories of evolution, adding that "the statute is unconstitutional because it is an unreasonable, arbitrary and capricious misuse by the legislature of the public funds."

Concluding the argument for the defense was Robert Keebler, who said that the case had attracted attention because it concerned academic freedom—and freedom from dogmatism.

It was time then for the state to present its argument. Edward Seay conceded that to have created such enormous interest in the case, there had to be something broader and deeper at stake than the question of whether the theory of evolution should be taught in the public schools. But to him, any interest in the trial was a function of the "revolutionary agitation" best symbolized by the ACLU. To him, the American Civil Liberties Union was a disreputable organization that supported people—revolutionaries, that is—who aimed to overthrow the government. Remember that Darrow had defended communists in Chicago.

"If you permit the teaching that the law of life is the law of the jungle," Seay continued, "you have laid the foundation by which man can be brought to accept the doctrines of communism and to the point where he believes it right to advocate murder."

"I want Your Honors to believe that the Tennessee legislature passed the law to stamp out worse things," he beseeched the justices. "I want you to believe the legislature thought it best to strangle the puppy rather than to kill the mad dog later."

Strangle the puppy? The room was silent.

On the next day, Tuesday, Judge Thomas Malone rose first to speak as a friend of the defense and represent, he said, those intelligent, devout citizens who were neither blind materialists nor bigoted literalists.

K. T. McConnico paid no attention. He too tore into the ACLU, into Hays, and especially into Darrow.

Known as a masterful speaker, McConnico blasted the ACLU as hiding their communism under a bushel of patriotism. He scoffed at the ACLU's statements about free speech, noting that Roger Baldwin had said any "advocacy of murder unaccompanied by an act" falls within the scope of free speech, and Hays had signed a document to that effect.

"Just open the sewer, hold your nose, and let them talk," McConnico exclaimed. And the ACLU had advocated sending "lewd matter" through the mails. "No censorship of any kind," McConnico lashed out. "That is the way their mind works."

"When people—radicals, civil liberty unions, iconoclasts and communists and anarchists—were invading Tennessee, and said that this act violated religious liberty," McConnico angrily continued, "I knew there was a missing link somewhere." To him, the missing link was the desire to overthrow the government. "Whenever a government is overthrown," McConnico portentously declared, "religion must be overthrown before the flag is lowered and chaos reigns."

"Today in Russia"—he was almost hysterical—"where the chaos of communism reigns and terror has stalked"—it was terrifying—"they have abolished religion, they have nationalized women and children."

"There is no truth in that," Darrow whispered under his breath.

McConnico took a swipe at what he called Darrow's "animal dogma" (the theory of evolution) and reminded the justices that the Chicago attorney had defended William Bross Lloyd and nineteen members of the Communist Labor Party of America—all "Reds"—in Illinois.

To prove his point, McConnico declared that "animal dogma" leads directly "to atheism, on to communism, on to the filthy cult of free love, on to the filthy cult of free thought, on to chaos, on to perversion, and on to degeneracy."

And the Tennessee legislature had been the necessary bulwark against all this. Good Christians do not tend that way. Good Tennesseans James Polk and Andrew Jackson and Andrew Johnson did not tend that way. Nor did that well-known Tennessean Sam Davis, the young Confederate scout who was captured in 1863 carrying papers that belonged to Union general Grenville

Dodge. When Dodge asked where young Davis had gotten the documents and the boy refused to answer, he was court-martialed and sentenced to death.

McConnico told the story: Just before his execution, General Dodge gave young Davis one more chance. Say who gave you the documents, and I will give your weapon back and convey you safely to the Confederate line. The good boy would not budge.

McConnico read the letter that Sam Davis wrote to his mother. " 'All Heaven is sanctioning the act I am about to take,' " wrote the noble boy, who was more than ready to die for the Confederacy.

"That is the type of citizenship we want in Tennessee," McConnico cried to great applause.

It wasn't clear if the clapping was for his oratory, the Butler Act, or the myth of the glorious Lost Cause: that is, how the South, undimmed by defeat, had defended and would continue to defend its honor and integrity and loyalty and valor—and, implicitly, slavery—against a rapacious North.

DARROW HADN'T SAID MUCH. When it was his turn, he mainly confined himself to the legal issues. But not entirely.

He took on McConnico's abuse of the ACLU. "From what I think I know of human nature I fancy there never will be a time when a league for the protection of individuals will not be a fine thing," Darrow declared with an edge. Quietly he added that we've had everything argued in this case except what "it seems to me should have been—a temperate, scholarly argument to the highest tribunal in this state." Darrow too knew how to appeal to the vanity of judges, though he did say that greatness and virtue might just exist in places other than Tennessee.

As for a little learning being dangerous, Darrow shrugged his large shoulders. Maybe so, he admitted, "but in spite of that, as long as man has an inquiring mind, he will seek to know and to find out. He is bound to do it."

He then launched into the case.

The theory of evolution was not a religious but a scientific theory. No chemist or civil engineer or doctor could ever build a bridge or treat the sick by reading the Bible alone. The Bible is not a scientific book. Similarly, the Bible never pretended to be a work of science. "The realm of religion, as I understand it, is where knowledge leaves off and where faith begins," Darrow explained, "and it never has needed the arm of the state for support, and wherever it has received it, it has harmed both the public and the republic that it would pretend to serve."

As for the schools of Tennessee, they were established to teach science and knowledge, not religion.

Darrow dissected the Butler Act, word for word, to demonstrate its ambiguities. This too had been said in Dayton, but Darrow was making those points all over again. The law didn't specify what a teacher could or could not teach, and for that matter teachers would have to know the entire Bible and be familiar with all the different versions of it before they could know whether they were in violation of the law. Don't forget that even Mr. Bryan did not interpret the Bible in strict literal terms any more than he believed, like some Holy Rollers did, that the earth was flat. In fact, Darrow continued, it would've been as logical for the state to have legislated that geography should not be taught, from the Holy Roller point of view, as it was logical to legislate against teaching the theory of evolution from the Fundamentalist point of view.

In this same vein, Darrow noted that moral precepts may be common to all religions. Take Greece, he said, which was civilized long before the Bible was written. But as it happens, Darrow emphasized, we're fighting for the same right today that was once fought in the Parthenon. We're fighting for intellectual freedom and the freedom to learn.

Darrow asked the court to set aside the conviction of Scopes and uphold constitutional guarantees of Tennessee and of the federal government.

Darrow too received applause. Tennessee reporters called him mild and scholarly and praised him for hewing close to the law.

AFTER ORAL ARGUMENTS were over, and shortly before nine o'clock on Tuesday night, Clarence Darrow strolled out of Nashville's Hermitage Hotel. He was on his way to Union Station, a cigarette dangling from his lips and on his head a jaunty straw hat. Reporters had been waiting for him, so he stopped for a brief chat.

"As time passes," Darrow observed, "the people will understand my views more and more." He was in a philosophical mood. "I realized early in life that I must be tolerant," he reflected. "I deny no man his beliefs, religious or otherwise."

IF THE TENNESSEE high court held the Butler Act constitutional, Darrow and Hays said they'd appeal the decision to the United States Supreme Court. But the ACLU was still, even now, not so sure that Darrow and Hays should be the ones to do it.

"Our feeling is that there should be a new set of counsel," Forrest Bailey wrote Darrow immediately after Darrow addressed the Tennessee Supreme Court. Now, as co-director of the ACLU, Bailey didn't waste any time letting Darrow know they wanted him to withdraw from the case. "We base that feeling on the theory that certain considerations more or less 'political' are bound to have influence before the United States Supreme Court. We believe that whoever argues the case before the United States Supreme Court should be utterly beyond the reach of the prejudices of certain members of that august body, and we seriously doubt whether you or Mr. Malone or Mr. Hays, for example, would meet this requirement."

"The psychology of course is what it is," Bailey added, somewhat superfluously. Darrow was incensed: "I have no idea that it will make the slightest difference to the Supreme Court of the United States who presents this case, provided it is well presented, and I have no idea that anyone else can present it better than it was done in Tennessee."

"Any possible prejudice that might exist as to Mr. Hays or me would be very much stronger against your Organization," Darrow noted with acerbity.

Darrow was hurt, his pride wounded, and though he rarely allowed himself to be seen as vulnerable, he sent the ACLU a letter that he'd received from Judge Malone. The judge had heard through the grapevine that Darrow had deeply impressed the State Supreme Court with his "very fair and conservative argument."

Forrest Bailey wasn't impressed. "To have Darrow appeal to the U.S. Supreme Court would be fatal to the case," Bailey told Roger Baldwin. "I think that we have to get Darrow out or get out ourselves."

Bailey was obviously troubled too by more editorials in the New York *World* claiming that the ACLU had made a huge mistake when they refused to enlist conservative attorneys at the outset of the Scopes case. Defending the organization, Bailey contacted Walter Lippmann and rehashed the origins of the case, what he called the "inside story" of Darrow and Malone's involvement: how Scopes, who was already working with John Neal, had accepted the offers of those two men and how even though "we did the very best we could to undo it," and how the ACLU had failed to convince Darrow and Malone—"right here in this office"—that "they did not belong." There was no way, then, to eradicate the "taint of the left wingers."

Darrow knew none of the specifics but decided to share his

correspondence with John Scopes. Scopes contacted Bailey. As if endorsing the ACLU's decision to invite only cautious lawyers to defend him, Scopes agreed that "right from the first we have all been very much interested in retaining the services of some outstanding conservative to fight our cause."

He then turned around. "Do you not think that showed a little cowardice?" Scopes asked. "Besides," he continued, "I believe that any radical cause, as this is, will be defended with more zeal and effect by radicals. I believe we would have made a larger mess of things at Dayton than we did if we had not shown our true colors, and if the case goes on up, personally I think we should still keep ourselves as we were there."

Yet Scopes didn't want to lose the support of the ACLU. "I do not mean that the personnel [of] lawyers should be the same, but if a change is made men of like standing should be used."

Roger Baldwin immediately answered Scopes. "We would not think for a moment of selecting a lawyer who would not have the cause as thoroughly at heart as those two gentlemen," he reassured the younger man. "But it is not a radical case, and does not require a man whose economic philosophy is radical to handle it. Furthermore, we believe that the importance of the issue demands that we should get the lawyer most likely to impress the Supreme Court, and certainly one who would not prejudice the court in advance," Baldwin explained. "There is something to the psychology of having appear before the court a man who is not an agnostic or atheist."

That is, Clarence Darrow was a liability: an agnostic, a showman, a tainted and too-public figure associated with causes too radical. The ACLU was a pragmatic organization. Causes were more important than personalities, and they wanted to win. If that seemed ruthless, it was. If they had promised Darrow that they wouldn't do anything during the summer, they weren't exactly breaking their word. Baldwin went on to say that the ACLU might be forced to withdraw from the case if Darrow and Hays insisted on staying. Either Scopes could make the choice of counsel himself—the defendant had a right to employ whom he chose—or he could let the ACLU decide who should bring the case before the Supreme Court.

"I note that you seem a little distressed at having to make this decision," Baldwin said, continuing to mollify Scopes, promising he'd make every effort to remove Darrow and Hays from the case surgically and without causing a rift.

That wouldn't be easy. At an informal meeting of ACLU lawyers, Wolcott Pitkin said he felt Darrow should never have been hired in the first place but didn't think it right for the ACLU to ditch him now. Morris Ernst didn't want to change counsel either. To him, it would be a tactical error suggesting weakness. Still, he recommended that any appeal headed to the United States Supreme Court be signed by nationally prominent lawyers who happened to be members of evangelical churches. That would be hard, Pitkin countered, with Darrow on board. And Samuel Rosensohn was dead set against Darrow. He still hoped to enlist Charles Evans Hughes to present the case from a cold constitutional point of view, which Darrow couldn't do, "even with the best intentions." Nothing was decided.

And no one wanted to buck Arthur Garfield Hays, who unfailingly supported Darrow. He never wavered. Never. "Nothing in life do I treasure more than that," Hays wrote later in life, reflecting on his long association with Darrow. "Nothing has been more inspiring or humanly helpful than his company, his example, and his friendship."

"He was, to me, the greatest man I ever met."

IT DIDN'T MATTER whether the ACLU convinced Darrow to resign from the case. It didn't matter that Darrow and Hays were tarred with a red brush, or that Bryan seemed a martyr, or that

Dayton resumed its quiet village life, almost as though nothing had happened there.

It didn't matter because the Tennessee Supreme Court's decision outwitted the defense and even the state.

Though it upheld the law as constitutionally valid, with just one justice dissenting, the court reversed the guilty verdict on a technicality. Judge Raulston had apparently erred when he levied the $100 fine against Scopes. In Tennessee any fine more than $50 had to be set by a jury, not a judge, so the jury should have determined the amount of the fine.

As Hays later said, "The decision was a subtle one." To say the least.

Chief Justice Green read aloud the court's conclusion. The court suggested that the state's attorney general drop the indictment and declare nolle prosequi (no longer prosecuting) to prevent any appeal.

"All of us agree," Justice Green read in a low voice, that "nothing is to be gained by prolonging the life of this bizarre case."

IT WAS JANUARY 15, 1927, when the four remaining Tennessee Supreme Court judges issued their ruling. (Justice Hall had died and his replacement recused himself.) Three of the four justices—Green, Cook, Chambliss—held the law to be constitutional, noting that the anti-evolution law did not infringe on individual liberty because it applied only to public employees, and since it didn't prescribe what to teach, it did not give preference to any one religion.

But Justices Green and Cook said the law prohibited only the teaching of human evolution, as opposed to plant or animal evolution, in the public schools. And Judge Chambliss stated that the Butler Act prohibited only a so-called materialist, as opposed

to a "theistic," theory of evolution. That is, if the theory of evolution didn't explicitly deny that God had some role in creation,
then it could be taught. In fact, one might even suppose that God
created humans over time: "The way is left open for such teaching of the pertinent sciences as is approved by the progressive
God recognizing leaders of thought and life." Judge Chambliss
could thus uphold the anti-evolution law and deny it. To him,
the law hadn't been violated.

As Hays remarked, Chambliss slyly, even brilliantly, managed to keep the law and suggest at the same time it should not
be enforced.

The fourth justice, Colin P. McKinney, dissented. To him, the
law was indeed vague and therefore unconstitutional.

And that was the end of it. In a matter of days, Chief Justice
Green denied a defense motion for a new hearing. There could
be no appeal to the United States Supreme Court.

Exasperated, Dudley Field Malone called the court's sleight
of hand "a typical country lawyer's trick" though in cooler mo-
ments proclaimed the verdict a victory since the state would
never permit another indictment to be brought under the Butler
Act.

Hays too interpreted the decision as a victory, as he almost
had to do, politically speaking. "I think the Anti-Evolution law
in Tennessee is dead, because the courts don't want to pass
upon it."

"We are dealing with astute church people," Hays remarked,
"and I guess we did not credit them with the astuteness that they
really possessed."

The decision was astute, no doubt about it. Darrow barely
mentioned it.

HE CONTINUED TO speak out. He could not stop. He would not
let himself stop. He refused to debate John Roach Straton but

appeared at the community church of his friend John Haynes Holmes in New York. Throngs of people waited at the door. "When the devil preaches, the churches are crowded," Mary Field Parton confided to her diary. Darrow spoke at the Brooklyn Jewish Center, where about 1,500 men and women showed up. He was funny. He was cutting. "Tennessee is composed of a singular aggregation of people belonging to the Nordic race— 90 per cent pure (I should say poor)." The audience laughed.

"All Nordics are of the super-race, so-called," he sardonically noted. "I'm a Nordic." He paused. "I apologize for it." More laughter.

It was clear that the issues in Dayton went beyond religion.

"What about the future life?" someone in the audience asked. "Do you leave man without a crutch?"

Darrow softened. He said that in the face of a relentless world, in the face of the terrible fact of death—the death of one's loved ones, of one's self—one needs some kind of comfort, some kind of drug. His was work, or crossword puzzles, or lecturing and taking a drink now and then. His voice was kind, gentle. "I knew again he was a man of sorrow & acquainted with grief," Mary Field Parton noted.

He continued to object to the state's intrusion into an individual's civil rights. Just two months after the Tennessee Supreme Court handed down its decision on the Scopes case, Darrow and his wife were in Alabama, presumably to rest. The strain of the Scopes case, followed by the Ossian Sweet case, followed by the Scopes appeal, had taken a toll. He was a weathered seventy-one, the lines in his face cut deeper than ever, and he had recently suffered what seems to have been a heart attack. But the Old Lion would not stay caged.

At the Tuskegee Institute, he reminded the students that no one race possesses more intrinsic intelligence than any other. At the Negro Industrial School in Daphne, Alabama, he was hustled out of the theater through the back door when he advised the

Black audience to defy "the white man who calls himself your 'friend' by hanging and burning you; by making you do his work, and use his back door; refusing to let you enter the best hotels and to use the best coach in the train, and by making you sit in the rear of the street car."

"The only front place the white man has ever given you is in the battle line," he cried.

The Ku Klux Klan had threatened to ride him out of town on a rail.

He continued to act and to speak out. He and Arthur Hays defended a Black woman, Blanche Brookins, pulled off a train in Florida and fined because she violated the state's Jim Crow laws. They recovered more than two thousand dollars for her when they sued the railroad. But a group of Black ministers, on behalf of the Interdenominational Ministerial Alliance, refused to let him speak in their churches in Washington because of his agnosticism. He spoke anyway, but in the open-air pavilion at the Suburban Gardens, an amusement park owned by Blacks, to an audience of about six hundred. When Bishop John Hurst of the African Methodist Episcopal Church stood up to leave, Darrow looked right at him as Bishop Hurst headed for the door. "Your battle," Darrow pointedly said, "will be fought here on earth, and victory will never come out of the clouds, for these same heavens witnessed the slave ships in the middle passages, the jettisons and hangings and burnings of negroes for 300 years, all in the midst of prayer on prayer."

"What do people mean when they talk about a race?" he asked. "They talk as if Almighty made a white man, a red man, a blue man, a black man and a yellow man, all different races."

With Arthur Hays, Darrow defended two Italian immigrants, Calogero Greco and Donato Carillo, both of them accused of murdering two Fascist supporters of Benito Mussolini, who then sent flowers to their funerals and arranged to have the bodies buried in Naples. Asked why he took the case, Darrow gave two reasons: "The first reason is that I detest Mussolini and everything he stands for; the second was the example of the Sacco-Vanzetti case."

Darrow was referring to the Italian-born anarchists, Nicola Sacco and Bartolomeo Vanzetti, executed in Massachusetts for allegedly murdering guards during an armed holdup—despite several motions for a new trial, several appeals, and a huge international outcry against the demonstrably biased judge and the failure of the American criminal justice system.

"I felt that prejudice, passion and feeling were largely responsible for the verdict," Darrow declared. "I didn't want to see it happen again."

He also said this case would be his last. Then, with a broad grin lighting his craggy face, he added, yes, it would be his last case—unless someone gets into trouble.

The Four Winds of the Sky

Law is born from despair of human nature.
—JOSÉ ORTEGA Y GASSET

The world is dark; but it is not hopeless.
—CLARENCE DARROW

"IT IS TOO EARLY, it seems to me, to send the firemen home," Henry Mencken reflected shortly after the trial. "The fire is still burning on many a far-flung hill, and it may begin to roar again at any moment. The evil that men do lives after them."

Mencken understood that the trial had been no silly circus—that, in fact, the Scopes trial raised issues that have perplexed America since its founding and still do today. The First Amendment to the Constitution was meant to protect free speech and the free exercise of religion and, by implication, to protect one's ability to inquire, to teach, and to learn. In Dayton in 1925, and in America, this was neither a joke nor theoretical—not to the churchgoers who reconciled faith and science nor to the churchgoers who read the Bible as the literal word of God; not to the people at home or abroad reading front-page news about the trial; not to those hugely popular evangelists, like Billy Sunday

or Aimee Semple McPherson, who considered evolution the devil's work; and certainly not to the lawyers arguing the case.

"The issue in the Tennessee case is not merely the issue of
academic freedom," the journalist Walter Lippmann warned before the trial began. "In this Tennessee case there is revealed at
last the full significance of the movement which in these last
years has as its spearpoint the Ku Klux Klan," Lippmann omi-
nously added. "That lawless and un-American and un-Christian
brotherhood has loudly insisted it was fighting for the preservation of American institutions from religious control." It was
doing no such thing, Lippmann declared. It was, instead, campaigning against American liberty.

"I wonder whether we don't have to develop some new doctrine to protect education from majorities," Lippmann then
wrote his friend Judge Learned Hand. "The size of the electorate, the impossibility of educating it sufficiently, the fierce ignorance of these millions of semi-literate, priest-ridden and
parson-ridden people have gotten me to the point where I want
to confine the actions of majorities."

To Lippmann, Bryan had reduced the principle of majority
rule to an absurdity. Though created equal, Lippmann pointed
out, not all humans were equally good scientists or equally good
parents or even equally good Christians. To invoke the will of
the majority and claim that it had a right to decide anything it
chose were the political ploys of a demagogue. In fact, the principle of majority rule wasn't so different from the idea that might
makes right, which Bryan had denounced, unaware of any contradiction.

What a travesty: "In Tennessee the people used their power
to prevent their own children from learning, not merely the doctrine of evolution, but the spirit and method by which learning is
possible. They had used their right to rule in order to weaken the
agency which they had set up in order that they might learn how

to rule," Lippmann wrote. "They had used the prerogatives of democracy to destroy the hopes of democracy."

WHEN DARROW HUMILIATED Bryan—for that's what he'd done—he had done so to educate the people and, in so doing, thwart the spread of majoritarian intolerance.

"To me it was perfectly clear that the proceedings bore little resemblance to a court case," Darrow reflected. Publicity was strategic. Yet while Darrow knew perfectly well that he'd litigated the Scopes case in the headlines, his strategy was not without its irony: he needed to woo the same people, or at least a subset of them, that Bryan did.

Yet to Darrow the law could take one only so far, since it was administered by fallible men and overseen by fallible judges. Still, Clarence Darrow never gave up on the law. Essential to a civil society—and a humane one—the law could provide a momentary stay against intolerance and ignorance.

After all, he said, "there is no limit to which fanaticism will not go."

For he also understood that behind the issue of what could or should be taught in the classroom—behind the question of separating church and state, behind the new gag laws, behind it all— lay prejudice, xenophobia, fanaticism.

"The sharpshooters of bigotry were picking off its victims in our schools and colleges," he recalled.

AFTER BRYAN'S DEATH, the Fundamentalists did for a time lose a leader who could create the politics of revivalism that feminist writer Doris Stevens had predicted. But fundamentalism as a political movement had obviously survived and would resurface, over and over, during that century and decidedly during the next.

In 1926, the year after the Scopes trial, Boston's New England Watch and Ward Society dubbed the April issue of Mencken's *American Mercury* obscene because it included the story of a prostitute in a religious town where the men who exploited her by night shunned her at church on Sunday. Henry Mencken hired Arthur Garfield Hays to defend him, and the two of them confidently rode up to Boston. On cue, they arrived at the corner of Park and Tremont Streets—a place locally known as Brimstone Corner—where five thousand people had gathered, many of them students and Mencken fans. Hooting and laughing, the crowd blocked traffic, waving copies of the magazine.

At Brimstone Corner, the society's secretary, Reverend J. Frank Chase, pretended to buy a copy of the magazine for a half dollar—which Mencken took and then bit, as if to test its authenticity—and then Chase yelled out to arrest the journalist. As the head of the Boston vice squad and a plainclothesman escorted Mencken to police headquarters a few blocks away, the crowd followed, still laughing and shouting.

Mencken was charged with possessing and selling a magazine that corrupted the morals of youth. Mencken huffed. His magazine had been founded on the principle of liberty. Judge James Parmenter took home a copy of the magazine and, finding nothing particularly objectionable, dismissed the complaint.

While Mencken addressed cheering students at Harvard and Felix Frankfurter praised him, Arthur Hays worried. "The country was coming to be governed not by law," Hays presciently declared, "but by threat of ruination made by various irresponsible groups of imposing title and supposedly pious purpose."

Nine books were boycotted in Boston. When Theodore Dreiser's *An American Tragedy* was banned in Boston for allegedly violating its obscenity laws, Clarence Darrow testified on behalf of Dreiser's publisher, Donald Friede, by reading aloud from the novel in the courtroom. Stunts like that didn't work in Boston. Convicted, Friede was fined $300.

"Massachusetts became the Tennessee of the North," Hays observed without humor.

MENCKEN'S REMARKABLE INFLUENCE didn't really extend much beyond the 1920s, although his swaggering and prose remained peerless, his Swiftian point of view shattering. In his writing, he continued to parade his antisemitism, racism, misogyny, and his downright mean-spiritedness, though in his actions he was often better, finer, more generous. An elitist though not a snob, and consistently devoted to free speech, he had published articles by Emma Goldman, he supported Sacco and Vanzetti, he continued to attack lynching, and by 1931 was advised to stay out of the Eastern Shore of Maryland because he had so vehemently denounced the white mobs there.

He left *The American Mercury* in 1933 and though still prolific he was soon called "the late Mr. Mencken," as if he were already an anachronism. Journalism, he once wrote, is fleeting. "The man who devotes his life to it," he said, "writes his history in water." A massive stroke devastated him in 1948, and he died in 1956 at the age of seventy-five.

NEITHER AS ABRASIVE as a Henry Mencken nor as Olympian as a Walter Lippmann, neither cynical nor supercilious, Arthur Garfield Hays liked to quote nineteenth-century abolitionist Wendell Phillips: "When the muse of time shall be asked to name the greatest of them all, she will dip her pen into the sunlight and write against the clear blue sky, 'Agitator.'"

Hays was an agitator but of a quieter sort than a Phillips or a Clarence Darrow, the men he most admired. "He had convictions and courage," Baldwin said of Hays. Hays refused to join the American Bar Association because it did not accept Blacks. When he and Darrow were preparing to defend the Scottsboro

boys, the American Communist Party, which was already involved in the case, demanded that they renounce their association with the NAACP. Hays and Darrow refused. "I hate to see
people pushed around," Hays said.

To him, the government had no right to snoop or to meddle
with individual rights or to protect people from their own
stupidity—"the right of the individual to be damned in his own
way," as Hays put it. A liberal to his bones, he was utterly critical of an America where "order has become the fetish, property
its handmaiden; respectability its emblem," he wrote. "Conformity is the watchword. Production, possessions, material success, the end."

As for the Scopes trial, while he publicly considered it a moral
victory, he differed from Mencken and the modernists who saw
it as a contest between supernaturalism and reason. "Bigotry is
not necessarily limited to church people, or to any class or creed
of church people," Hays wrote. "Freethinkers in attacking religion, often show the greatest intolerance."

"I believe in the fundamentals of democracy," Hays declared.
"I believe that we can safely risk the expression of any kind of
opinion by anybody." He said that early in his career, he said
that late in his career. "If we are to retain our traditional Constitutional rights," Hays wrote in 1936, " 'the humblest and most
hated member' in the community must be afforded the fullest
protection of American liberty guaranteed by the Bill of Rights.
Otherwise, the liberty of no one is safe."

Hays liked people, chess, and sports. He opposed the intern-
ment of Japanese Americans during World War II and criticized
the slanted prosecution of Ethel and Julius Rosenberg for allegedly passing secrets to the Soviets. He could be counted on to
defend liberty and the right to dissent. "To him, liberty transcended order," Roger Baldwin eulogized, "and the heart of liberty was the courage to resist oppression."

When he died in 1954 at the age of seventy-three, more than

three hundred men and women attended his funeral in New York City. In a matter of months, the Arthur Garfield Hays Memorial Fund was raised to support a program for the defense and strengthening of civil liberties, which was located at New York University, where it has since thrived.

"YOU COULDN'T BE angry with Dudley Malone," Arthur Hays once said of his friend. "He was too disarming." The room visibly brightened when Malone, spotless and freshly pressed, entered. "Extravagant demands from him would often meet with cheerful compliance," Hays recalled. "Everybody would want to please him." Likewise, Malone wanted to please everyone, it seemed, and he often did. He had a wide array of legal clients and friends, including actress Gloria Swanson, the heavyweight fighter Gene Tunney, and poet Edna St. Vincent Millay. He was urbane and outgoing and passionate about his causes until, as Arthur Hays noted, he lost interest. And when he did, he turned his back, with a "they can go to hell."

As if determined to ruin his own life, there was a recklessness about Malone. During the Depression, he had to give up the Paris branch of his law practice and return to New York, accompanied by his third wife, Edna Johnson, a woman twenty-five years his junior whom he'd met in London and married in 1930, shortly after his divorce from Doris Stevens. In 1935 he declared bankruptcy, listing his liabilities at a little more than $261,000. Though he owed money everywhere, including $25,000 to Stevens, he was still a sought-after speaker, admired for his warm oratorical power. He toyed with the idea of running for governor on any ticket, Republican or Democrat, since he'd campaigned for both Al Smith and Fiorello La Guardia. He also said he was writing his memoirs, "Through Irish Eyes." None of this came to anything.

After moving to California, Malone divorced again. In Los

Angeles, while employed on the legal staff of the Twentieth Century–Fox movie studio, he played Winston Churchill, another friend, in the 1943 Hollywood movie *Mission to Moscow*. He had grown to look like Churchill, whom he in no other way resembled.

"All lawyers and politicians are actors at heart," he said. Buffeted by time and circumstance and his own unquenchable need for attention, and despite his having outlived his fame, Malone retained his charm as a raconteur and bon vivant. In 1938, when he learned of Clarence Darrow's death, he immediately sent four dozen American Beauty roses to Ruby Darrow and boarded a plane to Chicago. Standing at Darrow's bier, he wept. "You may be sure he is in paradise, or no one else is there," Malone said. "For God always loved his integrity and his great heart."

"I WAS THE poor apostle of freedom," the feminist Doris Stevens told her estranged husband, Dudley Malone. "You were the communicant who profited by my doctrine," which involved sexual freedom—his, not hers.

In 1935, Stevens remarried, far more happily, the journalist Jonathan E. Mitchell, a contributor to *The New Republic*. She also founded and served as the first head of the Inter-American Commission of Women, which created an international alliance, investigated the condition of women in Latin America, and worked legislation that would have guaranteed full and equal economic and political rights for women, which she had long fought for. In 1939, after she was summarily removed from her post, she blamed United States State Department officials and Eleanor Roosevelt for "partisan monkeyshines." Although Stevens had continued to argue for an Equal Rights Amendment to the Constitution, ensuring political, economic, and social equality for women, Roosevelt and Labor Secretary Frances Perkins were concerned that such an amendment would undermine the

protective legislation that guaranteed working women, especially in industry, such provisions as a minimum wage. Stevens
argued that such protections just reinforce a stereotype: that
women are fragile creatures in need of protection. Women have
the same right as men to be overworked and underpaid, she
added with some sarcasm.

"I happen to be connected with a group which does not believe as the National Woman's Party does," Eleanor Roosevelt
replied. "I think they have a good argument on an ideal basis.
But we have to live in the world as it is."

Perhaps the peremptory dismissal changed Stevens. It's hard
to know. By the 1950s, both she and her husband, who by that
time was writing for *The National Review*, had become rabid
anti-communists.

IN THE SPRING of 1932, the seventy-five-year-old Clarence Darrow, suffering from heart disease, smoking too much, his breath
short and his flesh saggy, was defending four white people in
Honolulu who'd been accused of murdering Joseph Kahahawai,
a young Hawaiian native.

Kahahawai had been one of a group of five Hawaiians arrested and put on trial for the alleged rape of Thalia Fortescue
Massie, the attractive wife of Navy Lieutenant Thomas Massie,
who was stationed in Pearl Harbor. Released on bail after the
jury deadlocked, Kahahawai was awaiting a retrial when Lieutenant Massie; his wealthy mother-in-law, Grace Fortescue; and
two white sailors kidnapped, tortured, and shot him. The four
were caught trying to dispose of Kahahawai's bloody corpse,
wrapped in a bedsheet, that had been hidden in their automobile.

Grace Fortescue begged Clarence Darrow to take the case.
The fee would be large. But the case was controversial. Kahahawai's murder was widely regarded as nothing short of a racial
lynching.

Darrow had hesitated. "I had so long and decidedly been for the Negro and all so-called 'foreigners' that I could not put myself in a position where I might be compelled to take a position, even in a case, at variance with what I felt and stood for," he told a friend. He mailed Grace Fortescue a copy of his closing argument in the Ossian Sweet murder trial. But when Fortescue replied that race would not be an issue in the case, he conveniently believed her. He'd lost heavily in the stock market crash and needed the money. "I don't know what I should have done if now and then a fairly well-to-do client had not come my way," Darrow admitted with apparent—but not lasting—chagrin.

In Hawaii, he argued that the vigilante-style murder of Kahahawai was but an "honor killing" for the supposed rape of Thalia Massie. The jury didn't entirely buy it, and though they didn't find the defendants guilty of first-degree murder, they returned a manslaughter verdict. Dudley Malone contacted President Herbert Hoover. Initially said to be Darrow's co-counsel, Malone left the case before it began, but for some reason now intervened. He requested that Hoover override the Hawaii court and bring the quartet of defendants to the mainland where they could get a supposedly "fair" trial—that is, a trial among white people.

Hoover evidently telephoned Governor Lawrence M. Judd of Hawaii. Pressured also by Congress as well as by public opinion— white public opinion—Judd did commute the sentences from ten years to one hour served.

The NAACP debated whether to censure Darrow—it didn't— and much of the Black press excoriated Darrow as a white liberal dilettante and poseur. "Scottsboro has condemned white America nationally and Hawaii has condemned throughout the world," wrote the *Negro World*. Walter F. White of the NAACP had preferred that Darrow not defend Fortescue and the four sailors but accepted the decision of his friend. "He always did the thing which he in his heart felt was the right thing to do regardless of the consequences," White loyally insisted.

"I am not trying to excuse myself to colored people for hav-ing participated in this case," Darrow told the Black reporter Earl Wilkins (brother of Roy Wilkins, later the executive direc-tor of the NAACP). "Any colored person who reads and who knows my record is aware that I need neither excuse nor de-fense," he said. He sounded defensive, and he no doubt was.

"Many times I have been asked why I went to Honolulu. I was not sure then, and am not sure now," Darrow also remarked, as if covertly confessing he should not have gone. But like Bryan, he was not a man of regret, at least not in public. It was a disap-pointing twist in Darrow's late career, but there were always knots in his character. He was a moral amoral man.

"No one has ever been able to classify Clarence Darrow and I am quite sure he would not be able to classify himself," Eugene Debs mused. "He is simply not of the classifiable kind. He is neither republican, nor a democrat, nor a progressive, nor any-thing else in politics. I know for a fact that he hates politics and politicians and yet somehow he is always lined up with them."

In 1933, President Roosevelt selected Clarence Darrow to head an advisory board established to rebut criticism recently lev-eled at the National Recovery Administration, or NRA. Created to help spur business and industrial production during the De-pression, the NRA had instituted a set of wage, price, and other regulations, called codes, over most industries, large and small. To advertise their compliance, stores and restaurants and manu-facturers prominently displayed the NRA symbol, a big blue eagle, in their place of business. If they didn't, they risked losing patronage and prestige and could face bankruptcy.

But the NRA had been under fire for being unduly influenced by corporate lobbyists. Though apparently appointed as a fig-urehead, Darrow would never rubber-stamp anything, so his final reports, issued after three months of hard work, which in-cluded as many as sixty public hearings, accused the NRA of insolently discriminating against small businesses. However well-intentioned the NRA may have been, Darrow reported that it allowed corporate America to control the government, and the government in turn had legalized corporate malfeasance. "Not in many years have monopolistic tendencies in industry been so forwarded and strengthened as they have through the perversion of an act excellently intended to restore prosperity and promote general welfare."

In a way, the report revealed a paradox at the center of Darrow's thinking. He was a libertarian socialist who advocated free market competition while at the same time he advocated government ownership of industry. Sounding like William Jennings Bryan, he said, "We've got to keep the Morgans, the Mellons, and the others from controlling the money of the country."

In a series of blistering attacks, retired General Hugh S. Johnson, the head of the NRA, branded Darrow a "Red" who at seventy-seven wanted to show the world he was still alive.

Darrow resigned from the advisory board, which Roosevelt soon abolished.

EXHAUSTED AND FRAIL, the lines on his face more deeply grooved than ever, Darrow left Washington for New York City, this time to head an unofficial agency called the American Inquiry Commission on Social Changes in Germany. The brainchild of Arthur Garfield Hays, it publicized the recent and growing Nazi atrocities against Jews, Catholics, radicals, and the political enemies of Adolf Hitler. While in New York and quizzed by reporters, Darrow told them he hoped Hitler would be assassinated— this from the man who despised capital punishment.

Darrow's detractors jumped on the seeming inconsistency. He didn't mind. As he once said, "I have never murdered anybody, but on occasion I have read obituary notices with a certain degree of satisfaction."

.   .   .

ROBERT KEEBLER, THE Memphis lawyer who had worked with Darrow and Hays on the Scopes appeal, was the grandson of a Methodist minister, and though he'd gone up North to law school at Harvard, he fondly recalled earning his very first dollar selling copies of Bryan's paper, *The Commoner*. As a boy, he worshipped Bryan, as did all devout Democrats and Fundamentalists from the South, and he heard Bryan speak more than once. But he grew disillusioned. A Bryan speech heard over and over lost its shine. As did Bryan. Still, while in Washington, whenever Keebler passed by the big bronze statue of Bryan looming near the Potomac, he never failed to tip his hat.

To Keebler, the Butler Act was an insult to the state of Tennessee. Just after it passed, in a barn-burning speech at the annual meeting of the Tennessee Bar Association, he had called it crazy. His remark caused such a commotion that it was cut from the record, and Keebler's Fundamentalist friends forced him to resign from the Methodist church where he taught Sunday school.

Though Darrow's name was never mentioned in polite Tennessee circles, Keebler was curious enough in July 1925 to go to Dayton. By the time he left town, he felt that in Clarence Darrow he'd met a great man, humane, sensitive, and affectionate. The impression deepened when Keebler accompanied Arthur Hays and Darrow to Nashville to appeal the Scopes decision before the Tennessee Supreme Court.

"In my opinion he was another Socrates," Keebler lovingly concluded, "a sort of gadfly who bothered people and set their minds to working."

JOHN THOMAS SCOPES kept out of the public eye as much as he could, and over the years rarely granted an interview. He left graduate school in Chicago for Venezuela, where he was employed as a geologist for the Gulf Oil Company, and in 1930, he married and briefly returned to the University of Chicago. He then worked for the United Production Corporation, renamed the United Gas Corporation, first in Texas and afterward in Louisiana. He retired in 1963 and in 1966 decided to write his memoirs, with the assistance of a friend.

After the trial, Scopes evidently wanted nothing more to do with the local Dayton impresario George Rappleyea. Arrested in 1947 in Gulfport, Mississippi, Rappleyea was sentenced to a year in a Texas prison for a gun-running plot to smuggle submachine guns and grenades to Cuba. Later, Rappleyea moved to Miami, where he manufactured something called "Plas-Mo-Falt," which was the registered trade name for a plastic roofing compound derived from molasses. Scopes said Rappleyea always had to have an angle.

SCOPES HAD CONSIDERED the defeat in Dayton a mere legal setback since the trial did have widespread educational value. With extensive newspaper and magazine coverage, the trial explained, over and over, what was meant by evolution according to the scientists, many of them devout, come to testify. But by 1967, when his memoir was published, he had come to a different conclusion. "Dayton is not the only place in America where evolution is still thought to mean that *homo sapiens* descended from monkeys rather than common ancestors," Scopes wrote.

"Prejudice is not unique to Tennessee; it is ubiquitous and not easily eradicated," he added. "On its simplest level, prejudice means people are afraid of what they don't know and don't understand. By this criteria, who of us is not affected by prejudice?"

To him, then, Dayton wasn't about biology or science—or not those alone. It was about power and the exercise of political power over learning and freedom, whether in 1925 or in the future. "Liberty is always under threat," Scopes concluded, "and it literally takes eternal vigilance to maintain it."

He quoted Clarence Darrow: "You can only be free if I am free."

MAYNARD SHIPLEY, the president of the Science League of America, knew the anti-evolution crusade was not going to fade away. "The Fundamentalists have merely changed their tactics," he wrote. "As one of their leaders had worded it, 'We were too precipitate; we must go directly to the people themselves and not depend on the legislators.'" That meant the Fundamentalists were planning to censor books, strong-arm publishers, control libraries, alter textbooks, and harass teachers.

Still, in 1955, when some participants in the Scopes trial were still alive, Jerome Lawrence and Robert E. Lee wrote the play *Inherit the Wind*, a thinly disguised fictional account of the trial, which was adapted for the screen in 1960. Directed by Stanley Kramer, the film version portrayed the Bryan character, played by Fredric March, as a well-meaning, devious and skyward-looking zealot unable to change with the times—or to relinquish the power to move millions that he had once enjoyed. Less complex but far more endearing, the Darrow protagonist is the avatar of heroic, kindly, and incontestable reason whom Spencer Tracy plays in a lissome, witty, offhand way. The townspeople, particularly its women, were the film's real antagonists, bigots most of them, especially their fire-and-brimstone preacher: stereotypes galore.

Nominated for an Academy Award in the category of Best Adapted Screenplay from Another Medium, *Inherit the Wind* lost to *Elmer Gantry*, Sinclair Lewis's story of the evangelical huckster played to the hilt by Burt Lancaster.

· · ·

IN 1967, the Tennessee state senate repealed the Butler Act, and the next year the United States Supreme Court struck down an Arkansas law that criminalized teaching of evolution. In 1987, the United States Supreme Court also struck down as unconstitutional the Louisiana law stipulating that "creationism"—a Bryan-like, literal interpretation of Genesis—must be given equal time in the classroom if evolution was being taught there. The Court declared that Louisiana law violated the First Amendment's establishment clause, separating church and state. "Somewhere in heaven, John Scopes is celebrating," said the executive director of the ACLU.

But biologist Stephen Jay Gould keenly noted that the fight against the rule of reason and the discoveries of science is far from over. Academic freedom is in jeopardy. As are teachers, whose professional commitment is to teach real, not sham, science.

TOM STEWART, who had prosecuted the Scopes case, was a United States Senator representing Tennessee during World War II when he tried to intern American-born citizens of Japanese descent, calling them "yellow devils." He also tried to revoke their citizenship. The idea that all human beings shared a common ancestry—which was what the Scopes trial was about—still offended him. "Where there is one drop of Japanese blood," Stewart cried on the Senate floor in 1942, "there is Japanese treachery."

He led the Southern fight to defeat the passage of bills to preserve Franklin Roosevelt's civil rights directive, known as the Fair Employment Practices Commission, which had banned discrimination in the workplace. It was iniquitous and communist-tinged, Stewart said. The South didn't need any more carpetbaggers or anti-lynching legislation. He voted to protect the House Un-American Activities Committee.

In 1948, Estes Kefauver defeated Senator Stewart in the Democratic primary and won in the general election.

In 1965, when a reporter from *The New York Times* asked Stewart how he felt about evolution, Stewart replied, "Well, I just can't give a scientific answer."

BRYAN'S TRAGEDY, if it can be called tragedy, was that he lacked ability, over time, to do anything more than lurch toward a vision of a beneficent world by folding it back into a literal interpretation of the Bible, which contained the only language available to him.

According to Darrow, Bryan stifled whatever doubts he harbored, particularly about religion. Comparing him to that boy who passes by the graveyard at night, "whistling to keep up his courage," Darrow noted that Bryan's "very attitude showed that he was frightened out of his wits lest, after all, the illusions of his life might be only dreams."

Darrow too was frightened for the future although he bore his fear in a far different way. Complacent conformity and unthinking cruelty may have alarmed him, but they also inspired him to act. And while he called himself a determinist, which in many respects he was, he was a man who could not countenance resignation. "I won't be going very long," Darrow had told Mencken back in 1925, "and intellectually I am glad of it, though emotionally I presume I shall fight to the end." He did. He never submitted, never blinked, never walked away.

"He loved to pose as a pessimist and a cynic," recalled Victor Yarros, one of Darrow's law partners. "He loved life deeply and hated the fact of death." Or, as William Allen White said, Darrow sought the unattainable, and if hobbled by his cynicism, he nonetheless stumbled forward, "looking for the ideal which he could not accept without quibble or gibe."

He would also defend anyone who paid.

. . .

BUT TO CLARENCE DARROW, during the Scopes trial and after it, the trial mattered greatly; it mattered in 1925, and it would matter in the future. America itself was on trial, Darrow firmly believed. "The fundamental bedrock of liberty is tolerance," he said in July 1925. And as if he could darkly anticipate the implications of the Scopes trial not just for Bryan, or Tennessee, or 1925, but for the future of a nation that was said to cherish liberty, he explained, "Tolerance means a willingness to let other people do, think, act and live as we think is not right; the antithesis of this is intolerance and means we demand the right to make others live as we think is right, not as they think is right." Otherwise, as he had declared, no one was safe.

The Scopes trial was not a circus or a sideshow. Nor was the trial just about evolution. "If a law can stand against teaching science in one school, it can stand against teaching science everywhere," Darrow continued, growing emotional. "And if it can bar the teaching of one science, it can bar the teaching of any science; therefore, all science."

"DO YOU THINK I look eighty years old?" Darrow asked Russell Owen, who had been one of the reporters at the Scopes trial. "Mr. Darrow, you have always looked eighty years old," Owen replied. Darrow was amused.

Owen had come to interview him in the spacious Chicago apartment where he and Ruby had lived for more than thirty years. The two men were talking in Darrow's huge library. Six large windows overlooked the green trees of Jackson Park, and everywhere in that room there were books, shelves and shelves of books, science and philosophy, novels and poetry, books on the tables and the radiators and chairs and windowsills.

Darrow was not well. His health had been poor. And just shy

of his eighty-first birthday, Clarence Seward Darrow died in this apartment, on March 13, 1938, with Ruby at his side.

At his funeral, two hundred people crowded into the Bond Chapel at the University of Chicago, men and women, Black and white, young and old, rich and poor, workers and judges and lawyers and friends. Federal Judge William Holly, one of Darrow's former law partners, delivered the only eulogy.

"He loved mercy," Judge Holly said, ending the service with the poem Robert Burns had addressed to "The Rigidly Righteous": "Though they may go a little wrong," he read, referring to those who go astray, "To step aside is human." And yet, he continued, "One point must still be greatly dark, / The moving Why they do it."

That's the question Darrow had always asked. Why do they do it? Darrow never knew, which didn't stop him from asking.

THAT SAME YEAR, 1938, Tennessee Williams dedicated his three-act play, *Not About Nightingales,* to the memory of Clarence Darrow, "whose mental frontiers were the four corners of the sky."

"THE WAY OF the world is all very, very weird," Clarence Darrow observed.

"You may be sure that the powers of reaction and despotism never sleep," he also warned, "and in these days when conservatism is in the saddle, we have to be very watchful."

Then the defense rested.

Dramatis Personae

THE TRIAL OF JOHN THOMAS SCOPES

Presiding: Judge John T. Raulston

ARGUING FOR THE STATE OF TENNESSEE
A. Thomas Stewart (Tennessee)
Sue Hicks (Tennessee)
Benjamin McKenzie (Tennessee)
Herbert Hicks (Tennessee)
Gordon McKenzie (Tennessee)
William Jennings Bryan (Florida, formerly Nebraska)

LAWYERS FOR THE DEFENSE OF JOHN T. SCOPES
John Randolph Neal (Tennessee)
Clarence Darrow (Illinois)
Arthur Garfield Hays (New York)
Dudley Field Malone (New York)

PRESIDING
Raulston, John T. (1868–1956). Presiding judge at the Scopes trial. Born on a small farm in Tennessee, Raulston had been elected judge of the state's Eighteenth District in 1918. A Fundamentalist and great ad-

mirer of William Jennings Bryan, he did what he could to mollify all the lawyers involved in the case while always smiling for the cameras. After the trial, he took to the road as a lecturer but when he ran again for election in 1926, he was defeated. Ditto his run for governor. Raulston maintained throughout his life that he "did not think our children should be taught any theory that would tend to destroy their faith in the integrity of the Bible." With typical tact, John Scopes observed that "Judge Raulston was trying to do what he believed was right."

ARGUING FOR THE STATE OF TENNESSEE

Stewart, Arthur Thomas (Tom) (1892–1972). Lead prosecutor against John Scopes, Stewart was District Attorney General for the Eighteenth Circuit of Tennessee after the resignation of Ben McKenzie; elected to serve out the remainder of his term, he was reelected twice more. Later, running as a Dixiecrat, Stewart won a seat in the United States Senate.

Hicks, Herbert E. (1893–1946), and his brother **Sue K. Hicks** (1895–1980), named for his mother, who died after childbirth. Served on the team prosecuting John T. Scopes. Both graduated from the University of Kentucky and both practiced law together in Dayton. Sue Hicks and John Scopes had been friends; before the trial, they often went on double dates. It's said Sue Hicks's name inspired the song "A Boy Named Sue," recorded by Johnny Cash.

McKenzie, Benjamin G. (1866–1938). Member of the team prosecuting John T. Scopes; formerly District Attorney for the Eighteenth Circuit in Tennessee; before that, he was a special circuit judge and served one term in the Tennessee legislature. Slightly round, generally jovial, glasses balanced on his nose, and eager to tell a long story, he was assisted by his son, Gordon. "To know him, was to love him," McKenzie said of Darrow when Darrow died.

Bryan, William Jennings (1860–1925). In his novel *The 42nd Parallel,* John Dos Passos depicted Bryan as "the silver tongue of the plain people" whose "Pacifism, Prohibition, Fundamentalism" turned back the clocks. Novelist Willa Cather noted that she had seen Bryan without a coat but never without high moral purpose. Theodore Roosevelt called him shallow and formidable, although the Great Commoner, as Bryan was known, advocated such progressive reforms as trust-busting and the enfranchisement of women. But "Bryanism" also represented a patent ignorance of history, geography, religion, diplomacy, and science. Nominated by Democrats as their candidate for president three times, Bryan fought for the passage of the Prohibition amendment— and for keeping the theory of evolution out of the classroom. "He will have no trouble matching virtues with the saints," said an acquaintance, "even though the philosophers lift an eyebrow when he appears in their paradise."

LAWYERS FOR THE DEFENSE OF JOHN T. SCOPES

Neal, John Randolph (1876–1959). Chief defense lawyer during the Scopes trial, and the only Tennessee native on the defense team, Neal had taught at the University of Tennessee, where he had been dismissed in 1923. He opened his own private law school in Knoxville before becoming involved with the Scopes case. A descendant of a large landowning family and twice a member of the Tennessee legislature, Neal ran unsuccessfully for governor against Austin Peay, the man who signed into law the anti-evolution bill; later Neal ran again, unsuccessfully, for governor; he was a perennial candidate for either governor or senator and often both at the same time. A graduate of Vanderbilt University and an expert in constitutional law, he also earned a PhD from Columbia University, and after the Scopes case, became an early advocate for the Tennessee Valley Authority. He struck neighbors and colleagues as eccentric, distracted, outspoken, and courageous in his fight to preserve civil liberties and human rights, mostly at his own expense.

Hays, Arthur Garfield (1881–1954). Co-counsel at the Scopes trial, Hays was a corporate lawyer with a lucrative practice—though he was frequently derided as a "damned radical." He affirmed the right to assemble; defended the right of labor unions to organize; and like Darrow often worked without remuneration. He insisted that "if we are to retain our traditional Constitutional rights, 'the humblest and most hated member' in the community must be afforded the fullest protection of American liberty guaranteed by the Bill of Rights. Otherwise, the liberty of no one is safe." Long associated with the ACLU, he served as its general counsel. In 1951 he denounced Senator Joseph McCarthy as the most dangerous man in America, more dangerous to freedom than all the supposed communists in the country. To Hays, "liberty transcended order," Roger Baldwin eulogized, "and the heart of liberty was the courage to resist oppression."

Malone, Dudley Field (1885–1955). Co-counsel in the defense of John T. Scopes. Formerly Third Assistant Secretary of State under Woodrow Wilson and Collector of the Port of New York, Malone was sought after as a superb speaker—as good as Bryan—but he resigned from the Wilson administration over the question of women's suffrage, which he supported. He helped form the League of Oppressed People in 1919. Running for governor of New York on the newly formed Farmer-Labor Party ticket, he was denounced nationally as a Bolshevik and parlor socialist. And though he'd campaigned hard for Al Smith, by 1932, he supported Herbert Hoover against Roosevelt, arguing that Hoover's economic policies would soon succeed—even though thirteen million people were out of work. A mercurial man, Malone allegedly turned on Roosevelt for personal reasons. Malone was briefly married to the feminist Doris Stevens.

Darrow, Clarence (1857–1938). Celebrated lawyer who volunteered to defend John T. Scopes without a fee. Formerly a labor lawyer, then a criminal lawyer, a voracious reader, an almost compulsive lecturer, a skeptic, a brilliant storyteller especially in the courtroom, and a self-proclaimed agnostic, Clarence Darrow during the Scopes trial said, as he had many times before, that "if men are not tolerant, if men cannot respect each other's opinions, if men cannot live and let live, then no man's life is safe." At his death in 1938, it was claimed that Darrow wrote himself into American social history, not just with his defense of John Scopes but in his defense of murderers, labor organizers, and the friendless. When he was asked if he believed in progress, he said, "Well, it's a decent illusion."

And of course there was the **Defendant, Scopes, John T.** (1900–1970). Born in Paducah, Kentucky, Scopes was the "center of the storm," as he later described himself: he was the resolute and quietly courageous young man who agreed to act as a defendant to test the recently passed anti-evolution law and then and later dodged publicity. After the trial, with a scholarship raised by scientists associated with the trial, he attended the University of Chicago. When those funds ran out, in 1927, he was nominated for another fellowship, but the president informed Scopes, "As far as I am concerned, you can take your atheistic marbles and play elsewhere."

OTHERS, A SELECTION

Altgeld, John Peter (1847–1902). Born in Germany, raised in poverty, admitted to the bar, elected Superior Court judge in Cook County, Illinois, and then elected governor of Illinois, Altgeld was a wealthy real estate investor until he lost it all. Pardoning the three men still in prison for the horrific Haymarket bombing (1886), Altgeld was a reformer, a radical, a kingmaker, and an anti-imperialist. Poet Vachel Lindsay called him "the eagle that is forgotten," for to many, it was Altgeld and not Bryan who contributed to the progressivism of the Democrats at the turn of the twentieth century. If Darrow loved anyone, he loved Altgeld, whose book *Our Penal Machinery and Its Victims* (1884) demonstrated to the younger man that "our penal machinery seems to recruit its victims from among those who are fighting an unequal fight in the struggle for existence."

Baldwin, Roger (1884–1981). In 1920, Baldwin helped found the American Civil Liberties Union to protect dissidents, immigrants, and

radicals against unwarranted prosecution and what he called "the sinister use of patriotism to cover attacks on radical and labor movements." The ACLU depended on volunteer lawyers, such as Clarence
Darrow, when it challenged what it considered unconstitutional laws,
as it did in the Scopes trial. Earlier, declaring that he was opposed to
war in 1917, Baldwin refused to register for the draft. Arrested, at his
trial he said that conscription undermined American ideals about individual freedom, democratic liberty, and Christian teaching. He was
found guilty.

Darrow, Ruby (1878–1957). Formerly Ruby Hamerstrom, she wrote
under the name Ruby Stanleigh for the Chicago *Evening Post,* covering
aspects of the World's Fair, iron mining in northern Michigan, and
women's clubs. Around 1899, she met Clarence Darrow. She remembered that she wore a wine-colored jacket and that Darrow was lecturing on Omar Khayyam. They married in 1903. It was his second
marriage and her first.

Debs, Eugene V. (1855–1926). Gentle Gene from Terre Haute, Indiana, was a labor organizer and socialist who helped establish the American Railway Union in 1893; the next year, he and the ARU called for
a boycott that soon affected all the rail traffic in the United States. After
President Grover Cleveland used federal troops to break the strike, and
Debs was arrested, Clarence Darrow defended him. In 1897, Debs declared himself a socialist. He ran for president in 1900, the first of five
times. In 1912, he won almost one million votes. In 1918, when he opposed America's entrance into the war, he was arrested under the Espionage Act and sentenced to jail for ten years. He ran for president
again—this time from a prison cell.

Du Bois, W.E.B. (1868–1963). Black historian, social scientist, activist, editor, Du Bois was born in Great Barrington, Massachusetts, and
educated at Fisk University and Harvard, where he received a second
BA (Harvard didn't accept Fisk credits) and his PhD in 1895. In 1902,

he published *The Souls of Black Folk* in part as a response to Booker T. Washington's conservatism. Instrumental in the founding of the National Association for the Advancement of Colored People, Du Bois edited its monthly magazine *The Crisis;* early members of the NAACP included Clarence Darrow. "I do not think there is a brighter, finer, more philosophical mind in America than Du Bois," Darrow later proclaimed. In 1928 Du Bois defended Darrow when Black newspapers slammed him for apparently denouncing Black churches, and many a Black minister in Washington, D.C., refused to allow Darrow to speak in their churches. "Here is a man whose voice has been raised for righteousness in the face of flattery, money and fame. He has dared to use his unique genius to defend the rights of poor white labor and disfranchised Negroes," Du Bois said. "There is not a Negro church in the United States that ought not to throw wide its doors to Clarence Darrow."

Fosdick, Harry Emerson (1878–1969). Liberal minister who clashed with Bryan and other Fundamentalists, particularly after delivering a notorious sermon, "Shall the Fundamentalists Win?," in 1922. The controversy almost led to his censure by the Presbyterian General Assembly; he resigned from the First Presbyterian Church in New York. After John D. Rockefeller Jr. financed the construction of the massive and interdenominational Riverside Church—it sat 2,500—near the Hudson River in New York City, Fosdick became its founding pastor. He also was a member of the American Eugenics Society, presumably because it seemed a scientific application of morality distinct from Christian orthodoxy. William Jennings Bryan loathed him.

Haldeman-Julius, Emanuel (1889–1951), and **Marcet Haldeman-Julius** (1887–1941). Writer Emanuel Julius was editor of the socialist paper *The New York Call,* and later the *Appeal to Reason,* which he published in Girard, Kansas, the hometown of Anna Marcet Haldeman, an actor, author, and socialist, and the niece of Jane Addams. Marcet and Emanuel had met while both were in New York, they mar-

ried in 1916, and in Kansas they set up a publishing company that basically offered the first paperbacks, the Little Blue Books, which sold for
five cents each and included essays, stories, novels, plays, and lectures
by Henrik Ibsen, Oscar Wilde, George Sand, Clarence Darrow, Upton
Sinclair, Voltaire, Charles Lamb, Margaret Sanger, and Walter F. White.
Both Emanuel and Marcet were in Dayton, Tennessee, during the
Scopes trial; Marcet Haldeman-Julius wrote of it in the newspaper the
couple also published.

Huxley, Thomas Henry (1825–1895). The brilliant scientist known
as Darwin's Bulldog for his vehement public defense of the theory of
evolution, as well as of science and public education, Huxley is said to
have coined the term "agnostic." In 1876 he visited America as something of a superstar. He was the grandfather of the biologist, scientific
humanist, internationalist—and eugenicist—Julian Huxley and of the
novelist Aldous Huxley.

Lippmann, Walter (1889–1974). Journalist, urbane political philosopher, social critic, and later journalist-dean of public intellectuals,
Lippmann in 1923 managed and wrote for the New York *World*'s
editorial page. He denounced Prohibition, xenophobia, the Ku Klux
Klan, Fundamentalism, and William Jennings Bryan, but was repulsed
by the Scopes trial's implication of a dictatorship by majorities. To
him, the Scopes trial represented an assault on the freedom of worship
and the integrity of education. "It seems to me that majority rule is
after all only a limited political device and that where some great
interest like education comes into conflict with it, we are justified in
trying to set up defenses against the majority," Lippmann wrote a
friend in 1925.

Markham, Edwin (1852–1940). Inspired by the painting by Jean-
François Millet of a field hand, Edwin Markham's poem "The Man
with the Hoe" (1899) became an international success, much debated

and quoted as a cry against injustice. William Jennings Bryan adored the poem; Eugene Debs said it depicted the condition of the worker, although the more acerbic Ambrose Bierce claimed it was about as exciting as a dead fish. The railroad titan Collis Huntington said it all when he petulantly asked, "Is America going to turn to Socialism over one poem?"

Masters, Edgar Lee (1868–1950). The law partner of Clarence Darrow for eight years but who parted ways with him in 1911, Masters accused Darrow of not paying money owed him and their firm. Darrow and Masters had also invested in a bank, and when it failed, Masters blamed Darrow. (When Masters's wife sued for divorce, she chose Darrow as her lawyer.) Masters also turned against Bryan, who had also been a friend, and whom he had backed for president in 1896. In 1916, he bitterly described Bryan as a hypocrite: "A radical doesn't say: / 'This is true and you must believe it; / This is good and you must accept it, / And if you don't believe it and accept it / We'll get a law and make you.'" Of Darrow, Masters wrote, "A giant as we hoped, in truth a dwarf."

McPherson, Aimee Semple (1890–1944). Faith-healing evangelist, a friend of William Jennings Bryan, and the creator of the Angelus Temple, a mammoth house of worship that seated more than five thousand and where Sister Aimee, as she was known, held a style of revival that blended vaudeville and religion. Anticipating the televangelists who appeared later in the century, she knew how to use the new media, the radio. "If all the forlorn pilgrims she baptizes every year remained on her rolls," Henry Mencken tartly observed, "her Angelus Temple would swell to the proportions of a county, and shove Los Angeles into the Pacific." Called the Sarah Bernhardt of the Sawdust Trail, an evangelizing feminist, in her way, though deeply conservative, in 1926, McPherson staged her own kidnapping, presumably as a publicity stunt. Though she was prosecuted for fraudulent conspiracy, the case was dropped.

Mencken, Henry L. (1880–1956). Journalist, author, polemicist, humorist, and gadfly of tremendous influence, particularly in the 1920s, Mencken covered much of the Scopes trial with wit and vitriol. He also covered presidential conventions, fires, and literary trends, which he helped to create. Called the Bad Boy of Baltimore, the city where he was born and always lived, Mencken was a crusader in his own caustic way. He ridiculed Puritans, puritanism, Christian Scientists, philistines, Prohibition, and William Jennings Bryan, whom he called the Fundamentalist Pope. He also flung around such terms as "boobus Americanus" to satirize the complacency of American philistines, and he caricatured the American South as "The Sahara of the Bozart," "bozart" being a term he coined for the occasion, meaning something of an arid wasteland for the beaux arts.

Rappleyea, George W. (1894–1966). Instigator, or so he claimed, of the test case that became the Scopes trial after he read in a newspaper that the ACLU would support anyone who challenged Tennessee's recently passed anti-evolution law. Working in Dayton as a civil engineer, as he also claimed, and a friend of John Scopes, Rappleyea was born in New York City, served in the army during the war, and eventually settled in Tennessee, where he was managing what was left of the Cumberland Coal and Iron Company. Extremely helpful to those interested in his role in the Scopes case, especially during the trial but also long after he left Dayton for a peripatetic career, this man of imagination and invention liked to reminisce that "I was the only evolutionist there, and life became unbearable."

Riley, William Bell (1861–1947). Leader and founder in 1919 of the World's Christian Fundamentals Association, Riley had asked William Jennings Bryan to help prosecute the Scopes case. Born during the Civil War in Indiana (his father a proslavery Democrat), Riley was called to the ministry and in 1897 headed the First Baptist Church in Minneapolis, where he enlarged the congregation, partly by denouncing corruption, turning against Darwin, berating theological liberalism, and endorsing Prohibition. A vigorous speaker, nationally prominent and with wide grassroots support, Riley was the face of conservative evangelical Protestantism and in later years was known as a supporter of the antisemitic demagogue Father Charles Coughlin; Riley was himself an antisemite and a segregationist.

Stevens, Doris (1888–1963). Vice president of the National Woman's Party and author of *Jailed for Freedom* (1920), a history of the militant suffrage movement, as it was called, Stevens chronicled the experience of being imprisoned for having picketed the White House in 1917 to protest President Wilson's failure to back a federal amendment giving women the vote. "To be sure," Stevens later wrote, "women have often resented it deeply that so much human energy had to be expended for so simple a right." She observed that all participants in the Scopes trial were male—even the schoolchildren who testified. There was some talk about having girls testify too, she recalled, but it wasn't thought proper. Before the trial's end, she interviewed William Jennings Bryan.

Straton, John Roach (1875–1929). One of the most vehement of the Fundamentalists, who loathed the loose morals that he associated with the 1920s, and head of the Calvary Baptist Church in New York City, Straton blamed Darwinism for the "wave of immorality" breaking over youth. "Monkey men," he exclaimed, "make monkey morals." He called William Jennings Bryan "the outstanding intellect of the age." As for evolutionists, he called them cuckoo birds. Said to endorse the Ku Klux Klan, an accusation he hotly denied, Straton was accused of distributing Klan pamphlets from the pulpit. Bryan asked Straton to join him in Dayton, which Straton did not. After the trial, Straton offered to debate Darrow, who declined the invitation.

Sunday, William A. (Billy) (1862–1935). Formerly an outfielder for the Chicago White Stockings, Sunday was probably the most famous evangelist in the world in the early part of the twentieth century. A tireless performer who thumped the Bible and shadowboxed with Satan

onstage, Sunday had been ordained in 1903 and was more of a promoter than a theologian. Reputed to have delivered as many as twenty
thousand sermons during his lifetime, Sunday made a fortune shouting
that sin was no cream puff. During the Scopes trial, he wrote Bryan,
"Thank God for WJB" and offered Bryan his deeply unscientific advice:
"If man evolved from a monkey, why are there any monkeys left? Why
didn't they evolve into humans?" Mencken called Billy Sunday a
whooping and bellicose clown, which didn't bother Sunday in the
slightest.

White, Walter F. (1893–1955). A fair-skinned Black man who could
pass as white, the author and activist White traveled the South as field
secretary of the NAACP to investigate lynching, though when folks
discovered he was Black, he said he "found it rather desirable to disap-
pear slightly in advance of reception committees imbued with the desire
to make an addition to the lynching record." When Clarence Darrow
attended a small meeting of NAACP members, Darrow mistakenly assumed the NAACP vice president Arthur Spingarn was Black; Darrow
turned to White and said, "Well, with your blond hair and blue eyes,
I'd never make that mistake." White named his son, Walter Carl Darrow White, after Darrow.

The Butler Act

House Bill No. 185
(By Mr. Butler)

An Act prohibiting the teaching of the Evolution Theory in all the Universities, Normals and all other public schools of Tennessee, which are supported in whole or in part by the public school funds of the State, and to provide penalties for the violations thereof.

Section 1. Be it enacted by the General Assembly of the State of Tennessee, That it shall be unlawful for any teacher in any of the Universities, Normals and all other public schools of the State which are supported in whole or in part by the public school funds of the State, to teach any theory that denies the story of the Divine Creation of man as taught in the Bible, and to teach instead that man has descended from a lower order of animals.

Section 2. Be it further enacted, That any teacher found guilty of the violation of this Act, Shall be guilty of a misdemeanor and upon conviction, shall be fined not less than One Hundred ($100.00) Dollars nor more than Five Hundred ($500.00) Dollars for each offense.

Section 3. Be it further enacted, That this Act take effect from and after its passage, the public welfare requiring it.

Passed March 13, 1925.

W. F. Barry,

Speaker of the House of Representatives

L. D. Hill,

Speaker of the Senate

Approved March 21, 1925.

Austin Peay,

Governor

Acknowledgments

N O BOOK OF THIS KIND can be written without the tireless assistance of archives, archivists, libraries, and librarians, who, during the last five years and especially during Covid, offered help that was staunch and steadfast.

Among them, I want to thank the following institutions and people for assistance as well as permission to publish material from their archives: at the Abraham Lincoln Presidential Library and Museum, Christopher A. Achnell, Manuscripts Curator, and Michelle Miller, Manuscripts Librarian; the Archives of American Art, Smithsonian Institution; the Bancroft Library, University of California, Berkeley; the Beinecke Rare Book and Manuscript Library, Yale University, Paul Civitelli, Public Service Assistant; the Harry Ransom Humanities Research Center at the University of Texas at Austin, Jim Kuhn, Associate Director, and Hobby Foundation Librarian; Sarah Wharton, Curatorial Associate at the Harvard Law School Library, Historical and Special Collections; the Houghton Library, Harvard University; the Library of Congress, Manuscript Division: DeCarlos Boyd, Product Support, along with Kelly Dyson, Customer Service and Tomeka Myers and Chamisa Redmond in the Office of Business Enterprises, and Edith A. Sandler, Manuscript Reference Librarian; Lindsey Hillgartner, Digital Curator at the Nebraska State

Historical Society; Tal Nadan, Reference Archivist at the New York Public Library, Brooke Russell Astor Reading Room for Rare Books and Manuscripts; the Newberry Library, Graham Greer, Reference Services and Juan Molina Hernández, Digitization Technician; at the Niels Bohr Library & Archives, Max Howell, Manuscript Archivist; Pittsburg State: Sara DeCaro, Curator of Special Collections and University Archivist at Pittsburg State, and Sarah Hutcheon, at the Schlesinger Library on the History of Women in America, Harvard Radcliffe Institute; the Smithsonian Institution Archives, Heidi Stover, Archivist; the Tennessee State Library and Archives, Lindsay Hager, Archivist, as well as Perry G. Davis Jr., Digital Services; The State Historical Society of Missouri, Columbia, Missouri, Kevin R. George, Senior Librarian; Local History and Genealogy, Toledo Lucas County Public Library; Linda J. Long, Curator of Manuscripts, University of Oregon Library, Special Collections and University Archives, as well as Lauren Goss, Public Services Librarian and Randy Sullivan, Digital Production Manager; Kyle Hovious at the University of Tennessee, Knoxville; the University of Wisconsin, Milwaukee, UWM-Libraries and Archives; and Taylor Henning, University Archivist at the Walter P. Reuther Library, Archives of Labor and Urban Affairs, Wayne State University.

I am also grateful to the exceptional research assistance of Kiley Bense, my former student at Columbia University and herself a fine writer of history; to Evgeniya Dame for her meticulous attention to the bibliography and notes; and to William Pugsley of Austin, Texas, who asked of the Harry Random Humanities Research Center all manner of pertinent questions about L. Sprague de Camp, his papers, his interviews, and his correspondence. Thanks, too, to Claudia Anderson for introducing me to Bill Pugsley and to the extraordinary Bob Caro for introducing me to Claudia Anderson. I'm also grateful to Lawrence Wright for his Austin assistance and to Wendy Lesser, who brought the gifts of Evgeniya Dame to my attention.

While researching and writing this book, I taught in the MFA programs at the New School University and in Columbia University's School of the Arts. All of my talented colleagues in both places have offered support, guidance, and good humor over the years, and though I thank them all, I must mention only a very few: the recent and brilliantly competent chair of the department Lis Harris; the former head of nonfiction, the indefatigable Phillip Lopate; the former and acting head of nonfiction, Leslie S. Jamison; and Wendy Walters, most recently the very kind head of nonfiction, all at Columbia, and of course the late Richard Locke, that understandably beloved teacher and editor. At the New School, I'm indebted to the diligence and courage of John Reed, the present head of the Writing Program, and to the diligently caring Lori Lynn Turner. There too, I'm grateful for the sustaining friendship of Helen Schulman, the chair of the fiction concentration, and for the moral support and humor of Susan Cheever and the perspicacity of Robert Polito. As for the students in both places, they have been an ongoing delight.

As I put the finishing touches on this book, I was privileged to be working with the other fellows at the Dorothy and Lewis B. Cullman Center for Scholars and Writers at the New York Public Library. Their good cheer and support—and particularly that of the director, Salvatore Scibona and the deputy directors, Lauren Goldenberg and Paul Delaverdac—were distracting in all the best, most stimulating ways.

A mere thank-you doesn't begin to cover all I owe friends like the late and remarkable Robert Gottlieb, who, once again, read a very early version of this manuscript with the discernment for which he was justly famous. He was one of those very few people on whom nothing was lost. I treasure his notes, but more than that, I will forever be grateful for his friendship, his sensitivity, his outsized humor and his huge heart—and of course his capacious love of the written word in every form and genre. It was no surprise to me to learn that one of his earliest and dearest acquaintances, the poet and translator Richard Howard, was also one of my most beloved friends, whose advice, as I've said before, kept me aloft in dark times. The death of both of them—avid readers, avid writers, avid everything—is not just a loss to me personally, though it is that, but to the world of letters. I am lucky to have known and now to remember them.

For their unflagging encouragement and advice, for good times and good meals, for their illuminating conversations and their cheer, for the letters they've written on my behalf and for the morale they so generously offered during a very and almost indescribably bizarre five years—simply put, for their friendship—I thank these very special people: David Alexander, Alida Becker, Ina Caro, Robert A. Caro, Ron Chernow, Dan Collins, Gail Collins, David Ebershoff, Fernanda Eberstadt, Wendy Gimbel, Judith Ginsberg, Molly Haskell, the late Peter Heinegg, Rosemarie Heinegg, Bruce Handy, Virginia Jonas, Joe Klein, Victoria Klein, Paul LeClerc, Wendy Lesser, Doug Liebhafsky, Arthur Lubow, Michael Massing, Evangeline Morphos, Jed Perl, Claudia Roth Pierpont, Phil Primack, Richard Rizzo, Deborah Rosenthal, Max Rudin, Kent Sepkowitz, Ileene Smith, Howard Sobel, Deborah Solomon, Domna Stanton, Annalyn Swan, Benjamin Taylor, Michele Underwood, Paul Underwood, Sean Wilentz, and Robert Wilson.

My agent, Lynn Nesbit, deserves a paragraph of her own—and much more. She is unparalleled in all things, from book matters to matters more personal. For her intelligence, her wisdom, her loyalty, her perspicacity, her humor, her generosity, and her plain good sense, I'm forever in her debt. She is peerless, not just in her profession, which she is, but in all things, and most particularly in friendship. I'm also indebted to Mina Hamedi, my former Columbia writing student and herself a writer and agent, who has been Lynn's terrific assistant, and to all the people at Janklow & Nesbit that I have met through Lynn—

especially the exemplary Bruce Vinokour, the most considerate Michael Steger, and the ebullient Bennett Ashley.

At Random House, I have been lucky to work with another woman, sui generis: Kate Medina, my reliably conscientious and gifted editor, always available, always understanding, always promptly replying, always clear-sighted about what must be done—and what shouldn't be. She too is a legend among editors, and writers, and no wonder: her scrupulousness and kindness work together hand in hand. She's tops. And she brings with her a marvelous team that in my case consisted of Erica Gonzales, Noa Shapiro, and most recently her terrific assistant, Monica Rae Brown. I'm also indebted to other team players: Benjamin Dreyer, Vice President, Executive Managing Editor and Copy Chief; Rachel Rokicki, Vice President and Deputy Publisher; Rebecca Berlant, Senior Managing Editor; Elizabeth Rendfleisch, text designer; Ayelet Durantt, marketer; and Josh Karpf, copy editor. And for publicity, I want to thank Daniel Christensen, Senior Director, Online Content; Alison Rich, Senior Vice President and Deputy Publisher; Maria Braeckel, Vice President and Director of Publicity; Michelle Jasmine, publicist; and the incomparable Paul Bogaards.

And as for the person to whom I have dedicated this book, and my life, my husband, Michael Dellaira: there are no words. With daunting acuity—and sensitivity—he has read my manuscript with insight and wit and sheer brilliance, and he read it over and over until it became a book; he lights up everything he touches; he contains multitudes and brings sound and song to life; he is the best thing that has ever happened to me.

Notes

FREQUENTLY USED ABBREVIATIONS

All quotations from the Scopes trial taken from *The State of Tennessee v. Scopes,* published as *The World's Most Famous Court Trial: Tennessee Evolution Case.* Cincinnati: National Book Company, 1925.

PEOPLE

AGH: Arthur Garfield Hays
CD: Clarence S. Darrow
DFM: Dudley Field Malone
HLM: Henry L. Mencken
MBB: Mary B. Bryan
MFP: Mary Field Parton
THH: Thomas Henry Huxley
WJB: William Jennings Bryan

BOOKS

AGH, *City Lawyer:* Arthur Garfield Hays, *City Lawyer: The Autobiography of a Law Practice* (New York: Simon & Schuster, 1942).

AGH, *Let Freedom Ring:* Arthur Garfield Hays, *Let Freedom Ring* (New York: Boni and Liveright, 1928).

CD, *The Story of My Life:* Clarence Darrow, *The Story of My Life* (New York: Charles Scribner's, 1932; rpt. New York: Da Capo Press, 1996).

Farmington: Clarence Darrow, *Farmington* (Chicago: A. C. McClurg, 1904; rpt. New York: Da Capo Press; rpt. Charles Scribner's, 1932).

Forgue, *Letters:* Guy L. Forgue, ed. *Letters of H. L. Mencken* (New York: Alfred A. Knopf, 1961).

Prejudices, Fifth Series: Henry L. Mencken, *Prejudices, Fifth Series* (New York: Alfred A. Knopf, 1926).

Scopes, *Center of the Storm:* John T. Scopes, *Center of the Storm* (New York: Holt, Rinehart and Winston, 1967).

Tietjen, *Clutches*: *In the Clutches of the Law: Clarence Darrow's Letters*, ed.
    Randall Tietjen (Berkeley: University of California Press, 2013).
Verdicts out of Court: *Verdicts out of Court* ed. Arthur and Lila Weinberg
    (Chicago: Quadrangle, 1963; rpt. New York: Putnam, 1980).
WJB and MBB, *Memoirs*: William Jennings Bryan and Mary B. Bryan,
    The Memoirs of William Jennings Bryan (Philadelphia: John C. Winston
    Co., 1925).
WJB, *In His Image*: William Jennings Bryan, *In His Image* (New York:
    Fleming H. Revell, 1922).
WJB, *The First Battle*: William Jennings Bryan, *The First Battle*: *The Story of the
    Campaign of 1896* (Chicago: W. B. Conkey, 1896).

ARCHIVES AND COLLECTIONS

ACLU: American Civil Liberties Union papers, Library of Congress, Washington,
    D.C., and online: columbia.edu/cgi-bin/cul/resolve?clio15528034.
Berkeley: Fremont Older papers, Bancroft Library, Berkeley, California.
BU: Leo Cherne papers, Boston University, Boston.
CCOH: Columbia University Oral History Collection, Columbia University New
    York, New York (includes oral histories of Roger Baldwin, Felix
    Frankfurter, Walter Lippmann, August Mencken, A. Philip Randolph,
    Adela Rogers St. Johns, George Schuyler).
Harvard: Learned Hand papers, Harvard Law School Library, Harvard
    University, Cambridge, Massachusetts.
Houghton: Oswald Villard papers, Houghton Library, Harvard University,
    Cambridge, Massachusetts.
HRHRC: L. Sprague de Camp papers, Harry Ransom Humanities Research
    Center, Austin, Texas.
LC: Library of Congress, Washington, D.C. (includes papers of William Jennings
    Bryan and Clarence Darrow as well as Ruby Darrow, George F. Milton, and
    William Allen White).
Missouri: Winterton Conway Curtis papers, Center for Missouri Studies, The
    State Historical Society of Missouri, Columbia, Missouri.
NAACP: National Association for the Advancement of Colored People, Library
    of Congress.
Newberry: Clarence Darrow papers, Clarence Darrow and Mary Field Parton
    papers, Newberry Library, Chicago.
NYPL: Henry L. Mencken papers, New York Public Library, Brooke R. Astor
    Reading Room for Rare Books and Manuscripts, New York, New York.
Oregon: Mary Field Parton papers, University of Oregon, Eugene, Oregon,
    Knight Library, Mary Field Parton papers.
Schlesinger: Doris Stevens papers, Schlesinger Library, Harvard University,
    Cambridge, Massachusetts.
Yale: Edward Mandell House papers, Sterling Library, Yale University, New
    Haven Connecticut.

PREFACE: THE TRIAL OF THE CENTURY

xv   **"This trial was bound to take place somewhere"**: William G. Shepherd, "Monkey Business in Tennessee," *Collier's*, July 18, 1925, 38–39.

xviii   **"natural selection"**: see, for instance: "any being, if it vary however slightly in any manner profitable to itself, under the complex and sometimes varying conditions of life, will have a better chance of surviving, and thus be naturally selected," in Charles Darwin, *On the Origin of Species*, 5.

xix   **"God intended"**: "Communism Denounced," *New York Times*, July 30, 1877, 8.

xix   **"When men are ignorant and poor and weak"**: Ibid., 8.

xix   **"evolution robs the individual"**: "Scopes Convicted Before Case Opened," Washington *Star*, July 19, 1925, 4.

xix   **"The evolutionists bring their doctrine"**: Ibid., 4.

xx   **"When science strikes at that upon which man's eternal hope"**: *Trial*, fifth day, 197. As noted, unless otherwise indicated, all direct quotations from the trial are taken from the transcript, published as *The World's Most Famous Court Trial: Tennessee Evolution Case*.

xxi   **"At bottom, down in their hearts, they are equally at a loss"**: Frank R. Kent, "Dayton Trial Raises Issues Yet Unsolved," Baltimore *Sun*, July 13, 1925, 1.

xxi   **"Darwin is right inside"**: this and preceding examples from Charles A. Merrill, "Air of Both Camp Meeting and Fair," *Boston Globe*, July 8, 1925, A19.

xxii   **Men in black felt hats**: see Charles A. Merrill, "Religion Battles Evolution as Trial of Scopes Opens," *Boston Globe*, July 10, 1925, 1, 22.

xxii   **"Shall We Be Taxed to Damn Our Children?"** "Mountaineers Won't Hear Arguments on Evolution," *New York Times*, July 12, 1925, 16.

xxii   **Two chimpanzees**: see M. R. Werner, *Bryan*, 315.

xxii   **"morons and moral cowards"**: "British Condemn Charges," *New York Times*, July 10, 1925, 6.

xxii   **an American circus**: see, for instance, Edwin L. James, "Europe Sees Trial a Huge Joke on Us," *New York Times*, July 14, 1925, 3; "Scopes Case Stirs Berlin," *New York Times*, July 19, 1925, 2. See also "All Germany Watching Scopes' Evolution Trial," *Boston Globe*, July 10, 1925, 13; "Europe Is Amazed," *New York Times*, July 11, 1925, 1, 2.

xxii   **"Faith cannot"**: "Britons See Ape Trial Revival of Puritan Bigotry," *Chicago Tribune*, July 12, 1925, 4.

xxii   **"This is twentieth-century America?"**: Alan Bott, "Through a Londoner's Window," *The Sphere*, July 18, 1925, 90.

xxiii   **"I would have given anything"**: *The Letters of Rudyard Kipling*, vol. 5, 251.

xxiii   **"It was not in rural Tennessee"**: HLM, "In Tennessee," *The Nation*, July 1, 1925, 2.

xxiii   **"horde of pacifists, pro-Germans, German agents"**: Truman Hudson

Alexander, "War on Legion Fits Liberties Union's Record," *The Tennessean*, Aug. 30, 1925, 1.

xxiv   **"Rental for rooms? . . . for nothing":** W. O. McGeehan, "Why Pick on Dayton?" *Harper's Magazine*, Oct. 1925, 624, 625; see also W. O. McGeehan, "Darrow's Lavender Galluses Snap Crown of Thorns," *New York Herald Tribune*, July 11, 1925, 1.

xxiv   **He believed:** see the fine Lawrence W. Levine, *Defender of the Faith: William Jennings Bryan: The Last Decade*, which acutely discusses the irony of Bryan's crusades, esp. 53–54.

xxiv   **"Tennessee safe for Genesis":** "The Week," *New Republic*, May 27, 1925, 4.

xxv   **"one of the most dangerous lions of the U.S. Bar":** "Law: In the Bronx," *Time*, Jan. 2, 1928, 25.

xxv   **Darrow would fight desperately:** Bruce Catton, "Downtrodden Will Miss Clarence Darrow," *Ithaca Journal*, Mar. 17, 1938, 6.

xxvi   **"The powerful orator hulking his way":** Lincoln Steffens, "Attorney for the Damned," *Saturday Review of Literature*, Feb. 27, 1932, 550.

xxvi   **To them, Darrow:** See "Clarence Darrow," *Chicago Tribune*, Aug. 1, 1907, 8; "The Debs Movement," *People*, Nov. 24, 1990, 3.

xxvi   **Attorney for the damned:** Steffens, "Attorney for the Damned," 549.

xxvii   **"There is a contest pending today":** "Ingersoll," *Cincinnati Enquirer*, Nov. 26, 1900, 10.

xxviii   **"a universal republic":** quoted in Arthur Weinberg, ed. *Attorney for the Damned*, 407.

xxix   **"Most of the newspapers":** CD, *The Story of My Life*, 249.

xxx   **"Free thought is the most important issue":** quoted in Charles McCann, "Fundamentalism Must Lose Fight to Aid Science," *Atlanta Constitution*, July 12, 1925: 1, 7.

xxx   **"Democracy has shaken my nerves to pieces":** Henry Adams, *Democracy*, 370, 78.

xxx   **"Dayton, Tennessee, is America!":** W.E.B. Du Bois, "Scopes," *The Crisis*, September 1925, 218.

CHAPTER ONE: THE BEGINNING
OF WISDOM, 1858–1914

4   **"Corn, hogs, wheat":** *Sherwood Anderson's Memoirs*, 107, 108.

4   **His parents:** See Winterton Curtis, recollections of Darrow in "Fundamentalism vs. Evolution," 8, Winterton Curtis papers, Missouri.

5   **denied that the Bible was the literal word of God:** See "The Chronicle," *Western Reserve Chronicle*, Feb. 22, 1871, 3.

5   **John Stuart Mill:** *Farmington*, 37.

5   **"Doubt was the beginning of wisdom, and the fear of God was the end of wisdom":** CD, *The Story of My Life*, 38.

5   **Darrow was a sensitive child:** this and the chicken anecdote recounted in Ruby Darrow to Irving Stone, n.d., LC.

5   **told his first biographer:** see Charles Yale Harrison, *Clarence Darrow*, 3.

6   "I must have loved her": *Farmington*, 30.

6   he enjoyed: see CD, *The Story of My Life*, 29.

8   his real love: see Harry Barnard, *Eagle Forgotten: The Life of John Peter Altgeld*, 64.

8   "plays the game": quoted in "Interview with CD," 1918, p. 2, Illinois State Historical Library.

10 "If I do it . . . I will be a dead man politically": Ernest L. Bogart and Charles M. Thompson, *Centennial History of Illinois*, vol. 4, 187.

10 "A lying, hypocritical": "The Anarchist Governor of Illinois," *Chicago Tribune*, July 7, 1894, 12.

10 Theodore Roosevelt: see Harvey Wish, "Governor Altgeld Pardons the Anarchists," 441. See also Thomas Beer, *Hanna, Crane, and the Mauve Decade*, 53.

10 "a shameless advocate of rapine and assassination," Mencken, *Prejudices, Fifth Series*, 128.

10 "What in God's name": quoted in Beer, *Hanna, Crane, and the Mauve Decade*, 78.

10 "A man who won't meet his men": quoted in Ibid., 498.

11 "Forty years ago the slave power predominated": John Peter Altgeld, *Live Questions*, 460.

11 When Darrow defended Debs: Debs was denied the victory it had been clear he would've had; the judge refused to seat an alternate when a member of the jury took ill.

13 "I love trade unions": quoted in Weinberg, ed., *Attorney for the Damned*, 406.

14 "If you decree his death": quoted in William D. Haywood, *Bill Haywood's Book: The Autobiography of William Haywood*, 215–16.

15 frequently considered a possible candidate: see "Darrow May Get There," *Chicago Tribune*, Jan. 28, 1891, 6.

16 "He was absolutely honest in his ends": CD, 1918, Illinois State Historical Library.

16 "When bought, Darrow stayed bought": John A. Farrell, *Clarence Darrow: Attorney for the Damned*, 84.

16 "I came to Chicago . . . get it": CD to [Ellen Starr?], March 1895, Tietjen, *Clutches*, 76–78.

16 "I never have been able": CD to Fremont Older, July 26 [1911], Berkeley.

17 "I remember during . . . victims": quoted in Marcet Haldeman-Julius to Ruby Darrow, n.d., LC.

17 "Who Is This Man Darrow?": *Current Literature*, Aug. 1907, 157. The essay was often reprinted.

17 "He affects to be a brave man": Elbert Hubbard, *The Philistine: A Periodical of Protest*, July 1906, 52.

17 "Darrow, indeed": Hutchins Hapgood, *The Spirit of Labor*, 141.

17 "He was human as pie a la mode": Willis Thornton to Irving Stone, Feb. 19, 1940, LC.

18 on speaking terms: "Darrow, Hope of the Accused Mine Officers," *St. Louis Post-Dispatch*, May 26, 1907, 3B.

18   He smoked heavily: "Who Is This Man Darrow?," *Current Literature*, Aug. 1907, 157.

19   "The streets of the city": "Clarence Darrow's *Farmington*," *Chicago Tribune*, Oct. 1, 1904, 9.

19   "Clarence's first experience": Ruby Darrow to Irving Stone, April 2, n.y., LC.

19   "was everywhere, with everyone, men as well as women": Ruby Darrow to Irving Stone, "About Gertrude Barnum," n.d., LC.

20   "What a goddamn fool!": Ruby Darrow to Irving Stone, n.d., LC. Ruby Darrow added the comment about the apology, noting, "Fortunately, we could laugh off almost anything together."

20   "Perhaps he felt the need": MFP diary, n.d. [1911], Oregon.

21   "Sex [is] the only feeling": CD to MFP, Apr. 27, 1915, Parton-Darrow papers, Newberry Library.

21   "was not an indiscriminate petticoat chaser": William Allen White, *The Autobiography of William Allen White*, 510.

21   "Stand up": "Woes of the Peddlers," *Chicago Daily Tribune*, Mar. 25, 1901, 1.

21   Law was a luxury bought and sold: See "Suppression of Vice," Chicago *Inter Ocean*, Jan. 18, 1901, 2.

21   "Is there any reason ... any realization": CD, "The Problem of the Negro," 321, 325.

22   "The laws don't go far enough": see, for instance, "Socialist Advises Negroes to Strike," *New York Times*, May 13, 1910, 2.

22   "He was so brave and so fearless": George S. Leisure, "Reflections on Clarence Darrow," 414.

23   "I was drawn": Irving Stone, *Clarence Darrow for the Defense*, 471.

23   "No well-balanced": "The Folly of Darrow," *Rockford Morning Star*, May 18, 1910, 4.

24   But then Samuel Gompers: See Ruby Darrow to Irving Stone, Sept. 3, 1940, LC.

24   "I felt as does a doctor": "Clarence S. Darrow, Vegetarian," *Vegetarian Magazine*, Chicago, Sept. 1, 1912, 3.

25   "It was all the compensation": Lincoln Steffens, *The Autobiography of Lincoln Steffens*, vol. 2, 683.

25   "notorious corporation corruptionist": Eugene Debs to CD, Feb. 19, 1912, Eugene V. Debs collection, Indiana State University. For other information on Earl Rogers, see Adela Rogers St. Johns, *Final Verdict*, and Richard F. Snow, "Counsel for the Indefensible," 96–97.

26   Slumping listlessly: see "Darrow's Detective May Confess All," *New York Times*, Jan. 31, 1912, 1.

26   "I am as fitted for jury bribing": Weinberg, ed. *Attorney for the Damned*, 506.

27   "Life is a game of whist": "Jurors Weep as Darrow Pleads," *Chicago Tribune*, Aug. 16, 1912, 2. For a slightly different version, see Weinberg, ed. *Attorney for the Damned*, 529.

27   People in the courtroom sobbed: "Moved to Tears by Darrow's Plea," *Atlanta Constitution*, Aug. 16, 1912, 1.

27 **Darrow wiped:** see W. W. Robinson, *Bombs and Bribery*, 41.

27 **The sweeping denunciation:** see "New Trial March 31," *Boston Globe*, Mar. 9, 1913, 2.

28 **"he seemed a beaten man":** Hugh Baillie, *High Tension: The Recollections of Hugh Baillie*, 25.

28 **"Won't you & can't you do":** CD to Eugene V. Debs, Feb. 12, 1912, Debs collection, Indiana State University.

29 **"Almost firmly convinced of the innocence":** Samuel Gompers to CD, Mar. 16, 1912, Leo Cherne papers, BU.

29 **"Poor broken Darrow":** MFP, journal [n.d., 1911], Oregon.

29 **"an old-fashioned soul":** Edgar Lee Masters, *Across Spoon River*, 273.

30 **"According to some of the descriptions of Lincoln":** Ibid.

30 **"No one can find life tolerable without dope":** CD to MFP, July 4, 1913, Newberry.

30 **"I will never close my eyes again":** CD to MFP, Apr. 27 [1915], Newberry.

30 **"What an everlasting enigma":** CD to MFP, Dec. 6 [1915], Newberry.

CHAPTER TWO: A CROSS OF GOLD AND THE MAN WITH THE HOE, 1860–1908

32 **"Be sure":** Moses Koenigsberg, *King News: An Autobiography*, 195.

33 **Bryan had surprised many:** see Carter H. Harrison, *Stormy Years*, 72.

35 **The speech had mowed the audience down:** Waldo Browne, *Altgeld of Illinois*, 277.

35 **"A suffering people":** Francis Fisher Browne, *National Review* (London), 454.

35 **"We are not attacking a race":** WJB, *The First Battle*, 581.

36 **"I have been thinking over Bryan's speech":** CD, *The Story of My Life*, 92.

36 **"kindred forces against the common enemy—the Republican party":** Quoted in Paul V. Peterson, "William Jennings Bryan, *World-Herald* Editor," 353, history.nebraska.gov/wp-content/uploads/2022/10/NH 1968BryanEditor.pdf.

37 **"one of the foremost agencies":** quoted in Ibid., 362.

38 **"Bryan was a law unto himself":** quoted in Arthur Wallace Dunn, *From Harrison to Harding*, vol. 1, 188.

38 **"It was Hugo's vague hyperbolic"; books by quacks:** Willa Cather, "The Personal Side of William Jennings Bryan," 332. The article was originally published on July 14, 1900, under the pseudonym Henry Nickelmann.

38 **"The shelves might have been filled"; clothes seemed antebellum:** William Allen White, "Bryan," 237.

39 **"free from any accountability . . . question":** "An Address Delivered by Hon. Silas L. Bryan," *Salem Advocate*, Nov. 6, 1862, 1.

39   "to advance their peculiar views": see "Democracy Exultant," *Salem Advocate,* Aug. 18, 1858, 2.

39   **though he lost his seat:** see "Silas L. Bryan," *Salem Advocate,* Mar. 17, 1863, 2; see also "Copperhead Meeting in Monroe County," *Chicago Tribune,* Oct. 23, 1863, 2.

40   **Silas Bryan put it:** see "Announcements," *Nashville Journal,* Oct. 25, 1972, 7; see also "Judge Bryan," Belleville *Semi-Weekly Advocate,* July 26, 1872, 4.

40   **In 1864:** "Too Good to Be Lost," *Salem Advocate,* July 14, 1864, 3.

40   **unreconstructed rebel:** "Martin and Bryan," *Nashville Journal,* Oct. 25, 1972, 6.

40   **"Is there no relief":** "A Hard Case Question," *Marion County Herald,* Aug. 30, 1878, 1.

40   **rebel fossil:** see "Martin and Bryan," *Nashville Journal,* Oct. 25, 1872, 6; see also *Nashville Journal,* Oct. 12, 1876, 3; "Some Illinois Bourbons," *Chicago Tribune,* May 18, 1878, 2.

40   **"who for forty years has three times":** "Southern Illinois," *Chicago Tribune,* May 20, 1878, 2.

40   **"Every step in our progress":** "An Address Delivered by Hon. Silas L. Bryan," *Salem Advocate,* Nov. 6, 1862, 2.

40   **Silas opened:** see "Some Illinois Bourbons," *Chicago Tribune,* May 18, 1878, 3.

41   **"His devotion to the doctrines of the Democratic fathers":** "When Has the Exercise of Patience Ceased to be Virtuous?," *Marion County Herald,* Aug. 16, 1878, 1.

41   **Both father and son:** see Paolo E. Coletta, "Silas Bryan of Salem," 57.

41   **showcase:** Ibid., 4.

42   **"learn to make music on the hack saw":** WJB and MBB, *Memoirs,* 39.

42   **"When you have four pounds more of brains":** Ibid., 56.

42   **"I felt so unworthy":** Ibid., 242.

42   **"noble aims make noble men":** Ibid., 227.

43   **"It has enough dynamite":** quoted in William L. Stidger, *Edwin Markham,* 148.

43   **sick fish:** see Ambrose Bierce, "Prattle," San Francisco *Examiner,* Jan. 22, 1899, 13.

43   **"Is America going to turn to Socialism over one poem?"** quoted in Oscar Lewis, *The Big Four,* 241; see also "Markham's Poem," *New York Times,* Aug. 5, 1899, 17.

43   **"The good workman":** Collis P. Huntington, *California: Her Past, Present, and Future,* 21.

44   **a poor degenerate wretch:** see David Starr Jordan, *The Blood of the Nation: Study of the Decay of Races Through the Survival of the Unfit,* 25.

44   **"Is it the fault of God . . . heart":** WJB, "The Man with the Hoe," San Francisco *Examiner,* Apr. 1, 1900, 25.

45   **no peace without guns:** The speech was delivered in Omaha on June 14, 1898; it was Bryan's first lengthy comment on the war.

46   **Once ratified:** see WJB to Andrew Carnegie, Jan. 30, 1899, box 22, LC.

46 **What was that:** see *Speech of Hon. George F. Hoar in the Senate of the United States, April 17, 1900* (Washington, D.C., 1900), 6–8; "Senator Hoar Pleads for the Filipinos," *New York Times*, Apr. 18, 1900, 5; "Denby Smashes Bryan's 'Bogy,'" *Chicago Tribune*, Aug. 27, 1900, 1.

46 **"I was so incensed . . . found it":** Richard F. Pettigrew, *Imperial Washington: The Story of American Public Life from 1870 to 1920*, 270–71.

47 **"To advocate the incorporation":** WJB, "The Philippine Question," 2.

47 **"When conditions force the two races":** WJB, "The Negro Question," 2.

47 **influential Black journalist:** see *The Colored American*, Nov. 11, 1898.

47 **John E. Bruce:** See John E. Bruce, "Tammany and the Negro," *The Colored American*, Sept. 15, 1900, 2.

47 **"It does seem to me that Mr. Bryan":** *The Letters of Theodore Roosevelt*, vol. 2, 1385.

48 **Bryan's racial bias:** see, for instance, George Hoar, "President McKinley or President Bryan?," 478.

48 **"we are not ashamed":** U.S. Congress, Senate, S. Res. 174, 56th Congress, 1st session, Feb. 26, 1900, *Congressional Record*, 33, 2348.

48 **An Anglo-Saxon is an Anglo-Saxon:** see Benjamin Tillman, "Causes of Southern Opposition to Imperialism," 453. See also Edwina C. Smith, "Southerners on Empire: Southern Senators and Imperialism, 1898–1899," 89–107.

48 **Bryan praised:** see, for instance, "William Jennings Bryan," *Freeman* (Indianapolis), Nov. 3, 1900, 3, and WJB, "Tillman and McLaurin," *The Commoner*, May 31, 1901, 1.

48 **"more advanced race":** WJB, "The Negro Question," *The Commoner*, Nov. 1, 1901, 1.

48 **"social equality":** Ibid.

48 **"No advantage . . . is to be gained":** Ibid., 2.

49 **"He is not seeking":** William Allen White, "Bryan," 236.

49 **"No fluttering wings of doubt":** Ibid., 234.

49 **"Facts never budged him":** William Allen White, *Masks in a Pageant*, 254.

49 **"the very lightest weight":** *The Letters of Theodore Roosevelt*, vol. 2, 1359.

50 **"I remember well a Sunday":** Charles E. Russell, *Bare Hands and Stone Walls*, 319–20.

50 **Special trains:** see Werner, *Bryan*, 138.

50 **a standard fee of $250:** see Michael Kazin, *A Godly Hero*, 132.

51 **"had lost his grip":** HLM, "William J. Bryan, Once Powerful, Goes Down to Defeat Before the Forces That Will Nominate Chief Judge Parker," quoted in S. T. Joshi, *H. L. Mencken: An Annotated Bibliography*, 387.

51 **In 1896 Hearst:** see David Nasaw, *The Chief*, 118.

52 **"In his frayed alpaca":** HLM, *Heathen Days*, 282, 284.

52 **"if it is the choice of this Convention":** "Speech of William Jennings Bryan," *Official Report of the Proceedings of the Democratic National Convention Held in St. Louis, Mo., July 6, 7, 8, and 9, 1904,* reported by Milton W. Blumenberg, 241–42.

52 **Bryan may have been hoping:** see David Nasaw, *The Chief,* 181.

52 **"Some of you have called me dictator":** this speech has often been reproduced. I am using H. L. Mencken, *Heathen Days,* 284, for full effect.

53 **"His soul was marching on":** Ibid., 285.

53 **"Monticello of the West":** for this and other details about Fairview, including its cost and Bryan's 1908 income, see Verum, "William Jennings Bryan at Home," 8–11.

54 **"I fear the plutocracy of wealth":** WJB, *Speeches,* vol. 2, 362. The speech "The Price of a Soul" was launched in 1908.

54 **"runs the death of Little Nell":** Werner, *Bryan,* 138.

55 **he was more fully becoming:** see Paola E. Coletta, "The Youth of William Jennings Bryan," 24.

56 **"How long they will think this policy wise":** WJB, "An Ecclesiastical Factor," *The Commoner,* Dec. 4, 1908, 14.

56 **In Charleston, West Virginia:** see "No Negroes Wanted," Washington *Bee,* Apr. 4, 1908, 2.

56 **"The people in the Northern":** See, for instance, "Bryan's Views," the Orangeburg (SC) *Times and Democrat,* Apr. 4, 1907, 5. Bryan and Beveridge had debated each other in the pages of *The Reader Magazine,* and the debate on race, in the second installment, had been followed closely, especially in the South.

56 **"not in the darkest":** WJB and MBB, *Memoirs,* 10.

56 **"I cannot believe that man came from monkeys":** "Bryan on Religion," *New-York Tribune,* May 2, 1907, 14.

57 **"I have as much right to assume":** "Crowds Honor Bryan," Baltimore *Sun,* Apr. 15, 1907, 2.

57 **"Did you ever see a radish...don't":** "Bryan Greeted by Large Crowd," Washington *Evening Star,* Apr. 15, 1907, 12.

57 **"If the Father makes the acorn":** "'The Prince of Peace,'" *Great Falls Tribune* (Montana), Aug. 11, 1907, 8. See also WJB, *Speeches,* vol. 2, 283.

CHAPTER THREE: HUXLEY, NIETZSCHE, MENCKEN, 1876–1917

61 **"like a flash of light":** THH, "On the Reception of *Origin of Species,*" in Sir Francis Darwin, ed., *The Life and Letters of Charles Darwin,* vol. 1, 550.

62 **"No man can think in English ... enemy":** HLM, "Huxley," *Chicago Tribune,* Aug. 2, 1925, 1, 7.

62 **"His mind was an almost perfect instrument":** Ibid., 1.

62 **"Sit down before a fact":** *Life and Letters of Thomas Henry Huxley,* vol. 1, 219.

63 "believes only those propositions": THH, "Agnosticism and Christianity," *Science and Christian Tradition*, 310.

63 "If I had at my side all those": THH, "Agnosticism and Christianity," 230.

63 "My style of writing": *Letters*, 189.

63 "like all men who discover in themselves": HLM, "Darwin's Bulldog," 374.

63 primary colors: see Isaac Goldberg, *Mencken the Man*, 132.

63 "He calls you a swine": Walter Lippmann, "H. L. Mencken," 414.

64 "So many young men": Ernest Hemingway, *The Sun Also Rises*, 39.

64 "The gleam of fanaticism": Reinhold Niebuhr, "Treatise on the Gods," 18.

64 "was above that of a street-walker": HLM, "The Newspaper Man," 248.

65 "Looking back": "Notes on Newspaper Days," in HLM, *The Days Trilogy, Expanded Edition*, 694.

65 "I was disinclined": *My Life*, unfinished ms., Enoch Pratt Library.

66 After his mother died: see "'Mr. M: An Unpublished Memoir of H. L. Mencken' by James M. Cain," ed. David Roessel and Stephanie Maniaci, 169, 183.

66 "If I had to leave it": HLM, *Prejudices, Fifth Series*, 241.

67 "A language is not the master": HLM, "A Call for Help," Baltimore *Evening Sun*, Oct. 29, 1910, 6.

67 "Isn't the present sovereignty": HLM, "Trouble Ahead," Baltimore *Evening Sun*, Aug. 10, 1910, 6.

67 "The king was dead": HLM, "Hon. Henry G. Davis for Vice President," Baltimore *Morning Herald*, July 10, 1904, 1–2.

67 "Their lynchings are now conducted": HLM, "The Art of Lynching," Baltimore *Evening Sun*, June 17, 1910, 6.

67 "Lynchings, of course": HLM, "The Arts and Crafts Movement in Texas," Baltimore *Evening Sun*, July 25, 1910, 6.

67 "These noble men of God": "HLM, The Free Lance," Baltimore *Evening Sun*, Mar. 18, 1914, 6.

68 "he was handy": HLM, "The Free Lance," Baltimore *Evening Sun*, June 23, 1915, 6.

68 "the sort of patriotism": HLM, *Pistols for Two*, 21.

68 "My prejudices are innumerable": HLM, "Addendum on Aims," in Guy L. Forgue, ed., *Letters of H. L. Mencken*, 189.

68 "the Jews could be put down": HLM, *Treatise on the Gods*, 345.

68–69 "would cause him inconvenience . . . Ruston, La": HLM, "Help for the Jews," Baltimore *Sunday Sun*, Nov. 27, 1938, 8.

69 "an enchanting Mephistopheles": 'Mr. M: An Unpublished Memoir of H. L. Mencken' by James M. Cain," 174.

69 "What amazed me": Richard Wright, *Black Boy*, 293.

69 "Error was his enemy": HLM, *The Philosophy of Friedrich Nietzsche*, xi.

69 "given divine sanction": Ibid., 81.

70 "that burned the books": Ibid, 96.

70 "high priest": Ibid., viii.

70   "a counterblast": HLM, "Nietzschiana," Baltimore *Evening Sun*,
     Nov. 3, 1910, 6. See also HLM, *Men Versus the Man*, 69.

70   Mencken would distinguish himself: see Goldberg, *Mencken the Man*,
     58, 118; HLM, *Happy Days*, 259–61.

70   "Among human beings": HLM, *The Philosophy of Friedrich
     Nietzsche*, 93.

71   "Without this constant strife": Ibid., 105.

71   "the unfortunate ambiguity": THH, "Evolution and Ethics," in *Col-
     lected Essays*, vol. 9, 80.

71   "The joy of life comes": HLM, *The New Mencken Letters*, 45.

71   "a riddle solved": HLM, *Men Versus the Man*, 119–20.

71   "the intelligent, ingenious and far-seeing man": HLM, *The Philosophy
     of Friedrich Nietzsche*, 242.

71   "My own private view": HLM, *Men Versus the Man*, 205.

72   "whether we adopt Socialism": Ibid., 71.

72   "to make a dent in the cosmos": HLM, *George Bernard Shaw*, 71.

72   "There are chapters": see HLM, "The Literature of a Moral Republic,"
     152.

72   "Who has the courage": HLM, "The Horse-Power of Realism," *Smart
     Set*, June 1911, 152.

72   Henry James's: see HLM, "The Good, the Bad, and the Best-Sellers,"
     159.

73   "old Walt": HLM, "Novels for Hot Afternoons," *Smart Set*, July 1911,
     158.

73   "have an answer to my answer": HLM, "A 1911 Model Dream Book,"
     Smart Set, Sept. 1911, 155.

73   "I am an extreme libertarian": HLM, "Addendum on Aims," in Forgue,
     Letters, 189.

73   "Of what value": HLM, "On Free Speech," Baltimore *Evening Sun*,
     Mar. 25, 1911, 6.

74   "the cleansing shock of adversity": HLM, "The Free Lance," Baltimore
     Evening Sun, Mar. 14, 1914, 6.

74   "The American people . . . money": Ibid.

74   "liberty cabbage": HLM, *The American Language: A Prelimi-
     nary Inquiry into the Development of English in the United States*, 152.

74   "The country is in a state of moral mania": Forgue, *Letters*, 87.

74   Mencken himself: see John Edgar Hoover to [deleted], FBI, Department
     of Justice, Nov. 24, 1941. FBI files on Mencken.

74   "Eagle-eyed scientists . . . aniline dyes": HLM, "Star-Spangled Men,"
     118, 120.

75   "Neutral?": HLM, "The Free Lance," Baltimore *Evening Sun*, Sept 7,
     1914, 6.

75   He pointed out: Franz von Papen, the German intelligence officer, said
     in his memoirs that the ship did carry 12 crates of detonators, 6,026
     crates of bullets, and 492 cases of military equipment. Franz von Papen,
     Memoirs, 42.

75   "It is a first principle": HLM, "The Free Lance," Baltimore *Sun*,
     May 12, 1915, 6.

76   Convicted of trading with the enemy: Convicted of perjury related to

violation of the "Trading with the Enemy Act," Rumely was later pardoned by President Calvin Coolidge.

76   **"I have been engaged in propagandist":** HLM, "The Great American Art," 310.

76   **"in all human beings":** HLM, *The American Language*, 321.

CHAPTER FOUR: MAKING THE WORLD SAFE, 1912–1918

78   **"I never have known a case":** Dunn, *From Harrison to Harding*, vol. 2, 189.

78   **No one:** see Ellen Maury Slayden, *Washington Wife: The Journal of Ellen Maury Slayden*, 180.

78   **party's prophet and nemesis . . . led it to defeat:** see Henry Morgenthau, *All in a Life-Time*, 138.

78   **"could do something at once dignified and effective":** quoted in Arthur S. Link, *Wilson: The Road to the White House*, 353.

78   **"If anyone . . . Waterloo":** Morgenthau, *All in a Life-Time*, 142.

79   **"people through the country regard him as a hero":** Edward M. House, *The Intimate Papers of Colonel House*, vol. 1, 70.

79   **"When you are on a football team":** James M. Cox, *Journey Through My Years*, 413.

79   **"Wilson didn't knock Bryan":** for instance, *Daily Sentinel-Tribune* (Ohio), Apr. 22, 1913, 2.

79   **Secretary Bryan appeared ignorant:** see Rachel West, "The Department of State, at Home and Abroad, on the Eve of the First World War," 47–59, especially 58–64, 71–72.

80   **"valor of ignorance":** Sydney Brooks, "An English View of Mr. Bryan," 692.

80   **"Chaos prevails:"** Wilbur J. Carr, diary, Apr. 12, 1913, LC.

80   **The Russian ambassador:** WJB and MBB, *Memoirs*, 351.

80   **Bryan cared less:** see Wilbur J. Carr, diary, Apr. 11, 1913, LC. See also West, *The Department of State*, 49–51.

80   **Wilson offered the Chinese ambassadorship:** see House, *The Intimate Papers of Colonel House*, vol. 1, 104.

81   **"Pacifist Bryan":** see Albert J. Nock, "What the Right Hand Doeth," *Freeman* (Indianapolis), Nov. 20, 1921, 269.

81   **"soft pedal":** Edward M. House ms., June 24, 1915, MS 466, Edward Mandell House Papers, Series II, Diaries, Volume 3, Yale.

82   **"If I run again for the Presidency":** Arthur S. Link, *The New Freedom*, vol. 2, 113.

82   **"I have never had your full confidence":** Edward M. House, diary, June 24, 1915, Yale.

82   **"I go out in the dark . . . die for me":** David F. Houston, *Eight Years with Wilson's Cabinet*, 146.

82   **"A pistol-toting nation":** *The Commoner*, Oct. 1915, 3.

83   **"Bryan is as usual an ass":** quoted in Arthur S. Link, *Wilson: The Struggle for Neutrality*, vol. 3, 427.

83   Woodrow Wilson privately: see Edwin Tribble, ed., *A President in Love: The Courtship Letters of Woodrow Wilson and Edith Bolling Galt*, 60.

83   "the lower path of expediency and party regularity": Edgar Lee Masters, "The Christian Statesman," 397.

84   "I had some glimpses": WJB and MBB, *Memoirs*, 433.

84   "a race question": WJB, "Prohibition," *The Commoner*, Jan. 1, 1916, 13, 14.

85   "This reform is needed": "Woman's Suffrage in Ohio," *The Commoner*, Dec. 1, 1917, 4.

85   In 1917: "Not a Difficult Question," *The Suffragist*, June 30, 1917, 10.

86   If there weren't enough police: see, for instance, "Blames Capitol Police," *New York Times*, July 17, 1917, 9.

87   Originally from Nebraska: for a more full account of Stevens's life, feminism, and marriage to Malone, see Leila J. Rupp, "Feminism and the Sexual Revolution in the Early Twentieth Century: The Case of Doris Stevens," 289–90.

87   "What will you do": "Secretary of the Navy Strikes His Flag," *Riverside Daily Press* (California), June 13, 1916, 1.

87   "administration terrorism": see Doris Stevens, *Jailed for Freedom*, chapter 2.

87   "high-powered temperament": Morgenthau, *All in a Life-Time*, 145.

88   It was Malone: see Ray Stannard Baker memorandum, Baker papers, interview with DFM, Nov. 1, 1927, LC.

88   Five years later: see "La Follette 'Framed,' Dudley Malone Says," *St. Louis Post-Dispatch*, Oct. 29, 1920, 8.

89   A rumor spread: Colonel House had advised him to stay: July 26, 1917, MS 466, Edward Mandell House Papers, Series II, Diaries, vol. 5, Yale.

89   "I think it is high time": "To Rebuke Wilson Malone Resigns," *Atlanta Constitution*, Sept. 8, 1917, 1.

89   Ridiculed: see Aug. 27, 1918, MS 466, Edward Mandell House Papers, series II, Diaries, vol. 6, Yale.

89   "deluded creatures with short skirts and short hair." "House Moves for Woman Suffrage," *New York Times*, Sept. 25, 1917, 11.

90   "I know of nothing": quoted in Arthur S. Link, ed., *The Papers of Woodrow Wilson*, vol. 43, 313.

90   Malone never saw Wilson again: see Doris Stevens, *Jailed for Freedom*, 163.

90   Postmaster General Burleson refused: see Adam Hochschild, *American Midnight*, a recent, excellent summary of the repression and censorship inaugurated by the administration during the war.

90   "absolute power": quoted in *From Baltimore to Bohemia: The Letters of HLM and George Sterling*, ed. S. T. Joshi, 33.

91   "If a few are permitted": WJB, "Resisting the Draft," *The Commoner*, Aug. 1, 1917, 1.

91   "unpatriotic utterances," . . . abuse of free speech: WJB, "Abusing Free Speech," *The Commoner*, Aug. 1, 1917, 1.

92   "Repent?": Caroline Moorehead, *Troublesome People*, 71.

92   "Clarence Darrow was"; "I love him": Eugene Debs to Emanuel

Haldeman-Julius, Jan. 24, 1926, Debs collection, Indiana State University.

92   "While I was strongly": CD, *The Story of My Life,* 74.

92–93   "To keep in prison . . . deep wounds of war": Tietjen, *Clutches,* 233.

93   "It is he, not I, who needs a pardon": "Debs, Unrepentant, Denounces Wilson," *New York Times,* Feb. 2, 1921, 5.

93   "If I had it within my power": "Gene Debs, in Prison Cell, Turns the Other Cheek," *Appeal to Reason,* Feb. 12, 1921, 2.

93   "I have long ceased": Tietjen, *Clutches,* 235.

CHAPTER FIVE: REBIRTH OF A NATION: THE KU KLUX KLAN, 1919–1922

96   If Americans went into the war: "Wilson Jeered by Speakers at Rally of 3,000," 1, 2.

96   "No single nation got out": Harold Stearns, *Liberalism in America,* 197.

97   It was a time for brotherly love: see "Time for Action," *The Commoner,* Oct. 1, 1919, 2, and "Labor's Bad Advisors," *The Commoner,* Nov. 1, 1919, 2.

98   "All the complex machinery": "From the Diary of a Reviewer," *The Smart Set,* Feb. 1920, 143.

98   Jane Addams . . . Clarence Darrow: see Norman Hapgood, ed. *Professional Patriots.*

98   "My motto for the Reds": quoted in Walter Lippmann, "Leonard Wood,"79.

99   "We are ready to do anything": quoted in Robert K. Murray, *Red Scare: A Study in National Hysteria, 1919–1920,* 79.

99   "To be a red in the summer of 1919": John Dos Passos, *1919,* 454.

99   "prohibits the free exchange of ideas": HLM, "A Glance Ahead," Baltimore *Evening Sun,* May 25, 1920, 17.

100   "Names! Names of all parlor bolsheviki": quoted in Burl Noggle, *Into the Twenties,* 105.

100   Lusk and his henchmen; "A Radical Negro Publication"; and "to the left of Booker T. Washington": see J. M. Pawa, "Black Radicals and White Spies: Harlem 1919," 130.

100   "If the world cannot stand up": CD, "After the War," *Newark Leader* (Ohio), Apr. 4, 1919, 1.

100   "started on a mad career": CD, *Argument in Defense of the Communists,* 30. William Bross Lloyd was the son of Henry Demarest Lloyd.

100   "save only Mr. Wilson himself . . . Americanism": HLM, "A Carnival of Buncombe," Baltimore *Evening Sun,* Feb. 9, 1920, 8.

101   Its secret password: Norman Hapgood, "The New Threat of the Ku Klux Klan," 12. Hapgood ran a series on the Klan in early 1923; it was subsequently alleged that he must be Jewish and that he was an alcoholic.

101   "100 per cent of Americanism . . . white Americans": quoted in "The

Ku Klux Klan in Texas," *Fort Worth Star-Telegram Magazine*, Aug. 28, 1921, 1.

101   **It takes courage:** see William Pickens, quoted in NAACP investigation [James Weldon Johnson], "Darkest Mississippi," *The Crisis*, July 1919, 142.

102   **"The North is no paradise":** W.E.B. Du Bois, "Brothers, Come North," *The Crisis*, Jan. 1920, 105.

102   **Black men and women:** for information in this paragraph, see "The Looking Glass," *The Crisis*, Sept. 1919, 247.

102   **James Weldon Johnson:** "The Riots: An NAACP Investigation," *The Crisis*, Sept. 1919, 243.

102   **"of Rome . . . Anti-Saloon league":** HLM, "Répétition Générale," 1922, 43.

102   **"Ku Klux Klan is essentially a Methodist organization":** Ibid., 42.

103   **the war's repression of pacifists:** "Why Not Tell the Truth," July 19, 1922, Baltimore *Sun*, 13.

103   **"One of the chief causes":** William Howard Taft, *Anti-Semitism in the United States*, 3.

104   **"Negro blood":** see, for instance, Douglass K. Daniel, "Ohio Newspapers and the 'Whispering Campaign' of the 1920 Presidential Election," 156–64.

104   **governors:** see David Mark Chalmers, *Hooded Americanism: The History of the Ku Klux Klan*, 200.

104   **Their main offices:** the description taken from "Ku Klux Klan Rides North to Expand 'Invisible Empire,' " *New York Herald*, Jan. 16, 1921, section 7, 5.

105   **"It was real war":** W.E.B. Du Bois, "Opinion," *The Crisis*, April 1926, 269.

106   **"What is America going to do":** Walter F. White, "The Eruption of Tulsa," 839.

106   **About five thousand new:** "For and Against the Klan," *Literary Digest*, Sept. 24, 1921, 34.

106   **"drips with venomous attacks," "terrorize certain classes":** "Statement of Hon. Leonidas C. Dyer," Oct. 21, 1921, *The Ku Klux Klan, Hearings Before the Committee on Rules, House of Representatives*, 67th Congress, Session 1, 7.

106   **Mary Burnett Talbert and "The Shame of America":** see Philip Dray, *At the Hands of Persons Unknown*, 269–70.

107   **"more sympathy for the colored man":** quoted in J. F. Essary, "Bryan Against Special Tax to Defray Bonus," Baltimore *Sun*, Jan. 23, 1922, 1.

107   **"turn the attention":** "Anti-Lynch Bill Dropped," *The Commoner*, Dec. 1, 1922, 2.

107   **Lynching in the South:** see WJB, "Republican Partisanship," *The Commoner*, Jan. 1, 1922, 2.

107   **"In the south the whites":** WJB, "Convention Takes Up Task of Balloting," *The Commoner*, Aug. 1, 1920, 12.

CHAPTER SIX: PROHIBITION, SCRIPTURE, AND THE CROWN OF RIGHTEOUSNESS, 1920–1923

109   "I am stemming the tide": *The Commoner,* June 1920, 1.

109   "Remember that it is better": *Official Report of the Proceedings of the DNC Held in SF CA, June 28, 29, 30, July 1, 2, 3, 5, 6,* 208.

110   Texas Representative James Luther Slayden: see Ellen Maury Slayden, *Washington Wife: The Journal of Ellen Maury Slayden,* 292.

110   "I stand for the home": WJB, "Peace and Prohibition," *The Commoner,* July 1, 1920, 3.

110   "As he raged and leaped": HLM, "Mencken Describes Session in Which Wm. J. Bryan Was 'Murdered in Cold Blood,' " Baltimore *Evening Sun,* July 3, 1920, 3.

110   "Mr. Bryan, while applauded": William Allen White, "From the Cave of Gloom," *Omaha World-Herald,* July 7, 1920, 10.

110   "I never thought": Florence Jaffray Hurst Harriman, *From Pinafores to Politics,* 333.

110   "My heart is in the grave": Mark Sullivan, "The Stump and the Porch," 6.

111   "What strength he will develop": Franklin K. Lane, *The Letters of Franklin K. Lane, Personal and Political,* 1 [Jan. 3, 1920], 334.

111   "Four years from now": Werner, *Bryan,* 272.

111   "hysteria has turned to apathy": quoted in Ronald Steel, *Walter Lippmann and the American Century,* 170.

111   "was civilization nothing": John Dos Passos, *Three Soldiers,* 210.

111   "no wonder so many Young Intellectuals": HLM, "Glouglou Patriotique," Baltimore *Evening Sun,* Apr. 10, 1922, 15.

112   "from special scorn": quoted in Adam Gopnik, ed., *Americans in Paris,* 199.

112   "It was not what France gave you": Gertrude Stein, "An American and France," in *What Are Masterpieces,* 70.

112   "who cling to the great fundamentals": "Convention Side Lights," *The Watchman Examiner,* July 1, 1920, 835, quoted in Charles L. Cohen and Paul S. Boyer, eds., *Religion and the Culture of Print in Modern America,* 176.

112   "man-made": WJB, "The Fundamentals," *Forum,* July 1923, 1665–80.

113   "I believe the brute": WJB, *The Bible and Its Enemies: An Address Delivered at the Moody Institute of Chicago,* 43.

113   "the flower that blooms": WJB and MBB, *Memoirs,* 545.

114   "lawless human being": "The Superman Dead," *The Commoner,* Dec. 1, 1918, 1.

114   "Nietzsche's philosophy": "Sees Peace in League," *Washington Post,* Mar. 31, 1919, 3.

114   "Down beneath all the German propaganda": "Bryan Flays Atheists," Baltimore *Sun,* Jan. 6, 1919, 12.

114   "That man bears the image of God": WJB, "Back to God," *Brooklyn Daily Eagle,* Jan. 19, 1920, 22.

114   "cultured crowd": in one form or another, the sentence appeared in WJB's first Bible Talks, 1921, which were widely distributed. He slightly revised the sentence when he included his lecture in *In His Image*, 11.

115   "Inventive genius": WJB, "The War in Europe and Its Lesson for Us," *Aletheian*, Mar. 1916, 33. Bryan had not yet fingered Darwin as the great culprit.

115   "The intellectuals have led civilization": WJB, "Speech on Evolution," *Indianapolis Star*, June 14, 1922, 3. The speech was delivered at the National Convention of Baptists in Indianapolis and excerpted in *The Commoner*, July 1, 1922, 6.

115   "Why should the children be taught": WJB, "The Modern Arena," *The News and Observer* (Raleigh, North Carolina), July 24, 1921, 24.

116   "substituting the guesses of": *In His Image*, 187.

116   Bryan was told: see, for instance, WJB, *The Bible and Its Enemies*, 1921; see also 35–36.

116   Behind the scenes: quoted in Masters, "The Christian Statesman," 394.

116   "I leave him to the taxpayers": "Bible Critics Assailed by Bryan," *The Courier-Journal* (Louisville), Sept. 20, 1921, 2.

116   "outstanding in the world": "Bryan Heard by State Assembly," *Courier-Journal*, Jan. 20, 1922, 2.

117   "He doesn't even let us descend": "Bryan Stumps U.S. for God Against Ape," *El Paso Herald*, Jan. 24, 1922, 8.

117   "No time is to be lost": "Bryan, Called as Witness, Defends Bible Vigorously; Apology Made by Darrow," *Lexington Herald* (Kentucky), Jan. 20, 1922, 1, 10.

117   "there is a widely prevalent view": "Bryan's Ideas 'Buffoonery,'" *New York Times*, Apr. 5, 1922, 4.

117   He ate plate after plate: see "Bryan to Keep Watch over Next Democratic Convention," *Minneapolis Sunday Tribune*, Sept. 2, 1923, 5.

118   "Good for forty acres": Bruce Bliven, "Mother, Home, and Heaven," *The New Republic*, Jan. 9, 1924, 19.

118   "Speaking became his business": quoted in Cox, *Journey Through My Years*, 409.

118   He arranged: see "A Bible Talk: A Very Present Help in Trouble," *Atlanta Constitution*, Nov. 6, 1921, F6.

118   "People often ask me": "Bryan Explains Why He Is a Standpatter on Religion," *Miami Herald*, May 28, 1925, 1.

119   the significance of Christianity: see Harry Emerson Fosdick, "Tolerance," 714.

120   "We are all made of one blood": "Dr. Fosdick Says the Church Must Drop Spindling Issues to Meet Real Ones of Times," *New York Herald*, Dec. 24, 1922, 21.

120   "baboon booster": "Calls Minister Baboon Booster," *New York Times*, July 24, 1922, 10; see also "Bryan Attacks Fosdick," *New York Times*, Jan. 9, 1923, 6.

120   "the millennium": quoted in Felix Harcourt, "A Visible Empire: Ku Klux Klan and American Culture, 1915–1930," 259.

120   "the progressive unfolding": Harry Emerson Fosdick, "Shall the Fundamentalists Win?" *The Christian Century*, June 8, 1922, 715.

120   "Theistic evolution is an anesthetic": WJB, "The Fundamentals," *Forum,* July 1923, 1678.

102–121   "seriously proffered . . . forever trimmed": Harry Emerson Fosdick, "Mr. Bryan and Evolution," *The Christian Century,* March 23, 1922, 363, 364.

121   "incredible folly . . . their God": Harry Emerson Fosdick, "Attacks W.J.B.," *New York Times,* Mar. 12, 1922, section 7, 2.

121   "Do not teach men": Harry Emerson Fosdick, "Attacks W.J.B."

122   "the Government would be in danger . . . as well as for the black man": "Bryan Says North Would Act as South," *New York Times,* Mar. 18, 1923, section 8, 1.

122   "advanced race": see also "Race Problem" (1903), typescript in WJB papers, box 57, LC.

122   "Bryan's passion for democracy": Michael Kazin, *A Godly Hero,* 278.

122   "It did look as if Mr. Bryan . . . believe him to be?": *The Works of Francis J. Grimké,* vol. 4, 374, 375.

122   "Pray tell me what kind of Christianity": W. Thomas Soders to WJB, Feb. 23, 1923, LC.

123   Marcus Garvey: see "Government of Negros," *Negro World,* Mar. 3, 1923, 2.

123   thin ice: "Bryan Declares for White Supremacy," *The Fiery Cross,* Mar. 9, 1923, 1.

123   "I have had experience": "G.O.P. Presbyterian Leads Victory Against Bryan, Evolution Foe," *Nashville Tennessean,* May 23, 1923, 1.

123   "The colored people": see WJB to D. S. Kennedy, June 12, 1923, WJB Papers, box 37, LC.

123   while men like the Reverend Grimké: see Rev. W. E. Houston, "Presbyterians Endorse Dyer Lynching Bill," *Chicago Defender,* June 2, 1923, 5.

123   "this eloquent champion . . . inflicted upon them": *The Works of Francis J. Grimké,* vol. 4, 139, 373.

123   "religious Ku Klux Klan": "The Religious Ku Klux Klan," *The Christian Register,* Feb. 23, 1922, 170.

124   "I do not feel a burning sense of shame": Horace F. Ferry to WJB, Apr. 16, 1923, LC.

124   They'd heard he'd be running for president: see, for instance, WJB to Charles Scanlon, Mar. 31, 1923, LC; also John Marquis to WJB, May 1923, LC, and WJB to John Marquis, May 2, 1923, LC.

124   "We have preachers in this audience": "Bryan Loses Fight to Ban Darwinism," *New York Times,* May 23, 1923, 4.

125   "I wouldn't live in a generation like this": quoted in Robert Moats Miller, *Harry Emerson Fosdick: Preacher, Pastor, Prophet,* 145.

125   "oligarchy of professors . . . history": WJB to John F. Hylan, June 12, 1923, LC.

125   "I think you are right": WJB to John F. Hylan, June 12, 1923, LC.

126   "There is a scientific soviet": "Bryan to Keep Watch over Next Democratic Convention," *Minneapolis Sunday Tribune,* Sept. 2, 1923, 5; " 'Scientific Soviet' Attacked by Bryan," *Des Moines Register,* Oct. 2, 1923, 3.

126   **Henry Mencken drily observed:** see "Répétition Générale," *The Smart Set*, Feb. 1, 1923, 33.

126   **"Mr. Bryan is a typical democratic figure":** John Dewey, "The American Intellectual Frontier," *The New Republic*, May 10, 1922, 303, 304.

CHAPTER SEVEN: LEOPOLD AND LOEB AND THE BOOK OF LOVE, 1924

131   **institutionalized revenge:** see Hiram Johnson, *The Diary Letters of Hiram Johnson, 1917–1945*, 4.

131   **"What we need in this world":** quoted in "Darrow Flings Shaft at Blue Law Fanatics," *Minnesota Daily Star*, May 5, 1924, 5.

131   **"introduce some novelty":** "Editorial," *American Mercury*, January 1924, 27.

132   **"a bit bent, a bit scarred":** Arturo Giovannitti, "Communism on Trial," *The Liberator*, March 1920, 7.

132   **"It never occurs to me":** CD to MFP, July 1 [1923], Newberry.

132   **On May 21, 1924:** For quotes from the trial, see "Trial Transcript: *Leopold and Loeb v. Illinois*" (Chicago: Criminal Court of Cook County, 1924). Accounts of the trial that were also helpful, in addition to various newspaper coverage, and coverage in subsequent notes: Edward J. Larson, "An American Tragedy: Retelling the Leopold-Loeb Story in Popular Culture," 119–56. See also Paula S. Fass, "Making and Remaking an Event: The Leopold and Loeb Case in American Culture," 919–51; Maureen McKernan, *The Amazing Crime and Trial of Leopold and Loeb*; Robert Lee, "The Leopold Loeb Trial," in *Best News Stories of 1924*, ed. Joseph Anthony and Woodman Morrison; Kevin O'Kelly, "Leopold & Loeb: The Case That Capped Darrow's Career," 24–31, 35; S. K. Ratcliffe, "Leopold and Loeb," *New Statesman*, Sept. 20, 1924, 668–71.

133   **"jazzed" . . . powder":** Annie Laurie [Winifred] "Franks Death Case Declared Flower of Present Jazz Age," San Francisco *Examiner*, June 29, 1924, 24; see also, for instance, "Slayers Branded Victims of Jazz," *Wilmington Morning News*, June 7, 1924, 6.

133   **"Nowadays it is considered fashionable":** quoted in Harold Andrews, "Billy Sunday Says Gibbet Should Punish Boy Killers," *Atlanta Constitution*, June 5, 1924, 3.

133   **He too:** see Julian Huxley, "America Revisited: Fundamentalism," *The Spectator*, Nov. 22, 1924, 772.

135   **"No client of mine had ever been put to death":** CD, *The Story of My Life*, 232.

136   **The press quickly convicted:** see the *Chicago Daily News* items in Francis X. Busch, *Prisoners at the Bar*, 150.

137   **"Should two boys of this age":** Robert Lee, "The Leopold Loeb Trial," in *Best News Stories of 1924*, 36.

138   **"derangements of their emotional life":** see McKernan, *The Amazing Crime and Trial of Leopold and Loeb*, 4.

138   **"as easily"**: A. J. Lorenz, "Boy's Murder 'Experiment in Emotion,'" San Francisco *Examiner*, June 17, 1924, 2.

138   **"A 6-year-old-boy is justified in pulling"**: "Franks Boy Killed to Assist Science," *Washington Post*, June 2, 1924, 1.

139   **"because somewhere in the finite processes"**: McKernan, *The Amazing Crime and Trial of Leopold and Loeb*, 232.

139   **"If to hang these two boys"**: Ibid., 221.

139   **"I sometimes wonder whether I am dreaming"**: "Darrow Scores Public Demand," San Francisco *Examiner*, Aug. 24, 1924, 3.

140   **"We have preached it"**: see John Herrick, "Darrow Recites History of Hangings in His Closing Plea," *Chicago Tribune*, Aug. 26, 1924, 2.

141   **Called a philosopher of infinite mercy**: see Orville Dwyer, "Darrow Calls Slaying Mad Act of Fools," *Chicago Tribune*, Aug. 24, 1924, 1.

141   **"I know Your Honor"**: Ibid., 1.

141   **Across the street from the Loeb mansion**: see "Grewsome Symbol of Death Is Left Near Home of Loeb," *Chicago Tribune*, Aug. 19, 1924, 2.

142   **"There is nothing to be surprised at in Leopold and Loeb"**: Sidney Howard, "Our Professional Patriots, VI," 119.

CHAPTER EIGHT: A REVIVAL, 1924

143   **"you have signed your own political death warrant"**: quoted in George Seldes, *World Panorama, 1918–1933*, 167–68.

143   **"He might help us get a drink"**: CD to Negley D. Cochran, Apr. 6, 1924, Toledo; Tietjin, *Clutches*, 289.

144   **One of Smith's aides**: see Robert A. Slayton, *Empire Statesman: The Rise and Redemption of Al Smith*, 211.

144   **"If the wets expect to obtain control"**: WJB, "Law vs. Lawlessness Is Issue Raised by Wets," *Christian Science Monitor*, June 11, 1923, 1.

144   **"Those bilingual signs"**: William Allen White, *Politics: The Citizen's Business*, 79.

145   **"wandering around half dazed"**: HLM, "Convention's Only Reality is the Struggle for Jobs," Baltimore *Evening Sun*, June 25, 1924, 2.

145   **Ridiculing the convention**: see HLM, "Seeing Party's Hopes Ruined by Klan," Baltimore *Sun*, June 30, 1924, 2.

145   **He'd worked hard**: See, for instance, WJB to Duane Fletcher, Feb. 13, 1924, LC.

145   **"In presenting the name of Dr. Murphree"**: WJB to Frank Webb, Feb. 9, 1924, LC. See also Jack Mills, "The Speaking of William Jennings Bryan in Florida, 1915–1925."

146   **"The only"**: WJB George Wyman, Mar. 5, 1924, LC; Also, see Werner, *Bryan*, 273.

146   **"I do not care to discuss the matter"**: WJB to George Huddleston, Mar. 30, 1923, LC.

146   **He did not want to end his career**: see WJB to W. T. Brooks, Mar. 6, 1924, LC; WJB to J. E. Engstrom, Mar. 5, 1924, LC; WJB to Charles Bryan, Mar. 3, 1924, LC.

146   **"Mr. Bryan's religious convictions":** Heywood Broun, "It Seems to Me," *Boston Globe*, June 26, 1924, 16.

147   **One of these private corporations:** For the Teapot Dome scandal, see Laton McCartney, *The Teapot Dome Scandal: How Big Oil Bought the White House and Tried to Steal the Country.*

147   **McAdoo was presumed:** see Robert K. Murray's excellent *The 103rd Ballot*, 108.

148   **"I hate bigotry":** For all direct quotes from the convention floor, see *Official Report of the Proceedings of the Democratic National Convention Held in Madison Square Garden, New York City, June 24, 25, 26, 27, 28, 30, July 1, 2, 3, 4, 5, 7, 8, and 9, 1924, Resulting in the Nomination of John W. Davis (of West Virginia) for President and Charles W. Bryan (of Nebraska) for Vice-President*, ed. Charles A. Greathouse and Louis Grant.

149   **There were more than two hundred Klansmen:** see "M. E. Hennessy's Convention Sidelights," *Boston Globe*, June 30, 1924, 3.

149   **ratty and moth-eaten:** see "Editorial," *American Mercury*, Sept. 1924, 32.

149   **His eyes were harder:** See Mark Sullivan, "Science Took Silver Out of Bryan's Life," *New York Herald Tribune*, June 26, 1924, A1.

150   **"Calling on God":** George Sylvester Viereck, "Neither with God Nor His Enemies," *The American Monthly*, Aug. 1, 1924, 167.

150   **"combines about all the race prejudices":** WJB to Thomas J. Walsh, Dec. 30, 1922, LC.

151   **"Democrats catered to Klan's race hatred":** "Opinion of W.E.B. Du Bois," *The Crisis*, Aug. 1924, 152.

151   **"Saturday will always remain":** Will Rogers, "Will Rogers Runs Into One Delegation That He Admits He Is Unable to Rope," *New York Times*, June 30, 1924, 6.

152   **"You do not represent":** quoted in Slayton, *Empire Statesman*, 214.

152   **"Mr. Bryan has killed poor McAdoo":** quoted in Murray, *The 103rd Ballot*, 217.

152   **noted without sympathy:** see Raymond S. Tompkins, "WJB Seen in Shell of His Former Self," Baltimore *Sun*, July 3, 1924, 3.

152   **"The two factions lost everything":** HLM, "Post-Mortem," Baltimore *Evening Sun*, July 14, 1924, 15.

153   **"in on the beating":** Slayton, *Empire Statesman*, 214.

153   **"There is something about a national convention":** HLM, "Post-Mortem," Baltimore *Evening Sun*, July 14, 1924, 15.

154   **walked out of Madison Square Garden:** anecdote quoted in Lawrence W. Levine, *Defender of the Faith*, 324.

CHAPTER NINE: THE MAN EVERYBODY KNEW, 1925

155   **"Wist ye not":** For a fine interpretation of Barton, see T. Jackson Lears, "From Salvation to Self-Realization," in *The Culture of Consumption: Critical Essays in American History, 1880–1980*, ed. Richard Wightman Fox and T. J. Jackson Lears.

156 **"What I am you can be":** Bruce Barton, *The Man Nobody Knows: A Discovery of the Real Jesus,* 179.

156 **William Jennings Bryan:** See John Kimberly Mumford, "Who's Who in New York—Bruce Barton," *New York Herald,* July 5, 1925, A3. See also WJB to William C. Bobbs, Apr. 22, 1925, LC: "The discrediting of the supernatural side of Christ not only robs the book of power to be largely beneficial but leaves the impression that Mr. Barton has a very superficial understanding of the Master." So annoyed was he, WJB wrote again on April 29, 1925, LC.

156 **He loathed:** among many examples, see William Bell Riley, "Youth and the Babel in Religion," *Pilot,* November 1936, 41–42.

159 **"the spirit of God":** quoted in "The Spirit of Angelus Temple," *Los Angeles Times,* Dec. 29, 1923, 6.

159 **Sister Aimee dressed as:** see Anita Loos, *No Mother to Guide Her,* 23.

159 **She borrowed a camel:** see Sarah Comstock, "Prima Donna of Revivalism," *Harper's Magazine,* Dec. 1927, 11–19.

159 **"Now, the crowning blessing":** quoted in Tona J. Hangen, *Redeeming the Dial: Radio, Religion, and Popular Culture in America,* 69.

159 **"Our Lady of the Loudspeaker":** Constant Reader, "Reading and Writing," *New Yorker,* Feb. 25, 1928, 79.

159 **"You can't laugh Aimee McPherson off":** Quoted in Charles Barfoot, *Aimee Semple McPherson and the Making of Modern Pentecostalism, 1890–1926,* 232.

159 **"The Cathedral of the Air am I":** Aimee Semple McPherson, "The Cathedral of the Air," 6–7.

160 **She did warn them:** see "Denver Klansmen Deliver Love Gift," *Oklahoma Herald,* July 25, 1922, 1.

160 **"the triumph":** see Paxton Hibben, "Aimee and Tex," *New Yorker,* Mar. 5, 1927, 65.

160 **"ten thousand members . . . teachers":** Aimee Semple McPherson to WJB, July 12, 1925, box 47, LC. For more information on McPherson, see also Matthew Avery Sutton, *Aimee Semple McPherson and the Resurrection of Christian America.*

160 **"number my friends by the millions . . . a bird flies":** W. A. [Billy] Sunday, "To the Editor," *Harper's Magazine,* Feb. 1928, 395.

161 **"as a jack-rabbit knows about ping-pong":** Francis Hackett, "Billy Sunday, Salesman," *The New Republic,* Apr. 28, 1917, 370.

161 **"bughouse peddler of second-hand gospel":** Carl Sandburg, "To Billy Sunday," 11.

162 **"It is an honor to welcome you":** Ridley Wills, "Huge Throng Joins in Welcome to Sunday at Opening Meeting," Memphis *Commercial Appeal,* Feb. 6, 1925, 1, 7; "Billy Sunday Will Be Legion Speaker," Memphis *Commercial Appeal,* Feb. 8, 1925, 19.

162 **"the most useless war ever fought . . . the juice":** Wills, "Huge Throng Joins in Welcome," 1.

162 **"If anyone wants to teach":** "When Billy Banged Table," *Elmira Star-Gazette* (New York), Sept. 17, 1924, 2.

163 **"Darwin was a rotten old infidel":** Ridley Wills, "Get Right! Seek God! Judgement's Coming!," Memphis *Commercial Appeal,* Feb. 9, 1925, 2.

163   "The Three Krosses," "Attention, KKK!": ad in Memphis *Commercial Appeal*, Feb. 15, 1925, 18.

163   "You could hear the dragons flap": Ridley Wills, "Ku Klux Klansmen Hear Billy Sunday," Memphis *Commercial Appeal*, Feb. 19, 1925, 1.

163   Billy Sunday insisted: "Doings of the Race," Cleveland *Gazette*, Feb. 17, 1923, 2.

164   "He either doesn't know": *The Works of Francis J. Grimké*, vol. 1, ed. Carter G. Woodson, 556.

164   Does God evolve?: see, for instance, *The Works of Francis J. Grimké*, vol. 2, ed. Carter G. Woodson, 397.

164   "Beware, beware": quoted in the excellent article by Stephen Tuck, "The Doubts of Their Fathers: The God Debate and the Conflict between African American Churches and Civil Rights Organizations between the World Wars," 658.

164   "recent science declares": "Quadrennial Address of the Bishops of the Colored Methodist Church to the Fourteenth Session of the General Conference," *Colored Methodist Episcopal Church, General Conference 1922*, 6.

164   "Sunday school teachers": Guy T. Vishinski to WJB, Dec. 31, 1924, LC.

165   Bryan ostentatiously: for a discussion of why Bryan may have done this, see James Gilbert, *Redeeming Culture: American Religion in an Age of Science*, 23–35.

165   "If you would be entirely accurate": *Chicago Daily Tribune*, May 28, 1925, quoted in Stephen Jay Gould, "William Bryan's Last Campaign," *Natural History*, Nov. 1, 1987, 20.

166   "Simply say for me": "Bryan May Again Fling Hat into Ring," *Nashville Banner*, Apr. 28, 1925, 12.

166   "I regard the Senate": WJB to F. I. Robertson, Mar. 11, 1925, LC.

166   "I can render the party more service": WJB to R. L. Dean, Mar. 11, 1925, LC.

166   "I dread the thought of adding anything": WJB to Edward Keating, [1925], LC.

166   Bryan had been hired: "Bryan Stars as Ballyhooer for Florida Realty," *Chicago Tribune*, Mar. 21, 1925, 1.

167   "so we can have a pleasant little community": WJB to E. T. Meredith, July 29, 1924, LC.

167   "The Commoner will become The Realtor": "New York, Etc.: Under the Palm Trees," *New Yorker*, Apr. 4, 1925, 5.

167   Mark Sullivan assumed: "Bryan Talks Land," *New York Herald*, Apr. 19, 1925, A1, 12.

167   A preacher who came once a month: see "Fights Evolution to Uphold Bible," *New York Times*, July 5, 1925, E1.

168   "Ninety-nine people out of a hundred . . . politics": Marcet Haldeman-Julius, *Clarence Darrow's Two Great Trials: Reports of the Scopes Anti-Evolution Case and the Dr. Sweet Negro Trial*, 18.

168   "making monkeys of themselves": "Missing Link Sermon Stirs Legislators," Chattanooga *Daily Times*, Feb. 6, 1925, 1.

168   "blood relation with animals of a lower order," "flat as a fritter," and
      for other comments, see Howard Eskridge, "Senate Passes Evolution
      Bill," *Nashville Banner*, Mar. 13, 1925, 1, 10.

169   "The earth still revolves around the sun": "Communications: As to
      Evolution," *Nashville Tennessean*, Feb. 4, 1925, 4.

170   "they've got their nerve": Joseph Wood Krutch, "Tennessee: Where
      Cowards Rule," *The Nation*, July 15, 1925, 88.

170   "irreligious tendency": "Governor's O.K. on Evolution Ban in Schools,"
      The Knoxville Journal, Mar. 24, 1925, 1.

170   A group of university students: "Tenn. University Boys out After the
      Lizzies," Baltimore *Sun*, May 3, 1925, 10.

170   evolution as a cult: see, for instance, "Straton Says Modernism and
      Worldliness Threaten Church of Today," *News-Democrat* (Paducah,
      Kentucky), June 24, 1925, 2.

170   "outstanding intellect": quoted in Stanley Walker, "Saving Souls in
      New York," *American Mercury*, Mar. 3, 1925, 274.

170   cuckoo birds: "Modernists Cuckoo Birds," *New York Tribune*, Jan. 24,
      1924, 4.

170   "is not merely religious": "Dr. J. Roach Straton Challenges Clarence
      Darrow," *Chicago Daily News*, Aug. 18, 1925.

170   It would be better: see "Calls for Spread of Tennessee Law," *New York
      Times*, July 20, 1925, 18.

171   "Our radio system": "Calvary Installs Broadcast Plant," *New York
      Times*, Feb. 23, 1923, E1.

171   "Keep politics out of the pulpit": "Minister Calls Bryan in 1924 a Ca-
      tastrophe," *New York Tribune*, June 11, 1924, 3.

171   "It will be very interesting": "Dr. Potter Assails Anti-Evolution Bill,"
      New York Times, Mar. 25, 1925, 13.

171   "All living species": William Montgomery Brown, *Communism and
      Christianism*, 140.

172   "If you ask whether I am still a professing Christian": Ibid., 144.

172   "believes it is not right to think": "Bryan Attacked by Bishop," *Los
      Angeles Times*, July 7, 1925, 2.

172   found guilty, he said, of being innocent: see "Episcopal Bishop to Face
      Heresy Charge," *Tampa Tribune*, Feb 13, 1924, 1; Charles W. Wood,
      "Benign Heretic," *New Yorker*, Jan. 26, 1926, 17–18.

172   Liberal Christians: see "Timid Modernism," *Christian Century*, July 9,
      1925, 883.

173   troublemakers: William Bruce Wheeler, *Knoxville, Tennessee: A Moun-
      tain City in the New South*, 54; for a complete examination of Neal's
      career, see James R. Montgomery, "John R. Neal and the University of
      Tennessee: A Five-Part Tragedy."

173   "Every time one man": Krutch, "Tennessee: Where Cowards Rule,"
      The Nation, July 15, 1925, 88, 89.

CHAPTER TEN: THE HAND THAT WRITES
THE PAYCHECK

177   **"We have a tailor-made job for you"**: Lucille Milner, *Education of an American Liberal*, 30.

178   **"No economic or political question"**: "The Civil Liberties Bureau," *The Messenger*, May–June 1919, 10.

178   **"I seek no martyrdom"**: quoted in Robert Duffus, "The Legend of Roger Baldwin," *American Mercury*, Aug. 1, 1925, 411.

178   *The Liberator:* see Joseph Freeman, *An American Testament*, 292.

179   **"no matter whose lips would speak"**: Oswald Garrison Villard, "New Fight for Old Liberties," *Harper's Magazine*, June 1, 1925, 442.

179   **"The future of democracy"**: Milner, *Education of an American Liberal*, 71.

179   **"The American Civil Liberties Union *is* Roger Baldwin"**: quoted in Dwight Macdonald, "The Defense of Everybody—1," *New Yorker*, July 11, 1953, 31.

179   **"Take it to the Board on Monday"**: Milner, *Education of an American Liberal*, 93.

179   **"at scientific teaching . . . sustained"**: "Test Evolution Law Is Brewing," *The Knoxville Journal*, May 3, 1925, 4.

180   **"Any Professor at UT Feel Like Making a Fight?"**: *The Knoxville News*, May 4, 1925, 8.

180   **"Man from monkey"**: "Plan Assault on State Law on Evolution," *Chattanooga Daily Times*, May 4, 1925, 5.

180   **"The hand that writes the paycheck"**: see, for instance, WJB, "Mr. Bryan's New Book, *In His Image*," *The Commoner*, June 1, 1922, 7.

180   **Coal and iron**: Wallace Haggard to L. Sprague de Camp, May 19, 1966, HRHRC.

182   **"Everybody liked Rappleyea"**: de Camp, interview with Sue K. Hicks, Mar. 12, 1966, HRHRC.

182   **"I don't believe in evangelic Christianity"**: "Was Converted Through Science," *Chattanooga Daily Times*, May 21, 1925, 2.

182   **When the Tennessee legislature passed the Butler bill**: see "Lays Scopes Trial to Publicity Thirst," *New York Times*, Aug. 5, 1925, 10.

182   **he picked up the telephone**: There are many, many accounts of what Rappleyea did and when, especially at Robinson's drugstore, many of them recollected twenty or more years later, especially about the desire to put Dayton on the map, which was not the intention of Rappleyea or Scopes. My account is based on the account Rappleyea gave the local papers at the time.

182   **White sat in the back**: Warren Allem, "Backgrounds of the Scopes Trial," 58, trace.tennessee.edu/utk_gradthes/941. Much of Allem's account of what happened at Robinson's is also based on recollections long after the trial, but the cherry Coke detail rings true.

184   **Fresh out of the University of Kentucky**: John T. Moutoux, "Accused Evolution Prof Most Popular Man in Town," *Knoxville News-Sentinel*, May 11, 1925, 1.

185   "I don't see how any one can teach biology": quoted in George
       Fort Milton, "Testing the Monkey Bill," *The Independent*, Jun 13,
       1925, 660. See also L. Sprague de Camp to Sue K. Hicks, Mar. 24,
       1966, and de Camp, interview with John Scopes, Mar. 17, 1966,
       HRHRC.

185   "Have you a competent local attorney? . . . otherwise raising federal
       issue?": see "Scopes' Arrest Planned," Baltimore *Evening Sun*, June 30,
       1925, 2.

186   Years later: L. Sprague de Camp, interview with Sue K. Hicks, Mar. 12,
       1966, HRHRC.

186   "In that way I felt": Nellie Kenyon, "How Scopes Case Really Started,"
       Chattanooga News, June 29, 1925, 1, 2.

187   According to John Moutoux: see Moutoux, "Accused Evolution
       Prof," 3.

187   accent: see L. Sprague de Camp, interview with O. W. McKenzie,
       Mar. 13, 1966, HRHRC.

187   "His influence": E. F. Adams to WJB, May 24, 1925, LC.

187   "rank socialist": Ibid.

187   "long and loud . . . laws of our country": Rev. T. W. Callway, "Father
       of Scopes Renounced Church," *Chattanooga Daily Times*, July 10,
       1925, 14.

187   "He's a chip": "Sees Son on Trial," Bristol *News Bulletin*, July 14,
       1925, 1.

189   "the teaching of . . . antiradical and antipacifist measures": ACLU, sur-
       vey, April 1925, quoted in "Employers in Drive, Backed by Klan,"
       Daily Worker, May 5, 1925, A1.

190   Evolution is nuts: see "Commoner Believes Evolution Is Tommyrot,"
       Memphis *Commercial Appeal*, May 11, 1925, 1, 2.

190   "Mr. Bryan could do nothing else": William Bell Riley, "Bryan, the
       Great Commoner and Christian," *Christian Fundamentals in School
       and Church*, Oct.–Dec. 1925, 5.

190   "It's a fight to the finish . . . possible": "US Scientists 'Scoundrels,' As-
       serts Bryan," *New York Herald*, May 14, 1925, 4.

191   "The Scopes trial was weird": Russell Owen, "Hot Lands and Cold,"
       in *We Saw It Happen: The News Behind the News That's Fit to Print*,
       231.

191   "if Bryan could succeed": "Editorial," *The New Republic*, July 22,
       1925, 219.

192   "Bryan is a clever demagogue": Negley D. Cochran to G. B. Parker,
       May 22, 1925, Toledo.

192   "We cannot afford to have a system of education": "Bryan Agrees to
       Prosecute Evolutionist," Pittsburgh *Gazette Times*, May 13, 1925, 1, 4.

192   "The Bible rests . . . the distant future": WJB, "Indictment Against
       Evolution," n.d. (copy sent to J. R. Straton), LC.

192   "We cannot be caught . . .": WJB to Howard Kelly, June 17, 1925, LC.

193   "We will consider it a great honor": WJB and MBB, *Memoirs*, 483.

193   "I am glad": quoted in "H. G. Wells May Fight Bryan," Memphis
       Commercial Appeal, May 15, 1925, 1.

193 **"leads to idiotic action":** "Richmond Lost Darrow," *Richmond Times-Dispatch*, May 13, 1925, 18.

193 **"I realized that there was no limit":** CD, *The Story of My Life*, 249.

194 **"We are certain you need no assistance":** "Would Offset Bryan," *Washington Post*, May 17, 1925, 3.

194 **"As we see it . . . truth":** "Darrow and Malone Services Are Accepted," *Atlanta Constitution*, May 17, 1925, 6.

194 **"I am inclined to think . . . conscience and speech":** ED to Samuel D. Schwartz, Aug. 20, 1925, Tietjen, *Clutches*, 310.

195 **questions to the *Tribune*:** see "Darrow Asks W. J. Bryan to Answer These," *Chicago Tribune*, July 4, 1923, 1.

195 **"My controversy is not with atheists":** "Bryan Brushes Darrow Bible Queries Aside," *Chicago Tribune*, July 5, 1923, 15.

CHAPTER ELEVEN: THE GREAT RACE

197 **"spoiled our chances":** Forrest Bailey to Charles H. Strong, Aug. 17, 1925, ACLU vol. 274.

197 **"Messrs. Darrow and Malone":** Forrest Bailey to members of the Committee on Academic Freedom, May 27, 1925, ACLU, vol. 273.

197 **"If Mr. Scopes wants me to help him":** Philip Kinsley, "Is Darrow an Infidel or Not?," *Chicago Tribune*, May 27, 1925, 3.

197 **any association with a socialist:** see "Dayton Jolly as Evolution Trial Looms," *Chattanooga Times*, May 21, 1925, 1.

198 **"If you want this case to be tested only":** Oliver S. H. Garrett, "Jazz Faction Puts Malone Back in Case," *Chattanooga Times*, June 11, 1925, 1.

199 **Said to strut:** see John T. Scopes, *Center of the Storm*, 70; see also L. Sprague de Camp, interview with John Scopes, Mar. 17, 1966, HRHRC.

199 **Scopes, George Rappleyea, and John Neal:** the lunch included, for instance, the ACLU treasurer Helen Phelps Stokes, Lucille Milner, and Walter F. White, the assistant secretary of the NAACP.

199 **"headline hunter":** Scopes, *Center of the Storm*, 72.

199 **One of the ACLU lawyers:** see de Camp, interview with John Scopes, Mar. 17, 1966, HRHRC.

200 **"I want Darrow":** see, for instance, "Scopes' Defense Fight on Choice of Counsel," *Boston Globe*, June 9, 1925, 4.

200 **Now, in New York:** Ibid.

200 **"It's a circus already":** L. Sprague de Camp, interview with John Scopes, Mar. 17, 1966, HRHRC.

200 **"No . . . But there will be a lot of lawyers":** Robert D. Lusk, "Defense Lawyers in Scopes Case Finally Chosen," *Atlanta Constitution*, June 10, 1925, 8.

201 **Osborn asked him about life in Appalachia:** "Scopes and Darrow Say Farewell to New York," *New York Herald Tribune*, June 11, 1925, 15.

201 **"religion and education are the two greatest subjects known to man":** "Bryan Going to Work on His Scopes Speech," *Chattanooga Times*, June 11, 1925, 2.

201 "It is the *easiest* case I have ever found ... absurd": WJB to Sue K. Hicks, May 28, 1925, Grace Bryan Hargreaves ms., box 58, in WJB papers, LC.

202 menagerie: see "Scopes Defense Allied to 'Reds,' State Holds," *New York Herald,* June 11, 1925, 11.

202 To a large extent eugenics: see Daniel J. Kevles, *In the Name of Eugenics: Genetics and the Uses of Human Heredity;* see also Diane R. Paul, "Darwin, Social Darwinism and Eugenics," in *The Cambridge Companion to Darwin;* Matthew J. Tontonoz, "The Scopes Trial Revisited: Social Darwinism versus Social Gospel," 121–43.

203 non-eugenicist Henry Mencken: see HLM, "Specimens of Current Fiction," 142.

204 "Kansas' Best Crop": see Christine Rosen, *Preaching Eugenics: Religious Leaders and the American Eugenics Movement,* 113.

204 "Conservation of that race": Henry Fairfield Osborn, "Preface," in Madison Grant, *The Passing of the Great Race,* ix, x.

204 "America must be kept American": quoted in Daniel Okrent, *The Guarded Gate,* 336.

205 "enlighten government": "Eugenists Dread Tainted Aliens," *New York Times,* Sept. 25, 1921, 1.

205 "The bigoted and the ignorant": CD, "The Eugenics Cult," 136.

205 "If the stock of domesticated": George William Hunter, *A Civic Biology,* 193–96, 261–63.

205 the so-called Negro problem: see Dray, *At the Hands of Persons Unknown,* 298.

206 "the line should have ended ... its own image": CD, "The Edwards and the Jukes," 149ff.

206 "a system of breeding": WJB and MBB, *Memoirs,* appendix, 548.

CHAPTER TWELVE: DAYTON

207 Prosperous after the the Civil War: see A. D. Smith, *East Tennessee,* 435–36.

208 "aping" Dayton: quoted in Shepherd, "Monkey Business in Tennessee," 38.

209 "I'm perfectly willing to hold court": "Evolution Trial Raises Two Sharp Issues," *New York Times,* May 31, 1925, 4.

209 "We have a fine chance here": Howard K. Hollister, "In Dayton, Tennessee," *The Nation,* July 8, 1925, 61.

209 "He was a good man": L. Sprague de Camp, interview with Sue K. Hicks, Mar. 12, 1966, HRHRC.

209 On Monday, May 25: see Philip Kinsley, "Indict Scopes for Teaching of Evolution's Law," *Chicago Tribune,* May 26, 1925, 2.

210 Newspapers gleefully: see "Ask A. Conan Doyle," *Chattanooga Times,* May 21, 1925, 2.

210 "connected with an extremely tiresome lot of people": "Shaw, in Debate, Takes Aim at Bryan," *Knoxville News-Sentinel,* June 10, 1925, 6.

211 **People said:** for a fine description of the Mansion, see Marcet Haldeman-Julius, "Impressions of the Scopes Trial," 325.

211 **In the dining room:** Ibid., 324; see also Howard K. Hollister, "In Dayton, Tennessee," *The Nation*, July 8, 1925, 61.

211 **"more like a town prepared for a Billy Sunday revival":** Winterton Curtis papers, folder f148d, Missouri.

211 **"The trial .. appears to be a great joke":** Philip Kinsley, "Darrow Tells Plans," *Chicago Tribune*, June 26, 1925, 3.

212 **"That's from some poor soul ... suspenders":** "Darrow Will Meet Counsel in Scopes Case," *Chattanooga News*, June 22, 1925, 1.

212 **"Good morning, General":** Ibid.

212 **"I buy just as good clothes":** Winterton Curtis papers, f141d, Missouri.

212 **"What is God, ma'am?":** Marquis James, "Dayton, Tennessee," *New Yorker*, July 11, 1925, 8.

212 **"I voted for William Jennings Bryan":** John T. Moutoux, "Darrow Tells Dayton Folk His Idea of Life," *The Knoxville News*, June 23, 1925, 1.

213 **"Those poor, poor unfortunate people!":** Scopes, *Center of the Storm*, 81.

214 **"Race, color, poverty ... cause":** John T. Moutoux, "Jibes at Law by Darrow Win Throng," *The Knoxville News*, June 24, 1925, 10.

214 **As a young man:** see "Darrow Reveals His Philosophy of Life," *The Knoxville Journal*, June 24, 1925, 1.

214 **"No part of freedom":** "Gala Atmosphere for Scopes Trial Decried by Colby," *Washington Post*, June 25, 1925, 4.

215 **"Darrow is disgusted":** Negley Cochran to G. B. Parker, July 4, 1925, Toledo.

215 **"Unless we land it in the federal courts":** "US Judge Declines to Halt Scopes Case," Memphis *Commercial Appeal*, July 6, 1925, 1.

215 **"this is an increasingly serious matter ... this law":** "Dayton Protests New Scopes Move," Baltimore *Sun*, July 4, 1925, 1.

215 **"Dayton Keeps It":** George Fort Milton, "Dayton Happy Plot to Steal Show Is Foiled," Baltimore *Evening Sun*, June 7, 1925, 2.

216 **"brilliant Jew":** "Dayton, Tennessee," *The Baptist Record*, Aug. 6, 1925, 4.

217 **"My general view on these civil liberties cases":** AGH to Roger Baldwin, Sept. 1, 1932, ACLU, vol. 508.

217 **"some Jewish lawyer":** WJB to Sue K. Hicks, June 10, 1925.

217 **"never heard of":** Grace Bryan Hargreaves, memoir, box 58, Bryan papers, LC, 6.

218 **"This is the first time":** "Scopes Lawyer Asked His Views in Religion," *New York Times*, June 24, 1925, 15. See also "Lawyers in Scopes Case Answer Query on Religious Belief," *Nashville Tennessean*, June 23, 1925, 1.

219 **"I believe religion is greater than education":** Raymond Clapper, "Tennessee Evolution Law Faces Court Test Today," *Atlanta Constitution*, July 10, 1925, 2.

220 **"a good tip-off to Bryan's scientific knowledge":** Scopes, *Center of the Storm*, 86.

220 **It was going to lead the country back:** see Charles A. Merrill, "South

Revealed to Him as Defender of Faith," *Boston Globe,* July 9, 1925, 1; see also, for instance, "Case Presents Duel to Death," *Nashville Banner,* July 8, 1925, 3.

221 **"One man's liberty":** Jack Lait, "Darrow Loud in His Protest," *Nashville Banner,* July 8, 1925, 3.

221 **Pegler:** see L. Sprague de Camp, interview with Warner B. Ragsdale, Apr. 3, 1966, HRHRC.

223 **"To call a man a doubter":** HLM, "Mencken Likens Trial to Religious Orgy," Baltimore *Evening Sun,* July 11, 1925, 1.

223 **lead the campaign to put the Bible in the United States Constitution:** see Forrest Davis, "Evolution Ban by U.S. Seen as Bryan's Object," *Philadelphia Inquirer,* July 9, 1925, 1.

CHAPTER THIRTEEN: DAY ONE

All quotations in this chapter and subsequent chapters referring to the trial testimony have been taken from the trial transcript.

227 **"tall, gaunt, thin, underfed, sad":** Mary Bryan, Grace Bryan Hargreaves memoir, 13, box 58, Bryan papers, LC.

230 **"There were many among them . . . pants":** HLM, "Heathen Days," in *The Days Trilogy, Expanded Edition,* 553.

231 **"feeling of unrest . . . the traditional language of prophecy":** Walter Lippmann, *A Preface to Politics,* 100.

231 **"Democracy to him":** Masters, "The Christian Statesman," 391, 392.

231 **"I have always been right":** Dunn, *From Harrison to Harding,* vol. 2, 49.

232 **"The new front is the religious front":** McAlister Coleman, "Is America Civilized?," 6.

232 **"Therein lies their difficulty":** "If Monkeys Could Speak," *The Chicago Defender,* May 23, 1925, 10. For the widespread distribution of the *Defender,* see Shantá R. Robinson, "A Crusader and an Advocate: The Black Press, the Scopes Trial, and Educational Progress," 5–21, and especially 8.

232 **"The law of evolution cannot be overthrown":** William Pickens, "Bryan and Evolution," *New York Amsterdam News,* 16.

233 **"Look at this Mr. Scopes":** quoted in W. O. McGeehan, "Darrow's Lavender Galluses Snap Crown of Thorns on Mr. Bryan," *New York Herald Tribune,* July 11, 1925, 1.

234 **gold watch chain:** see Mary Bryan, July 11, 1925, Grace Hargreaves ms., Bryan papers, LC.

235 **"We have a beautiful jury":** E. Haldeman-Julius, "Scopes Trial Opens; Bryanites Plan to Write Bible Amendment into U.S. Constitution," 1.

235 **"It is as we expected":** Philip Kinsley, "Get Scopes Jury," *Chicago Tribune,* July 11, 1925, 1.

235 **"offensive":** "Hostility Grows in Dayton Crowds; Champions Clash," *New York Times,* July 12, 1925, 1.

235 **"some thousand different religions":** Ibid.

235 **"Foreign scientists should be barred from Dayton"**: Forrest Davis, "Fears Scopes Trial Will Fizzle," *New York Herald Tribune*, July 12, 1925, 1.

236 **"I've been here three years"**: Charles A. Merrill, "Dayton Minister Quits in Row over Evolution," *Boston Globe*, July 13, 1925, 1.

237 **"a little oligarchy . . . truth"**: Philip Kinsley, "Dayton Ousts Evolutionist," *Chicago Tribune*, July 13, 1925, 1.

237 **"The once great"**: Charles F. Potter, *The Preacher and I: An Autobiography*, 285.

237 **"How many more wars"**: Nellie Kenyon, "Bryan Fears Too Much Education," *Chattanooga News*, July 13, 1925, 1.

237 **"You probably laughed at the prohibitionists"**: HLM, "Darrow's Eloquent Appeal Wasted on Ears That Heed Only Bryan," Baltimore *Evening Sun*, July 14, 1925, 1, 2.

238 **"It is purely a question of power"**: E. Haldeman-Julius, "Scopes Trial Opens; Bryanites Plan to Write Bible Amendment into US Constitution," 1.

238 **Bryan suggested**: see N. D. Cochran, "Clear Evolution Trial of Burlesque Features," *Pittsburgh Press*, July 8, 1925, 1–2; see also N. D. Cochran, "Bible in School 'Aim' of Bryan," *Cincinnati Post*, July 9, 1925, 1.

CHAPTER FOURTEEN: AND IT WAS GOOD

239 **"A grinning, long-jawed, mountain product"**: Mary Bryan, July 20, 1925, 19, Grace Hargreaves ms., box 58, Bryan papers, LC.

241 **Also, the law did not specify what was meant by "teach"**: see, for instance, AGH, "The Strategy of the Scopes Defense," *The Nation*, Aug. 5, 1925, 156.

241 **"as forward and self-asserting"**: Mary Bryan, July 20, 1925, 18, Grace Hargreaves ms., Bryan papers.

241 **"old war horse of the Tennessee Bar"**: AGH, *Let Freedom Ring*, 42.

244 **"Isn't it difficult to realize"**: Ibid., 28.

245 **"with a transition too quick to be noticed,"** Joseph Wood Krutch, "Darrow vs. Bryan," *The Nation*, July 29, 1925, 136.

246 **The hole in his shirt**: Philip Kinsley, "Darrow Rips into Bigotry," *Chicago Tribune*, July 14, 1925, 1.

248 **His wife thought he looked tired**: Mary Bryan, July 20, 1925, 19, Grace Hargreaves ms., Bryan papers, LC.

248 **"No subject possesses"**: Phillip Kinsley, "Darrow Makes Great Plea for Liberty of Church, Press and School," *The Montgomery Advertiser*, July 14, 1925, 2.

248 **"rose like a wind"**: HLM, "Darrow's Eloquent Appeal Wasted on Ears That Heed Only Bryan," Baltimore *Evening Sun*, July 14, 1925, 1.

249 **"It was the greatest speech"**: William L. Losh, "Judge Studies Scopes Dismissal," *Indianapolis Times*, July 14, 1925, 11.

249 **Though there were some faint hisses**: Charles A. Merrill, "Darrow's Attack on Tennessee Law," *Boston Globe*, July 14, 1925, 13; see also

George Fort Milton, "Bryan, Enigma of Trial," *Chattanooga News,* July 14, 1925, 1.

249 **"the denizens commented . . . good":** AGH, *Let Freedom Ring,* 46.

CHAPTER FIFTEEN: RENDER UNTO CAESAR

250 **"The fellow is full":** HLM, "Darrow's Eloquent Appeal Wasted on Ears That Heed Only Bryan," *Baltimore Evening Sun.* July 14, 1925, 2.

250 **"on the common ground":** HLM, "Mencken Likens Trial to Religious Orgy," Baltimore *Evening Sun.* July 11, 1925, 1–2.

250 **"100 per cent American":** "Heard and Seen in Dayton at Scopes' Trial," *Atlanta Constitution,* July 15, 1925, 6.

250 **"Ask Us About Tampa, Florida":** Nellie Kenyon, "Ample Room on Dayton Streets," *Chattanooga Times,* July 15, 1925, 11.

253 **"The plain fact was that he sincerely longed to appear":** Marcet Haldeman-Julius, "Impressions of the Scopes Trial," *Haldeman-Julius Monthly,* Sept. 1925, 323.

255 **"I came all the way from New York . . . great":** John T. Moutoux, "Malone's Wife Calls Herself 'Miss Stevens,'" *Knoxville News-Sentinel,* July 17, 1925, 6.

258 **As Arthur Hays would say:** see AGH, *Let Freedom Ring,* 43.

262 **"I know where you can get a copy":** W. O. McGeehan, "Court Shudders as Lads Repeat Scopes Ape Tale," *New York Herald Tribune,* July 16, 1925, 1.

263 **"In view of the fact":** HLM, "Mencken Declares Strictly Fair Trial Is Beyond Ken of Tennessee Fundamentalists," Baltimore *Evening Sun,* July 16, 1925, 1.

265 **"It is a tragedy indeed to begin life . . . elsewhere":** HLM, "Mencken Declares Strictly Fair Trial Is Beyond Ken of Tennessee Fundamentalists," 2.

CHAPTER SIXTEEN: THE FEAR

266 **"L.L.L.":** Raymond Clapper, "Darrow Sips Red Soda Pop as He Reads Stacks of Mail," *Atlanta Constitution,* July 17, 1925, 1.

270–71 **"What a travesty . . . stand":** Rev. T. W. Callaway, "Monkey Is Kin Only in Court," *Chattanooga Daily Times,* July 17, 1925, 3.

271 **"anything but a weak face":** Marcet Haldeman-Julius, "Impressions of the Scopes Trial," 333.

272 **Malone's mouth fell open:** see HLM, "Malone the Victor," Baltimore *Evening Sun,* July 17, 1925, 2.

275 **"I never saw him quite so agitated":** Mary Bryan, circular letter, July 20, 1925, Grace Hargreaves ms., box 58, Bryan papers, LC.

275 **"Once the voice had":** W. O. McGeehan, "Outtalked at Last, Bryan Wilts in Court: Malone Puts Plumed Knight of Fundamentalist Flat on Back," *New York Herald Tribune,* July 17, 1925, 1

275 **"amen":** in addition to the court transcript, see Frank R. Kent, "Bryan's Speech at Dayton," *Baltimore Sun,* July 17, 1925, 1.

275   succumbed to the heat: see Scopes, *Center of the Storm*, 148.
275   "with his own naked voice": HLM, *Heathen Days* in HLM, *The Days Trilogy, Expanded Edition*, 557.
278   "The speech of Dudley Field Malone was a wow": W. O. McGeehan, "Bryan Speech Grieves Dayton," *Los Angeles Times*, July 17, 1925, 2.
278   "Great God!": HLM, *Heathen Days*, 557.
278   "Dudley . . . make it": Scopes, *Center of the Storm*, 155. Also, the conversation is quoted in several newspaper accounts.
279   "These Tennessee mountaineers . . . fundamentalism": HLM, "Malone the Victor," Baltimore *Evening Sun*, July 17, 1925, 2.
280   Spectators heartily applauded: see W. O. McGeehan, "Outtalked at Last, Bryan Wilts in Court," *New York Herald Tribune*, July 17, 1925, 1.

CHAPTER SEVENTEEN: IT IS IN

281   "today we have won": Fay-Cooper Cole, "A Witness at the Scopes Trial," 128.
282   "As matters now stand": Mary Bryan, circular letter, July 20, 1925, Grace Hargreaves ms., box 58, Bryan papers, LC.
283   "It was felt by us that": AGH, *Let Freedom Ring*, 6–8.
284   "I'd like to have heard the evidence": "Author of the Law Surprised at Fuss," *New York Times*, July 18, 1925, 1.
284   "People who have never thought before": Philip Kinsley, "Scientists Write Views for High Court," *Chicago Tribune*, July 18, 1925, 1.
284   "Just as a World War": Watson Davis, "Science Stirred to New Crusade by 'Mock Trial,'" *New York Herald Tribune*, July 18, 1925, 2.
284   "Bryan, who blew loud trumpet": see, for instance, "Bryan Now Regrets Barring of Experts, *New York Times*, July 18, 1925, 2.
285   "They expect Bryan": Paul Y. Anderson, "Arguments for and Against Scientific Testimony by Bryan and Malone," *St. Louis Post-Dispatch*, July 17, 1925, 2.
285   "uncovered the conspiracy": Raymond Clapper, "Bryan and Darrow Assail Each Other in Bitter Attacks," *Atlanta Constitution*, July 12, 1925, 1.
285   "Holy Church": Marion Elizabeth Rodgers, *Mencken and Sara: A Life in Letters*, 219.
285   "All that remains": HLM, "Battle Now Over," Baltimore *Evening Sun*, July 18, 1925, 1.
285–87 "Nearly twenty-five years ago . . . politically": Doris Stevens, "Fears Bryan Soon to Wield Great Power," *Chattanooga Daily Times*, July 26, 1925, 1–2.

CHAPTER EIGHTEEN: COME UNTO ME

288   There were about one hundred: see Allene Sumner, "The Holy Rollers on Shin Bone Ridge," 137.
288   During the war: see Coleman, "Is America Civilized?," 1.

289 **"spouted from his lips," "barbaric grotesquerie":** HLM, "Yearning Mountaineers' Souls Need Reconversion Nightly, Mencken Finds," Baltimore *Evening Sun,* July 13, 1925, 2.

289 **"It is all they have":** Richard J. Beamish, "Duel at Dayton in Silly Stage," *Philadelphia Inquirer,* July 19, 1925, 6.

290 **"They are better than Bryan":** "Tennessee Demands That Judge Punish Darrow for Dare," *St. Louis Globe-Democrat,* July 19, 1925, 2.

290 **"Take heed of hypocrites":** Beamish, "Duel at Dayton in Silly Stage," 6.

290 **"Yes . . . in the courtroom":** "Darrow Goes to 'Church' ": *Kansas City Star,* July 19, 1925, 2.

290 **"We had been looking":** Russell Owen, "Hot Lands and Cold," in *We Saw It Happen: The News Behind the News That's Fit to Print,* p. 232.

293 **tears welling:** see Forrest Davis, "Bryan Fights to Bar Science, Malone Pleads for Evolution," *New York Herald Tribune,* July 17, 1925, 1.

293 **"Maybe Bryan and the Solid South":** Howard Brubaker, "Of All Things," *New Yorker,* June 13, 1925, 6.

293 **Comparing Black people:** see, for instance, David Brion Davis, *The Problem of Slavery in the Age of Emancipation.*

294 **"the hypothesis that links man":** WJB, *In His Image,* 88.

294 **"Shall [schoolchildren] be detached":** WJB, *The Menace of Darwinism,* 17, 33, 63.

294 **"dean of the Simians . . . battle":** George S. Schuyler, "This Simian World," *Pittsburgh Courier,* Nov. 22, 1924, 16.

294 **"Bryan from the pulpit":** J. A. Rogers, "The Critic," 270, 271. For a fine analysis of Darwinism, white supremacy, and the Scopes trial, see Richard Allen Bolar, "There's Power in the Blood: Religion, White Supremacy, and the Menace of Darwinism in America."

295 **"conflicts with the South's idea":** "If Monkeys Could Speak," *Chicago Defender,* May 23, 1925, 10; WJB, *The Menace of Darwinism*; J. A. Rogers, "The Critic," 271.

CHAPTER NINETEEN: THE WITNESS

As usual, all quotations in this chapter have been taken from the transcript of the trial, except as indicated.

312 **"Hell is going to pop now!"** Scopes, *Center of the Storm,* 165.

CHAPTER TWENTY: SALT OF THE EARTH

313 **"I'm going to put . . . 'Wire instructions' ":** Charles Francis Potter, "Ten Years After the Monkey Show, I'm Going Back to Dayton," *Liberty Magazine,* Sept. 28, 1935, 36–37.

313 **"test his views in open court under oath":** "Bryan Now Regrets Barring of Experts," *New York Times,* July 18, 1925, 2.

314   "Like lightning": "Darrow and Hays Talk 'Old' Times," Austin *Sunday American-Statesman*, Jan. 21, 1934, 3.

314   "How in blazes": see Kirtley F. Mather to L. Sprague de Camp, June 14, 1965, HRHRC.

314   Was the earth made in six literal days?: see "Darrow Asks W. J. Bryan to Answer These," *Chicago Tribune*, July 4, 1923, 1, 12.

316   "It will go out to the world": see, for instance (among the many accounts of Bryan's testimony), Paul Y. Anderson, "Science vs. Fundamentalism," *St. Louis Post-Dispatch*, July 21, 1925, 2.

323   A few gasps: see Ray Ginger, *Six Days or Forever?*, 172.

328   broken, crushed: see George Fort Milton, "A Dayton Postscript," 551, and Paul Y. Anderson, "Science vs. Fundamentalism," 1.

328   He may have prevented a riot: see Forrest Davis, "Dramatic Scenes in Trial," *New York Herald Tribune*, July 21, 1925, 1.

CHAPTER TWENTY-ONE: THE VERDICT

329   ignorance was so pitiful: see Watson Davis, "Lays Emphasis on the Importance of Bryan's 'Pitiful Exhibition of Ignorance' When Put on Stand," *Chattanooga Times*, July 21, 1925, 1.

329   "near hysterics": Forrest Davis, "Darrow Grills Bryan," *New York Herald Tribune*, July 21, 1925, 2.

329   "intellectually butchered": Henry Hyde, "Chicago Lawyer Offered Apology to Court," Baltimore *Evening Sun*, July 21, 1925, 1.

329   Running for cover: see Sterling Tracy, "Darrow Quizzes Bryan," Memphis *Commercial Appeal*, July 21, 1925, 1; see also Charles A. Merrill, "Bryan Grilled by Darrow," *Boston Globe*, July 21, 1925, 1, 7.

329   "innate goodness of Mr. Bryan's heart": "The Cost of Bad Manners," *The Independent*, Aug. 1, 1925, 113.

330   "the grim, deft, sneering man": Merrill, "Bryan Grilled by Darrow," 1, 7.

330   "obliged to show his gross ignorance": "Bryan and Darrow Pour Out Ridicule Upon Each Other," *Atlanta Constitution*, July 22, 1925, 7.

332   Malone placed his hand on Scopes's shoulder: "The Trial by Watch Ticks," *Chattanooga Daily Times*, July 22, 1925, 4.

334   "there was nothing else we could do": Charles A. Merrill, "Scopes Appeals on Fine of $100," *Boston Globe*, July 22, 1925, 1.

335   "We all wanted to hear": "Crowd at the End Surges to Darrow," *New York Times*, July 22, 1925, 2.

335   "Mr. Bryan has been organizing ... in America": Forrest Davis, "Scopes Guilty," *New York Herald, New York Tribune*, July 22, 1925, 1.

336   "Mr. Bryan's convulsions ... answers": "Dayton Hears Parting Shots," *Nashville Banner*, July 22, 1925, 4.

336   "Of course I speak for myself": "Evolution Battle Rages out of Court," *New York Times*, July 22, 1925, 2.

336   "I do not pretend to know": Merrill, "Scopes Appeals on Fine of $100," 1; see also Charles A. Merrill, "Scopes Case Goes to Higher

Court," *Boston Globe*, July 22, 1925, 14; "Now Bryan Quizzes Darrow, *Chicago Daily Tribune*, July 22, 1925, 1.

CHAPTER TWENTY-TWO: KEEPING THE FAITH

339   **"Keep Kongress Klean"**: Thomas L. Sokes, "Thousands March in Klan's Parade Through Capital," *Atlanta Constitution*, Aug. 9, 1925, 4.

339   **It was "grander and gaudier"**: HLM, "Parade Unlike Anything Since the Days of Roosevelt," Baltimore *Sun*, Aug. 9, 1925, 1.

339   **Spectators**: See, for instance, "Klan Host Parade in Capital," *New York Herald Tribune*, Aug. 9, 1925, 1; "40,000 Klansmen Parade in Washington as 200,000 Spectators Look on Quietly," *New York Times*, Aug. 9, 1925, 1; "White Robed Klan Cheered on March," *Washington Post*, Aug. 9, 1925, 1.

340   **He posed as the driver**: "Klan March at Capital to Tune of Hymns," *Philadelphia Inquirer*, Aug. 9, 1925, 14.

340   **"We have long looked forward"**: "The Klan Parade," Baltimore *Sun*, Aug. 10, 1925, 6.

340   **"I cannot conclude"**: "Klan's Big Rally Ends with Oratory," *New York Times*, Aug. 10, 1925, 26.

340   **He listed**: "Bryan Plans University," *Los Angeles Times*, July 23, 1925, 1.

340   **And in addition**: see "Ignorance Charge Denied by Bryan," *New York Times*, July 25, 1925, 10.

341   **"necessary to protect my family"**: John Herrick, "Dayton Slips Back into the Shadows Again," *Chicago Tribune*, July 23, 1925, 2.

341   **"victorious defeat"**: "Malone Talks at Follies," July 24, 1925, *New York Times*, 13.

341   **"I love you"**: Ben McKenzie to CD, Aug. 6, 1925, LC.

341   **The next year**: see L. Sprague de Camp, *The Great Monkey Trial*, 436; "Scopes' Prosecutor Held on Charge of Bootlegging," *Johnson City Chronicle*, Feb. 17, 1926, 1.

342   **"red meat"**: see "Bryan, Fundamentalism and the Democratic Party," *Chicago Tribune*, July 26, 1925, 8.

342–343   **"Christian faith" ... "I think I can,"**: WJB and MBB, *Memoirs*, 485–86.

343   **"the mountain peak of my life's efforts"**: quoted in George Fort Milton, "The Story of the Last Message," WJB, *The Last Message of William Jennings Bryan*, 9.

343   **"who come into daily contact"**: Ibid., 14.

343   **"No more repulsive doctrine"**: Ibid., 51.

344   **"down to the brute level"**: Ibid., 36.

344   **"descended from some"**: Ibid., 21, 23.

344   **"if morality rests on religion"**: WJB to William S. Woods, Apr. 5, 1923, box 37, LC.

344   **"Capitalism, supported by force ... wages"**: WJB, *In His Image*, 230.

345   **"to noble deeds"**: WJB, *The Old World and Its Ways*, 79.

345 **As his biographer:** see Michael Kazin, *A Godly Hero,* 303.

345 **"a system under which":** WJB, *The Last Message of William Jennings Bryan,* 53–54.

345 **"Science needs religion":** Ibid., 66.

345 **"Now we are told that newly":** Ibid., 67.

346 **"That cannot be the answer":** Ibid., 69.

CHAPTER TWENTY-THREE: I HAVE FINISHED THE RACE

349 **Though some:** see Raymond Clapper, "Bryan Succumbed Fighting for God as He Saw Light," *Atlanta Constitution,* July 27, 1925, 1.

350 **"I firmly believe . . . Amen":** Paul Y. Anderson, "Bryan More Powerful in Death than Life," *St. Louis Post-Dispatch,* July 29, 1925, 2.

350 **On the way:** see Paul Y. Anderson, "Bryan Funeral Party on Its Way from Tennessee to Washington," *St. Louis Post-Dispatch,* July 29, 1925, 1.

351 **"This last journey":** WJB and MBB, *Memoirs,* 489.

351 **"God aimed at Darrow":** Joseph Wood Krutch, *More Lives Than One,* 154.

351 **Magazines:** see "Publishers Destroy Caricatures on Bryan," *Reading Times,* July 29, 1925, 2.

351 **"died within the borders of our state":** "Gov. Peay Issues Proclamation," *Chattanooga Daily Times,* July 31, 1925, 1.

351 **In Oklahoma, Arkansas, and Arizona:** see "Burial," *Time,* Aug. 10, 1925, 5.

351 **Standing for hours in a drenching rain:** for this and other details, see Paul Y. Anderson, "Taps Sounded at Burial of Bryan," *St. Louis Post-Dispatch,* Aug. 1, 1925, 2.

352 **"a death from an ordeal of faith":** George Fort Milton, "A Dayton Postscript," *The Outlook,* Aug. 19, 1925, 551.

352 **"that others might live":** Michael Williams, "WJB," *The Commonweal,* 303.

352 **"He was the golden voice":** Felix Frankfurter, Oral History, 1956, p. 10, CCOH.

353 **"The forces which are embodied":** John Dewey, "The American Intellectual Frontier," *New Republic,* May 10, 1922, 303–5.

353 **as the British journalist:** see Brooks, "An English View of Mr. Bryan," 29.

353 **"Mr. Bryan never has been wrong":** "Wm. A. White Names Bryan Diagnostician," Memphis *Commercial Appeal,* Apr. 26, 1925, 3; "A Remarkable Man," Memphis *Commercial Appeal,* Apr. 29, 1925, 6.

353 **"for his fearless stand on issues":** "Debs and Scopes Speak," *Boston Globe,* July 28, 1925, 15.

353 **"I have known Mr. Bryan since 1896":** "Darrow in Tribute to Late Adversary," *Chattanooga News,* July 27, 1925, 1, 3.

354 **"Broken heart nothing":** Ruby Darrow to Irving Stone, n.d., LC.

354   "Mr. Bryan will always be affectionately . . . ending": "Malone Lauds Bryan," *New York Herald, New York Tribune*, July 28, 1925, 3.

354   "apology, not praise . . . Domingo?": HLM, "Editorial," *The American Mercury*, Oct. 1925, 159.

354   Though Bryan's sudden death: see, for instance, "Theaters Eliminate Scenes," *Billboard*, Aug. 8, 1925, 9.

354   "He was crafty as a Talleyrand": Hugh Nugent Fitzgerald, "Bryan, Cut by Texas Votes, Swayed Voters," Austin *Sunday American-Statesman*, Aug. 2, 1925, 1.

354   "It is pathetic to think of the hero": "William Jennings Bryan," *The Nation*, Aug. 5, 1925, 154.

355   "How did they thank me . . . calculation": "A Note on Bryan," *The American Monthly*, Sept. 1, 1925, 197–98.

355   "the riches that came to him": James Morgan, "With Bryan in Eight Conventions," *Boston Daily Globe*, Aug. 2, 1925, B2.

355–56   "The cause of human progress . . . penitentiary": Eugene V. Debs, "The Truth About Bryan," *The American Monthly*, Oct. 1, 1925, 8.

356   "the unity and homogeneousness of our nation": WJB, "The Yellow Peril," *The Commoner*, Dec. 6, 1901, 1.

356   "if every American could visit China": WJB, *The Old World and Its Ways*, 137.

356   "One race problem is enough": Ibid., 146.

356   "more advanced civilization": WJB, "The Race Problem Again," *The Commoner*, Oct. 2, 1903, 1.

356   "We stand with the Commoner": Floyd Calvin, "The Digest," *Pittsburgh Courier*, Aug. 8. 1925, 16; see also "Bryan and the American Press," *Pittsburgh Courier*, Aug. 1, 1925, 16.

356–57   "a sort of speculating and dealing . . . 'shell game' . . . religion": Chandler Owen, "William Jennings Bryan," *The Messenger*, Dec. 1925, 392–93.

357   "Bryan at his best": HLM, "Bryan," Baltimore *Evening Sun*, July 27, 1925, 15.

357   "This talk of sincerity": HLM, "Editorial," *American Mercury*, Oct. 1925, 159.

357   "The job before democracy": HLM, "Bryan," Baltimore *Evening Sun*, July 27, 1925, 15.

357   "No man of his time": "President Gives Bryan Eulogy," May 4, 1934, *Chicago Daily Tribune*, 20.

359   progressive Democrat: see Franklin Delano Roosevelt to WJB, June 23, 1923, LC.

CHAPTER TWENTY-FOUR: A LITTLE LEARNING IS A DANGEROUS THING

360   "pained eyebrows": "Darrow, Hayes [*sic*] and Malone Made Brave Fight," *The American Guardian*, July 31, 1925, 6.

360   The main issue: see Frank R. Kent, "Scopes Trial Result Is Said to Be Negative," Baltimore *Sun*, July 23, 1925, 1.

361   **"Apostle of the Morons"**: "The Bigot's Progress," New York *World*, June 3, 1925.

361   **"Great Realtor . . . state"**: "The Rise of Sectarian Politics," New York *World*, July 10, 1925.

361   **"for or against the Christian religion"**: "A Blunder by the Scopes Defense," New York *World*, July 21, 1925.

361–62   **"Lippmann evidently has not any sense . . . freedom"**: CD to HLM, Aug. 5, 1925, NYPL.

362–63   **"to show that such laws . . . expert"**: AGH, "The Strategy of the Scopes Defense," *The Nation*, Aug. 5, 1925, 157.

363   **"no sympathy"**: "The Wandering Defense," New York *World*, July 22, 1925, 10.

363   **There's no education in that:** "The Baiting of Judge Raulston," *The New Republic*, July 29, 1925, 249–50.

364   **"it would be disastrous"**: See Walter Nelles, "The Conduct of the Scopes Trial," *The New Republic*, Aug. 19, 1925, 332.

364   **The lawyer Walter Nelles:** Ibid., 347.

364   **"kept idealists"**: HLM, *A Book of Prejudices*, 183.

364   **"Darrow did more for them"**: HLM, "Aftermath," *Chattanooga News*, Sept. 18, 1925, 4.

365   **"Cold feet"**: CD to AGH, Sept. 14, 1925, in Tietjen, *Clutches*, 314.

365   **Behind closed doors:** See Walter Nelles to Forrest Bailey, Sept. 5, 1925, ACLU, vol. 274.

365   **"we all feel as you do"**: Roger Baldwin to Raymond Fosdick, Oct. 21, 1925.

365   **"urging Dr. Neal"**: Minutes, executive board meeting, Aug. 3, 1925, ACLU, vol. 279.

365   **"besieged with criticism"**: Forrest Bailey to John Neal, Aug. 3, 1925, ACLU, vol. 274.

365   **"baiting of Mr. Bryan"**: Forrest Bailey to John Neal, Aug. 3, 1925, ACLU, vol. 274; see also Brewer Eddy to John Neal, Sept. 10. 1925, copy enclosed in Brewer Eddy to Forrest Bailey, Sept. 11, 1925, ACLU, vol. 274; and Forrest Bailey to Charles H. Strong, Aug. 12, 1925, ACLU, vol. 274.

365–66   **"there seemed to be difficulty . . . personality"**: Forrest Bailey to John Neal, Aug. 12, 1925, and Aug. 3, 1925, ACLU, vol. 274.

366   **"If there is any graceful way"**: Forrest Bailey to John Neal, Aug. 12, 1925, ACLU, vol. 274.

366   **"quiet, modest, scholarly"**: Forrest Bailey to John Neal, Aug. 3, 1925, ACLU, vol. 274.

366   **"The last thing in the world"**: Forrest Bailey to John Neal, Aug. 12, 1925, ACLU, vol. 274.

366   **"the man who spiritually and literally crucified Bryan . . . Supreme Court"**: George Rappleyea to Forrest Bailey, Aug. 7, 1925, ACLU, vol. 274.

366   **"personal feelings"**: George Rappleyea to Forrest Bailey, Aug. 7, 1925, ACLU, vol. 274.

366   **"It must be understood"**: George Rappleyea to Forrest Bailey, Aug. 25, 1925, ACLU, vol. 274.

367   "deepest appreciation . . . in Knoxville": Forrest Bailey to George Rappleyea, Aug. 10, 1925, ACLU, vol. 274.

367   "meeting the prosecution": Forrest Bailey to David Starr Jordan, July 29, 1925, ACLU, vol. 274.

367   "delicate factors": Forrest Bailey to Charles Strong, Aug. 12, 1925, ACLU, vol. 274.

367   "You employed": Brewer Eddy to John Neal, Sept. 10, 1925, ACLU, vol. 274.

368   "I am not at all sure that religion . . . drive them away": CD to Oswald Garrison Villard, Oct. 2, 1925, quoted in Tietjen, *Clutches*, 315, 316.

368   "I never at any time . . . existed": Forrest Bailey to CD, Sept. 2, 1925, ACLU, vol. 274.

369   "Of course . . . mean": CD to Forrest Bailey, Sept. 4, 1925, ACLU, vol. 274.

369   "I am not willing to have conservative lawyers": AGH to Walter Nelles, Sept. 9, 1925, ACLU, vol. 274.

369   "Dr. Neal is neither communicative": Forrest Bailey to John Scopes, Sept. 29, 1925, ACLU, vol. 274.

369   "absolutely hopeless": CD to AGH, Sept. 17, 1925, ACLU, vol. 274.

370   "It would be a grave mistake . . . counsel": Forrest Bailey to John Scopes, Oct. 7, 1925, ACLU, vol. 274.

370   The executive committee: see Forrest Bailey to John Scopes, Oct. 16, 1925, ACLU, vol. 274.

371   "This case is a cross-section": quoted in Walter F. White to N. K. McGill, Oct. 6, 1925, NAACP papers.

CHAPTER TWENTY-FIVE: THE LOST CAUSE

372   "If any other suggestions": Forrest Bailey to AGH, Jan. 7, 1925, ACLU, vol. 299.

372   "The pressure upon me": Forrest Bailey to AGH, Feb. 2, 1926, ACLU, vol. 299.

374   "A Little Learning Is a Dangerous Thing . . . 'lower order of animals' ": "Reply Brief and Argument for the State of Tennessee," *State vs. John T. Scopes* (1926), 326–27.

374   "soiled or even red banner": Ibid., 80.

374   "overthrow the existing order": Ibid., 326.

374–75 "pathetic," "perverted," "hysterical," and "repulsive," "which is the safeguard": Ibid., 328, 331, 337.

375   "the doctrine of communism": Ibid., 203–4.

376   "scientific infidelity": "Supreme Court Hears Scopes Case," *Nashville Banner*, May 31, 1926, 1.

376   "the freedom of education": Ibid.; see also W. P. Hoffman, "Sidelights on Scopes Case," *Nashville Banner*, May 31, 1926, 4.

377   "revolutionary agitation": Ibid.

377   "If you permit the teaching that . . . later": "Anti-Evolution Law Called 'Capricious,'" Memphis *Commercial Appeal*, June 1, 1926, 1; "Supreme Court Hears Scopes Case," *Nashville Banner*, May 31, 1926, 1.

377   **"advocacy of murder"**: W. P. Hoffman, "Sidelights on Scopes Case," *Nashville Banner,* June 1, 1926, 20.

378   **"Just open the sewer . . . There is no truth in that"**: "McConnico Excoriates Those Who Would Force 'Animal Dogma' on State," *Nashville Tennessean,* June 6, 1926, 1, 5, 6.

378   **"animal dogma"**: John P. Fort, "Scopes Case Fire Leaps Up Again," *Chattanooga News,* June 2, 1926, 1. See also Truman Hudson Alexander, "Scopes Hearing to Close with Forensic Duel," *Nashville Tennessean,* June 1, 1926, 1, 6.

378–79 **"to atheism . . . citizenship we want in Tennessee"**: "McConnico Excoriates Those Who Would Force 'Animal Dogma' on State," *Nashville Tennessean,* June 6, 1926, 6.

379–80 **"From what I think I know . . . pretend to serve"**: "Darrow, Defending Scopes, Says Scientific Truth Is Inevitable," *Nashville Tennessean,* June 7, 1926, 3.

381   **reporters called him mild**: see "Religious Issue Flares in Scopes Case Pleas," *Chattanooga Times,* June 1, 1926, 1.

381   **"As time passes"**: "Darrow Enjoys Nashville Trip," *Nashville Tennessean,* June 2, 1926, 16.

381–82 **"Our feeling is that there should . . . is what it is"**: Forrest Bailey to CD, June 3, 1926, ACLU, vol. 299.

382   **"I have no idea . . . Organization"**: CD to Forrest Bailey, June 9, 1926, ACLU, vol. 299.

382   **"very fair"**: Thomas Malone to CD, June 12, 1926, ACLU, vol. 299.

382   **"To have Darrow appeal to the U.S. Supreme Court"**: Forrest Bailey to Roger Baldwin, June 11, 1926, ACLU, vol. 299.

382   **"I think that we have to get Darrow out"**: Forrest Bailey to Roger Baldwin, June 12, 1926, ACLU, vol. 299.

382   **"inside story . . . left wingers"**: Forrest Bailey to Walter Lippmann, June 12, 1926, ACLU, vol. 311.

383   **"right from the first . . . used"**: John Scopes to Forrest Bailey, Aug. 8, 1926, ACLU, vol. 299.

383   **"We would not think"**: Roger Baldwin to John Scopes, Aug. 10, 1926, ACLU, vol. 299.

384   **"I note that you seem"**: Roger Baldwin to John Scopes, Sept. 20, 1926, ACLU, vol. 299.

384   **"even with the best intentions"**: Wolcott Pitkin to Felix Frankfurter, Nov. 10, 1926, ACLU, vol. 299.

384   **"Nothing in life do I treasure"**: AGH, *City Lawyer,* 227.

384   **"He was, to me"**: Ibid., 208.

385   **"The decision was a subtle one"**: AGH, *Let Freedom Ring,* 81.

386   **"typical country lawyer's trick"**: "Called Country Trick," *Washington Post,* Jan. 17, 1927, 3. The comment was repeated in newspapers nationwide.

386   **"I think the Anti-Evolution law"**: "Revival of Scopes Case Barred," *New York Times,* Jan. 22, 1927, 15.

386   **"We are dealing with astute church people"**: "Expects to Fight Decision," *New York Times,* Jan. 17, 1927, 19.

387 **"Tennessee is composed"**: "Darrow Lashes Evolution Foes," *Birmingham News,* Dec. 13, 1925, 2.

387 **"What about the future life? . . . grief"**: MFP, diary, Dec. 13, 1925, Oregon.

388 **"the white man who calls himself your 'friend'"**: "Darrow Almost Mob-Handled After Pleading Racial Justice in Southern Cities, Is Report," *The Cincinnati Enquirer,* Mar. 9, 1927, 1. See also "Education, Money, Are Power, Darrow Tells Tuskegeeans," *The New York Age,* Jan. 22, 1927, 3.

388 **"Your battle . . . prayer"**: "Negroes Must Give More for Freedom," *Washington Post,* Apr. 23, 1928, 8.

388 **"What do people mean"**: "Full Text of Clarence Darrow's Speech," *Afro-American,* Apr. 28, 1928, 1.

389 **"The first reason . . . happen again"**: "Fascist 'Frame-Up' Doubted by Darrow," *New York Times,* Feb. 20, 1926, 15.

EPILOGUE: THE FOUR WINDS OF THE SKY

391 **"It is too early, it seems to me"**: HLM, "Editorial," *American Mercury,* Oct. 1925, 160.

392 **"The issue in the Tennessee case"**: quoted in "Shall We Have an Established Church," *Chicago Tribune,* May 30, 1925, 4.

392 **"I wonder whether . . . majorities"**: Walter Lippmann to Learned Hand, n.d. [spring 1925], Harvard Law School Archives, Hand papers.

392–93 **"In Tennessee the people . . . hopes of democracy"**: Walter Lippmann, *Men of Destiny,* 49.

393 **"To me it was perfectly clear"**: CD, *The Story of My Life,* 74.

393 **"there is no limit to which fanaticism"**: CD, letter to *The Nation,* May 22, 1929, quoted in Tietjen, *Clutches,* 379.

393 **"sharpshooters of bigotry"**: CD, *The Story of My Life,* 276.

394 **"coming to be governed not by law,"** AGH, *Let Freedom Ring,* 170.

394 **Convicted, Friede was fined $300:** see, for instance, "Dreiser Testifies at Friede's Trial," *Boston Globe,* Apr. 17, 1929, 11; "Darrow Gives Public Reading in Courtroom," *Boston Evening Transcript,* Apr. 17, 1929, part 1, 7; "Tried for Boston Sale of Dreiser Book," *New York Times,* Apr. 17, 1929, 14.

395 **"the Tennessee of the North"**: AGH, *Let Freedom Ring,* 184.

395 **"When the muse of time"**: quoted in AGH, *Let Freedom Ring,* 281.

395 **"He had convictions and courage"**: Roger Baldwin to de Camp, Oct. 14, 1965, HRHRC.

396 **"I hate to see people pushed around"**: AGH, *City Lawyer,* xi.

396 **"the right of the individual to be damned"**: AGH, *Let Freedom Ring,* xviii.

396 **"order has become the fetish"**: Ibid., 10.

396 **"Bigotry is not necessarily limited"**: Ibid., 88.

396 **"I believe in the fundamentals of democracy"**: AGH, "Should Radicalism be Suppressed," *Forum,* May 1929, 291.

396 **"retain our traditional Constitutional rights"**: Brief, *Hering v. State Board of Education*, AGH papers, box 26, folder 8, Department of Rare Books and Special Collections, Princeton University Library.

396 **"To him, liberty transcended order"**: "Memorial to A. G. Hays: Civil Rights Champion," *New York Times*, Mar. 17, 1955, 30.

397 **"You couldn't be angry" . . . they can go to hell"**: AGH, *City Lawyer*, 157; see also John Reddy, "Magnificent Failure," *Esquire*, August 1951, 29, 109–10.

397 **he owed money**: see Doris Stevens to Dudley Malone, Dec. 27, 1929, folder 41, and Stevens to Mr. Conner, June 23, 1927, folder 43, Stevens collection, Schlesinger.

398 **"All lawyers and politicians are actors at heart"**: "Dudley Field Malone Funeral Will Be Held in Beverly Hills," *New York Herald Tribune*, Oct. 7, 1950, 12.

398 **"You may be sure he is in paradise"**: "Messages to Mrs. Darrow," *Unity*, May 16, 1938, 96.

398 **"I was the poor apostle of freedom"**: Doris Stevens to DFM, June 21, 1927, folder 43, Stevens collection, Schlesinger.

398 **"partisan monkeyshines"**: Alice Hughes, "Yes, She's Bellicose," *Miami Herald*, Dec. 5, 1939, 11A.

399 **Stevens argued**: see "Women of Today," *The Daily Worker*, Feb. 27, 1939, 5.

399 **"I happen to be connected"**: Quoted in Eleanor Roosevelt, *The White House Press Conferences of Eleanor Roosevelt*, 94–95. See also Bredbenner, Candice Lewis. *A Nationality of Her Own: Women, Marriage, and the Law of Citizenship*, excerpted at ark.cdlib.org/ark:/13030/ftog500376/; and Paula F. Pfeffer, "Eleanor Roosevelt and the National and World Woman's Parties," 39–57.

399 **suffering**: see "Eyes of World on Honolulu Trial," *Pittsburgh Courier*, Apr. 9, 1934, 4.

400 **"I had so long and decidedly"**: CD to Harry Elmer Barnes, Mar. 5, 1932, quoted in Tietjen, *Clutches*, 431.

400 **"I don't know what I should have done"**: CD to Harry Elmer Barnes, Mar. 12, 1932, quoted in Tietjen, *Clutches*, 432.

400 **He requested**: "Malone Wires That Family Should Be Brought to Mainland," *Washington Post*, Apr. 30, 1932, 1.

400 **Hoover evidently**: see George S. Leisure to Irving Stone, Aug. 1, 1940, LC. Leisure was a young attorney working with Darrow on the Massie case. See also Farrell, *Clarence Darrow*, 529.

400 **much of the Black press**: see "Unmasking the Anglo-Saxon," *Negro World*, May 14, 1932, 3.

400 **"Scottsboro has condemned"**: "Echoes of Other Editors," *Negro World*, May 14, 1932, 3.

400 **"He always did the thing"**: WW to Ruby Darrow, July 1, 1932, NAACP files, June 1, 1932–July 31, 1937, LC.

401 **"I am not trying to excuse myself"**: E. W. Wilkins, "Darrow Tells Negro Reporter His Views on 'Honor Slaying,'" *Philadelphia Tribune*, May 26, 1932, 1.

401 "Many times I have been asked": CD, *The Story of My Life*, 444.

401 "No one has ever been able to classify": Eugene V. Debs to Emanuel Haldeman-Julius, Jan. 4, 1926, Debs collection, Indiana State University, indstate.contentdm.oclc.org/digital/collection/evdc/id/3882.

402 "Not in many years have monopolistic": "Findings of Third Darrow Report," *New York Herald Tribune*, July 2, 1934, 10.

402 In a way: see the brilliant essay by Henry Steele Commager, " 'Regimentation': A New Bogy," *Current History*, July 1934, 385–91.

402 "We've got to keep the Morgans": "Clarence Darrow, on Akron Visit, Says He's Content to Watch Roosevelt's Experiment Move 'To the Left,' " *Akron Beacon Journal*, Aug. 26, 1933, 11.

402 Darrow a "Red": see, for instance, "Darrow's 'Wonder If I'm Dead,' Caused NRA Job Acceptance," *New York Times*, May 2, 1934, 7.

402 "I have never murdered": quoted in AGH, *City Lawyer*, 236.

403 "In my opinion": Robert S. Keebler to Irving Stone, May 30, 1940, LC.

404 "Dayton is not the only place": Scopes, *Center of the Storm*, 270.

404 "Prejudice is not unique to Tennessee": Ibid., 269.

405 "Liberty is always under threat": Ibid., 272.

405 "You can only be free": Ibid., 277.

405 "The Fundamentalists": Maynard Shipley, "Growth of the Anti-Evolution Movement," *Current History*, May 1930, 330.

406 "Somewhere in heaven": Rita Ciolli, "A Rebuff for Creationism," *Newsday*, June 20, 1987, 3.

406 biologist Stephen Jay Gould: See Stephen Jay Gould, "The Verdict on Creationism," *New York Times Magazine*, July 19, 1987, 32.

406 "one drop of Japanese blood": see *Congressional Record*, 78th Congress, Second Session, Apr. 22, 1943, 3,702.

407 "I just can't give a scientific answer": Sherwin D. Smith, "The Great 'Monkey Trial,' " *New York Times Magazine*, July 4, 1965, 15.

407 "whistling to keep up his courage": see Darrow on Bryan as early as 1929, when reviewing M. R. Werner's biography of Bryan: CD, "Bryan," 364.

407 "very attitude showed": CD, *The Story of My Life*, 247.

407 "I won't be going very long": CD to HLM, Aug. 25 [1925], NYPL.

407 "loved to pose as a pessimist": Victor S. Yarros, "My 11 Years with Clarence Darrow," 9.

407 "sought the unattainable": William Allen White, *The Autobiography of William Allen White*, 511.

408 "fundamental bedrock of liberty . . . all science": Jack Lait, "Darrow Loud in His Protest," *Nashville Banner*, July 8, 1925, 3.

408 "Do you think I look": Russell Owen, "Darrow—A Pessimist with Hope—Is Eighty," *New York Times Magazine*, Apr. 18, 1937, 5.

409 "The way of the world": CD, *The Story of My Life*, 428.

409 "powers of reaction and despotism": CD to Roger Baldwin, May 19, 1929, in Tietjen, *Clutches*, 377.

Select Bibliography

(All newspaper articles are fully cited in the notes.)

Adams, Henry. *Democracy*. 1880; rpt. New York: Henry Holt, 1908.

Allem, Warren. "Backgrounds of the Scopes Trial at Dayton, Tennessee." Master's thesis, University of Tennessee, 1959.

Altgeld, John Peter. *Live Questions*. Chicago: George S. Bowen, 1899.

———. *Our Penal Machinery and Its Victims*. Chicago: A. C. McClurg & Co., 1886.

Anderson, Sherwood. *Sherwood Anderson's Memoirs*. New York: Harcourt, Brace, 1942.

Anthony, Joseph, and Woodman Morrison, eds. *Best New Reports of 1924*. Boston: Small, Maynard, 1925.

Arnold-Fisher, Tom. "Rethinking the Scopes Trial: Cultural Conflict, Media Spectacle, and Circus Politics." *Journal of American Studies*. February 2022: 142–66.

Bagby, Wesley M. *The Road to Normalcy*. Baltimore, Md.: Johns Hopkins University Press, 2019.

Baillie, Hugh. *High Tension: The Recollections of Hugh Baillie*. New York: Harper & Brothers, 1959.

Baldwin, Hanson W., and Shepherd Stone, eds. *We Saw It Happen: The News Behind the News That's Fit to Print*. New York: Simon & Schuster, 1938.

Bare, Daniel R. *Black Fundamentalists: Conservative Christianity and Racial Identity in the Segregation Era*. New York: New York University Press, 2021.

Barfoot, Charles. *Aimee Semple McPherson and the Making of Modern Pentecostalism, 1890–1926*. London: Routledge, 2014.

Barnard, Harry. *Eagle Forgotten: The Life of John Peter Altgeld*. New York: Duell, Sloan and Pearce, 1938.

Barton, Bruce. *The Man Nobody Knows: A Discovery of the Real Jesus*. Indianapolis: Bobbs-Merrill, 1925.

Bashford, Alison. *The Huxleys: An Intimate History of Evolution*. Chicago: University of Chicago Press, 2022.

Beer, Thomas. *Hanna, Crane, and the Mauve Decade*. New York: Alfred A. Knopf, 1941.

———. *The Mauve Decade*. New York: Alfred A. Knopf, 1926.

The Bible and Its Enemies: An Address Delivered at the Moody Institute of Chicago. Chicago: Bible Institute, 1921.

Bliven, Bruce. "Mother, Home and Heaven." *The New Republic*. Jan. 9, 1924: 172–75.

Bode, Carl. *Mencken*. Baltimore, Md.: Johns Hopkins University Press, 1986.

Bogart, Ernest L., and Charles M. Thompson. *Centennial History of Illinois*, vol. 4. Edited by Clarence W. Alvord. Springfield: Illinois Centennial Commission, 1920.

Bolar, Richard Allen. "There's Power in the Blood: Religion, White Supremacy, and the Politics of Darwinism in America." University of California, San Diego, 2014. Dissertation.

Bott, Alan. "Through a Londoner's Window." *The Sphere*. July 18, 1925: 90.

Bourne, Randolph. "War and the Intellectuals." *The Seven Arts*. June 1917: 133–46.

Boyle, Kevin. *Arc of Justice: A Saga of Race, Civil Rights, and Murder in the Jazz Age*. New York: Henry Holt, 2004.

Bredbenner, Candice Lewis. *A Nationality of Her Own: Women, Marriage, and the Law of Citizenship*. Berkeley: University of California Press, 1998.

Brooks, Sydney. "An English View of Mr. Bryan." *North American Review*. July 1913: 27–39.

Brown, William Montgomery. *Communism and Christianism*. Bradford Brown Educational Company, 1921.

Browne, Francis Fisher. *National Review* (London). December 1896: 454.

Browne, Waldo. *Altgeld of Illinois*. New York: B. W. Huebsch, 1924.

Bruce, John E. "Tammany and the Negro." *The Colored American*. Sept. 15, 1900, 1–2.

Bryan, William Jennings. "Abusing Free Speech." *The Commoner*. Aug. 1, 1917: 1.

———. "An Ecclesiastical Factor." *The Commoner*. Dec. 4, 1908: 14–15.

———. "Anti-Lynch Bill Dropped." *The Commoner*. Dec. 1, 1922: 2.

———. "Convention Takes Up Task of Balloting." *The Commoner*. Aug. 1, 1920: 12.

———. *In His Image*. New York: Fleming H. Revell Company, 1922.

———. "Mr. Bryan's New Book, *In His Image*." *The Commoner*. June 1, 1922: 7.

———. "Peace and Prohibition." *The Commoner*. July 1, 1920: 1–3.

———. "Prohibition." *The Commoner*. Jan. 1, 1916: 13, 14.

———. "Republican Partisanship," *The Commoner*, Jan. 1, 1922: 2.

———. "Resisting the Draft." *The Commoner*. Aug. 1, 1917: 1.

———. *Speeches of William Jennings Bryan*. 2 vols. New York: Funk & Wagnalls, 1913.

———. *The First Battle: The Story of the Campaign of 1896*. Chicago: W. B. Conkey, 1896.

———. "The Fundamentals." *Forum*. July 1923: 1,665–731.

———. *The Last Message of William Jennings Bryan*. New York: Revell, 1925.

———. *The Menace of Darwinism*. New York: Fleming H. Revell, 1922.

———. "The Negro Question." *The Commoner*. Nov. 1, 1901: 1–2.

———. *The Old World and Its Ways*. Saint Louis: Thompson Publishing Co., 1907.

————. "The Philippine Question." *The Commoner.* Oct. 2, 1903: 2.

————. *The Prince of Peace.* New York: Funk & Wagnalls, 1916.

————. "The Race Problem Again." *The Commoner.* Oct. 2, 1903: 1–2.

————. "The Yellow Peril." *The Commoner.* Dec. 6, 1901, 1.

————. "Tillman and McLaurin." *The Commoner.* May 31, 1901, p. 1.

Bryan, William Jennings, and Mary B. Bryan. *The Memoirs of William Jennings Bryan.* Philadelphia: John C. Winston Co., 1925.

Busch, Francis X. *Prisoners at the Bar.* Indianapolis: Bobbs-Merrill, 1952.

The Cambridge Companion to Darwin. New York: Cambridge University Press, 2004.

Cather, Willa. "The Personal Side of William Jennings Bryan." *Prairie Schooner.* Winter 1949: 331–37.

Chalmers, David Mark. *Hooded Americanism: The History of the Ku Klux Klan.* Durham: Duke University Press, 1987.

Clark, Constance Areson. *God—or Gorilla: Images of Evolution in the Jazz Age.* Baltimore: Johns Hopkins University Press, 2008.

Cohen, Charles L., and Paul S. Boyer, eds. *Religion and the Culture of Print in Modern America.* Madison: University of Wisconsin Press, 2008.

Cole, Fay-Cooper. "A Witness at the Scopes Trial." *Scientific American.* January 1959: 1.

Coleman, McAlister. "Is America Civilized?" *The New Leader.* July 7, 1925: 1, 6.

Coletta, Paolo E. "Silas Bryan of Salem." *Journal of the Illinois State Historical Society.* March 1949: 57–79.

————. "The Youth of William Jennings Bryan." *Nebraska History.* March 1950: 1–24.

————. *William Jennings Bryan,* vol. 1: *Political Evangelist, 1860–1908;* vol. 2: *Progressive Politician and Moral Statesman, 1909–1915;* vol. 3: *Political Puritan, 1915–1925.* Lincoln, Nebraska: University of Nebraska Press, 1964–1969.

Commager, Henry Steele. "'Regimentation': A New Bogy." *Current History.* July 1934: 385–91.

Comstock, Sarah. "Prima Donna of Revivalism: Aimee Semple McPherson." *Harper's Monthly Magazine.* December 1927: 11–19.

Cowen, Geoffrey. *The People vs. Clarence Darrow.* New York: Times Books, 1993.

Cox, James M. *Journey Through My Years.* New York: Simon & Schuster, 1946.

Crunden, Robert M. *Ministers of Reform: The Progressives' Achievement in American Civilization, 1889–1920.* New York: Basic Books, 1982.

Daniel, Douglass K. "Ohio Newspapers and the 'Whispering Campaign' of the 1920 Presidential Election." *Journalism History.* Winter 2001–2: 156–64.

Darrow, Clarence. *Argument in Defense of the Communists.* Chicago: Charles H. Kerr & Co., 1920.

————. "Bryan." *The New Republic.* May 15, 1929: 363–64.

————. *Can the Individual Control His Conduct?* Girard, Kans.: Haldeman-Julius, 1928.

————. *Farmington.* Chicago: A.C McClurg, 1904; rpt. 1932.

————. *Resist Not Evil.* Chicago: Charles H. Kerr, 1902.

————. "The Edwards and the Jukes." *The American Mercury.* October 1925: 147–57.

————. "The Eugenics Cult." *The American Mercury.* June 1926: 129–37.

———. "The Problem of the Negro." *The International Socialist Review,* vol. 2. November 1901: 321–35.

———. *The Story of My Life.* New York: Charles Scribner's Sons, 1932.

Darwin, Charles. *On the Origin of Species.* 1859. New York: D. Appleton, 1896.

———. *The Life and Letters of Charles Darwin,* ed. Sir Francis Darwin. 3 vols. New York: D. Appleton, 1893.

Davis, David Brion. *The Problem of Slavery in the Age of Emancipation.* New York: Alfred A. Knopf, 2014.

De Camp, L. Sprague. *The Great Monkey Trial.* Garden City, N.Y.: Doubleday, 1968.

Debs, Eugene V. "The Truth About Bryan." *The American Monthly.* Oct. 1, 1925: 231–32.

Dewey, John. "The American Intellectual Frontier." *The New Republic.* May 10, 1922: 303–5.

Dos Passos, John. *1919.* New York: Signet; rpt. 1969.

———. *Three Soldiers.* New York: George Doran, 1921.

Dray, Philip. *At the Hands of Persons Unknown: The Lynching of Black America.* New York: Modern Library, 2002.

Du Bois, W.E.B. "Brothers, Come North." *The Crisis.* January 1920: 105–6.

———. "Opinion" [on the Tulsa massacre]. *The Crisis.* April 1926: 267–70.

———. "Scopes." *The Crisis.* September 1925: 218.

Duffus, Robert. "The Legend of Roger Baldwin." *The American Mercury.* Aug. 1, 1925: 408–14.

Dunn, Arthur Wallace. *From Harrison to Harding, 1888–1920.* 2 vols. New York and London: G. P. Putnam's Sons, 1922.

Farrell, John A. *Clarence Darrow: Attorney for the Damned.* New York: Vintage, 2012.

Fass, Paula S. "Making and Remaking an Event: The Leopold and Loeb Case in American Culture." *Journal of American History.* December 1993: 919–51.

Fitzgerald, F. Scott. *The Great Gatsby.* 1925; rpt. Signet, 2021.

———. *This Side of Paradise.* New York: Scribner's, 1920.

Fitzgerald, Frances. *America Revised.* New York: Vintage, 1980.

Fosdick, Harry Emerson. "Mr. Bryan and Evolution," *The Christian Century,* March 23, 1922: 363–65.

———. "Shall the Fundamentalists Win?" *The Christian Century.* June 8, 1922: 713–77.

———. "Tolerance." *Harper's Monthly Magazine.* Dec. 1925: 710–14.

Fox, Richard Wightman, and T. J. Jackson Lears, eds. *The Culture of Consumption: Critical Essays in American History, 1880–1980.* New York: Pantheon, 1983.

Freeman, Joseph. *An American Testament.* New York: Farrar & Rinehart, 1936.

Furniss, Norman F. *The Fundamentalist Controversy, 1918–1931.* 1954; rpt. Hamden, Conn.: Archon Books, 1963.

Gilbert, James. *Redeeming Culture: American Religion in the Age of Science.* Chicago: University of Chicago Press, 1997.

Ginger, Ray. *Altgeld's America: The Lincoln Ideal Versus Changing Realities.* New York: Funk & Wagnalls, 1958.

———. *The Bending Cross: A Biography of Eugene Victor Debs.* New Brunswick, N.J.: Rutgers University Press, 1949.

———. *Six Days or Forever? Tennessee v. John Thomas Scopes.* 1958; rpt. New York: Oxford University Press, 1974.

Giovannitti, Arturo. "Communism on Trial." *The Liberator.* March 1920: 5–8.

Goldberg, Isaac. *Mencken the Man.* New York: Simon & Schuster, 1925.

Gopnik, Adam, ed. *Americans in Paris.* New York: Library of America, 2004.

Gordon, Linda. *The Second Coming of the KKK.* New York: Liveright, 2017.

Gould, Stephen Jay. *Ever Since Darwin.* New York: W. W. Norton, 1977.

———. *The Mismeasure of Man.* New York: W. W. Norton, 1981.

———. "William Bryan's Last Campaign." *Natural History.* Nov. 1, 1987: 16–26.

Grant, Madison. *The Passing of the Great Race.* New York: Charles Scribner's Sons, 1922.

Grimké, Francis J. *The Works of Francis J. Grimké,* ed. Carter G. Woodson. 4 vols. Ann Arbor: University of Michigan Press, 1942.

Hackett, Francis. "Billy Sunday, Salesman." *The New Republic.* Apr. 28, 1917: 370–72.

Haldeman-Julius, Emanuel. "Scopes Trial Opens; Bryanites Plan to Write Bible Amendment into U.S. Constitution." *Haldeman-Julius Weekly.* July 18, 1925: 1.

Haldeman-Julius, Marcet. *Clarence Darrow's Two Great Trials: Reports of the Scopes Anti-Evolution Case and the Dr. Sweet Negro Trial.* Girard, Kans.: Haldeman-Julius Company, 1927.

———. "Impressions of the Scopes Trial." *Haldeman-Julius Monthly.* September 1925: 323–47.

Hangen, Tona J. *Redeeming the Dial: Radio, Religion, and Popular Culture in America.* Chapel Hill: The University of North Carolina Press, 2000.

Hapgood, Hutchins. *The Spirit of Labor.* New York: Duffield & Co., 1907.

Hapgood, Norman. "The New Threat of the Ku Klux Klan." *Hearst's International.* January 1923: 8–12.

Hapgood, Norman, ed. *Professional Patriots.* New York: Albert and Charles Boni, 1927.

Harcourt, Felix. "A Visible Empire: The Ku Klux Klan and American Culture, 1915–1930." George Washington University, 2014. Dissertation.

Harriman, Florence Jaffray Hurst. *From Pinafores to Politics.* New York: Henry Holt, 1923.

Harrison, Carter H. *Stormy Years.* Indianapolis: Bobbs-Merrill, 1935.

Harrison, Charles Yale. *Clarence Darrow.* New York: Jonathan Cape & Harrison Smith, 1931.

Hays, Arthur Garfield. *City Lawyer: The Autobiography of a Law Practice.* New York: Simon & Schuster, 1942.

———. *Let Freedom Ring.* New York: Boni and Liveright, 1928.

———. "Should Radicalism Be Suppressed." *Forum.* May 1929: 290–93.

———. *Trial by Prejudice.* New York: Covici, Fried, 1933.

———. "The Strategy of the Scopes Defense." *The Nation.* Aug. 5, 1925: 157–58.

Haywood, William D. *Bill Haywood's Book: The Autobiography of William Haywood.* New York: International Publishers, 1929.

Hemingway, Ernest. *The Sun Also Rises.* 1926; rpt. New York: Penguin, 2022.

Hibben, Paxton. "Aimee and Tex." *The New Yorker.* Mar. 5, 1927: 65–67.

Hoar, George. "President McKinley or President Bryan?" *North American Review.* October 1900: 473–86.

Hochschild, Adam. *American Midnight.* New York: Mariner Books, 2022.

Hoffman, W. P. "Sidelights on Scopes Case." *Nashville Banner.* May 31, 1926: 4.

Hofstadter, Richard. *Anti-Intellectualism in American Life.* 1963; rpt. New York: Library of America, 2020.

———. *Social Darwinism in American Thought.* 1955; rpt. New York: G. Braziller, 1959.

———. *The Age of Reform.* New York: Alfred A. Knopf, 1955.

———. *The American Political Tradition.* 1948; rpt. New York: Vintage, 1989.

Hollister, Howard K. "In Dayton, Tennessee." *The Nation.* July 8, 1925: 61–62.

House, Edward M. *The Intimate Papers of Colonel House,* ed. Charles Seymour. 4 vols. Boston: Houghton Mifflin, 1926.

Houston, David F. *Eight Years with Wilson's Cabinet.* Garden City, N.Y.: Doubleday, Page & Co., 1926.

Howard, Sidney. "Our Professional Patriots, VI." *The New Republic.* Oct. 1, 1924: 119–23.

Hubbard, Elbert. *The Philistine: A Periodical of Protest,* vol. 23. East Aurora, N.Y.: Society of the Philistines. July 1906: 52.

Hunter, George William. *A Civic Biology.* New York: American Book Company, 1914.

Huntington, Collis P. *California: Her Past, Present, and Future.* San Francisco: n.p., 1900.

Huxley, Julian. "America Revisited: Fundamentalism." *The Spectator.* Nov. 22, 1924: 772.

Huxley, Leonard, ed. *Life and Letters of Thomas Henry Huxley.* 2 vols. New York: D. Appleton, 1901.

Huxley, Thomas Henry. "Agnosticism and Christianity" in *Science and Christian Tradition: Collected Essays,* vol. 5. London: Macmillan, 1894.

———. *Collected Essays.* 9 vols. London: Macmillan, 1893–94.

Israel, Charles A. *Before Scopes: Evangelicalism, Education, and Evolution in Tennessee, 1870–1925.* Athens, Ga.: University of Georgia Press, 2004.

James, Marquis. "Dayton, Tennessee." *The New Yorker.* July 11, 1925: 6–9.

Johnson, Hiram. *The Diary Letters of Hiram Johnson, 1917–1945.* Edited by Robert E. Burke. New York: Garland Publishing, 1983.

Johnson, James Weldon. "The Riots: An NAACP Investigation." *The Crisis.* Sept. 1, 1919: 241–43.

Jordan, David Starr. *The Blood of the Nation: Study of the Decay of Races Through the Survival of the Unfit.* Boston: Unitarian Society, 1902.

Joshi, S. T. *H. L. Mencken: An Annotated Bibliography.* Metuchen, NJ: Scarecrow Press, 2009.

Kazin, Michael. *A Godly Hero: The Life of William Jennings Bryan.* New York: Alfred A. Knopf, 2006.

———. *The Populist Persuasion: An American History,* rev. ed. Ithaca, New York: Cornell University Press.

Kerston, Andrew. *Clarence Darrow: Attorney for the Damned.* New York: Hill & Wang, 2011.

Kevles, Daniel J. *In the Name of Eugenics: Genetics and the Uses of Human Heredity.* 1985. Cambridge: Harvard University Press, 1995.

Kipling, Rudyard. *The Letters of Rudyard Kipling.* Edited by Thomas Pinney. 5 vols. Iowa City: University of Iowa Press, 2004.

Koenig, Louis W. *Bryan: A Political Biography.* New York: Putnam's, 1971.

Koenigsberg, Moses. *King News: An Autobiography.* Philadelphia: F. P. Stokes, 1941.

Krutch, Joseph Wood. "Darrow vs. Bryan." *The Nation.* July 29, 1925: 136–37.

———. *More Lives Than One.* New York: W. Sloane, 1962.

———. "Tennessee: Where Cowards Rule." *The Nation.* July 15, 1925: 88–89.

The Ku-Klux Klan: Hearings Before the Committee on Rules, House of Representatives, 67th Congress, First Session. Washington: Government Printing Office, 1921.

Lane, Franklin K. *The Letters of Franklin K. Lane. Personal and Political,* ed. Anne Lane Wintermute. Boston: Houghton Mifflin, 1922.

Larson, Edward J. "An American Tragedy: Retelling the Leopold-Loeb Story in Popular Culture." *American Journal of Legal History.* April 2010: 119–56.

———. *Summer for the Gods: The Scopes Trial and America's Continuing Debate over Science and Religion.* New York: Basic Books, 1997.

———. "The Scopes Trial and the Evolving Concept of Freedom." *Virginia Law Review.* April 1999, 503–29.

Leisure, George S. "Reflections on Clarence Darrow." *Virginia Law Review.* April 1959: 414–18.

Levine, Lawrence W. *Defender of the Faith: William Jennings Bryan: The Last Decade, 1915–1925.* New York: Oxford University Press, 1965.

Lewis, Oscar. *The Big Four.* New York: Alfred A. Knopf, 1938.

Lienesch, Michael. *In the Beginning: Fundamentalism, the Scopes Trial, and the Making of the Antievolution Movement.* Chapel Hill: University of North Carolina Press, 2007.

Link, Arthur S. *The New Freedom.* 2 vols. Princeton: Princeton University Press, 1947.

———. *Wilson: The Road to the White House.* Princeton: Princeton University Press, 1947.

———. *Wilson: The Struggle for Neutrality.* Princeton: Princeton University Press, 1960.

Link, Arthur S., ed. *The Papers of Woodrow Wilson.* Princeton: Princeton University Press, 1966.

Lippmann, Walter. *A Preface to Politics.* New York: Mitchell Kennerley, 1914.

———. *American Inquisitors: A Commentary on Dayton and Chicago.* New York: Macmillan,1928.

———. *Drift and Mastery.* New York: Mitchell Kennerley, 1914.

———. "H. L. Mencken." *Saturday Review of Literature.* December 1926: 414.

———. "Leonard Wood." *The New Republic.* Mar. 17, 1920: 76–80.

———. *Men of Destiny.* 1927; rpt. New York: Macmillan, 2003.

Loos, Anita. *No Mother to Guide Her.* New York: Avon Press, 1961.

Lukas, J. Anthony. *Big Trouble: A Murder in a Small Western Town.* New York: Simon & Schuster, 1997.

Macdonald, Dwight. "The Defense of Everybody—1." *The New Yorker.* July 11, 1953: 31–32, 34–36.

Marsden, George. *Fundamentalism and American Culture: The Shaping of Twentieth-Century Evangelicalism.* New York: Oxford University Press, 1980.

Masters, Edgar Lee. *Across Spoon River.* 1936; rpt. Urbana: University of Illinois Press, 1964.

———. "The Christian Statesman." *The American Mercury.* Dec. 1924: 385–98.

McCartney, Laton. *The Teapot Dome Scandal: How Big Oil Bought the White House and Tried to Steal the Country.* New York: Random House, 2008.

McGeehan, W. O. "Why Pick on Dayton?" *Harper's Magazine.* October 1925: 624–27.

McKernan, Maureen. *The Amazing Crime and Trial of Leopold and Loeb.* Chicago: The Plymouth Court Press, 1924.

McPherson, Aimee Semple. "The Cathedral of the Air." *The Bridal Call Foursquare.* June 1924: 6–7.

Mencken, Henry L. *A Book of Prejudices.* New York: Alfred A. Knopf, 1917.

———. "A 1911 Dream Book," *The Smart Set.* September 1911: 153–58.

———. "Darwin's Bulldog." *The Nation.* Mar. 30, 1932: 374.

———. *George Bernard Shaw.* New York: Boston, J. W. Luce & Co., 1905.

———. *Happy Days.* New York: Alfred A. Knopf, 1940.

———. *Heathen Days.* New York: Alfred A. Knopf, 1943.

———. "In Tennessee." *The Nation.* July 1, 1925: 2.

———. *Letters of H. L. Mencken,* ed. Guy Forgue. New York: Alfred A. Knopf, 1961.

———. *Notes on Democracy.* New York: Alfred A. Knopf, 1926.

———. "Novels for Hot Afternoons," *The Smart Set.* July 1911: 153–58.

———. *Pistols for Two.* New York: Alfred A. Knopf, 1917.

———. *Prejudices, Fifth Series.* New York: Alfred A. Knopf, 1926.

———. "Specimens of Current Fiction," *The Smart Set.* Feb. 1, 1923: 138–44.

———. "Star-Spangled Men." *The New Republic.* Sept. 29, 1920: 118–20.

———. *The American Language: A Preliminary Inquiry into the Development of English in the United States.* New York: Alfred A. Knopf, 1919.

———. "The Great American Art." *The Smart Set.* April 1916: 304–10.

———. *The Days Trilogy, Expanded Edition,* ed. Marion E. Rodgers. New York: Library of America, 2014.

———. "The Good, the Bad, and the Best-Sellers." *The Smart Set.* November 1908: 155–57.

———. "The Horse-Power of Realism," *The Smart Set.* June 1911: 152–58.

———. "The Literature of a Moral Republic." *The Smart Set.* October 1915: 150–56.

———. *The New Mencken Letters,* ed. Carl Bode. New York: Dial Press, 1976.

———. "The Newspaper Man." *The American Mercury.* June 1924: 248–50.

———. *The Philosophy of Friedrich Nietzsche.* Boston: Luce and Co., 1908.

———. *Treatise on the Gods.* New York: Alfred A. Knopf, 1930.

Mencken, Henry L., and George Jean Nathan. "Répétition Générale." *The Smart Set,* Jan. 1, 1922: 41–45.

———. "Répétition Générale," *The Smart Set.* Feb. 1, 1923: 33–45.

Mencken, Henry L., and George Sterling. *From Baltimore to Bohemia: The Letters of H. L. Mencken and George Sterling,* ed. S. T. Joshi. Madison, N.J.: Fairleigh Dickinson University Press, 2001.

Mencken, Henry L., and Robert Rives La Monte. *Men Versus the Man: A Correspondence.* New York: Henry Holt, 1910.

Merriam, Charles. *Four American Party Leaders.* New York: Macmillan, 1926.

Miller, Robert Moats. *Harry Emerson Fosdick: Preacher, Pastor, Prophet.* New York: Oxford University Press, 1985.

Mills, Jack. "The Speaking of William Jennings Bryan in Florida, 1915–1925." University of Florida, 1948. Unpublished master's thesis.

Milner, Lucille. *Education of an American Liberal.* New York: Horizon Press, 1954.

Milton, George Fort. "A Dayton Postscript." *The Outlook.* Aug. 19, 1925: 550–51.

Montgomery, James R. "John R. Neal and the University of Tennessee: A Five-Part Tragedy." *Tennessee Historical Quarterly.* Summer 1979: 214–31.

Moorehead, Caroline. *Troublesome People.* Maryland: Adler & Adler, 1987.

Moran, Jeffrey P. "Reading Race into the Scopes Trial: African American Elites, Science, and Fundamentalism." *The Journal of Southern History.* Dec. 1, 200: 95–120.

Morgenthau, Henry. *All in a Life-Time.* Garden City, N.Y.: Doubleday, Page, and Co., 1922.

Murray, Robert K. *Red Scare: A Study in National Hysteria, 1919–1920.* Minneapolis: University of Minnesota Press, 1955.

———. *The 103rd Ballot.* New York: HarperCollins, 1976.

Nasaw, David. *The Chief.* New York: HarperCollins, 2000.

Nelles, Walter. "The Conduct of the Scopes Trial." *The New Republic.* Aug. 19, 1925: 347.

Niebuhr, Reinhold. "Treatise on the Gods." *The Atlantic Monthly.* June 1930: 18.

Nock, Albert J. "What the Right Hand Doeth." *The Freeman.* Nov. 20, 1921: 268–70.

Noggle, Burl. *Into the Twenties.* Urbana: University of Illinois Press, 1974.

Numbers, Ronald L. ed. *Galileo Goes to Jail and Other Myths about Science and Religion.* Cambridge, MA: Harvard University Press, 2009.

O'Kelly, Kevin. "Leopold & Loeb: The Case That Capped Darrow's Career." *Experience: The Magazine of the Senior Lawyers Division.* Fall 2009: 24–31, 34.

Official Report of the Proceedings of the Democratic National Convention Held in Madison Square Garden, New York City, June 24, 25, 26, 27, 28, 30, July 1, 2, 3, 4, 5, 7, 8, and 9, 1924, Resulting in the Nomination of John W. Davis (of West Virginia) for President and Charles W. Bryan (of Nebraska) for Vice-President, eds. Charles A. Greathouse and Louis Grant. Indianapolis: Bookwalter-Ball-Greathouse, 1924.

Official Report of the Proceedings of the DNC Held in SF CA, June 28, 29, 30, July 1, 2, 3, 5, 6. Indianapolis: Bookwalter-Ball Printing Co., 1920.

Official Report of Proceedings of the Democratic National Convention Held in St. Louis, Mo., July 6, 7, 8, and 9, 1904, ed. Milton W. Blumenberg. New York: Press of the Publisher's Printing Company, 1904.

Okrent, Daniel. *The Guarded Gate.* New York: Scribner, 2019.

———. *Last Call: The Rise and Fall of Prohibition.* New York: Scribner, 2010.

Osborn, Henry Fairfield. "Evolution and Daily Living." *Forum.* February 1925: 169–77.

Owen, Chandler. "William Jennings Bryan." *The Messenger.* December 1925: 392–93.

Owen, Russell. "Darrow—A Pessimist with Hope—Is Eighty." *New York Times Magazine.* Apr. 18, 1937: 5, 31.

———. inter alia. "Hot Lands and Cold." In *We Saw It Happen: The News Behind the News That's Fit to Print.* Edited by Hanson W. Baldwin and Shepherd Stone. New York: Simon & Schuster, 1938.

Pavuk, Alexander. "The American Association for the Advancement of Science Committee on Evolution and the Scopes Trial: Race, Eugenics, and Public Science in the USA." *Bulletin of the Institution of Historical Research.* February 2018: 137–59.

Pawa, J. M. "Black Radicals and White Spies: Harlem 1919." *Negro History Bulletin.* October 1972: 129–33.

Peterson, Paul V. "William Jennings Bryan, *World-Herald* Editor." *Nebraska History* 49 (1968): 348–71.

Pettigrew, Richard F. *Imperial Washington: The Story of American Public Life from 1870 to 1920.* Chicago: Charles H. Kerr, 1922.

Pfeffer, Paula F. "Eleanor Roosevelt and the National and World Woman's Parties." *The Historian.* Fall 1996: 39–57.

Postel, Charles. *The Populist Vision.* New York: Oxford University Press, 2007.

Potter, Charles F. *The Preacher and I: An Autobiography.* New York: Crown, 1951.

———. "Ten Years After the Monkey Show, I'm Going Back to Dayton." *Liberty Magazine.* Sept. 28, 1935: 38.

"Quadrennial Address of the Bishops of the Colored Methodist Church to the Fourteenth Session of the General Conference." *Colored Methodist Episcopal Church. General Conference 1922.* Chicago: Gentry-Mayham Print. Co., 1922.

Rampersad, Arnold. "Mencken, Race, and America." *Menckeniana.* Fall 1990: 1–11.

Ratcliffe, S. K. "Leopold and Loeb." *New Statesman.* Sept. 20, 1924: 668–71.

Reddy, John. "Magnificent Failure." *Esquire.* August 1951: 29, 109–10.

Riley, William Bell. "Bryan, the Great Commoner and Christian." *Christian Fundamentals in School and Church.* October–December 1925: 5–11, 37.

———. "Youth and the Babel in Religion." *Pilot.* November 1936: 41–42.

Robinson, Shantá R. "A Crusader and an Advocate: The Black Press, the Scopes Trial, and Educational Progress." *The Journal of Negro Education.* Winter 2018: 5–21.

Robinson, W. W. *Bombs and Bribery.* Los Angeles: Richard J. Hoffman, 1969.

Rodgers, Marion Elizabeth. *Mencken and Sara: A Life in Letters.* New York: McGraw Hill, 1987.

———. *Mencken: The American Iconoclast.* New York: Oxford University Press, 2005.

Roessel, David, and Stephanie Maniaci, eds. "Mr. M: An Unpublished Memoir of H. L. Mencken by James M. Cain." *Resources for American Literary Study.* November 2017: 169–206.

Rogers, J. A. "The Critic." *The Messenger.* July 1, 1925: 169.

Roosevelt, Eleanor. *The White House Press Conferences of Eleanor Roosevelt.* Edited by Maurine Beasley. New York: Garland, 1983.

Roosevelt, Theodore. *The Letters of Theodore Roosevelt.* Edited by Elting E. Morison. 2 vols. Cambridge: Harvard University Press, 1951.

Rosen, Christine. *Preaching Eugenics: Religious Leaders and the American Eugenics Movement.* New York: Oxford University Press, 2004.

Rupp, Leila J. "Feminism and the Sexual Revolution in the Early Twentieth Century: The Case of Doris Stevens." *Feminist Studies.* Summer 1989: 289–309.

Russell, Charles E. *Bare Hands and Stone Walls.* New York: Charles Scribner's Sons, 1933.

Sandburg, Carl. "To Billy Sunday." *The Masses.* September 1915: 11.

Scopes, John T. *Center of the Storm.* New York: Holt, Rinehart and Winston, 1967.

Seldes, George. *World Panorama, 1918–1933.* Boston: Little, Brown, 1933.

Shepherd, William G. "Monkey Business in Tennessee." *Collier's.* July 18, 1925: 8–9, 38–39.

Shipley, Maynard. "Growth of the Anti-Evolution Movement." *Current History.* May 1930: 330–32.

Slayden, Ellen Maury. *Washington Wife: The Journal of Ellen Maury Slayden.* New York: Harper & Row, 1963.

Slayton, Robert A. *Empire Statesman: The Rise and Redemption of Al Smith.* New York: Free Press, 2007.

Smith, A. D. *East Tennessee.* Chattanooga: A. D. Smith & Co., 1893.

Smith, Edwina C. "Southerners on Empire: Southern Senators and Imperialism, 1898–1899."*Mississippi Quarterly.* Winter 1977–78: 89–107.

Smith, Sherwin D. "The Great 'Monkey Trial.'" *New York Times Magazine.* July 4, 1965: 15.

Snow, Richard F. "Counsel for the Indefensible." *American Heritage.* February/March 1987: 96–97.

St. Johns, Adela Rogers. *Final Verdict.* Garden City, N.Y.: Doubleday & Co., 1962.

Stannard, David E. *Honor Killing: Race, Rape and Clarence Darrow's Spectacular Last Case.* New York: Viking Penguin, 2005.

State vs. John T. Scopes. Nashville, 1926.

Stearns, Harold. *Liberalism in America.* New York: Boni and Liveright, 1919.

Steel, Ronald. *Walter Lippmann and the American Century.* 1980. New York: Routledge, 2017.

Steffens, Lincoln. "Attorney for the Damned." *Saturday Review of Literature.* Feb. 27, 1932: 550.

———. *The Autobiography of Lincoln Steffens.* 2 vols. New York: Harcourt, Brace, 1931.

Stein, Gertrude. *What Are Masterpieces.* New York: Pitman Publishing Co., 1970.

Stevens, Doris. *Jailed for Freedom.* New York: Boni and Liveright, 1920.

Stidger, William L. *Edwin Markham.* New York: Abingdon Press, 1933.

Stone, Irving. *Clarence Darrow for the Defense.* Garden City, N.Y.: Doubleday, Doran & Co., 1941.

Sullivan, Mark. "The Stump and the Porch." *Collier's.* Oct. 9, 1920: 5–6.

Sumner, Allene. "The Holy Rollers on Shin Bone Ridge." *The Nation.* July 29, 1925: 137–38.

Sunday, W. A. [Billy]. "To the Editor." *Harper's Magazine.* February 1928: 395.

Sutton, Matthew Avery. *Aimee Semple McPherson and the Resurrection of Christian America.* Cambridge: Harvard University Press, 2007.

———. *American Apocalypse: A History of Modern Evangelicalism.* Cambridge, MA: Harvard University Press, 2014.

Taft, William Howard. *Anti-Semitism in the United States*. Chicago: Anti-Defamation League, 1920.

Tierney, Kevin. *Darrow: A Biography*. New York, Crowell, 1979.

Tietjen, Randall, ed. *In the Clutches of the Law: Clarence Darrow's Letters*. Berkeley: University of California Press, 2013.

Tillman, Benjamin. "Causes of Southern Opposition to Imperialism." *North American Review*. October 1900: 439–46.

Tompkins, Jerry R., ed. *D-Days at Dayton: Reflections on the Scopes Trial*. Baton Rouge, La. Louisiana State University Press, 1965.

Tontonoz, Matthew J. "The Scopes Trial Revisited: Social Darwinism Versus Social Gospel." *Science as Culture*. June 1, 2008: 121–43.

"Trial Transcript: Leopold and Loeb v. Illinois." Chicago, Criminal Court of Cook County: 1924.

Tuck, Stephen. "The Doubts of Their Fathers: The God Debate and the Conflict Between African American Churches and Civil Rights Organizations Between the World Wars." *Journal of Southern History*. August 2020: 625–78.

Verum. "William Jennings Bryan at Home." *Town & Country*. July 18, 1908: 8–11.

Viereck, George Sylvester. "Neither with God Nor His Enemies." *The American Monthly*. Aug. 1, 1924: 167.

Villard, Oswald Garrison. "New Fight for Old Liberties." *Harper's Magazine*. June 1925: 440–46.

Von Papen, Franz. *Memoirs*. London: Andre Deutsch, 1952.

Walker, Samuel. *In Defense of American Liberties: A History of the ACLU*. New York: Oxford University Press, 1990.

Walker, Stanley. "Saving Souls in New York." *The American Mercury*. Mar. 3, 1925: 270–77.

Weinberg, Arthur and Lila Weinberg, eds. *Verdicts Out of Court*. Chicago: Quadrangle; rpt. New York, Putnam, 1980.

Weinrib, Laura. *The Taming of Free Speech: America's Civil Liberties Compromise*. Cambridge, Ma.: Harvard University Press, 2016.

Werner, M. R. *Bryan*. New York: Harcourt, Brace, 1929.

West, Rachel. "The Department of State, at Home and Abroad, on the Eve of the First World War." Indiana University, 1972. Dissertation.

Wheeler, William Bruce. *Knoxville, Tennessee: A Mountain City in the New South*. Knoxville: University of Tennessee Press, 2005.

White, Walter F. *A Man Called White: The Autobiography of Walter White*. Athens: University of Georgia Press, 1995.

———. "The Eruption of Tulsa." *The Nation*. June 29, 1921: 909–10.

White, William Allen. "Bryan." *McClure's*. July 1900: 232–37.

———. *Masks in a Pageant*. New York: Macmillan, 1928.

———. *Politics: The Citizen's Business*. New York: Macmillan, 1924.

———. *The Autobiography of William Allen White*. New York: Macmillan, 1946.

Williams, Michael. "William Jennings Bryan." *The Commonweal*. Aug. 5, 1925: 303.

Wills, Garry. *Under God: Religion and American Politics*. New York: Simon & Schuster, 1990.

Wilson, Woodrow, and Edith B. Galt. *A President in Love: The Courtship Letters of Woodrow Wilson and Edith Bolling Galt,* ed. Edwin Tribble. Boston: Houghton Mifflin, 1981.

Wish, Harvey. "Governor Altgeld Pardons the Anarchists." *Journal of the Illinois State Historical Society.* December 1938: 424–48.

Wood, Charles W. "Benign Heretic." *The New Yorker.* Jan. 23, 1926: 17–18.

The World's Most Famous Court Trial: Tennessee Evolution Case. Cincinnati: National Book Company, 1925.

Wright, Richard. *Black Boy.* 1945; rpt. New York: Harper Perennial, 1965.

Yarros, Victor S. *My 11 Years with Clarence Darrow.* Girard, Kans.: Haldeman-Julius Publications, 1950.

Index

Morgan, James, 355
Morgan, J. P., 99, 153
Mormons, 55
Morrow, Edwin, 116
Moyer, Charles, 15
Muir, John, 73
Münsterberg, Hugo, 74
Murphee, A. A., 145, 146, 152
Murphy, Frank, 373
Mussolini, Benito, 221, 388, 389

Nashville, Tennessee, 165, 167
Nathan, George Jean, 73, 131, 132
Nation, The, 354, 362, 368
National Academy of Sciences, 263
National Association for the
    Advancement of Colored People
    (NAACP), 101–3, 106, 217, 231,
    371, 373, 396, 400, 401
National Association of Colored
    Women, 106
National Civil Liberties Union, 178
National Guard, 105
National Library Association, 126
National Negro Committee, 21–22
National Recovery Administration
    (NRA), 401–2
National Review, The, 399
National Women's Party, 85, 87
natural selection, xviii, 62, 203, 268,
    295
Neal, John Randolph, xvi, 186–88,
    200, 215, 223
    American Civil Liberties Union
        (ACLU) and, 199, 365–69
    appeal in Scopes case and, 376
    Darrow, Clarence and, 212
    as defense attorney in Scopes trial,
        194, 197, 198, 228, 240–42, 244,
        255, 282, 304, 334, 365, 382
    photographs of, 173, 198, 304
    as university professor, 173
Nebraska, 33, 35, 49, 77
Nebraska National Guard, 45
Nebraska State Journal, 352
Negro Industrial School, Daphne,
    Alabama, 287
Negro World, 400
Nelles, Walter, 199, 365

Nelson, Wilbur A., 267, 290, 296–97
New England Watch and Ward Society,
    394
Newman, Horatio Hackett, 267, 290,
    296, 298
New Republic, The, 111, 142, 191,
    361, 363–64, 398
New York Avenue Presbyterian
    Church, Washington D.C., 351–52
New York Call, The, 90
New York City, 143–54, 170–71
New York Commercial Advertiser, 17
New Yorker, The, 72, 167, 293
New York Evening Mail, 75
New York Society for the Suppression
    of Vice, 73
New York Times, The, 102, 343, 407
New York World, xxv, 106, 361, 382
Nicaragua, 81
Nicholas II, Czar, 97
Niebuhr, Reinhold, 64
Nietzsche, Friedrich, 69–71, 111,
    113–14, 117, 133, 138, 140,
    273–74, 286, 345
Noah, 115, 195, 314, 319–21
Nockels, Ed, 24
No-Conscription League, 91
Norris, Frank, 72
North Carolina, 47, 104, 169
Not About Nightingales (Williams),
    409
Notes on the State of Virginia
    (Jefferson) xiii–xiv

Oberlin College, 263
Occoquan Workhouse, 86, 87, 89
O'Gorman, James, 87
O'Hare, Kate Richards, 91
Ohio, 4, 6, 37, 91, 189
Ohio Northern University, 181
Oklahoma, 104, 105, 154
Omaha, Nebraska, 102
Omaha World-Herald, 36–37
O'Neill, Eugene, 73
On the Origin of Species (Darwin),
    xvii, xxvii, 61, 291, 334
Oregon, 104
Osborn, Henry Fairfield, 201
Otis, Harrison Gray, 24

About the Author

BRENDA WINEAPPLE is the author of seven books, including *The Impeachers: The Trial of Andrew Johnson*, named by *The New York Times* as one of the 10 best nonfiction works of 2019; *Ecstatic Nation: Confidence, Crisis, and Compromise, 1848–1877*, named a best book of the year by *The New York Times*, among other publications; *White Heat: The Friendship of Emily Dickinson and Thomas Wentworth Higginson*, a National Book Critics Circle Award finalist; and *Hawthorne: A Life*, winner of the Ambassador Award. A recipient of a Literature Award from the American Academy of Arts and Letters, a Pushcart Prize, a Guggenheim Fellowship, and an American Council of Learned Societies Fellowship, she has also received three National Endowment Fellowships, including its Public Scholars Award. Her essays and reviews regularly appear in *The New York Review of Books*, *The New York Times Book Review*, and *The Wall Street Journal*. In 2023, she was selected a Fellow at the Dorothy B. and Lewis Cullman Center for Scholars and Writers at the New York Public Library.

About the Type

This book was set in Sabon, a typeface designed by the well-known German typographer Jan Tschichold (1902–74). Sabon's design is based upon the original letter forms of sixteenth-century French type designer Claude Garamond and was created specifically to be used for three sources: foundry type for hand composition, Linotype, and Monotype. Tschichold named his typeface for the famous Frankfurt typefounder Jacques Sabon (c. 1520–80).

PG 206: "IF THE STOCK OF
          DOMESTICATED ANIMALS...

No............

SUBPOENA

THE STATE

vs.

Jno. Thos. Scopes

Issued *July 9,* 1925

E. B. Ewing, Clerk.

Officer's Return

STATE OF TENNESSEE RHEA COUNTY